Praise for *A New Shoah*

"This most impressive work is a valuable publication that presents a comprehensive picture of the many acts of terrorism against Israeli citizens. It is a very useful tool that fills the information gaps that unfortunately exist among many in the international community—including the media—and even decision makers, in regard to events in Israel and to our daily struggle for survival. There is no doubt that making this information readily available, together with the detailed descriptions that help increase awareness of the cruel impact of terrorism on the victims, is a very important contribution to a better understanding of life in Israel."

> —Reuven Rivlin, Speaker of the Knesset

"With eloquence and compassion, Giulio Meotti puts a human face on the atrocities suffered by nearly two thousand Israelis killed in terrorist incidents."

> —Daniel Pipes, director of the Middle East Forum and distinguished visiting fellow at the Hoover Institution

"Giulio Meotti belongs to this precious and tiny group of people to whom the Western world owes the preservation of its honor, freedoms, and dignity in a time of totalitarian media control, unlimited oil corruption, terror and violent anti-Semitism. In our time of fashionable cowardice, Meotti's book is a monument of love and courage dedicated to the forgotten Israeli and Jewish victims of Islamic jihad in Israel and in the world."

> —Bat Ye'or, author of the bestseller *Eurabia: The Euro-Arab Axis*

"We have become accustomed to talk blandly of 'terrorism' as if it were some sort of abstraction. But Giulio Meotti in meticulous fashion puts human faces on the body count from the organized Palestinian terrorist killing of Israeli civilians—and thereby reminds us that this is not a morally equivalent struggle, but a systematic effort to extinguish Israelis and the civilization that they have created."

—Victor Davis Hanson, senior fellow at the Hoover Institution and author of *Carnage and Culture*

"Meotti gives the reader a clear and clean view on the people of Israel for what they are: heroic in their daily democratic normality."

—Fiamma Nirenstein, journalist, vice president of the Commission for Foreign Affairs of the Italian Parliament, and member of the Global Forum for Combating Antisemitism

"Roger Scruton writes in the preface that Meotti 'tells the story in detail': the details of the lives cut short that generally fade into the collective forgetfulness. This book measures the appalling costs that the rebirth of anti-Semitism, fueled by an absolute and undying hatred for Israel as such and for its citizens, is imposing on the whole planet—not just in Tel Aviv or Jerusalem."

—Pierluigi Battista, deputy editor of the leading Italian daily *Corriere della Sera*

"Reading *A New Shoah* by Giulio Meotti, I immediately wondered why an Italian reporter, who doesn't belong to the nationalist Jewish Right, felt the need to spend four years gathering the testimonies of victims and survivors of Arab terrorism in Israel. He did it to give them a name amidst a public opinion, dominated by anti-Zionist and anti-Semitic propaganda, that denies them one. . . . And Meotti wanted not only to give them a name, but to tell their stories, their hope, and often, their acts of heroism."

—Vittorio Dan Segre, former Israeli diplomat, academic, and author of several books

A New Shoah

THE UNTOLD STORY OF
ISRAEL'S VICTIMS OF TERRORISM

Giulio Meotti

translated by Matthew Sherry

ENCOUNTER BOOKS
NEW YORK · LONDON

First American edition published in 2010 by Encounter Books, an activity of Encounter for Culture and Education, Inc., a nonprofit, tax exempt corporation. Encounter Books website address: www.encounterbooks.com

Originally published in Italy as *Non Smetteremo di Danzare: Le storie mai raccontate dei martiri di Israele* in 2009 by Lindau s.r.l.

Manufactured in the United States and printed on acid-free paper. The paper used in this publication meets the minimum requirements of ANSI/NISO Z39.48 1992 (R 1997) (Permanence of Paper).

FIRST AMERICAN EDITION

LIBRARY OF CONGRESS CATALOGING-IN-PUBLICATION DATA

Meotti, Giulio.
[Non smetteremo di danzare. English]
A new Shoah : the untold story of Israel's victims of terrorism / by Giulio Meotti.
p. cm.
Includes bibliographical references and index.
ISBN-13: 978-1-59403-477-0 (hardcover : alk. paper)
ISBN-10: 1-59403-477-X (hardcover : alk. paper)
1. Terrorism—Israel. 2. Victims of terrorism—Israel—Biography.
3. Jews—Persecutions—History—20th century. 4. Arab-Israeli conflict.
5. Israel—Ethnic relations. I. Title.
HV6433.I75M4613   2010
363.325095496—dc22
2010012395

Contents

Against the Last Wave of Anti-Semitism

Roger Scruton

F or nearly two thousand years, following the destruction of Jerusalem by the Roman imperial army, the Jews lived in exile from their holy places, keeping their religion, language, and customs alive in an unparalleled act of collective memory. Less a race or a tribe than what Giulio Meotti calls a "metaphysical family," the Jews have remained faithful to their culture and their calling through continuous suffering, targeted wherever they settled by the resentment and xenophobia of their hosts, yet never forgetting Jerusalem—the holy city of their dreams. No other people in history has experienced so much undeserved suffering, or devoted so much energy to remembering and mourning its dead.

And when, in the mid twentieth century, the greatest of all disasters wiped out the Jews of Central Europe—and with them a vital part of our European identity—the world seemed to undergo a brief fit of remorse. The United Nations voted overwhelmingly to recognize the State of Israel as an independent member and as a homeland in which the Jews could at last protect themselves. Israel was, for the Jews, a bid for freedom, a way of achieving the self-government that they had kept alive through two thousand years of memory. As we know, the hatred began again, now directed at Israel and its Jewish residents.

In this book, Giulio Meotti tells the story in detail, reminding us of the terrorist crimes of which the Israeli people have been the victims, of the rising anti-Semitism in the Middle East, and of the unwillingness of so many Western politicians and thinkers to recognize the malice of the Muslim states toward their neighbor. Meotti has given us a moving work of mourning, a new "Shoah" in memory of the many victims of the new wave of anti-Semitism. He invites us to put our duplicity behind us, and to recognize the right of Israel to exist and of its people to defend themselves.

The "blame Israel" approach to Middle Eastern politics is now the semi-official attitude of the European Union. It is an example of the same feeble-minded appeasement that allowed the last wave of anti-Semitism to triumph in Europe. But, as Meotti eloquently reminds us, Israel is not the cause but the target of the current belligerence, and there can be no solution in the Middle East that does not place the blame on those who live by hatred, and who have nothing to offer save destruction. Let us hope that this book will awaken Europeans to their duty toward the Jews, whose vigil down the centuries has been an example to us all.

The Unsung Dead of Israel

"He said that while it was true that time heals bereavement it does so only at the cost of the slow extinction of those loved ones from the heart's memory which is the sole place of their abode then or now. Faces fade, voices dim. Seize them back .... Speak with them. Call their names. Do this and do not let sorrow die for it is the sweetening of every gift."

CORMAC McCARTHY, *THE CROSSING*

"Just as for the victims of the Holocaust** we say 'every Jew has a name,' so also the victims of terrorism today have names." The words are from Uri Baruch, a French Jew born to Holocaust survivors, who lost a daughter in a terrorist attack. It was September 20, 2001, nine days after the assault on the Twin Towers in New York. The Baruch family had gathered to celebrate the Jewish New Year in Hebron, the city of the patriarchs south of Jerusalem. Together with Uri and his wife, Francine, were their daughter, Sarit; her husband, Shai Amrani; and their children: four-year-old Zoar, two-year-old Ziv, and Raz, just three months old. Sarit wanted to go back to their home in Nokdim, in the Judean desert. Francine convinced them to spend another night in Hebron because it would be safer for them to make the drive in the daylight. They left at dawn the next day.

A little while later, Uri received a telephone call from Shai's mother. She had heard on the radio that there had been a terrorist attack on the road to Nokdim. She had called her son's home, but no one answered. Uri immediately called Francine, who was working at a medical clinic. She contacted the army, and then called her husband. "You need to come. It's them."

On the way home, Palestinians had pulled their car up alongside Shai's. He had rolled down the window to ask if they needed help, and the terrorists responded with bullets. The first went through Sarit's heart, killing her instantly. The three shots fired at the children miraculously missed their targets. Shai was struck four times in the throat, once in the heart, and once in the lungs. He spent thirteen hours in surgery and two weeks in a coma. When he woke up, he saw Uri sitting there. "Forgive me," he said. "I couldn't save your daughter."

In Jerusalem, at the Yad Vashem memorial, visitors can peruse the giant archive that houses the names of the Holocaust victims. Of all the monuments dedicated to the Holocaust, which by their nature are monuments of emptiness, these plain walls with their endless expanse of names are the most poignant. They are an authentic *hazkara,* an act of remembrance. In its combination of breadth and individuality, the litany of those Jewish names creates a physical sensation of the immensity of the slaughter as well as the tragedy that each victim experienced. One comes away with something like a sense of betrayal. The territory of Israel is covered with plaques bearing the names of thousands of terror victims; they are displayed along city streets, in schools and synagogues, in cafes and restaurants, in markets, in parks and gardens. Like pinpricks of blood, these plaques form a memorial of the Holocaust, not forcefully but with tender love. For me, giving a voice to Israeli families destroyed by terrorism, letting them speak as the memories are beginning to fade and are shared only with loved ones, was a form of incarnation like those stark walls of names at the Holocaust memorial. Uri Baruch explained it to me this way: "Like Sarit's grandparents, who decided to go on living despite the pain and sadness for their slain families, we also decided to live commemorating our daughter."

Judaism teaches that there is something primordial behind the name given to a new life that comes into the world. When someone converts to Judaism, he must choose a new name, like Chaim, "life," Baruch, "blessed," or Rafael, "God heals." Rafael was the name of one of Uri Baruch's neighbors. He was a Jewish convert from Holland, and was killed in Hebron because he was a Jew. Before anything else, the Holocaust was an ontological attack against the Jewish name. In 1938, the Nazi official Hermann Göring ordered that "Israel" be added to the name on identification cards for Jewish males, and "Sarah" for females. The Jews were taken by the millions to anonymous, desolate places, where all of their luggage, letters, and photographs of loved ones were taken away. Then they were separated from their mothers, sisters, children, wives. They were stripped naked, and their documents, their names, were thrown into the fire. Finally, they were pushed into a hallway with a low, heavy ceiling. And they were gassed like insects. The nowhere land of the Holocaust was the engine of extermination for six million European Jews. Islamic terrorism and denial of the Holocaust, which spread through the world like wildfire after September 11, 2001, feed on this annihilation of the Jewish victim.

Even while the threat of a new extermination of the Jews is today a reality and a promise, the custodians of memory in the West usually distinguish between anti-Semitism, which is piously condemned in homage to the Holocaust, and anti-Zionism, a hatred for Israel that is eagerly accepted and propagated. European culture maintains that nothing can be compared to the Holocaust; that the Israelis killed today because they are Jews have nothing to do with their parents killed in the gas chambers; that the anti-Semitism behind the Holocaust is a singular evil of the past, where its lessons may be safely buried. In reality, it is not only a historical phenomenon, but also a terribly modern one; not just a form of obscurantism, but a crime against a people and its descendants, both theological and genetic. It is the same old evil with new, "enlightened" faces.

Being Jewish in the century of Hitler and the Islamic Republic of Iran means having a club membership that never expires. On the contrary, it is carried in a person's name. When terrorists hijacked a plane full of Israelis in Entebbe, in 1976, they selected hostages by making them state their names, and they detained the 105 Jews aboard. Some of them were concentration camp survivors who had experienced that same kind of selection more than thirty years earlier. One of them, Pasco Cohen, was killed in front of his daughter. When the *Wall Street Journal* reporter Daniel Pearl was murdered by al-Qaeda in Pakistan, the Islamic terrorists forced him to say his name, then those of his father and mother, both Israeli citizens: "My father is Jewish, my mother is Jewish, I am Jewish." In the grimmest photo, Pearl has his head lowered, a chain around his wrists. A man with his face covered is clutching him by the hair, pointing a pistol at his temple. In another, his bare feet can be seen, a bit of the chain dangling from his oversized sweatpants.

Those bare feet reminded me of a young man named Ofir Rahum, who lived in Ashkelon. One day, he received a message on his computer from an older Palestinian girl who lived in Ramallah. Without telling anyone, Ofir put on his best clothes and took the first bus he could. The girl came to pick him up in Jerusalem. He didn't even realize when the car entered Ramallah, in Palestinian territory. It is difficult to describe what they did to him. He was Jewish, poor, naïve and innocent. That is why he was chosen as "wood to be burned in hell," according to the propaganda of the Islamic fundamentalists. They assaulted and shot him. They tied his body to the car bumper and drove toward the city. Then they got rid of the body. That's how life ended for one sixteen-year-old Jewish boy. Why has Ofir's story never been held up as an example of what ethnic-religious hatred can do?

Why doesn't anyone know the name of Eliyahu Asheri? He was eighteen years old, the son of an Australian convert to Judaism. He looked at life with a smile, and was hitchhiking home when they caught him. Whenever a Palestinian dies, even a suicide bomber, the newspapers fall all over themselves to publish his story and photographs. Eliyahu wasn't even named in the newspapers; they just said "Israeli settler." He was only a kid, executed with a bullet in the head on the day he was kidnapped. Then the murderers took his identification card and used it to extort money from his family.

If a Nazi officer in Auschwitz had filmed a Jew, before entering the gas chamber, in the throes of physical and psychological suffering, like Daniel Pearl, and had made him say "I am a Jew," today that video would be shown to students all over the world to explain what racism is. But the stories of Daniel, Ofir, and Eliyahu have been forgotten. Daniel's father, Judea, should be invited to speak at every school.

The history of Israel has been buried under a mound of falsehood: Israel from the beginning accepted the UN Partition Plan for Palestine and the Arabs violently rejected it. Israel generously offered territory through Ehud Barak's and then Ariel Sharon's unilateral withdrawal, and each time received the same response: that the solution isn't land but Israel's disappearance. All of Israel's governments, right and left—from Menachem Begin, giving up the Sinai; to Yitzhak Shamir, attending the Madrid Conference; to Yitzhak Rabin, making peace with Jordan and signing the Oslo Accords; to Ehud Barak, retreating from Lebanon and going to the Camp David summit; to Ariel Sharon, withdrawing from Gaza—all have repeated the word that Israel's neighbors never say: *peace*. For a large sector of the Islamic world, the cities, skyscrapers, hospitals, cinemas, and schools on this tiny sliver of land are merely real estate that will be restored to Islam once this malefic form is swept away.

Peace can come only with the recognition in the Middle East of Israel as a national state of the Jewish people; the addition of the State of Israel to all the maps used in schools in the Islamic world; the elimination of the extensive anti-Israeli propaganda campaigns in the Muslim media and schools; the promotion of interactions among scientists, scholars, artists, and athletes; the abandoning of the delegitimization of Israel at the United Nations; the outlawing of terrorist groups devoted to the killing of Israelis and the destruction of Israel; the end of the economic boycott against Israel; the institution of full diplomatic relations with Jerusalem as Israel's capital; and last but not least, the proclamation of theological fatwas prohibiting the murder of "infidels," Jews, and Christians.

In 1968, just months after Israel's victory in the Six-Day War, the American philosopher Eric Hoffer wrote an op-ed in the *Los Angeles Times* in response to the proliferation of anti-Israel sentiment in the international community. His words now sound prophetic: "I have a premonition that will not leave me; as it goes with Israel so will it go with all of us. Should Israel perish the holocaust will be upon us." The Jewish condition is again the focal point of an enormous battle of identities. Israel can be threatened existentially because it does not exist on the maps studied by generations of Arabs and Iranians. It can be assailed because its history is denied in Europe—denied as a human occurrence made up of immigration, wars against Arab rejection, the struggle for independence under the British Mandate; denied as a right sanctioned by the United Nations and sanctified by the dignity of its victims. How can peace be constructed in the Middle East if Israel's victims are forgotten?

Two years ago, in Jerusalem, a terrorist killed eight young Jewish seminarians who were studying the Torah. Afterward, a survey by the Palestinian Center for Policy and Survey Research showed that 84 percent of the Palestinians justified the attack. Itamar Marcus, who has spent many years monitoring and exposing Palestinian anti-Semitic propaganda as director of Palestinian Media Watch, maintains that the heads of propaganda for Hamas and for the Palestinian Authority's TV station—with their televised sermons, cartoons, comic books, and schoolbooks—have created a machine to incite killing similar to that of the Hutu journalists who fomented genocide against the Tutsis in Rwanda. The Islamic movement describes the Jews as "children of monkeys and pigs" to be exterminated, just as the Hutu supremacists spoke of the Tutsis as "serpents" to be crushed. European countries first prosecuted hate speech on a par with war crimes during the Nuremberg trials of Nazi officers, and after this in the proceedings at an international court in Tanzania in 2003, when the Hutu journalists Hassan Ngeze, Fernand Nahimana, and Jean-Bosco Barayagwiza were found guilty of using Radio-Télévision Libre des Mille Collines and a biweekly magazine to incite the extermination of Tutsis and publish lists of people to be killed.

Hamas and Hezbollah, two of the terrorist organizations that seek the destruction of Israel, call the Jews "pigs," "cancer," "garbage," "germs," "parasites," and "microbes." Iran's president Mahmoud Ahmadinejad uses the expression "dead rats." This terminology is the contemporary version of the Nazi *schmattes,* Yiddish for "rags." As the great historian Robert Wistrich has explained, "the Islamic movement calls the Jews 'children of pigs and monkeys' because dehumanization comes before genocide." In Israel, terrorists have killed those who inherited the names of their parents and grandparents murdered in the gas chambers and in the forests of occupied Europe. When the siren sounds on Yom Hashoah, Holocaust

Remembrance Day, all Israelis stop wherever they are, like statues of pain, because living Israelis feel that they are the continuation of the Judaism that was cut off in Europe. They are linked by an invisible chain that explains to the whole world why Israel exists. It is no accident that the siren is the same one that warns Jews to take shelter in case of bomb attacks.

Abraham Joshua Heschel wrote that it was words, not machines, that produced Auschwitz. The Palestinian historian and TV host Issam Sissalem said that the Jews "are like a parasitic worm that devours a snail and lives inside of its shell. We will not allow them to live in our shell." This is the basic message conveyed by Palestinian sermons, academic lectures, and even performances for children. On March 12, 2004, in a mosque in Gaza, Sheikh Ibrahim Mudeiris, who draws a salary from the Palestinian Authority, declared, "We will fight the Jewish cancer." Shortly afterward, dozens of Israelis would be blown up by suicide bombers. In February 2008, Wael al-Zarad, an *ulema* of Hamas, launched a televised appeal for the extermination of the Jews. A few days later, a terrorist gunned down eight Jewish students.

Al-Aqsa TV, controlled by Hamas in the Gaza Strip, broadcast an interview with two young children in March 2007. "You love your mommy, right? Where is she now?" "In paradise." "What did she do?" "She chose martyrdom." "Did she kill Jews? How many of them did she kill?" The children on the program were the sons of Rim Riashi, who on January 4, 2004, had blown herself up at the Erez checkpoint. The five-year-old boy held out the fingers of his hand: "This many." "How many is that?" "Five."

For many years, since the Oslo Accords, Israel became self-hypnotized with the fable of a pacified, normalized, territorially integrated post-Zionist society. The dream of peace seemed close at hand, but then collapsed miserably under Islamic genocidal belligerence—a new, potentially fatal chapter in the story of the Jewish people. Over the past fifteen years, the Jewish state has been struck in its most vital and routine places. Scores of young people and children, women and elderly incinerated on buses; cafes and pizzerias destroyed; shopping centers turned into slaughterhouses; Jewish pilgrims picked off with rifle fire; mothers and daughters killed in front of ice cream shops; entire families exterminated in their own beds; infants executed with a blow to the base of the skull; teens tortured and their blood painted on the walls of a cave; fruit markets blown to pieces; nightclubs eviscerated along with dozens of students; seminarians murdered during their studies. Husbands and wives have been killed in front of their children; brothers and sisters, grandparents and grandchildren murdered together; children murdered in their mothers' arms.

This is the Ground Zero of Israel, the first country ever to experience suicide terrorism on a mass scale: more than 150 suicide attacks carried out, plus more than 500 prevented. It's a black hole that in fifteen years swallowed up 1,557 people and left 17,000 injured. Israel is a tiny country—a jet can fly from one end to the other in two minutes. If a proportion of the population equivalent to those 1,557 victims were murdered in the United States, there would be 53,756 Americans killed. Israeli figures of those wounded in terror attacks, extrapolated to the population of the United States, would be the equivalent of close to 664,133 injured. Since the beginning of the Second Intifada (al-Aqsa Intifida) in September 2000, more Israelis have been murdered by terrorists than in all previous years of Israel's statehood. Jerusalem is the suicide-terrorism capital of the world.

The stories told here are breathtaking also in their horror and shock. Israelis are deliberately attacked at the times when the largest numbers of people can be killed and in the most indiscriminate manner possible, in the name of eradicating Jews from the Middle East. A flier from the Ezzedeen al-Qassam

Brigades, the military wing of Hamas, shows a drawing of an ax destroying the word *al-Yahud,* meaning Jews, and says, "We will knock at the gates of Paradise with the skulls of the Jews in our hands."

There were sixteen million Jews in the world before the arrival of Adolf Hitler; now there are thirteen million. The extinction of European Judaism took place amid the complete and tragic failure of European culture. Today in the West there is a faulty conscience—indifferent to the parade of young Palestinians putting on explosive belts, the daily demonization inflicted on Jews in the Arab world, the crowds delirious over the lynching of two Jewish soldiers who had lost their way and whose dismembered bodies were displayed as trophies. This faulty conscience has obliterated the fate of thousands of Israelis murdered because they were Jews; it has erased one of the reasons for Israel's existence.

Who in the West still remembers that eighty-six Israelis lost their lives during the First Gulf War, killed by Iraqi missiles, by the panic, by suffocation? Linda Roznik, a ninety-two-year-old Holocaust survivor, was buried under the rubble of her home. The same thing happened to Haya Fried, another Holocaust survivor. During the fighting, the Jews of Israel took gas masks with them everywhere they went. Saddam Hussein had come up with a monstrous idea: people could be gassed in Israel just as in a gas chamber, without being able to lift a finger to defend themselves. For this reason, the *Jerusalem Post* proposed nominating as "person of the year" the sixty-nine Holocaust survivors living in the south of Israel in run-down apartments without any underground shelters or security exits, bombarded by Palestinian rockets after the Iraqi ones stopped falling—

people such as Frieda Kellner, from Ukraine, who had survived the Holocaust but was killed by Hezbollah rockets.

The terrorists have always selected their targets in Israel very carefully, to cause as much destruction as possible. One suicide bomber in Rishon Lezion massacred a group of elderly Jews who were enjoying the cool air on the patio, where they had no protection. And then there are the shopping malls like in Efrat, pedestrian areas like in Hadera, bus stops like in Afula and Jerusalem, train stations like in Nahariya, pizzerias like in Karnei Shomron, nightclubs like the one in Tel Aviv, buses full of students like at Gilo, or of soldiers like at Megiddo, bars and restaurants like in Herzliya, and cafes like in Haifa. The reserve soldier Moshe Makunan had just enough time to ask his wife, "Tell our girls that I love them."

Two brutal sets of murders took place in November 2002 within a few days of each other. Twelve Israelis were murdered in Hebron; and gunmen entered Kibbutz Metzer, killing five people. Terrorist bullets didn't differentiate between religious settlers in Hebron and dovish liberals in Metzer. The victims in Hebron were all adults; in Metzer, a mother and her two young children were murdered in cold blood. In Hebron, many of the victims were soldiers; in Metzer, the victims were all civilians.

There is a long, heartbreaking list of teenage Jewish girls whose lives were cut off in a moment by a suicide bomber. Rachel Teller's mother decided to donate her daughter's heart and kidneys: "That is my answer to the hyena who took my daughter's life. With her death, she will give life to two other people." Rachel wore her hair very short and had a wistful smile. Her friends remembered the last time they saw her. "We said 'Bye-bye,' a little bit bored, like it was nothing. Instead, it was the last time we said goodbye to Rachel."

Abigail Litle was returning home when she was killed. "She loved humanity and nature," her family said. Abigail was part of an Arab-Jewish project for peace. Her family comes from a community of American Baptists who hold their worship services in Hebrew and call themselves Jewish, but believe in Jesus Christ and practice baptism. Their existence is one little tile in the great Israeli mosaic. "For Abigail it was always important for a person to be valued as a person," her father said. "She never looked at persons as objects that have to be defined according to their nationality. Now she is in a better place." Her brother added, "She knew that God loved her, and she loved him, too."

Shiri Negari's mother had just taken her to the bus stop when she heard a loud boom. She went back and saw only the smoking remains of the bus her daughter had boarded. Shiri's sister Shelly was in training at the emergency room that morning. She saw the ambulances arriving but didn't know that her sister was in one of them. Shiri had long blond hair that she refused to have cut; it was like her trademark. She was a teacher in the army, and she signed her e-mails "Shiri Negari— Voyager in the world."

Noa Orbach had just left school and was chatting with two friends at the stoplight. A man dressed in black approached them and opened fire on the teenagers. Her teacher said, "Noa was the first to start singing on field trips, the first to help a friend in trouble, the first to raise the level of discussion in class. I knew her for three years, and I was looking forward to the satisfaction of seeing her grow up, seeing what she would make of her life. I can't believe that tomorrow I won't see her sitting at her desk." The newspaper published a card she had created, which said: "Getting angry means punishing yourself for someone else's stupidity . . . ," with a drawing of a heart and Noa's signature.

In almost all the attacks on buses or markets or bar mitzvah celebrations, soldiers have died. The terrorists have never distinguished between "civilian" and "military" victims, because the Israeli army is at the heart of the Jewish state, with its permanent exposure to the Islamist war. There is compulsory military service of three years for men, almost two for women, and reserve duties lasting to age fifty. There are no officer academies, so generals are made by rising up through the ranks. Young men come from all over the world to fight in the Israel Defense Forces; they are called *haial boded,* lone soldiers. They arrive with no money but plenty of idealism, and are taken in by the kibbutzim, eating with adoptive families on Friday evenings, or they share an apartment to save money. These young men have also died by the hundreds at the hands of terrorists.

"The Israelis were soldiers before they were athletes," noted Abu Daoud, the architect of the Munich massacre in 1972. "Joseph Romano, the weightlifting champion, participated in the Six-Day War in the West Bank and the Golan Heights." Soldiers before they were athletes; soldiers before workers; soldiers before scholars of the Talmud; soldiers before craftsmen; soldiers before husbands, brothers, sons. At the funeral of Afik Zahavi-Ohayon, a child who was killed by a rocket, the former Russian dissident Natan Sharansky said, "You must have dreamed of being a hero; you must have dreamed of being a soldier. Here every child becomes a soldier, and the entire country is a front. You fell as a soldier." Those who have fallen are Israel's human shield.

Corporal Ronald Berer had arrived from Russia fourteen years before he was killed. His mother didn't want to see him in uniform; she was afraid. He told her, "Mom, they're killing women and children. Someone has to protect them. If I don't do it, who will?" That's what almost all the soldiers say. Benaya Rein's mother recalled of her son, "The last time he said goodbye, I said 'Be careful,' and he replied, 'You and Dad have taught me to give everything. But you have to know that sometimes everything really does mean everything.'"

The truth about the broken destinies of these Jewish martyrs is reincarnated in the combination of a name and a place, in a life that continues on the ashes and embers of suffering, in the recollections of the parents and siblings and spouses that I have gathered and presented in these pages. Telling the victims' stories as one indissoluble chain has been, for me, the only way to keep them from slipping away. Reading these stories is an act of solidarity against the abandonment and dereliction of these thousands of victims, young and old, children and infants, women and men. They were coming from work or from school, going to the cinema or shopping when they passed into the next world, pulverized by an explosion. They were Jews whose only crime was that of "living ordinary lives in an extraordinary country," in the words of the friends of Motti Hershko and his son Tom, militants of the pacifist left who were blown up on a bus in Haifa.

Gadi Rajwan was an Iraqi Jew who employed seventy Arabs and came from a prominent family known in Jerusalem for its wealth and generosity. He went to the factory every day at six o'clock in the morning and was well liked by his employees. Gadi didn't even have time to look up before being shot in the face by a young Palestinian who had worked there for three years. At the funeral, Gadi's father, Alfred, kept shaking his head: "How could it have happened to us, to us who have always worked to do so much for everyone?"

Jamil Ka'adan, an Arab who taught Hebrew and worked as a supervisor in the Arab schools, was blown up in Hadera. "He had never believed in violence. He was a man of peace, and I'm not just saying that because he's gone," one friend said. Shimon Mizrachi and Eli Wasserman were killed in an industrial area where many Palestinians worked. Mizrachi's daughter said that "he helped all the workers; he loved to build and create things." Every morning he met with his Arab employees. Shimon's wife recalled that "he had a special relationship with the workers.

He believed in coexistence, and he liked to help people." His dream was to open a kitchen for the needy.

For a parable of Israel's condition in the Middle East, you can look to the exchange of one innocent boy, Gilad Shalit, an inexperienced Israeli army corporal held in cruel confinement by a gang of thugs, with 1,400 Palestinian prisoners condemned by the most rigorous processes of justice. Among them were at least a hundred life convicts, murderers, serial killers of women and children. Israel, so small and abandoned to itself, is deeply united around the value of life.

Until now, there was not one book devoted to Israel's dead. This book is written without any prejudice against the Palestinians; it is motivated by love for a great people in its marvelous and tragic adventure in the heart of the Middle East, and through the whole twentieth century. Every project to exterminate an entire class of human beings, from Srebrenica to Rwanda, has been commemorated in grand fashion; but this does not seem to be allowed for Israel. Throughout its history, a quick scrub has always been made of the blood of the Jews killed because they were Jews. Their stories have been swallowed up in the amoral equivalence between Israelis and Palestinians, which explains nothing about that conflict and even blurs it to the point of vanishing. This book is intended to rescue from oblivion an immense reservoir of suffering, to elicit respect for the dead and love for the living.

Every day in Israel there are memorials for victims of terrorism. It wasn't possible to tell about all of them. Many families, like the Rons of Haifa or the Zargaris of Jerusalem, enclosed themselves in a dignified silence. In four years of research, the most beautiful gift was given to me by the Israelis who opened their ravaged world and laid bare their sufferings to me, a

stranger, a non-Jew, a foreigner. They shook my hand and spoke
about their loved ones—the families of Gavish, Shabo, Hatuel,
Dickstein, Schijveschuurder, Ben-Shalom, Nehmad, Apter,
Ohayon, Zer-Aviv, Almog, Roth, Avichail, and others. I wanted
to tell some of the great Israeli stories full of idealism, suffering,
sacrifice, chance, love, fear, faith, freedom, and the hope that
Israel will triumph in the end.

Lipa lost his entire family in the gas chambers, and then
lost a son and granddaughter in terrorist attacks. The English-
man Steve, after saying goodbye to his wife, learned to live in a
wheelchair along with his daughter, and then built a family
larger than before. David lost everything, his wife and four little
daughters, and is still heroically able to reveal what it means to
be Jewish. There is something contagious about his compassion. After the death of his son, Yossi kept his memory with the
wisdom of the psalmist. There is a woman, the wonderful Adriana Katz, who heals civilian victims at the most heavily bombed
place in the world, Sderot.

Also among the survivors are the doctors who worked
beside Dr. Applebaum, who lived with a defibrillator under his
bed, and was killed together with his daughter the day before
she was to be married. Arnold, the living testament of two families decimated in the concentration camps, lost his daughter in
a restaurant bombing and has honored her memory through
acts of "true kindness." There are incredible people like the
obstetrician Tzofia, who lost her father, a rabbi, her mother and
her little brother, but today helps Arab women give birth.
There's Ron, whose grandfather escaped from the Nazis and
whose daughter was killed on a bus. There's Yitro, a Torah
copyist who converted to Judaism and whose son was kidnapped and executed by Hamas. There are the farming settlers
Elisheva and Yehuda, whose family had been lost in Auschwitz,
and whose daughter Yael was killed by remorseless terrorists
simply because "she wanted to live the Jewish ideal."

Many victims were settlers, the "colonists," people who pay a very high price for that kind of life—from political antagonism to an extremely intense relationship with death, but above all a pervasive solitude. The settlements endured hundreds of deaths during the Second Intifada, with the days full of fear, the nights spent standing guard in the isolated houses, the sudden massacres of families, infants and unborn babies, the drives through darkened streets in helmets and bulletproof vests, which offer little protection. The settlers' lives are simple, faithful, centered on lots of children. Their story is a tragic embrace of religion, compassion, toughness, honor, and fanaticism.

"When 'settlers' were killed, it was intolerable to read in the newspapers, stuck in a corner of the page: 'Settler woman killed,' or worse, 'Settler child strangled,' as if the twofold stigma of Jew and settler made the murder understandable, justified it and dismissed it from our attention," wrote Claude Lanzmann, the director of the monumental film *Shoah.* "When the 'martyrs' blew themselves up, practically every day and several times a day in Jerusalem, Tel Aviv, Netanya, Haifa, in the nightclubs, in the markets, on the buses, in the wedding halls and in the synagogues, the event rapidly became routine. This time, it was not the 'settlers' who were being attacked, but all of Israel. All of Israel had become a 'settlement,' and this procured and carefully administered death meant nothing other than the savage claim of a Greater Palestine, the manifest desire for the uprooting of Israel."

There's Steve, whose daughter was "too noble for this world," and Naftali, who lost a wonderful young son whose idea of paradise was "a Talmud and a candle." Bernice's daughter had left her comfortable life in the United States. Their stories speak to us about sacrifice and courage. Tzipi's father, a rabbi, was stabbed to death, and where his bedroom used to be there is now an important religious school. Ruthie's husband and David's brother was a great humanist doctor who treated everyone, Arab and Jew alike. There's the rabbi Elyashiv, whose son, a seminarian, was taken from him, but who believes that "everything in life makes the strong stronger and the weak weaker."

Sheila lost her husband, who took care of children with Down syndrome; she talks about the coming of the Messiah. Menashe lost his father, mother, brother, and grandfather in a night of terror, but continues to believe in the right to live where Abraham pitched his tent. Alex consecrated every day to the memory of his beautiful little daughter, nicknamed "Snow White." Miriam saw her husband, a musician, taken from her after they had come from the Soviet Union. Elaine lost a son during the Shabbat dinner, and for more than a year she didn't cook or make any sound. Yehudit lost her daughter too soon, coming back from a wedding together with her husband. Uri lost his daughter who volunteered for the poor and who studied the Holocaust, from which her family had miraculously escaped.

Orly had a happy life in a trailer in the Samarian hills until her son was killed, before he could put his kippah back on his head. There's Tehila, one of those God-fearing but modern women who populate the settlements, who loved the pink and blue plumage of Samaria's flowers. Dror lost much of his family in the Holocaust, and buried his son with his inseparable Babylonian Talmud. The terrorists took away Galina's husband after they had left everything in Russia so that their grandchildren could be born in Israel, a story that began with the Stalinist repression. Norman is a rich businessman from New York who gave up every convenience imaginable in order to live in Israel; his wife used to guard Rachel's Tomb in Bethlehem. There's also the marvelous Yossi, whose son went out every Friday to give religious gifts to passersby, and sacrificed his own life in order to save his friends. Rina had created a pearl in the Egyptian desert and thought of herself as a pioneer; her son was taken from her, along with his pregnant wife.

With his hymn to life, Gabi has honored his idealistic brother who was murdered at the university. There's also Chaya, who embraced Judaism together with her husband; conversion for them was "like marrying God." Dr. Picard left France, where his grandparents had fled from the cattle cars of the Vichy government, only to lose a son at a Jewish seminary. There's the devout Yehuda, who takes care of the bodies after terror attacks. Finally, special mention should be made of Ben Schijveschuurder, who lost his parents and three siblings at a pizzeria, and who likes to remember his father smiling and making the "V" for victory in front of the gates of Auschwitz.

These stories all speak to us of a state that is unique in the world, born from the nineteenth-century philosophy of secular Zionism, which brought back to their ancient homeland a people in exile for two thousand years and cut down to less than half its prewar size. They are stories of courage, desperation, faith, of defending hearth and home through "honorable warfare" in the only army that permits disobeying an inhumane order. This is the epic of a people that has suffered all of the worst injustices of the world, and is reborn time and again thanks to its moral strength.

One of the most excruciating scenes in *Shoah,* Claude Lanzmann's masterpiece, took place in the Polish *shtetl* of Grabow. In late December of 1941, all of the Jews there were asphyxiated in the Chelmno gas vans, and the Poles of the village took possession of their homes. In front of a beautiful carved door, Lanzmann talks with a rural woman, toothless and with upturned nose, who tells him with complete nonchalance that she lives in a Jewish house. Lanzmann asks if she knew the owners. "Of course." "What were their names?" Silence. She doesn't remember. Even their name has been lost. This was the second death of the Jews of Grabow. We cannot leave the Israeli victims of terrorism to the same fate by forgetting their names. Making up for the heartbreaking obscurity of these innocent victims is one of the deepest and truest reasons for the State of Israel to exist. As Gabi Ashkenazi, chief of the Israel Defense Forces and the son of Holocaust survivors, explains it, "In Israel there will never again be numbers instead of names; there will be no more ashes and smoke instead of a body and a soul."

Where a suicide bomber has struck, the victims are arranged near the carcass of the bus. They are placed in heavy black bags, to which are attached a Polaroid photo, a preliminary report, and a card with a number. Many of the victims still have the number assigned to them by the Nazis tattooed on their arms. If the ashes of the Holocaust have led back to the names of the millions killed, the bodies torn apart in suicide bombings have led us back to the individual destinies of Israel, to a name, to the spirit that illuminated a life—even the small, obscure life of an immigrant, dirt poor, who dreamed of living in that land of refuge. In many cases, the victims are identified by their teeth, by a watch, by DNA or blood analysis. There are mothers who go home from the morgue with just the little pieces of jewelry that had belonged to a daughter. Is there anything closer to the Holocaust than this black hole that swallows up lives with hardly a trace?

Ben-Zion Nemett talks about his daughter who survived an attack on a restaurant in Jerusalem: "Shira told me that when the explosion happened, the children were injured. They were burning. The youngest was crying and shrieking, 'Daddy, Daddy, save me!' And her father shouted back, 'Don't worry, recite the *Shema Yisrael* with me. Hear, O Israel: the Lord is our

God, the Lord is One.' Finally, there was silence. And I, the son of my father, the only member of his family to survive the Holocaust, who grew up with the *Shema Yisrael* that the Jews recited before being killed, I heard this same story from my daughter. The camp in Treblinka and the Sbarro restaurant became one and the same thing. A genetic code connects the holy victims of the Holocaust and those of the Sbarro. Holy victims whose only crime was that of being part of the Jewish people."

As Lanzmann remarked, "the Nazis had to look past the dead." In Ponari and Chelmno, where Jewish fathers and brothers and sons were forced to dig up the remains of their loved ones so they could be burned in huge open-air incinerators, the bodies were called *schmattes*, "rags." Things had to be done without describing them, without naming what was being done. The members of the Sonderkommando in Auschwitz, the team of Jews selected to work in the gas chambers and crematory ovens, had scattered hundreds of teeth belonging to victims all over the camp, so that there would still be some trace of them left. Serious reflection should be given to this image of people sowing thousands of human teeth around the camps. In the extermination camp at Sobibor, where 250,000 Jews disappeared, the gas chambers were replaced with fir trees, planted by the Nazis who were fleeing to the West. Those trees—what is it that nourishes them?

At Sobibor, the bodies had been thrown into mass graves with their heads facing downward, like herring. Withered and dry, they crumbled like clay when touched. The Jews were forced to dig with their hands, and the Germans would not allow them to use words like "dead" and "victims"; they were called "figures," and they no longer had names or faces. In the air, the flames turned red, yellow, green, violet. The largest bones, like the leg bones, were crushed into fragments by other Jews, and the ashes were put into bags and thrown into the rivers. Poles grew tomatoes and potatoes a few hundred feet from the death machines of Treblinka, where almost a million Jews were killed. Today, hens scamper around where the Sobibor camp once stood. The history of European Judaism did not end with a grave where Jews can now go to pray; the only pilgrimage possible is to contemplate a stormy sky, in pain, anger, and sadness. Likewise, the families of terror victims often have no chance to weep over the bodies of their loved ones. They rush to the place of the attack, only to find a carpet of human fragments.

In Chelmno, 150,000 Jews disappeared in a few months. Where are their remains? It's impossible to recreate the scene; even the survivors can't do it. "There was always a great silence, even when they were burning two thousand people a day," said Simon Srebnik, one of only two Chelmno survivors, who died of cancer in September 2006. "No one shouted; there was great calm and tranquility." That sensation is relived today in the silence observed on Yom Hashoah, Holocaust Remembrance Day, when thoughts turn to the names of the dead, but above all in the silence that follows an attack in the middle of a crowd. Yehuda Meshi-Zahav, the ultra-Orthodox Jew who founded the organization that identifies the victims of attacks, explains that "after the bomb goes off everything is quiet; you can only hear the voices of the wounded. It is in those moments that you know what you have to do: make order before the hysteria explodes around you." The silence of Chelmno and the silence after a suicide bombing, the Zyklon B of the Nazis and the explosive belts of Hamas have this in common: the total destruction of the victim.

Of the three thousand dead at the World Trade Center, one thousand have never been found—not even through DNA analysis. Three hundred bodies were found at Ground Zero. Few families have had the opportunity to identify loved ones with their own eyes. Memorial services were held without human remains. The harder task was identifying the shredded, charred and pulverized remains of the majority of victims—the most detailed and painstaking identification process. When fires rage and concrete crumbles, consuming most other tissues of the human body, only teeth survive. Israeli forensic experts pioneered the method of identification through dental records. Teams of up to one hundred dentists worked day and night shifts in Manhattan. Others performed the clinical task of extracting from cells the unique genetic recipe that identifies every human being.

In the village of Srebrenica, the site of Europe's worst mass killing since World War II, Serb troops secretly moved the bodies from one mass grave to another in an effort to hide the crime. The murderers also ordered their victims to change clothes before killing them, to make it harder to investigate the crime. From Srebrenica to Ground Zero and Israel, the annihilation of the victim is the mark of the devil. A Jewish headstone in Ashkelon is marked "anonymous." It is for an unidentified bombing victim who was buried in Israel in 2002. Fifteen years ago, before DNA analysis, most Jewish victims would never have been identified; they would have been buried in a common grave.

In one attack, two young Israeli women with similar features were killed. When a tearful husband arrived at the hospital, he embraced the wrong woman for several minutes before realizing his mistake and locating the body of his wife. Most of the victims in the Park Hotel bombing in Netanya, many of them elderly Holocaust survivors, were maimed beyond recognition, making it impossible to establish identity by fingerprints or birthmarks, scars or tattoos. Even dental records could not always be used, because in some cases the teeth were damaged by the scorching heat. The blast was so powerful that many relatives arrived at the forensic institute to discover that only a hand was still intact. The doctors and social workers accompanied these relatives as they went to the mortuary to touch and kiss the severed hand or leg in a gruesome and desperate farewell. Sometimes it has been necessary to use mass graves because distinguishing among the remains has been impossible. Speaking about the victims again is a form of vindication. It is the purest meaning of memory.

The hero of the Jewish resistance to Nazism in Europe, Abba Kovner, once said that "we Jews have nothing except for our blood." The Jewish question emerged in the concrete context of genealogy, of the religious and ethnic identity of a people, the genetic identity: Jewish son of a Jewish mother. Reminding us of this are the terrorists who tie up a Jew in front of a video camera and make him say the name of his mother. Men are "accused of a crime that they did not commit, the crime of existing," as Benjamin Fondane wrote before he was swallowed up by Auschwitz.

Just as Holocaust survivors never say "I" but always "we," speaking in the name of the dead, the families of terror victims have found suffering to be a source of unity for a country so often torn by politics. Many survivors of attacks, the families and friends of the victims, have talked about how Israel became so much closer to their hearts when they buried their loved ones. The Talmud says that in Israel, the dead protect the living. After the devastating attack on the Dolphinarium nightclub in Tel Aviv, in June 2001, it was said, "The land is won through work and blood. The more friends you bury in this land, the more it becomes yours."

The first on the scene after an attack are the thousand-odd volunteers of Zaka. The Israelis call them "those who sleep with the dead"; their own motto is *Chesed shel Emet,* "true kindness." They reverently gather every human remain, every scrap of flesh and tuft of hair, so that, in keeping with Jewish tradition, the body may be reassembled and buried with dignity. They are the God-fearers filmed at every massacre, bent over among policemen and nurses, gathering drops of blood, "because all men are made in the image of God, even the suicide bombers, and all of the bodies must be honored, so that God may smile again." They say that their task is sanctifying the Name—of God, and of the dead—and allowing the fulfillment of Ezekiel's prophecy according to which the dead will find their bodies in the messianic age, and the divine spirit will breathe in them again. "Son of man, can these bones come to life?" Ezekiel asked. And the bones began to move and reassemble themselves: "The spirit came into them; they came alive and stood upright, a vast army." In the thick of the extermination, in Dachau, Rabbi Mordechai Slapobersky said, "And the flesh and the skin formed around the dried bones that we left behind."

It was European civilization that died during the Holocaust, swallowing up all of the Jewish communities in its own nothingness; and after Passover in 2002, when the greatest single massacre of Jews since the Second World War was perpetrated in Israel, the Jewish state became the symbol of a war of civilizations. It is not easy to enter this place where suffering reigns, to remember all the victims of terrorism, the "unknown martyrs" of Israel, as Menachem Begin called them in his memoirs of the Soviet gulags. The region that is revealed to the visitor is peopled by the shadows of the dead, and illuminated by what Abba Kovner called "the candle of anonymity."

What, over the centuries, has permitted the survival of the most persecuted people in history? What has kept them from depression? After pogroms and repressions, what has driven them to put themselves again at the center of history? The birth of Israel is the only political event worthy of joy, hope, and gratitude in a century that became a slaughterhouse to hundreds of millions of human beings—because the twelve million Jews who insist on living in this world despite the gas chambers and the terrorism are the essence of liberty. Israel teaches the world love of life, not in the sense of a banal joie de vivre, but as a solemn celebration. Israel's national culture is like a miraculous continuation of the Jewish life that flourished in Israel until the Romans—first in 70 CE and then in 135 CE—reduced Jerusalem to ruins. The miracle was represented in the Israeli men who danced in the streets when David Ben-Gurion proclaimed that the Jewish nation had returned home after two thousand years, and right after the Nazi genocide.

What is the spirit that saves Israel from living under the emblem of fear and allows it to fight? The last protection against suicide attacks is a spontaneous form of civil defense, mainly by newly discharged soldiers and by students trying to earn a living, together with a coterie of middle-aged Russian and Ethiopian immigrants who also need a job. They are, in the words of one security guard, "the bulletproof vest of the country." Human shields, they stand for hours in the cold or the heat so people can shop, sip coffee, and go about their business without worrying about getting blown up.

Rami Mahmoud Mahameed, a young Arab Israeli, prevented a bomber from boarding a bus, but not from exploding; Rami was badly injured. Eli Federman, guarding a Tel Aviv disco, faced the speeding car of a suicide bomber heading straight for the club and coolly fired, blowing up the car before it could enter. Tomer Mordechai was only nineteen years old when he was killed after stopping a car loaded with explosives that was heading for downtown Jerusalem. Tamir Matan died while preventing a suicide bomber from entering a busy cafe. A suicide terrorist at a shopping center in Netanya left hundreds wounded and five dead, including Haim Amram, a working student who was guarding the entrance to the mall. A pregnant policewoman, Shoshi Attiya, had chased down the terrorist.

While some are heroes, the Jewish victims are almost always defenseless people. Massoud Mahlouf Allon was an observant Jewish immigrant from Morocco. He was mutilated, bludgeoned and beaten to death while giving poor Palestinians the blankets he had collected from Israelis. The disabled Simcha Arnad was blown up in the seat of his motorized wheelchair in Jerusalem's Mahane Yehuda market. Nissan Cohen was a teenager when he fled from Afghanistan. His neighbors called him "a saint," noting that "When he heard that people had died in an attack, he wept. He visited the sick and prayed for them." Nissan opened the synagogue in the morning, and in the evening he went back to turn off the lights. During the daytime he helped handicapped children, and at night he studied the Gemara, the commentary on the Law. A bomb killed him at the entrance to the Mahane Yehuda market.

"The great majority of victims are poor or close to the poverty threshold," explains Yehuda Poch. "Generally they are people who use the bus instead of a car, they shop at the market instead of the supermarket, and they live here in the poorer neighborhoods or downtown instead of in the nicer suburbs." Poch works with the One Family Fund, the association that for years has taken care of the victims of terrorism.

The stories of these martyrs speak of something that does not emerge from the brutal statistics on the numbers of victims. The International Institute for Counter-Terrorism in Herzliya, the most important center for analysis in Israel, has calculated that only 25 percent of the Israeli victims have been soldiers; the majority have been Jews in civilian dress. Europeans believe that Israel is the stronger side in the conflict, with the military, the technology, the money, the knowledge base, the capacity to use force, the friendship and alliance with the United States— and that before it stands a pitifully weak people claiming its rights and ready for martyrdom in order to obtain them. But the stories of these victims prove otherwise.

And still, the Israelis have shown that they love life more than they fear death. The buses circulate even if they leave burned carcasses here and there, and the stops are always crowded. The supermarkets stay open. Every time a bomb explodes, the signs of the blast are quickly removed; windows are repaired; bullet holes are patched. The places that were blown up reopen after two days. The terrorists of the "road without glory," as the Jew and French Resistance member Bernard Fall called it, have killed hundreds of teachers and students, but the schools have never closed. They have killed doctors, but the hospitals have continued to function. They have massacred 452 uniformed Israeli soldiers and policemen, but the list of those who volunteer has never shrunk. They have shot up buses of faithful, but the pilgrims continue to arrive in Judea and Samaria. They have committed massacres at weddings and forced young people to wed in underground bunkers, but life has always won over death. When a terrorist began to shoot and throw grenades into the crowd at Irit Rahamin's bachelorette party at the Sea Market restaurant in Tel Aviv, Irit threw herself to the ground, and from under the table called her fiancé and told him that she loved him—amid the screams and the dying.

The Jewish martyrs are common people with an identity that exposes them to the slaughter of many centuries. It is a story inhabited by people whose names have been lost or forgotten, as if there were nothing left of all those lives. Every time I encountered difficulty in telling their stories, I remembered the wonderful "iron mama" Faina Dorfman, whose grandfather, a rabbi, was burned by the Nazis in Russia. She lost her only daughter in a nightclub in Tel Aviv, but continues to believe in the Jewish saying *Yihye besseder,* "Everything will turn out well." She thanked me for "bringing the truth to the world." For me, pronouncing the names of Israel's martyrs was an act of piety—accompanying them to the end, dying with them, so that they remain among us.

The Beginning

There *is no difference between the terrorism* that kills Jews in Israel and the terrorism that strikes them abroad. In Rome, in 1982, the little boy Stefano Tachè was murdered by Palestinian terrorists. In Entebbe, in 1976, the Jews were selected on the basis of the names on their passports. On the ship *Achille Lauro*, in 1985, an American Jew in a wheelchair, Leon Klinghoffer, was picked from among all the other passengers and thrown into the ocean by Palestinian terrorists. In 1980, in Nairobi, a bomb devastated the Israeli-owned Norfolk Hotel, killing fifteen people. Five years later, in Sinai, an Egyptian policeman fired wildly on a group of Israeli tourists, killing seven of them, four of whom were children. Then there were the attacks on the airports in Rome and Vienna, with more than twenty killed. In 1986, in Istanbul, twenty-two faithful were killed in the Neveh Shalom synagogue. Between 1992 and 1994 in Buenos Aires, more than one hundred died in the Jewish schools. In Mombasa, in 2002, at a hotel used by Israeli tourists, guests were killed by a bomb in the hall. That same year, a suicide bomber blew himself up outside the ancient Tunisian synagogue of Djerba. And the list continues with the barbaric killing of Rabbi Holtzberg and his wife, in her fifth month of pregnancy, in Mumbai in December 2008.

Ilan Halimi, a young French Jew who worked at a cell phone shop, was kidnapped in 2006 in the heart of Paris and taken to a suburb where he was tortured and murdered. The neighbors heard him screaming, but no one intervened to stop the slow execution. The den where Ilan was held hostage resembled a "homemade concentration camp." Until the trial, the French government pretended that nothing serious had happened. Almost thirty people participated in the torture of Ilan, who was seized in plain sight, passed from one tormentor to another, starved and then given nourishment, and killed slowly, over a period of three weeks. The killers, young Muslims from the *banlieues,* stabbed him, broke his fingers, burned him with acid, and finally set him on fire. Ilan did not wear a long black robe, or the ritual tassels, or even the kippah. The name he bore was enough for Ilan Halimi to be a marked man. It was the most serious episode of anti-Semitism in France since the Second World War.

Thousands of French Jews vanished in Nazi death camps with hardly a murmur of protest from their Christian countrymen. Sixty years later, the chief rabbi of France, Rabbi Joseph Sitruk, advises Jews not to wear yarmulkes in the streets due to rampant anti-Semitism. It's the same in Norway, where Jews are advised not to speak Hebrew too loudly on the streets. For the first time since the war, French Jews are afraid. Shmuel Trigano, professor of sociology at the University of Paris, has openly questioned whether there is a future for Jews in France. Sébastien Sellam, a young disc jockey at a Parisian nightclub, was killed in 2003 in an underground parking lot by a Muslim neighbor, who slit his throat twice and mutilated his face with a fork, even gouging out his eyes. The assailant announced to Sellam's horrified mother, "I have killed my Jew. I will go to heaven."

Anti-Semitism—and not only in the guise of anti-Zionism—is in vogue again at European universities, in labor unions, in newspapers, among the political and cultural elite. Shouts of "Death to Jews" have filled the streets, and the crocodile tears spilled for Jews killed during the Holocaust make it much easier to demonize the living ones in Israel. The Dutch leftist parliamentarian Harry van Bommel attended a demonstration in Amsterdam where Muslims shouted, "Hamas, Hamas, Jews to the gas!" Anti-Semitism in the Netherlands is stronger today than it has been during any other time in the last two centuries except for the Nazi occupation. The percentage of Germans who hold unfavorable opinions of Jews has climbed from 20 percent in 2004 to 25 percent today. In France, which has the third-largest Jewish population in the world, after Israel and the United States, 20 percent of people view Jews unfavorably—up from 11 percent four years ago. In Spain, where all Jews were expelled in 1492 and synagogues are historic monuments, the figures are even more striking: negative views of Jews climbed from 21 percent in 2005 to nearly 50 percent this year. January 2009 was the most intense period of anti-Semitic attacks to have been recorded in Britain in decades. Anti-Semitism in Western Europe in 2009 was the worst since World War II, according to the Jewish Agency. In recent years, there have been thousands of attacks specifically aimed at Jewish targets outside Israel, and the attack on the United States has been connected by the terrorists to the war against the Jews. The Israeli national airline has suffered dozens of attacks since 1968. During various terrorist strikes like the one in Entebbe, the Jewish passengers have been separated from the non-Jews. It is a hunt for the Jews "wherever they may be," from the outskirts of Paris to the desert of Yemen.

After 2,500 years, the epic of the Yemeni Jews ended in November 2009, when U.S. forces rescued the last Jews from Sana'a, the magnificent city founded by Shem, the son of Noah, not far from the mountain where Noah's Ark came to rest when the flood subsided. One year earlier, a Muslim extremist shot Moshe Yaish Nahari five times with an AK-47 assault rifle as he prepared to take his mother shopping for food to make the Shabbat dinner. The killer called out, "Jew, accept Islam's message." Moshe died in his mother's arms. Five hundred Salafi Muslim extremists chanted *"Allahu Akbar wa itbakh al-Yahud,"* "Allah is great and death to the Jews."

If one is to identify a beginning of the massacre of Israeli civilians, one must return to that infamous morning in September 1972, at 31 Connollystrasse in the Olympic Village in Munich. Some of the Israeli athletes assassinated by Arafat's death squads were Holocaust survivors, the fruit of the night of Auschwitz and the wind of Chelmno; the disappearance of European Judaism had left its mark on their faces, together with the miraculous reconstruction in Israel. Others were *sabra,* born in Israel. Each of their stories calls up weeping and prayer. Today, before leaving for the Olympic Games, every Israeli athlete pays homage at the graves of his compatriots killed in Munich. What could have been more repugnant than the massacre of innocent Jews at the Olympics? But the episode became a great media event to stress the problems of the Palestinians, rather than a serious terrorist attack to be condemned.

On 31 Connollystrasse that day, a squad of eight Palestinians took Israeli athletes hostage and opened fire with AK-47s, shooting the coach Moshe Weinberg through the cheek. The Black September terrorists demanded the release of many fedayeen imprisoned in Israel in exchange for the hostages. The terrorists had been educated in the West. Like the suicide attackers who brought down the World Trade Center in 2001, "Issa," the leader of the squad, had studied in Europe, getting an engineering degree in West Germany. The document claiming responsibility for the killing of the "Zionists," the Jews, was written in perfect English. The terrorists of Black September were not after an exchange or negotiations; they just wanted to kill Jews. They wanted the young representatives of the Israeli people, hosted by the nation that once planned their industrialized extermination. It was a spectacular escalation in the war of the Islamist movement to wipe Israel from the face of the earth. The building that housed the Israeli athletes is located less than ten miles from the Dachau concentration camp. They were the first Jews killed in Germany for being Jewish since 1945.

When the hostages and terrorists were taken on three helicopters to the airport of Fürstenfeldbruck, a Lufthansa airplane was waiting on the runway to take them to Algeria. But when the first terrorist climbed into the cockpit, he realized that the flight crew was not there. German agents opened fire and turned on the floodlights. Two terrorists were struck and killed. Instead of returning fire or surrendering, the surviving terrorists completed their mission, throwing a hand grenade into the helicopter where the nine hostages sat. With the Jews dead and their objective attained, the three surviving Palestinians surrendered. Thirteen years later, on August 30, 1985, the Palestinian leader Abu Daoud would explain the significance of this action to the Tunisian weekly *Realité:* "The Zionist state is a military entity, and its citizens must be considered as combatants." From Munich to Tel Aviv, nothing has changed over the past thirty years.

That day in Munich, Islamic terrorism cut short eleven Jewish stories. Every one of them was a member of the great body of Israel. There was Moshe Weinberg, a Jewish son of Israeli liberty, with a winning smile and the joy of living stamped on his face. Amitzur Shapira, the father of four beautiful children, was a teacher in Herzliya. Shaul Ladani, who escaped the massacre in Munich, had been deported at the age of seven to the concentration camp of Bergen-Belsen, where his parents were exterminated. He contracted typhoid fever, but was saved and went to live in Israel. There was the great Yosef Romano, a Jew of Libyan origin who before dedicating himself to sports had fought like a lion in the Six-Day War. He was killed just five months after the birth of his third child. As Yosef's friends would say, "courage was his religion." The day before he was killed, Romano had said, "This is my last competition; I don't have enough time for my children." Yosef was so different from David Berger, a Jew from Cleveland, from one of the many American Jewish families who "make the aliyah" to Israel to discover their "roots." He was supposed to get married after returning from the Olympics. His father said that David knew the risks he had taken on by moving to Tel Aviv; he was proud of David, the idealist, the pacifist, who felt the injustice of the world, who wrote poetry about the war in Vietnam.

There was Mark Slavin, who kissed the Jewish soil upon his arrival in Israel. He came from Minsk, and had fought against the Communists who imprisoned and silenced thousands of Russian Jews who, like him, wanted to reach Jerusalem. Mark's grandmother, Griša, said that "he was a true Jew; he had always felt that he was an Israeli, and he was the one who convinced everyone to leave the Soviet Union." He was made of the same mettle as the famous "Prisoner of Zion" Ida Nudel, who recalled, "I arrived in the land of my dreams not as a refugee looking for just any sort of place under the sun. I am in the land of my people, I am free among my people." Mark had the calling of a liberator, and helped give a million Soviet Jews, a tribe absorbed and lost behind the Iron Curtain, the opportunity to find their freedom in the land of their fathers. He studied Hebrew in a kibbutz; he wanted to relive the history of the pioneers, and his parents were welcomed by the devout, ultra-Orthodox Jewish community of Bnei Brak.

Mark Slavin's story is the story of many thousands of Russian Jews who fought in the prisons and in the squares against Communist obscurantism that kept them from having an identity and reclaiming the right to emigrate to the land of their fathers. They had nothing but their typewriters, which they used to translate the samizdat, or clandestine manifestos, inciting the people to resistance and rebellion. It was the power of the Exodus. They threatened the Kremlin and the greatest totalitarian empire of the twentieth century not with weapons and bullets, but with slogans like "Let our people go" or "Freedom for Israel." Those dissidents gave a new meaning to the Jewish Passover expression *zman heruteinu*, "the time of our freedom." Their Judaism grew in the Soviet prisons, nourished by a fervent underground movement that was undermining the Soviet colossus from within. The refuseniks, the Jewish dissidents, had the special serenity of those who know they are in the right.

In Munich, there was Ze'ev Friedman, who was born in Siberia, and whose father was deported to a labor camp on the Vistula. He spoke a wonderful mixture of Yiddish and Russian. His mother lost everyone in Treblinka, the extermination camp that in a few months obliterated hundreds of thousands of Jews from all over Europe. The first Jews from Warsaw arrived at Treblinka—that place with the strange and beautiful name, surrounded by conifer forests and little ponds—on the ninth day of the month of Av, the same day on which the Temple was destroyed. The Jews of Treblinka were "trunks endowed with legs," slaves of a new species of men. The "Jews of death" took care of the corpses of their brothers and sisters, their mothers and fathers, their sons and daughters, pulling them out of the gas chambers by the legs, removing their gold teeth, cutting their hair, and throwing them into the open-air incinerators.

Ze'ev Friedman, who grew up with these stories, had distinguished himself in action against the fedayeen in Metula, a city on the Lebanese border. His father appeared on television asking for Ze'ev to be released, and recounting the fate that his family had already met. Upon learning of his son's death, he said that if Israel did not respond to the massacre, "Hitler will have won from the grave." Hannah and Shlomo were the only two survivors of the family. Ze'ev would have been the last male. Germany—like all of Europe—was indifferent to the silent martyrdom of Ze'ev Friedman.

Another martyr of Munich was Kehat Schorr, who arrived in Israel from Romania in 1963, where he had fought against the Nazi troops in the Carpathian Mountains. With him was Yakov Springer, who taught school in Bat Yam, near Jaffa. He was one of the few survivors of the armed revolt in the Warsaw ghetto on April 19, 1943.

Yakov was a veteran of Via Mila, the heart of Jewish resistance against Nazism. During the war, the European newspapers noted that in Warsaw, for the first time in two thousand years, the Jews had fought in a battle. "Who knows if the spirit of Israel will not rise again from the ashes of Warsaw," one Polish newspaper mused. Yakov took part in the revolt of two hundred Jewish young people. For them it was simply a question of how they were going to die. They wanted to show that they were not insects. "We wanted to choose to die our own way," said Stefan Grayek, a leader of the uprising. He lived the rest of his life in a little house on the outskirts of Tel Aviv. "On the street we saw scenes that the human mind cannot imagine: infants, alive, in the arms of their dead mothers, piles of dead children, and around them other children squatting on the ground, waiting for their turn." Yakov Springer, a man much like Grayek, would also fight for possession of East Jerusalem, where a little bit of his marvelous Jewish Warsaw had been planted, the Warsaw of rabbis, street kids, intellectuals—a city that by then existed only in the faded memories of the few who had survived its extinction.

It was partly with Springer in mind that Yitzhak Rabin, on April 19, 1993, paid homage in Warsaw to those who had taken up arms against the oppressors: "Where are the writers? And the rabbis? And the doctors? And the musicians? And the children? Where is Janusz Korczak? Doesn't my people exist anymore? In human history, the rebels of the ghetto will be remembered as those who kept the embers of honor alive. We have risen from the ashes of the martyrs; the courage of the combatants in the ghetto is the cornerstone of Israel's foundation."

The community of Bat Yam paused to weep for its noble fellow citizen, and Yakov Springer's daughter came back from Sinai, where she was serving in the army.

There was also Andrei Spitzer, who lived with his wife, a convert to Judaism, in a suburb of Tel Aviv. Andrei had immigrated from Communist Romania in 1967, the year in which the tiny Jewish state was attacked by the Arab powers. His wife received death threats from Black September after Andrei's murder, and agents from Mossad, the Israeli secret service, flew to Holland to bring her to safety in Israel. Another of the victims in Munich was Eliezer Halfin, the son of Lithuanian Jews who had lost all their relatives in the Holocaust. The Nazis had killed twenty of Eliezer's relatives. The USSR had denied him an expatriate visa dozens of times and even prohibited him from participating in international competitions, out of fear that Eliezer "the Zionist" would make statements in favor of Israel. He was the last Halfin male. The last victim of Black September was Yosef Gutfreund, who also left Romania, after spending months in prison under the accusation of "Zionist propaganda." He was legendary for his generosity toward Egyptian soldiers dying of thirst in Sinai.

The day after the massacre of the athletes, all the Israelis in Germany put on the kippah in mourning, as did the Jewish athletes from the French, English, and American delegations. The shameful decision not to bring everything to a halt was morally bankrupt, and gave a green light for future massacres. The distribution of medals started again, gold and silver stained with blood. The Olympic celebration was dead, but the competition went on and on and on. Israeli rabbis came to drape the coffins with flags bearing the Star of David. In Frankfurt that night, about fifty Jewish graves were vandalized. None of the Arab delegations sent any condolences to Israel. Not one.

When the bodies arrived at the Lod Airport, there was no fanfare to greet them, only silence and a dignified sadness. Waiting for them was the great Moshe Dayan, with the look of a *kibbutznik* who had interrupted his work in order to weep for his children. There was also Yigal Allon, who had started fighting in the clandestine Jewish army at the age of thirteen. There wasn't a single shop open in the entire country; the Jewish people were unified in suffering, just as they had been throughout their history. Tunisia offered to take the bodies of the terrorists—everyone wanted them. Libya won. Ambassadors from all the Arab countries were present at the burial in Tripoli. They were there to celebrate the "martyrs' wedding." The atmosphere in Israel was different. After reciting the Jewish Kaddish over the graves, the People of the Book went back to their homes. The next day was the beginning of the Jewish New Year, but there was no room for joy. That new year opened with all thoughts turned to the children of the eleven victims. Those children were, and are, the *why* of Israel.

Three Righteous Men

There is one image that explains Israel better than an abundance of words: it is the dance for disabled members of the army. During the grand opening ceremony for the celebration of independence, the disabled dance in their wheelchairs, led by young people who leap around them, take them by the hand, dart away and back again. There is joy, not sadness, on those faces that are at once so young and so mature. Their pain, their disabling, is part of Israel, a citadel-state that for more than half a century has tragically walked between life and death.

On Israeli television we saw a celebration of the return to life of three people in a bar on a pedestrian street in Jerusalem. In 2002, a suicide bomber had blown himself up there, killing eleven people. A girl who had been there, and had believed herself dead but then recovered, cajoled her friends into having a little party. Another victim had returned almost to normal after four years of therapy; he brought along his brother, who was hit in the head and could no longer talk or move normally, and who will never get better. The one young man didn't let go of his disabled brother's hand for a minute; he hugged his brother, made him eat and smile. The others in the group joined his efforts.

Disabled war heroes are often the protagonists of Israeli soap operas. Much attention goes into sports for the disabled;

at the Special Olympics in Athens in 2004, Israeli competitors obtained first-place results. Among them were Keren Leibowitz, a swimmer whose legs were paralyzed in an accident while she served in the army, who won a gold medal and two silver. Yizhar Cohen, a forty-one-year-old blind swimmer, came home with three gold medals. Yitzhak Mamistalov, who has cerebral palsy and swims with only his right hand, earned two gold medals and one silver. Inbal Pezaro, eighteen years old and wheelchair-bound due to a malformation of his dorsal spine, won a silver and a bronze medal in swimming.

More than ten thousand people have been wounded by terrorism; Israel itself is a giant wound. During the darkest times of terrorism, the hospitals have become repositories of anguish and ravaged bodies. The victims arrive in shreds. Staff have been hired to help the relatives of the victims recognize what is left of their loved ones. Those who plant the bombs are aiming for total destruction. It is a war against the hearts, souls, and bodies of the Jewish nation. Nearly four in ten Israelis have survived attacks, lost family members, or had family or friends wounded. Civilian victims and survivors often come from disadvantaged families. The most vulnerable are deaf and blind people.

Immediately after an attack, while the ambulances are taking the injured away, they are classified as *anush* (serious), *benoni* (moderate), and *kal* (light). The classification includes psychological trauma. Pieces of metal are added to the explosive in the terrorist's vest or backpack, and the blast sometimes completely severs limbs. Many children have had their faces burned or their hands rendered useless; some have had their sight ruined forever. There are trembling elderly people, totally dependent. There are people who go insane and don't want to live anymore because they are haunted by the sound of the explosion, and they seclude themselves in their homes. Naturally, the focus has been mainly on the people killed in terror attacks, but more than eight times as many have been wounded. This is the true face of the war against the Jewish people: Jews scathed and scarred, living reminders of the horror of the bombings. They require years of costly and complicated physical and mental rehabilitation. Israeli doctors estimate that 40 percent of the injured will have permanent disabilities. In a small nation like Israel, the wounded produce a ripple effect through society.

Some Israelis are still hospitalized from injuries sustained in suicide attacks years ago; many more require repeated hospital visits and multiple operations. Many are unable to work. Thousands of families have been forced to alter their lives to care for a wounded family member. Eran Mizrahi was celebrating his sixteenth birthday at a restaurant in Jerusalem when a suicide bomber blew himself up. A nail went through Eran's skull, leaving him paralyzed and in a catatonic state.

Dr. Michael L. Messing's remarkable report "Radiology of Suicide Bombing Terrorism" permits us to understand how the perfect weapon of the Palestinian "martyr" has literally and figuratively destroyed thousands of lives. He gives the example of Sharone K., who went to Ben Yehuda Street to meet a friend, Sharone M., for his birthday celebration. They stood fifteen feet away from one of the suicide bombers and were knocked unconscious by the blast. Sharone K.'s entire body, from head to toe, was imbedded with metal fragments measuring from millimeters to centimeters. Sharone M. was similarly wounded, but with one critical exception: a nail penetrated his skull and lodged in his brain. "From the X-ray images I saw, I estimated that Sharone K. had approximately 300 individual fragments, including many still recognizable as nails," Messing writes. "Several of the fragments penetrated his vital organs. He sustained a punctured colon, a collapsed lung and a lacerated liver and kidney. I could actually feel the nails under his skin where they had burrowed and lodged."

Earlier generations of bombs were packed with small ball bearings; during the Second Intifada, terrorists used heavier, deadlier metal. From screws and nails, to scrap metal found at construction sites, to rat poison, the additives boost the devastating impact of each explosion. The poison works as a blood thinner, causing victims to bleed profusely and die quickly. Shock waves from the explosion, especially in enclosed places like buses or restaurants, reverberate violently through the human body, collapsing lungs, breaking small bones, and destroying internal organs. Nuts and ball bearings are packed into the explosive vests to inflict unbearable pain and suffering on Jewish bodies.

Victoria Ogurenko was severely wounded in the Dolphinarium bombing that claimed the lives of twenty-one teenagers, including two of her close friends. They were standing outside the nightclub in Tel Aviv when a suicide bomber detonated his deadly explosives. A bone jutted out of Victoria's left arm. Her body was peppered with nails, screws, and ball bearings. A nail had pierced the bone near her heart. A screw penetrated a bone in her left leg, and ball bearings punctured the length of her left arm and leg.

Unlike people in a conventional war zone, the victims are often riding to work or eating a meal. Nahum Barnea, the premier Israeli newspaper columnist, gave this description of the scene of a suicide bombing. "Everything is fast, so businesslike, so well executed, that it seems for a moment that it was all a show prepared in advance. A few dozen yards away life went on supposedly as usual. People sat in cafes. Bought books. Sat in their offices. That is an optical illusion. Concealed beneath this energetic routine lies deep despair." The randomness of the attacks, the bombers' ability to strike anywhere at any time, has created among Israelis a sense of living a kind of collective Russian roulette. Many avoid taking buses or going to movies, shopping malls, any crowded place. The terrorists' aim is to force Israelis to place armed guards at kindergartens, to search bags at the entrance to movie theaters, to be afraid of sitting in their favorite cafes or restaurants. Crowded pedestrian malls, bar mitzvah celebrations, pool halls, foreign workers, public transport—these have been very popular terror targets. Islamic terrorism has tried to demolish Israel's right to exist in its ordinary activities.

Aharon Barak, as chief justice, made this point in the summer of 2005 when he opened his judgment on a petition brought by Palestinians who were appealing the legality of the separation fence: "Most of the terrorist attacks were directed toward civilians. They struck at men and at women; at the elderly and at infants. Entire families lost their loved ones. The attacks were designed to take human life. They were designed to sow fear and panic. They were meant to obstruct the daily life of the citizens of Israel. Terrorism has turned into a strategic threat. Terrorist attacks are committed inside of Israel and in the *area* [Judea, Samaria, and Gaza]. They occur everywhere, including public transportation, shopping centers and markets, coffee houses, and inside of houses and communities."

Every bomb is followed by a flurry of cell phone calls: "Are you all right?" Emergency workers are often traumatized and need counseling. Some unconscious children have been listed as "anonymous" because they didn't have identification cards and the doctors were searching for their parents. For all those killed, there are many, many more left alive but burned, scarred, blinded, hearing-impaired, or missing limbs. Many sustain fractures, vascular injuries, paralysis, or brain damage. Magen David Adom, the Red Star of David, has been putting aside extra blood. Hospitals have purchased walkie-talkies, ventilators, outdoor showers, and all sorts of antibiotics.

During the Second Intifada, Israeli hospitals continued to provide medical care to Palestinian patients without interruption, although in the first year of terrorism, seventy-one Israeli

ambulances that arrived to treat the injured in areas of confrontation were attacked and damaged by terrorists. The number of Gaza Palestinians being treated for medical conditions
of all sorts in Israel's hospitals has increased significantly,
despite the Hamas takeover of the Gaza Strip and the barrage
of rocket attacks. In 2007, according to an Israeli report published on January 13, 2008, more than seven thousand Palestinians were able to travel to hospitals in Israel and in the West
Bank—an increase of 50 percent over the figure for 2006.
Close to eight thousand more Palestinians were allowed to
accompany them. Israeli officials commented that Israel took
great risks in encouraging such visits, which on numerous occasions had been abused by Palestinians to attempt terrorist
attacks on Israeli hospitals or other targets. Israeli medical
cooperation with the Palestinians has resulted in the total erad-
ication of tetanus and measles from the Palestinian population,
a dramatically reduced death rate among Palestinian infants,
training projects for Palestinian doctors in cardiac and brain
surgery, and assistance in opening intensive care units.

Dr. Mario Goldin, who had immigrated from Argentina,
treated dozens of terror victims and helped them get back to
their lives again. His objective in life was to reduce "the pain of
those who suffer." He was considered a pioneer in pain management and "every patient's best friend," according to his
coworkers. A bomb killed Dr. Goldin while he was waiting for
the bus, planning to visit a few shut-ins. He had treated many
Arabs and Palestinians at the Beit Levinstein Rehabilitation
Hospital, some of them seriously injured in terror attacks. "He
treated everybody equally," said Ya'akov Hart, the director of
Beit Levinstein. "A patient recently sent me a letter saying that
Dr. Goldin had treated his pain, which was so bad that he
couldn't walk for six months. He went to Dr. Goldin for treatment and he was up on his feet again. He asked me to thank
Mario, who he said had called him every three days to see how

he was feeling. He was very caring and humane, charming, and dedicated. His death is a terrible loss." Dr. Goldin was one of many doctors killed by terrorist bombs.

The terrorist attacks in Israel have produced images that never go away. When the smoke cleared from the explosion on Allenby Street in Tel Aviv, Jacob Heyn saw a heart, still beating, lying on the sidewalk amid the shattered glass. "There was no body, just a heart beating. I didn't think such a thing could happen. But I saw it and others saw it," said Heyn, eighty-seven years old. He had been standing with his son in front of a bookstore that his family owns, filled with displays of children's books. It was a normal day on a busy street. Bret Stephens, then editor of the *Jerusalem Post,* called it "the amazing and horrifying quiet—that was the quiet of ten murdered souls."

Seconds after a suicide bomber killed a woman and her granddaughter, Danit Margolinski, standing with her five-year-old son at a video arcade next door, sprinted to offer help. Bleeding and broken bodies lay everywhere, as screaming women protected shrieking babies. Margolinski scooped up one baby from a mother sprawled on the floor and swaddled her in her shirt. Margolinski remained frozen on the spot, as if she were in a coma. "Slowly, I will become myself again, but the problem is: How will I forget the babies crying, and the women screaming, 'Save me. Save me!'?"

Added to the physical injury is mental trauma, which some experts say is particularly acute in the case of suicide attacks. Post-traumatic stress disorder, depression and anxiety affect not only the victims of the attacks, but all of Israeli society. There has been a significant increase in antidepressant and sedative use by the general public. Studies after the 1995 bombing that devastated a federal office building in Oklahoma City found that 16 percent of Americans living within a hundred-mile radius of the blast suffered from post-traumatic disorder, including acute stress, flashbacks, or anxious reactions to

loud bangs. In Israel, the number of people who find themselves in similar circumstances is enormous. According to Dr.
Danny Brom, director of the Israel Center for the Treatment of
Psychotrauma, thousands of Israelis are affected by difficulty
sleeping, nightmares, anxiety, fear of leaving home, light or
severe depression, chronic headaches and terrible flashbacks.

In 2004, one report estimated that 40 percent of the population in Jerusalem have some degree of post-traumatic stress
disorder. Some cannot sleep because the smell of burned flesh
will not leave them. More than half of those surveyed said they
felt a "loss of control on factors that influence" their lives due to
the violence. There are very few studies examining the psychological impact of mass terrorism in Israel. One is an extraordinary document by Marie-Thérèse Feuerstein, *Burning Flowers,
Burning Dreams: Consequences of Suicide Bombings on Civilians in
Israel, 2000–2005*. It is the culmination of a research project
involving specialists in trauma and bereavement counseling, as
well as frontline health professionals at the cutting edge of
emergency medicine in Israel following terrorist attacks.

Among the hundreds of people disabled by terrorism, there
are many stories of redemption that bear witness to the victory
of Israel. One is the story of Tomer Gamadani, a police officer
who suffered from serious burns caused by a terrorist bombing.
After months of struggling heroically to overcome pain and
despair, Tomer married the love of his life. "He was completely
burned," said Irit, his wife. "We had already set the date of our
wedding, but I saw death nearby, and I prayed that Tomer
would not die." She asked Tomer, "What will we do about the
wedding?" He embraced his fiancée and promised her, "We will
get married, Irit." And they did.

Eyal Neufeld was injured in an attack in Meron. After
being in a coma for two months, he woke up blind and deaf,
not knowing where he was. "Angry?" he said. "It was a miracle.
I was sitting next to the terrorist, and I survived." Nine people

were killed in the attack. Eyal's lungs were damaged, his spleen had to be removed, and his jaw, eye sockets, and nose were broken. His skull was fractured in two places, two of the vertebrae in his neck were collapsed, and at first it was thought that he would be paralyzed. His disabled right hand has been operated on dozens of times. The terrorists took away his eyesight, but it took him only two weeks to learn to read Braille and to get around with a cane. As soon as his hearing aid was put in, he was able to hear again.

"There are difficult times," Eyal acknowledges. "There is this darkness that drives me crazy twenty-four hours a day, seven days a week. A total obscurity—an unmoving black space, without end, without form, without color. I try not to think about it. When I am attacked by dark thoughts about what to do with my life, about what would have happened if I hadn't been injured, I try to distract myself. Someone else might have jumped out the window, but me? I may be deaf and blind, but I'm not retarded. Life is too important to me now; I try to see the glass as half full. I'm alive."

The doctors struggled for five days to save the life of Orly Virani, a survivor of the massacre at the Matza restaurant in Haifa in March 2002. They were afraid she wasn't going to make it. "My body was full of shrapnel," Orly said, "and they told me that a person with those kinds of injuries had less than a 20 percent chance of survival. At that time, no one talked about the possibility of getting pregnant and having a child, but I knew that I would survive. I fought for my life. It is a great victory."

Orly's story is very similar to that of another miraculous survivor. In June 2002, a terrorist entered the home of the Shabo family in the settlement of Itamar and fired a hail of bullets, killing Rachel Shabo and three of her children. Asael, nine years old, was hit by a series of bullets that took off his leg. Today he walks thanks to a sophisticated prosthesis designed in the United States. At first he was depressed and didn't want to hear about wearing an artificial limb. Then he met Shlomo Nimrod, a disabled veteran who wears a prosthesis designed to allow him to run and play sports (similar to the one used by the South African Olympic champion Oscar Pistorius). Nimrod convinced Asael to have a prosthesis like his own made. "Dad, I can run on two legs," Asael told his father before returning to Israel.

Since a Palestinian rocket hit her clinic in Ashkelon, Dr. Mirela Siderer lives with a piece of shrapnel an inch and a half long lodged in the left side of her back. The doctors say it is too close to the spinal cord to be removed. "I felt something like a ball of fire whirling inside of me, and all of my teeth were knocked out," Siderer told the United Nations commission set up to investigate the Israeli counteroffensive against Hamas in the Gaza Strip in January 2009. "What was my offense? That I am a Jew living in Ashkelon? I studied medicine to help people all over the world, and I have also helped many women from Gaza."

A volunteer from Zaka, David Dvir, removed a young woman who had just died from the ambulance to make room for an injured person. "And then I recognized her: it was my friend Nava Applebaum. She was twenty years old; she was supposed to get married the next morning." Her father, Dr. David Applebaum, had saved dozens of people torn apart by the bombs. He had immigrated from Cleveland more than twenty years earlier along with his wife, who like him was a scholar of the Torah. After directing Magen David Adom in Jerusalem, Dr. Applebaum founded an innovative emergency care center. The Knesset honored him for helping the injured in an attack on King George Street, before the flames had even been extinguished.

"His entire life was dedicated to saving the lives of others. Thousands of Jerusalem residents owe their lives to him."

Dr. Applebaum had just made a presentation at a conference on terrorism in New York, two years after the September 11 massacre. Israelis have been advising American hospitals on how to prepare for a terror-related mass casualty event, and the country has sent and received international delegations for hospital visits. In New York, Dr. Applebaum had shown slides illustrating how it is possible to treat "forty-four injured people in twenty-eight minutes," as he had done after one attack in Jerusalem. Then he returned home immediately and took his daughter Nava to Cafe Hillel, the day before her wedding was supposed to take place. Both of them were killed by the explosion at the cafe, along with five other people. Nava had just finished her national service with an organization that helps children who have cancer. "She will be an eternal bride," said her brother.

One year after the attack, fifteen American doctors emigrated to Israel in the name of Dr. Applebaum. It is one of the many legacies of this extraordinary doctor. His coworkers call him "revolutionary," a man who was always first to help the victims. Todd Zalut was his assistant for many years at the Shaare Zedek Medical Center. "David was the kind of doctor everyone dreams of becoming," Zalut tells us. "During the 1980s, David was the first volunteer doctor to work in the ambulances. He slept with a defibrillator next to his bed in case of emergency. He helped many to stay alive. At the end of the 1980s, he was frustrated because the Israeli health care system couldn't guarantee standard treatment for all. Regardless of their ability to pay, David gave everyone access to his intensive care unit. No waiting, quality medicine, and helping the patient as if the doctor were a friend." These efforts eventually led to the creation of the David Applebaum Memorial Foundation for the Advancement of Emergency Medicine.

"Everyone had his cell phone number; they called him in the middle of the night, on Shabbat and holidays. He was always there to help. Sometimes he took the patient to America simply because it was too risky to operate on him in Israel," recalls Zalut. He describes Dr. Applebaum as "more than a boss—he was a mentor, he was a friend. We will continue to fight for every patient, Jewish or Arab. And we will win this fight, because it is just and because we had a good teacher."

Dr. Margalit Prachi says of Applebaum, "I worked with him for seventeen years. The patients' families adored him. When he became head of the department, he revolutionized everything: he eliminated inefficiencies and organized a system for gathering family members quickly at the same hospital, children with their parents, in case of attacks or major catastrophes. It is difficult to express what he meant to us."

Dr. Yonatan Halevy, director of Shaare Zedek, remarks, "The fact that a man, three days before his daughter's wedding, would go to America to teach others what he had learned about medical preparation for a terrorist attack—a field in which the Israeli hospitals unfortunately have extensive experience—speaks of the stature of this person and of his complete dedication to both his work and his family." Professor Halevy was Applebaum's supervisor for many years. "David was an extraordinary human being," he says. "Outside of his medical profession, he was known as a scholar and a man of vision; he cared for every human person with respect. In the field of emergency medicine, David was a pioneer and developed many of the systems that are used in emergency rooms. He also organized a network for clinics that don't have access to the resources of the big hospitals. David wanted every patient to receive equal compassion and attention, always. No case was ever too much for him, and he stuck to this until the last days of his life."

Asked how Applebaum reacted to suicide attacks, Halevy replies, "David lived a few minutes from our hospital, so he was always one of the first to arrive. His presence helped to manage the chaos that follows such an attack. Although these attacks are sensational in their scope and nature, it is essential for a doctor to remain calm and give everyone the same attention. David always had the same level of compassion for the victims of attacks."

Dr. Applebaum always showed the close connection between medicine and Judaism, says Todd Zalut. "David was a rabbi, and studied with one of the greatest rabbis of our time, Aharon Soloveitchik. David also taught at the seminary for women. He was an ardent Zionist who thought that Jews all over the world should come to Israel, the land that God gave to the Jewish people."

Applebaum's name has been placed alongside those of the great Jewish masters. According to Yonatan Halevy, "David was a teacher of religion, and, like Maimonides, he was also a doctor. Medicine and Halakhah, the Jewish law, complement each other. There is no doubt that David's faith in the tradition and values of Judaism had a great impact on his role as a doctor, and in particular on the sense of compassion that he demonstrated to all." His death was a tremendous loss for all of Israel. "There are no words to explain this tragedy. The irony is that he was killed in an attack, when he had helped many victims to recover after similar attacks. The medical community will never get over his death. He was a true giant, and his example inspires many students of medicine here in Israel and all over the world. His witness lives on in the Weinstock Department of Emergency Medicine here at the Shaare Zedek hospital."

Applebaum's father-in-law, Shubert Spero, said this at his funeral: "Dear David, you should have accompanied your daughter to the *khupah* (wedding canopy), and instead we are accompanying both of you to your final resting place." Nava's fiancé, Chanan, put the wedding ring on her finger, saying, "She will always be my wife." Nava's grandfather said that "God gave man the ability to weep, but sometimes the tragedy is so painful that the mind refuses." There are many ways to mourn the dead. "At the celebration of the Tabernacle, the high priest Aaron saw his two sons die, but remained silent. When Job saw his family die, he said, 'God gives and God takes away, may the name of God be blessed forever.' We must talk about those who have passed away. David was a born leader, a wonderful father, a husband, a scientist, a teacher, and a friend. He saved human lives every day."

Addressing his family, someone quoted the words of Rabbi Soloveitchik, who said that Applebaum wanted them to live "a life according to the Torah, in the Holy Land." Israel's chief rabbi, Yisrael Meir Lau, compared Applebaum to the greatest saints of Judaism: "He was a true descendant of Maimonides. David and his daughter were great souls." His grandson Natan called him "one of the thirty-six just of the earth." According to an old legend, every generation has thirty-six righteous people, *lamedvavnikim* or *tzadikim,* upon whose piety the fate of the world depends. It is the minimum number of righteous men required to prevent the destruction of the world. The biblical book of Proverbs (10:25) says that the just man is the basis of the world's existence: "When the storm wind passes, the wicked is no more, but the righteous is an everlasting foundation." A *tzadik* is a just man, a saint and a sage, chosen by God to share his gifts with the rest of humanity. That was David Applebaum.

Israel's determination in tackling head-on the physical problems that arise either from natural causes or from war is astounding. There is an amazing quantity of research, inventions, new techniques for curing the ill and helping the blind and the paralyzed return to normal life. It is common to see children with Down syndrome or other disabilities on television programs and in the military. One leader in this work was Moshe Gottlieb.

"A *tzadik*," sobbed the mother of one of Gottlieb's patients. In Israel, Moshe was known as the healer of Down syndrome children and someone who could help people deemed by others to be untreatable. He was murdered on his way to another day's work of charity in behalf of the sick and disabled. Moshe Gottlieb was one of the nineteen victims of the suicide attack in Jerusalem on June 18, 2002.

After leaving a high-paying job at a fur coat factory in New York, Moshe had studied chiropractic in Los Angeles. He visited Israel in 1972 and fell in love with it. Six years later, he went with his wife and children to live in Jerusalem, where he expanded his medical practice and began an intensive study of the Torah. It was in a Jerusalem clinic for the chronically ill that he saw most of his patients, including a girl who was diagnosed with a brain tumor, whose wedding he attended as a guest of honor.

"We moved to Israel after spending a summer there a few years before," says Dr. Gottlieb's son, Seymour. "Simply put, my father 'fell in love' with the land and the people there. His love for community service was so great that he would usually prefer to stay home for the Sabbath and tend to the religious and social services of his community in the Gilo neighborhood of Jerusalem rather than take a weekend off to visit his children and grandchildren living elsewhere. He was also instrumental in creating the core of the neighborhood community services, and he continued to play an active role in these services for over twenty years, until his very last day."

Moshe Gottlieb lived at the far southern end of Jerusalem. For months, during the Second Intifada, the neighborhood was hit day and night by rockets and mortar rounds from the Palestinian suburb of Beit Jalla. Moshe always kept his chair in front of the window, where he could see all of Jerusalem. "His chair will always be there," says his wife, Sheila.

Every Tuesday, Moshe Gottlieb took the bus to Bnei Brak, the impoverished suburb of Tel Aviv inhabited by Orthodox devotees, and worked free of charge in a center for children with Down syndrome. He chose Tuesdays because in the Jewish tradition it is a day "twice as good," and therefore one must give twice as much glory to the Lord. Every other day, Gottlieb saw patients in his office starting at 8:15 on the dot. Many of them were desperate cases, chronic patients and the seriously disabled. "Moshe started working with one girl with Down syndrome when she was two years old," Sheila recalls. "At first she was completely withdrawn and terrorized; she didn't even want to be touched. She had been abandoned by her natural parents, and Moshe cared deeply about her adoptive parents. He always worked with special people. Well, to make the story short, the girl is about ten years old now and she plays the piano very well."

On Tuesdays and Thursdays, Moshe worked with seriously ill patients at Tel Chai. He cared for a woman in a vegetative state for thirteen years, with impressive dedication. Every time he visited New York, he bought expensive medical equipment to help that woman. He also worked at Aleh, a residential care facility for disabled children, always bringing gifts; and he did charity work for orphans.

Moshe woke up at 3:30 every morning, studied the Torah, and prepared the lessons on the Mishnah that he would be giving to a class of Russian immigrants. At sunrise and sunset, he went to pray at the synagogue of Gilo, which he had helped finance. "The synagogue was home to him," said Eliyahu Schlesinger, the chief rabbi of Gilo. "He was the first to arrive and the last to leave, and he was always ready to teach and to encourage us with his wisdom and his smile." A painting in his honor had been unveiled in the synagogue a short time earlier;

now it is dedicated to his memory, and his eulogies were delivered beneath it. Moshe helped the ultra-Orthodox Haredim families in which the men didn't work so they could continue to study. He was never without his religious books. It was the same way that fateful June day, as he walked serenely to the bus stop with his books under his arm.

"He was a very special person, my husband," Sheila tells us. "Two years before his death, Moshe had begun to work with children who had Down syndrome. He had two hundred patients from all over Israel. Everyone loved him. Moshe used to say, 'the body speaks.' . . . And with his hands and the divine guidance of Hashem, he was able to help many people. He was very close to our rabbi in Gilo, Eliyahu Schlesinger. Moshe had financed his synagogue. Now everyone misses his love, his guidance, his presence. His patients, friends, and family, they all mourn him. I hope that one day we can all be together again in *techiyat hametim,* the resurrection of the dead. And to be witnesses to the coming of the Messiah."

Sheila says, "My faith in Hashem, in God, and my love for my children and their families have sustained me during the years after Moshe's death. Now, in his memory, I volunteer with Alzheimer's patients." The famous biblical commentator Rashi said that when a *tzadik* leaves a place, everyone senses his absence, but a *roshem,* a spiritual presence, remains behind.

Dr. Shmuel Gillis lived in Gush Etzion, the most important bloc of settlements south of Jerusalem. "For us," says his wife, Ruthie, "Gush Etzion was part of the national consensus; there were settlements there since the 1920s." Dr. Gillis was killed on February 1, 2001, while returning home after work in the Hadassah Hospital in Jerusalem. One of his Arab patients, Omrina Pauzi, called him "the angel in the white coat." At his funeral, Ruthie told her children that their father had built bridges across religious, ethnic, and political differences. For a hematologist, all blood is the same, and Gillis was a pioneer in hematology. He might not have met his death that day on his way home if he had not waited for one of his colleagues, Dr. Hussein Aliyan, an Arab, who had asked him for help on a case of childhood leukemia.

Dr. Gillis had a warm, contagious smile; he loved the land and hiking in the desert of Judea. He was a humble person, but also a luminary. "Shmuel dedicated himself in everything to the preservation of human life," says his brother David, a pediatrician in the same hospital. "He would always look at the surrounding villages and say, 'I have a patient there, and two there.' It was hard on him that he couldn't go visit them without risking his life. What he loved about the hospital was that all divisions disappeared there; he could be a human being taking care of another human being."

Shmuel was born in England and he arrived in Israel at age eleven. He joined the air force and served in the Lebanon War. "He is still remembered for his compassion for the Arab prisoners of war, for how he treated them," his brother says. "Many years later, he would treat some of Yasser Arafat's associates in the same way." According to one of his patients in Tel Aviv, "He was the closest thing to an angel. He made no distinction between Arabs and Jews; he treated everyone wonderfully." His approach to his patients, his care for children with cancer, his attentiveness to infertile women, his joy at the circumcision of wailing little boys, and the happiness with which he greeted victory over the most terrible illnesses are still associated with the Gillis name.

"Shmuel was a very simple man, famous only among his colleagues and patients," says David Gillis. "As his brother and a doctor, I can tell you that I heard many times about his brilliant solutions during hematology conferences. Colleagues would often stop me in the hallway to tell me, 'You really have a special brother.' The hematologists tell me that Shmuel would reach a certain diagnosis through a Talmudic form of reasoning; they use a term for him that indicates a genius in the Talmud, *iluy*. Professor Pollack, a well-known hematologist who specializes in the diagnosis and treatment of lymphoma, once said that he felt as though he could consult with Shmuel over a difficult case for help in making a diagnostic decision. Shmuel's specialty was blood coagulation, and in this field he often came into contact with gynecologists and traumatologists. He helped the gynecologists to realize that in many cases, miscarriage is caused by blood coagulation problems, and Shmuel was close to women with problems in pregnancy. After his death, I came into contact with some women at Hadassah who recognized me because of my resemblance to Shmuel. Without waiting for me to tell them my own stories, these women told me, 'Look at this child—he is alive thanks to your brother.' In traumatology, Shmuel was involved in treating patients who had lost a lot of blood. The head of the traumatology ward at Hadassah talks about Shmuel's contribution to survival rates."

David describes Shmuel as "an incomparable researcher and teacher. He authored some pioneering works, becoming famous at the international level. Shmuel taught many students, including one Palestinian doctor. One year after his death, this doctor went to a conference in the United States through a fund established in Shmuel's memory. And this is what my brother would have wanted; he was a great humanist who never nursed any hatred toward the Arabs. He never mixed medicine and politics. He had served in the Israeli army as a doctor in the special forces, taking part in spectacular military operations, but he never lost his humanity or dignity during those actions. He always wanted to be sure that the soldiers were treated with dignity, even the enemy soldiers. Many of the things he did in the army became known only after his death."

The story of the Gillis brothers begins in Eastern Europe and winds through England. "One of our relatives was a rabbi in Lithuania, the last in a chain of rabbis that had spanned twelve generations," David tells us. "He was one of the *ohave Tzion,* the lovers of Zion, predecessors of the Zionist movement. And he wrote a book proposing that the Jews be brought back to their ancient land, in a movement in which the majority of Orthodox rabbis said would have to take place through divine intervention. He titled it *Love of Zion and of Jerusalem,* and demonstrated that most of the Jewish laws and traditions favored a physical return to Zion by means of human enterprise. Thanks to his fame, he was invited to Manchester, England, to become the rabbi of the main synagogue. Nonetheless, he never gave up on his Zionist ideals, and raised his children in the dream and ideology of returning to Zion. Our father and his brothers and sisters were raised as fervent Zionists, and over the years they all came to Israel. The first was my father's brother Joseph Gillis, who immigrated in 1948 and became a great mathematician, the designer of Israel's first computer, and the dean of the mathematics faculty at the Weizmann Institute of Science in Rehovot. Our father was very active in the Zionist movement in England, and we made the aliyah in 1970. Shmuel was eleven years old, and he quickly became one of the best students. We immediately fell in love with this land and this people."

David says that "Shmuel believed in the sanctity of the land of Israel, and after he married Ruthie they decided to build their house in the settlements of Judea and Samaria. The historical connection between the Jewish people and these places dates back to the time of the patriarchs. Shmuel was an enthusiast for the history and geography of these places, and he believed in peaceful coexistence with the Arab inhabitants. His view was that there was room for everyone in Israel, and that everyone should be able to live in peace."

After one year in the farming settlement of Beit Yatir in the Hebron Hills, the Gillises moved to Carmei Tzur. "In the first settlement, Shmuel was always happy to lend a hand with the 'dirty work,' like cleaning the chicken coop," his brother recalls. "Carmei Tzur also has a core of academics, scientists, and teachers, all people who believe in the idea of inhabiting the land while enhancing their Jewish ideals. Shmuel was always sought out by the other inhabitants of the settlement when they needed medical help, even on Shabbat, when they couldn't take a car to Jerusalem, or the roads were blocked by snow."

Shmuel was a man of great faith. "When he went to conferences all over the world, my brother always ate kosher, observed Shabbat, and took part in religious services. To those who asked how he was able to be an Orthodox Jew in a secularized world, Shmuel mentioned the extremely difficult dietary laws and the rules of Shabbat. Unlike some religious fanatics, such as the many Muslims who have a fundamentalist view hostile to everyone, Shmuel and Ruthie tolerated other people's ideas. Their love of neighbor was strong; they considered it their central religious principle. Tolerance was a way of life for Shmuel. His last patient before he died was an Arab woman. She had thanked him, calling him 'an angel of heaven.'"

Ruthie Gillis is the principal of a religious school in Jerusalem, and her family went through the Holocaust. "Shmuel was a very brilliant man, the first in his class in medicine," she says. "But at the same time, he was a very humble man; he never said 'I'm the best.' He was a man of science, an angel who wanted to take care of every patient. He felt that everyone, Arabs and Jews, had the same dignity."

In a 1997 interview with the *Jerusalem Post*, Shmuel said, "We were looking for simplicity, and Carmei Tzur fascinated us." Ruthie comments, "For us, Israel is everywhere. Shmuel and I thought that as Jews, we had the right to live anywhere, and that if we had left Carmei Tzur, one day they would also have asked us to leave Tel Aviv. We have to protect ourselves. Every morning, I pass the place where my husband was killed. And I know that we will never be able to live completely at ease." Ruthie has never thought about leaving her village in Gush Etzion, however. "I have to move forward. Every day is a battle, but I could never leave Carmei Tzur. Where would I go? Tel Aviv? Ashkelon? Terror is everywhere here. Shmuel got up every morning to pray; he believed in the Torah and that living in *Eretz Yisrael* is part of the Jewish faith itself. He was an optimist, and he always said that he had to do everything he could for the good of Israel."

Ruthie Gillis believes that the conflict with the Palestinians is not a conflict over land. "Anyone who lives here, like me and like many others, sees how many bare hills and valleys there are here. There's plenty of room for everyone, for us and for them. What is missing is room in their hearts. That's why the murderers are not fighting to obtain territory. The murderers murder Jews because they are Jews. That is anti-Semitism and racism for its own sake. Their war is against a different identity living alongside them, here in Carmei Tzur, and in Haifa and in Tel Aviv and in Jerusalem and in Tiberias—to them there is no difference. They are fighting against the Jew because he is a Jew. The land is a secondary factor in their struggle."

68.864 Was My Name

The siren begins on a rising note before settling into
a mournful steady tone. For two long minutes, the signs
of human movement simply stop. Everyone is overwhelmed by the mysterious solidarity of the moment. It is Yom
Hashoah, the solemn commemoration of the Holocaust. Drivers get out of their cars to recall the Nazi extermination of six
million European Jews.

The same single-tone siren was used as the all-clear signal in
the Gulf War, when Saddam Hussein's Iraq threatened to
"burn half of Israel." The specter of chemical warfare was a special nightmare, one that recalled memories of the annihilation
in Europe and brought forth feelings of helplessness and fear.
To its 4.6 million people, Israel distributed gas masks, syringes
of an anti-nerve-gas agent, and powder to absorb vapor
droplets on the skin, evoking dark memories for elderly citizens
whose families perished in Nazi gas chambers. The fact that
Saddam's missile power was aided by German companies drew
a line in Israeli minds from gas masks in Tel Aviv to gas chambers at Auschwitz and Treblinka. "The echoes and reverbera-
tions of the past returned," said Elie Wiesel, the Holocaust
survivor and Nobel Peace Prize laureate. "Once more we spoke
of gas, we spoke of Germany." Israeli infants had to be
put inside a greenhouse-like plastic tent called a *mamat*, and

parents could touch them only through stiff plastic gloves. "Another dictator using gas on the largest Jewish population in the world," said Theodore Weiss, a survivor of three concentration camps and president of the Holocaust Educational Foundation, in Wilmette, Illinois. At times of crisis, the memories of the Holocaust always surface from the Jewish unconscious, from places where Israel did not even know they were hidden.

For Israel, there is no moment more significant than Yom Hashoah: when the siren sounds, people stop in the streets; they stand at attention after getting out of their cars; they freeze while shopping in the supermarkets, studying in the universities, marching in the army, doing business. It is like a great wall of silence, full of suffering and vitality. All of Israel focuses its devotion on one memory. Some thought goes to the uprisings in the ghettos and in the camps, the pinnacle of Israel's national spirit.

This is why, when Ilan Ramon died, the country united around his name—because the soft-spoken young man with a humble expression had brought the memory of the Holocaust into outer space. As the first Israeli astronaut, he had carried with him a copy of a drawing that Petr Ginz made in the ghetto of Theresienstadt before he was killed in Auschwitz at the age of sixteen. Ramon was excited about bringing along the drawing by "a boy imprisoned within the walls of the ghetto, walls that could not imprison his spirit. His drawings are the testimony of the triumph of his spirit." Ilan also brought a Torah scroll and a coin from 69 CE, minted in Jerusalem, with the inscription "Salvation for the people of Israel." Ramon identified himself as the son of a German Jew who had taken refuge in Israel and a woman who had survived Auschwitz. He had taken into space the memory of the Holocaust, which his mother had escaped, unlike his grandfather and other relatives, and of the struggle for independence, in which his father had participated. Ilan died when the Space Shuttle *Columbia* exploded on February 11, 2003, killing the seven astronauts aboard.

The Torah scroll that Ilan brought into space, the first ever to have gone there, was the one that Joachim Joseph had used to prepare for his bar mitzvah in the Bergen-Belsen concentration camp. Early one Tuesday morning, before the alarm went off, the prisoners put blankets over the windows and lit candles, and Joachim chanted his passage from the Torah, as every Jewish boy has done for centuries. Then Rabbi Simon Dasberg, who had given him the scroll, said to him, "I will not get out of here alive; here, take the scroll, and tell the story." Joachim gave it to Ilan as "a symbol of the Jewish resistance even in the extermination camps, of the determination to survive." The Torah scroll, he noted, "came out of the most profound darkness, and Ilan took it into the dazzling light of space."

Ilan Ramon is buried in Moshav Nahalal in the Jezreel Valley, a place where death and malaria once reigned before the Jewish pioneers turned it into one of the most fertile areas in Israel. And beside him is the liberator of Jerusalem, Moshe Dayan. The diary entry with his *dvar Torah*, message from the Torah, has not come down to us. It will remain forever indecipherable. Just as in the legend about the Jewish mystic Baal Shem Tov: He met the Messiah and asked when he would come down to earth. The answer was, "When your message arrives in heaven."

Several months after the *Columbia* explosion, a group of Israeli pilots made a highly symbolic flight. Ignoring the protests from the Auschwitz museum, the Israeli jets, piloted by children of Holocaust survivors, flew over the concentration camp that had swallowed up a million Jews. The demonstration was led by Brigadier General Amir Eshel, whose grandmother had been murdered down there in the gas chambers of Birkenau. "We pilots promise to be a shield for the Jewish people and for Israel," Eshel said. "There was the platform where the selection took place, the railway line, the green fields, an innocent silence. That is how hell appeared on earth, in the heart of Europe. As an Israeli who had been taught that the Jews had gone 'like sheep to the slaughter,' I felt the courage of the millions who faced infinite suffering in the ghettos, in the forests, in the cattle cars. Representing their memory was a great honor for us. We understood the enormity of our responsibility, in guaranteeing the immortality of our people and bearing their greatness upon our wings."

On the occasion of Israel's fifty-eighth anniversary, Eliezer Shkedi, then commander of the air force and a man with a contagious smile, had his father, a Shoah survivor, get aboard his F-1. "For me it is clear that my duty is to restore value to human history," Shkedi said, "and for this reason I followed the path of my father, and my father today is somewhat compensated." The chief rabbi, Yisrael Meir Lau, a survivor of Auschwitz, said that Israel represents a special form of revenge: "The revenge is that we are here, the revenge is that we are home, the revenge is that we have a country, the revenge is that we are here in this place with the blue and white flag and the Star of David."

For Jews, the fact of the Shoah is a justification for Israel's existence. For the Iranian president Mahmoud Ahmadinejad, denial of the Shoah is reason enough to pursue a war of extermination against Israel. According to Ahmadinejad's logic, Israel was created after the Shoah (a historical fallacy); Jews have used the Shoah as an excuse to reclaim their nation (another historical fallacy); and therefore, since the Shoah didn't happen, Israel may consequently be obliterated. This is why, when a Holocaust survivor is killed by a suicide bomber or loses a relative in a terrorist attack, the entire country reads the story with anguish. It is a perfect murder—the conclusion of a project begun sixty years earlier in Europe. The aim to annihilate the Jews has left a long trail of darkness down through the generations.

George and Anna Yakobovitch had gotten on the train to Auschwitz together. He was able to get away before they reached the gate of death. She came to the ramp of Dr. Joseph Mengele, along with her father, mother, and siblings. They were gassed immediately, but she made it out alive. Thirty years later, George and Anna met again by chance and got married. At a Passover supper in 2002, a suicide bomber killed George on the spot, together with twenty-seven other people. "Sons of pigs and monkeys," the terrorist had called them before blowing himself up.

Another victim of terrorism was Mendel Bereson, from Saint Petersburg, who had lost all his relatives in Europe; today his family in Israel says he was "a true Zionist," someone who "said that the Jews have only one state." Leah Levine had just found out that her brother, the only other member of their large family to have escaped the genocide, was living in Russia. She is remembered as "a wonderful wife, always happy, and the mother of four boys." Leah Strick, a survivor of the massacre in the Bialystok ghetto in Poland, was blown up in a bus on a Sunday morning while she was going to visit her sister in a geriatric clinic.

"We came here by ourselves because our parents were killed in the Holocaust," said the brother of the artist Miriam Levy, who was killed in Jerusalem in June 2003. Her grandson noted that his "elegant and intelligent grandmother had emerged from the abyss of the Holocaust aboard the ship *Exodus*." Miriam had come to Israel on the legendary ship that in 1947 defied the British blockade by trying to reach Palestine with 4,515 Holocaust survivors. "We swore to them then: never again another Auschwitz," Commandant Yossi Harel would say later. "I like to think that Israel was born then, on those ships crammed with refugees considered illegal immigrants." The *Exodus 1947* was fired on by the English in the Bay of Haifa, and with dead and wounded aboard, Harel had to surrender. One girl on the ship had escaped being killed by the Nazis because she was buried under a pile of corpses; she could no longer close her eyes because her eyelid muscles had contracted.

Elsa Cohen and Bianca Shichrur, also victims of terrorism, had much in common. Both had survived the Second World War, and both had a mentally disabled son living in the same area of Jerusalem. Bianca, born in Italy, had come to Israel forty years earlier. Elsa had lost her whole family in the Holocaust, and was one of the children of Kinder Transport in London after the outbreak of the war. About ten thousand Jewish children were sent to Great Britain, without their parents, from Austria, Germany, Poland, and Czechoslovakia. Elsa made the journey with one of the children of Robert Wasselberg, who had to decide which of his three children would take the last spot available on a Kinder Transport.

Arno Klarsfeld is the son of Serge and Beate Klarsfeld, who dedicated their lives to hunting down Nazi war criminals. Arno said that he "broke intellectually and morally" with France in September 2001, after the attacks on the Twin Towers. He moved from Paris to a small apartment in Tel Aviv, refusing the subsidies provided for immigrants and taking up the study of Hebrew. He was outside the Mike's Place pub in Tel Aviv on April 30, 2003, right after an attack by a suicide bomber with an English passport who had come from London to massacre Jews. Those charred bodies, those human remains lying there on the pavement, gave Arno the last push toward enlisting in the Israeli army. One of those lifeless bodies was that of Yanay Weiss, the son of Lipa Weiss.

The saga of Lipa Weiss is emblematic of how much the survivors of the crematory ovens have suffered from Islamic fanaticism. He was fourteen years old when he was deported to Auschwitz, where in a few hours he saw his entire family vanish in the gas chambers—his parents, his grandparents, his brothers and sisters. After the war, he joined a kibbutz in Israel. Two years before his son Yanay was killed at Mike's Place, Lipa had lost his granddaughter Inbal in a suicide attack.

Lipa's story, recounted here at length for the first time, began in Zdeneve, a tiny village in the Carpathians, in December of 1924. "Mine was a classic Jewish family," he says. "As a child I studied in a *cheder;* I learned Hebrew and the Bible, translating our sacred language word by word into Yiddish, which was spoken at home. Up until the age of fourteen, I studied at both the Jewish school and the public school. I learned the stories of Adam and Eve, Isaac and Jacob, about how Joseph was sold by his brothers, about the captivity in Egypt, about Moses and the liberation and the conversations with the Pharaoh, the Exodus, the desert and the Ten Commandments, about Joshua at Jericho. These stories were the origin of my faith. Hebron, Bethlehem, and Jerusalem were my homeland, and I wanted to see them in person. This was the origin of my faith in Judaism, my faith in God and Jewish values. When I got older, my father questioned me every Sunday morning about the previous week's reading from the Torah. All this was done in a kind and respectful way, and this instilled in me a profound respect for my father and mother. She cooked my favorite dishes for me when I came back from school."

Until 1938, under the democratic Czechoslovakian government, the Jews were not discriminated against, and those years had a very strong impact on Lipa's personality: "Respect for Shabbat, the prayers in the synagogue, strengthened my faith in a merciful God, and this would give me the strength to confront the horrific period that would follow. I believed that God would save us."

The Weisses went through years of dire poverty. "Farming was the way of life in our region, growing potatoes for domestic consumption, and working in the forests. There were no industries or businesses. The Jews sold basic necessities to non-Jews. When Hungary came back to power in 1939, new economic laws were imposed on the Jews. The men, including my father, were conscripted to work on the fortifications, because we were on the border between Poland and Hungary. My family was not able to support itself, and since I was the oldest child I went to work in the forests to permit my mother to buy oil, sugar, and salt. We had two cows, and they gave us about a gallon of milk a day. We also had the potatoes that my parents grew in a little garden plot. Over time we were even able to buy clothes, which were mended and passed from one child to another."

With the Molotov-Ribbentrop Pact between the Nazis and the Soviets, the Polish region on the border with Hungary was put under Soviet control. And the Jews were accused of being Communist spies. "The most difficult thing was proving Hungarian citizenship from generation to generation, and it was too expensive to bribe the official," Lipa recalls. "My father returned home for the feasts of Rosh Hashanah and Passover, and two more children were born." During that period, the fate of the Jews was bound to the success of the Germans. The worse the war went, the more ferocious the SS became. "After the fall of Stalingrad in 1943 and the beginning of the German retreat, the Nazis started to deport the Jews to Ukraine, and the Ukrainians killed them by every means possible. They took families out onto the Dniester River, or killed them in the forests with axes and knives. When the Russians approached our area, the Jews were banned from leaving the villages. I was allowed to work in the forests, but not to enter a non-Jewish house."

The Hungarian regime under Horthy understood that the war was coming to an end, and withdrew its army to the east. The Germans entered, and together with the Hungarian fascists they began to confine the Jews to ghettos. "In April of 1944, at the end of Passover, when my father was at home, we were told to pack our bags, one bag weighing forty pounds for each person, and to get ready to leave our home. The next day we were deported to the ghetto of a city named Mukachevo. There was no water, no bathrooms or kitchens. Whole families packed together, one next to another. There were no medicines, and the sick died, the elderly died. Every day the bodies were burned in the communal crematory in the cemetery. We cooked potatoes and beans, and every day a list was drawn up of the people to be deported to Auschwitz."

Lipa Weiss would be one of the few Jewish survivors of the death machine of Adolf Eichmann, who deported the entire Hungarian Jewish community to the gas chambers. The *Ungarische Aktion* was the apex of the German capacity for extermination. About one-third of the victims of Auschwitz came from Hungary. Twelve thousand Hungarian Jews arrived every day, and Eichmann needed just twenty officers and a hundred functionaries to annihilate one of the largest Jewish communities in Europe.

Lipa remembers very clearly the time he saw the SS: "They were looking for the important men in the community. They pulled them out of the roll-call line, in front of their wives and children, and began to torture them. They ordered them to remove their hats, cut off their beards, and whipped them to the point of exhaustion. For us, these men were the highest authorities, models of honesty, morality, and piety, and they were publicly humiliated. When they were no longer able to react, they were left to die where they were lying. The stronger ones, who stayed alive longer, were shot. On the lists were the names of the people to be deported—entire families, the sick, pregnant women, the elderly."

Then came the day of deportation. "No one was allowed to bring more than ten pounds of luggage. There was barbed wire on the boxcar windows, and when the deportation began the German and Hungarian prisoners began shouting. Everyone, regardless of age or physical ability, had to get into the boxcars. An SS official checked to make sure they were full. We had no food or water. We didn't know where they were taking us, but we were on the train for four days. At the few stops, they threw out the urine and feces. Without warning, the train arrived at its destination. The doors were opened, and we were ordered to get out fast, without taking anything with us. We came down a ramp, and that was the first time we saw the prisoners who were already there. Their job was to separate the men from the women and children. I don't know how, but suddenly I found myself among the men. My mother, my seventeen-year-old sister, who was holding my one-year-old brother, and the other children all disappeared, and I didn't see them anymore. It was night, and they took us away. In a camp, the SS inspected us to see who was able to work. Those who were able went to the right; otherwise they joined the women and children."

Lipa looked out between two strands of barbed wire. "On my left, I saw the smoke of the crematories, and what looked like dead bodies being lifted by the hands and feet and thrown into the fire. We heard terrible screams. Later we found out that the gas chambers were there. They divided us into groups of ten and ordered us to run. We hadn't had any food or water. We came to a big shower room, where the men and women were stripped and beaten, and examined to see if they were hiding any valuables. The hot water was turned on for a few minutes, and then suddenly it turned cold. We went into another room where the barbers cut our hair. We were given a uniform, a hat, and an aluminum mess tin. That was all we had left in the world." The mess tin was the most important thing— without it you didn't eat. "The next morning, the men and women walked in two parallel lines. I saw the girls from my section, and I could see who had survived and who hadn't. I was the only one left from my family. All the others, my parents, sisters, brothers, the relatives with us on the train, they were all exterminated the night before."

Only Lipa and a cousin on his father's side were still alive. "From there we went to the barracks of Birkenau; we spent hours in the *Appellplatz,* famished and exhausted. We had not had anything to eat or drink since the ghetto. We had to support the prisoners who were about to fall down. The barracks was full of beds. We had to ask permission to go to the toilet, which was a barrel with planks on it. They ladled vegetable soup into our mess kits; the Germans called it *Durgensuppe.* It had no flavor, but we had to fill our stomachs. During those two terrible weeks, the journey by train, the time in the barracks, I had to learn to live in a new way. In the ghetto, I had slept with my parents, I had a blanket, but here I was alone. The few things I had to make my life happy had been taken away from me when I got on the train. There was no drinking water. We had to bathe ourselves standing up, in front of the others. How could human beings do this? The only things of your own were your shoes, and if they were good shoes you would live longer; you had less chance of getting sick. Any kind of help, like giving someone a glass of water, was forbidden. If you helped a sick person, you were risking your own life. The sick and the injured were left where they were until they died. If they were lucky, they went to the *Revier,* a sort of hospital. There you were subjected to every sort of medical experiment until you died. Those who could work went to Commando X or Y; those who couldn't went to Commando Himmel, the clinic. And then they were burned in the crematory. You always had to watch what was happening around you. The policy of the Germans was always *Vernichtung,* annihilation. And there were two ways of achieving this: gassing the unfit, the women, the children, the sick, and the elderly; and working the fit to death. The saying was *Vernichtung durch Arbeit.*"

Lipa was always thinking about his loved ones. "You thought about your parents who had died in that horrible way, and about the fact that you were left alone. There was no one to tell you what was happening. But the others were all alone, too. There were some who were trying to make it through the pain, and some who just couldn't. They threw themselves against the high-voltage wires, or killed themselves in other ways. In Auschwitz, I thought that I would be strong, the Germans would need me. One day we were taken to the train station in Birkenau. The orchestra was playing. Our only 'property' was the mess kit and a piece of bread. The train left in the evening, and the bread was our only food for four days. We had no water."

On a Sunday morning, the train stopped in Mauthausen, in Austria, not far from where Hitler was born. "We walked for four miles, toward an uninhabited place, and on a hill we could see guard towers. And the SS opened the huge gate. We entered the *Appellplatz*. There were two marble buildings in front of us, built by the prisoners with stones from the nearby quarry. From the balcony, the commandant informed us of the rules we had to follow. After that, we went through another door. The ground was covered with gravel, and there were barracks on both sides. On the right were the gas chambers, the crematory, and the laundry. Our barracks were empty, no tables or beds. We had to state our names and birthdates, one by one. They told you that from that moment on, you would be called by your registration number. My name was 68.864. When they called out your name, you had to respond *'Jawohl,'* that's me. That number was stamped on both of my pants legs and on my jacket, together with a red triangle and the letter J." It was the initial for *Juden*, Jew.

"In the afternoon, they gave us soup and three and a half ounces of bread, and we were sent to the barracks for the night. It was the end of June, it was hot, the sun was blazing, and we were not given anything to drink. There were no mattresses, and we were crammed together side by side. Our sleep was disturbed by cries and wails of pain. We stayed like this from Sunday to Thursday, when they took us to the trains going to Melk, on the Danube, to a concentration camp in the mountains. On the gate it said 'Pioneern Kaserme,' and it was the base of the military engineers. In one building was the general headquarters, and in another were the kapos. We slept in the garages. We were divided into work groups, and I was put together with a friend from my village. Our job was to build the tunnel walls."

The plant was used by Daimler-Benz to build modern aircraft. "An engineer in the SS was in charge of the work. The entire process was carried forward with German precision. There was an electric fence to keep us from escaping. In the evening, after counting us and counting those who had died that day, they brought us back to the camp. Occasionally they gave us cigarettes as a reward, and these could be exchanged for some soup, some bread, or a good pair of shoes taken from the dead. But the food was never enough to satisfy us; there were too few calories, and our bodies had no energy reserves. Many died and were burned in the crematory."

Lipa was able to assess the progress of the war from three things: "from what the trains were transporting, from the number of tanks, and from the mood of the Germans. After D-Day, we saw the airplanes that were going to bomb the German cities. We were overjoyed to see the four-plane formations in the sky. But in the camp, the Germans' dedication to the extermination never waned. When the Russians took Vienna, forty miles away from us, instead of letting us go the Germans took us to Linz. On the fourth day of the march, we were sleeping in the Austrian cold. Many died, or were shot because they couldn't walk."

They arrived in Ebensee, where there was another Daimler complex. "There were three sleeping in the same spot, and in the morning you realized that the one sleeping next to you was dead. There wasn't enough food, and the death rate rose dramatically. Death was present everywhere. Our job was to build new train tracks to replace the ones that had been bombed. One Friday, I was assigned to work in the tunnels. In the afternoon, we were taken outside to have some soup. The SS officer told us that just this once we would have the chance to be 'normal' people. We didn't return to the tunnels after lunch. It was a fantastic day. Each of us found a spot to lie in the sun. We felt we would be set free any day. One morning, the commandant announced that the Americans were going to try to take the camp, and that the SS were going to fight. He told us that if we wanted to save ourselves, we would have to go into the tunnels. We refused, and he disappeared; we never saw him again. There was no more order in the camp. Some went around looking for food, while the stronger prisoners lynched the kapos."

The Americans arrived on Sunday, but they left almost immediately. "My friends and I, blood brothers whose cooperation had been the secret of our survival, found ourselves free again. It was as if we had been reborn. The memories of our families exterminated in Auschwitz, the knowledge that we were alone in the world and far from home ... who could we talk to about this? Who could advise us? My friend and I were exhausted, without enough strength to walk. Our last meal had been some bread the day before. And we left the camp for the city. We had grown accustomed to the images of our imprisonment—so the lake, the mountains, the farming village all fascinated us."

They came to the city of Ebensee, to another labor camp. "We stayed there for three weeks, drinking milk, eating eggs, eating chocolate. I signed the list of people from Czechoslovakia, and we were divided by nationality. I wanted to find somewhere new to go, not go back to the place where I was born and see the people who for years had ignored our sufferings. I had lost my faith in God on the night in Auschwitz when I saw that horror, the innocent Jews walking to their death, their faith in God still strong. Their only crime was that they were Jews. Then I thought: how could the world ignore what was happening to the Jews? Europe knew and saw. Hitler had been very clear about his intention: the final solution to the problem of the Jews. I wanted no part in that world. One day the Jewish soldiers from Israel, called the Brigade, and the English and Americans brought faith and hope to the camp. They helped us believe that the Jews could defend themselves and have a state of their own. They could be 'Jews in Palestine.' Then why not build their state there? Europe had been destroyed, the cities had been razed to the ground, and the Allied armies were there. Normal life hadn't resumed yet."

After more than a month in the camp, Lipa was taken to Prague. "The Czechs welcomed us and gave us medicine, they invited us to eat in their homes, and they wanted to know what had happened. I saw some of the others reunite with their relatives, and I desperately wanted to meet one of my own. I knew that my parents were dead, but I thought I might be able to find some other relative. I went back home, but I discovered that all of the Jewish homes had been burned. So I went to Budapest, where I met one of my father's cousins; he was in the Czech army outfit that had entered Auschwitz, where he had found one of his sisters. I got work in a Jewish orphanage, but while I was living in Prague, the Communists interrogated me about the reason why I had not gone back to my country."

Meanwhile, the Zionist leaders had sent emissaries from Palestine to Europe, to organize the new Jewish state. "The young Zionists prepared our immigration into Israel, the aliyah. I joined the socialist group Hashomer Hatzair. They gave us lessons on Jewish history and Zionism. But the British had put restrictions on immigration, so we stayed in the camp until March of 1948. I remember the vote at the United Nations, an incredible historical event. Just two years earlier, in the camps, we had no future. Now there was recognition of the right of the Jews to the land of their fathers, Abraham, Isaac, and Jacob. We knew that the Jewish army, the Palmach, was smaller than the Arab armies. We were eager to take part in the war."

On May 14, 1948, Lipa found himself in Marseilles, where he would take the first ship bound for Israel. "We set sail knowing that we had a state. When we arrived in Haifa, there was excitement in the air. The Jewish army enlisted us immediately. The women were taken to Kibbutz Masaryk, and we were left to guard them. Then to another kibbutz, Ein Hashofet. While I was still at Kfar Masaryk, I married Judith in a religious ceremony, but without any celebration." Lipa was alone in the world. There was no one to share his joy. "I worked in the dairy for one year, and then I was enlisted in the artillery for two more."

In November 1950, Avner was born. "Avner means 'memory of my father.' We wanted to honor my father and Judith's father, who had been exterminated in Auschwitz. Two years later I became a reservist, and I returned to my job at the dairy. It was hard; the kibbutz depended on our work. But it was very satisfying—rewarding in a way that can't be measured in monetary terms. The kibbutz became my life. The standard of living was low, but the quality of education was very high, and that was the most important thing for me. I hadn't received any formal education since middle school, and this way of life allowed me to study. I made up the ground that I had lost. I saw the progress and success of the kibbutz as a living testimony to the expertise of Jews who had been viewed as less than human in the camps. We Jews now had a country, where we did every sort of agricultural work and sold the fruits of our labors. We were capable of defending ourselves. I found myself in a country where the Jews were laborers, farmers, merchants, actors, musicians—in other words, a normal country. We were independent, and we didn't exploit anyone."

In 1956, Lipa had another son, Yanay—the one who would be killed by a suicide bomber in Tel Aviv. "I was no longer a refugee. I had my family, even if it looked different from the outside. The hours I spent with my children were the best hours of the day. After living in a tent, we moved into a real building, into a little apartment that was very cozy, a source of satisfaction. I began working on a state-of-the-art chicken farm. All over the country, Israeli agriculture had moved from primitive to modern and scientific. We were innovators in many fields. During these years, I was frequently called up from the reserve."

The years went by, and in 1965 there was a third son, Gidi. "Avner played the flute and oboe. Yanay loved to listen to stories. On Sundays we went for walks, and we spent many hours in the swimming pool that the members of the kibbutz had built by themselves." Later, recalls Lipa, "Yanay developed a great talent for music; he played the violin and the guitar, and the kibbutz paid for his lessons. We wanted our children to develop their talents."

When war broke out in 1967, all Israeli men had to enlist, and Lipa did his duty as a reservist. "I worked on the farm for twenty-one years," he recounts, "and then I studied management on behalf of the kibbutz and began working in the field of management. I worked until I was seventy-nine years old, when I had to retire for health reasons. Since my retirement, I have been active in the senior citizens' center." Judith and Lipa divorced in 1981, and Lipa married Pnina, who was also a member of the kibbutz. "We spent twenty splendid years together, in mutual love and respect. Pnina got kidney disease and had to undergo dialysis, but although we had done everything we could, she died in September of 2000."

All three of Lipa's sons served in the army: Avner in the artillery, Yanay in the music band, and Gidi in the aviation sector. "Although I myself had been a reserve soldier for twenty-six years, my anxiety and concern for my sons has been a constant in my life," Lipa says. He has found great joy in his grandchildren. Avner's first daughter, Inbal, was born in 1979, followed by Avital, Ami, and Daniel. "To hold a grandchild in my arms, receive a kiss, be called *Saba*, 'Grandpa,' the laughter, the games, the delight of their first words—all of this has been a joy."

The first of the Weiss family to fall victim to a suicide bomber was the charming Inbal. "She had served as a teacher in the army. One day a week, she went to the archives of Beit Lohamei HaGeta'ot, the center that documents the Jewish resistance against the Nazis—the partisans, the clandestine fighters, and those who rebelled in the ghettos. She was motivated by compassion, and by her connection to her grandparents and the Jewish people. Inbal and I had a special relationship, we talked about many things, she admired me and I admired her." After her military service, it was time for Inbal to enter college. "She went to Emek Yisrael College. She started bringing me books, and she did a project on the policies of the Jewish Agency for Israel in my kibbutz. I admired her tenacity and determination. She was sent to the dean's office, where she was told that she had been chosen for a special program. I remember that it was November 29, 2001, and Inbal called to tell me; she was excited, proud, and happy. I planned to see her that Friday at dinner at her parents' house in Zichron Ya'akov. She always took the bus home. But that Thursday, she took a different route to meet her parents and go to the restaurant. The route wound through a number of Arab villages. Her parents called her on her cell phone to find out where she was. Two minutes later, the suicide bomber blew himself up. The bus was almost empty; there were three dead. Inbal was one of them."

Israeli television interrupted its broadcasts to report on the attack. "I was nervous. I called Avner at home and the children told me that Avner and Marianne had gone to wait for Inbal at the bus stop. I called his cell phone and asked him where she was. I realized that Inbal had been on the bus. Later they went to identify the body. It was a horrible night. I went to Zichron to watch the children. We sat down in shock; no one said a word. We were alone with our sadness and our anger. Their parents returned in the middle of the night. We sat up until the morning, waiting for the funeral. It was rainy, another note of sadness. Pnina, my second wife, had died the year before, and I missed her deeply. I sat down to write my eulogy for Inbal. I don't think I wept the way I did that night in Auschwitz, when my whole family was killed, maybe because I had to think about the things I had to do. But I had not wept since that night in the camps. Now everything made me weep. I missed Inbal so much; I woke up in the middle of the night thinking about her. I decided that I couldn't let this crush me. I focused on my sons and returned to my routine. Inbal had been killed because she was a Jew, just like my parents, my relatives, and six million more."

Yanay Weiss, Lipa's second son, had left the kibbutz after his military service. "He wanted to become a musician, to make a living with music, although he would do any kind of work." In Tel Aviv he married Orna, whose father was a survivor of Auschwitz and whose mother, together with her twin sister, had been among the "Mengele twins" who were subjected to horrifying medical experiments. "Orna taught at a nursery school and then worked as a therapist. Because they lived far away, I didn't see them as often as I wanted. We saw each other once a month and at the holidays. Yanay gave up his dream of being a musician to work for a high-tech company, but he never gave up on music. He organized a band and a choir for the employees. On Tuesday night they were playing at Mike's Place, and many of their friends and fans were there. The pub was full of people who had come to listen to them. They weren't being paid anything; their only compensation was joy. Yanay had a family full of warmth and love."

On April 29, 2003, Holocaust Remembrance Day in Israel, Orna was at Ben-Gurion University in Beersheba, happy because they were going to give her an award for her work. "They decided to meet at the station in Tel Aviv. Yanay came with a bouquet of flowers, they had coffee, and then she went home and he went to the pub. That evening Yanay's brother was at the pub, but he left a few minutes before the attack. The suicide bomber was stopped at the door by the bouncer, who was thrown back a few yards but survived. Yanay had gone outside to get some fresh air, and he was killed. The next morning I woke up at the usual time, 4:40, and turned on the radio. I heard that there had been an attack at Mike's Place and that there were three dead. I was very anxious; I didn't know the name of the pub, though I knew that Yanay played in Tel Aviv every Tuesday night. But I knew that the odds were against another horror in my family. Inbal had been killed a year and a half before. For two hours, I forced myself not to call. I thought that if Yanay were at home and if I called before seven o'clock, I would wake everyone up. Then the door opened. It was Avner—he had come to tell me the news. Yanay had been killed. It was as if my entire world had collapsed on me. Inbal had left her parents and relatives behind; Yanay left a widow and two orphans, a terrible tragedy. Avner took me to Orna. She was sitting down. She told me about the last time she had seen him, their last kiss. This time I couldn't do it, I couldn't write a eulogy for my son."

During the shivah, the seven days of mourning, hundreds of people from Yanay's workplace and from the music world came to pay their respects. One of his coworkers created a memorial website. "The terrorists were not from the Palestinian Territories; they were English citizens, well educated and from respectable families. Terrorism was based on hatred of Jews.

Inbal and Yanay were not killed as soldiers in battle, but as innocent citizens. The occupation is not the result of direct government policies, but a consequence of the fact that we must defend ourselves. I have suffered many losses in my life. The death of my family in the Holocaust had become a faint twinge of pain; my joy and pride in my sons and their families, and the satisfaction of my participation in the kibbutz and in Israel, had overshadowed the memory of those I had lost. But the tragic, cruel killing of my dearly beloved granddaughter and of Yanay, who was in the prime of life, who loved others and was himself loved, this has hit me very hard. I could never have imagined that I would bury my son and granddaughter in my lifetime—that I would be alive and they would be dead, that I would mourn for them in a eulogy. This has devastated both me and Judith. It robbed us of the satisfaction we had found in life. I had a family that was growing, and it has been reduced in such a cruel way."

Both Inbal and Yanay believed in coexistence with the Arabs. "Judith and I had raised them that way. My kibbutz was very left-wing; the motto was 'Zionism, socialism, and brotherhood.'" I had great respect for the Arabs, and I identified with this ideology. Even after the attack, I was not angry with the Arabs, but with the extremists and fanatics who want to kill us. In spite of everything, our lives have been touched by hatred, cruelty, and fanaticism. Before they died, we gathered around the table for birthdays, for the Jewish holidays, we sang, we joked, we talked about our lives. It was the purest form of pleasure for me. But now when we get together, our joy is mingled with sadness. We don't say it out loud, but inside we feel the absence of Inbal and Yanay. It is the sorrow that stains our happiness."

These days, Lipa thinks about his childhood in the village in the Carpathians, about the death camps, and about rebirth in Israel. "I was born in the early decades of the last century, and I survived the horrors of the years that followed. I found happiness in life in the kibbutz, in the house I lived in for sixty years, and in Israel, which has made unbelievable progress. I am proud of who we are, and of what I and the other members of the kibbutz achieved through our work. Today, at the age of eighty-four, I am retired, and the kibbutz takes care of everything for me. My love for all of them, Avner, Marianne, Orna, Gidi, Dorit, and the other children, and my love and concern for Judith is what gives me the strength to move forward and to try to live a normal life. We talk about our losses openly and freely; we mention Inbal and Yanay all the time. But we also enjoy what we have."

The story of Lipa Weiss is a story about destruction and heroism, about death and rebirth. It is the sacred story in which every life that ends is linked to another being born. It is Israel with its silent ranks of six million souls that march, hand in hand, until the ranks form an unbroken circle. One of the greatest mysteries of the past two thousand years is how one-third of God's chosen people—six million men, women, and children—were reduced to ashes during the Holocaust, and no more than a blink of an eye later, the same battered people won independence and freedom in Israel for the first time since the destruction of the Holy Temple. "We, your children, were born to survivors of the Holocaust, and constitute irrefutable proof to those who tried so hard to extinguish the Jewish nation," said Avner Weiss, speaking at his father's kibbutz, Ein Hashofet. "Our existence is also a partial compensation for the inconsolable loss of your loved ones, who were taken from you with such brutality. We were born in this land, as members of a kibbutz, growing up as the new nation and society were being formed. We were the sons and daughters of parents who had undergone unbelievable sorrow and anguish, who were now seeking for themselves love, support, security, and peace—a home. I stand before you in awe, filled with admiration that you were able to overcome such tremendous obstacles and to bestow on your lives a new and special meaning, as living witnesses to the Holocaust that annihilated whole families and loved ones."

The marvelous optimism of Lipa Weiss, his prodigious face of tears and smiles that is the very place of Shoah; the quiet smiles of Inbal and Yanay, emanating earnestness, seriousness, determination, moral strength and courage; the admirable spirit that carries Avner and Marianne through their almost unbearable pain—these will be forever part of this everlasting mystery. This is the best and most honorable part of Israel, and of all humanity.

A Clock Frozen at 2:04

A *rnold Roth traveled from Jerusalem* to The Hague so he could hold a photograph of his daughter, Malka, in front of the International Court of Justice as it began its deliberations over the legality of Israel's security fence. Malka was killed along with fourteen other people by a suicide bomber while enjoying lunch in Jerusalem's Sbarro pizzeria on August 9, 2001. "Do I feel bad about the destruction the fence is causing? I do," Roth said. "But do not compare the murder of my daughter to the inability of a Palestinian to get to work by 9:00 A.M." Since construction of the security fence began, the number of terrorist attacks has declined by more than 90 percent, and the number of Israelis murdered and wounded has decreased by more than 70 percent and 85 percent, respectively.

Avi Ohayon brought a bullet to The Hague. He had found it under a pile of toys in the bedroom corner where his two sons huddled with their mother when a terrorist shot all three to death. Ohayon held it up before a crowded room a few short blocks from the International Court, where a panel of fifteen judges in black robes ruled that Israel's security fence was a violation of humanitarian law. Israel was on trial for protecting its citizens.

Fanny Haim had the presence of mind to write an open letter to the judges: "Today, in The Hague, you will sit in judgment. Today, I will bury my husband, my heart—which has been cut in two. I am not a politician. I am appealing to you as someone who has lost her husband, a woman whose heart has been silenced—and a woman whose tragedy the separation fence could have prevented. Today, as you begin your deliberations with open eyes, think, just for a moment, about the ordinary people behind this bloody conflict. Think for a moment about the golden heart of my husband, Yehuda, and about our young son, Avner. Maybe you can explain to him—he's only ten years old—why in God's Name he doesn't have a father anymore. This evening, you will go home, kiss your spouses, hug your children—and I will be alone. Today, I am burying my husband; don't you bury justice."

Creating a river of faces, Israeli supporters and families marched through the Dutch city to the triangular plaza near the courthouse, holding posters of victims. Already parked there was the bombed-out shell of the No. 19 bus, in which eleven people were killed in Jerusalem. The organization Christians for Israel had helped bring the bus to The Hague, and held a silent march in front of the court with portraits of 927 terror victims. Paramedics from Magen David Adom read out the names of the dead. Some of the demonstrators were holding up a sign with a picture of the bodies rapped in plastic, and a banner saying: "The people who used this bus in 29.1.2003 were on their way to work and to school. Some of them never got there."

When the suicide bomber blew it up, the Sbarro restaurant had its usual crowd of families and office workers on their lunch break; there were children, teenagers, mothers with infants in strollers, elderly couples. A clock on the wall froze at 2:04, the time of the explosion. For hours, a bitter odor of explosives and burned bodies hung in the air. "I saw a man lying on the street shaking like he was being electrocuted and a child that looked dead in another man's arms," said a survivor. "A woman soldier sat motionless in shock inside, with the table that should have been in front of her gone." Blood pooled on the floor and stained the pitted plaster walls. Two strollers were overturned on the pavement amid broken glasses, blood splotches, fragments of tables, a charred chair back, a half-opened purse with a small teddy bear as a good-luck charm. There were clots of hair everywhere, and a splinter from a victim's arm. From the ceiling hung electrical wires, shattered signs, the chimney from the oven. Outside, the ultra-Orthodox Jews of Zaka, the guardians of Jewish piety, picked up even the tiniest scraps of the bodies. Beneath a blanket was the torso of a woman without legs. "The most striking thing I saw, which I will never forget, was a child sitting in a stroller outside of a shop: he was dead, and soon afterward his mother came out and started screaming," said Naor Shara, a soldier who was passing by the restaurant. All that remained of the building facade was the red, white, and green sign reading: "Sbarro: the Best Italian Choice. Kosher."

Today there is a plaque in Sbarro that reads: "In memory of the shadows that have fallen upon us. From the Sbarro family, the city of Jerusalem, and the entire Jewish nation."

Before going to lunch, the last thing Malka Roth and Michal Raziel did was decorate the room of a friend who was returning to Israel later that day. By the time the friend came back, the girls were no longer alive; they had made a date for Sbarro. "Malka was an extraordinary young woman; her life was an act of beauty," says her father, Arnold. She took care of handicapped children, and her sister was also disabled.

"We were old-school Zionist—we wanted to raise our children where the Jewish life could be truly lived," Arnold explains. He met his wife, Frimet, in New York, and they moved to Melbourne. "Before getting married, we promised each other that we would emigrate to Israel in a few years. We both believed in the centrality of Israel for the life of Jews. We are both devout in the Orthodox sense. In 1988, we went to live in an apartment in Jerusalem." Asked where he found the strength to go on after the death of his daughter, Roth replied, "Living a 'normal life' and rebuilding it after the death of a daughter is not an end or a result. It is a process—a process that has dominated our lives for seven years, since Malka was taken away from us. There are times when the battle gets the better of you. Each person is different from the next. It is so abnormal to bury your children, victims of an act of barbarity and hatred."

Roth has nothing rhetorical to say about Israel. "This is no place for angels, but a fascinating place with a unique history. The people of Israel are very similar to others, neither better nor worse, ordinary like all the rest. But the spirit of Israel and its history are special. We don't live here for the weather. We came here to raise our children where our nation was formed and where its ethical and religious traditions were created. To Jews, Israel is unique, and we live here because we believe it is the natural and normal place for Jews." The land is part of this hope. "The other members of the Jewish people who have come to live here also give us hope. The education of our children and the religion in which we are raising them give us hope. Nonetheless, nothing changes the sadness and remorse that we feel over the death of our daughter. No culture, hope, or tradition can comfort us over the tragic loss of her wonderful life."

We ask him what the victims of terrorism represent. "Jewish history is full of tragedy. It isn't easy to understand. But the questions that families like ours ask are questions that have already been posed by others before us. We also know that there are few answers. This does not make us any less devout, because in Judaism we can ask questions and know that sometimes the answers are elusive and impossible."

Frimet Roth was born in a secularized family in New York; Arnold has severed roots in Europe. "I was born in Melbourne, to parents who had survived Auschwitz and had lost everything there," says Arnold. Both of his parents came from Poland. "My mother, Genia, survived together with three of her sisters; they were deported to the ghetto and then to a death camp. After the war, they discovered that their parents and their three brothers had been killed by the Nazis. My father was the youngest of a large family. He and his oldest brother survived; all the others were exterminated by the Nazi machine. My uncle Shaya had decided that the prewar anti-Semitism in Poland was intolerable, so he survived thanks to his decision to emigrate to Tel Aviv. His children, my cousins, are authentic Palestinians, Jews who escaped Nazism and whose parents decided to take them to Palestine. So we know that our lives are an inseparable part of an organic nation with strong connections to the past. I was a child without grandparents. We didn't talk about our uncles, cousins, and grandparents who had been killed as heroes. They died because they were Jewish, and those who murdered them did so in the name of hatred and racial prejudice."

Arnold remarks, "I never would have expected to see the past tragedies of our people return into our lives. But it has happened, and today it is impossible for us to see what has happened to our daughter, her death as a martyr, without connecting it to the centuries in which we were dominated by those who hated us, by racists and by the ignorant. This is the reason why we have become so involved in the debate on terrorism, and it frightens and disturbs us that civil society is so reluctant to understand the danger." Unfortunately, in Israel there does not yet exist a shared memory of terrorism. "Israeli society wavers endlessly between the expression of force and determination on the one hand, and

of compassion for the victims on the other. In Israel we have
learned that terrorism is not a fluke, but a constant. It is a form
of war in which one act of terror is a prelude to the next. They
will strike as long as they can, until we have stopped them."

Arnold has founded a nonprofit association in Malka's
name. The Malki Foundation has no politics, but optimistically
celebrates life and the human spirit. "We wanted the foundation dedicated to Malka to be the antithesis of terror. We
wanted to honor her memory through practical actions that
would unite people, apart from race and religion—Jews, Christians, and Muslims. The most difficult thing for the parents of a
daughter who has been killed is to get up in the morning. This
gives us the strength. We have financed 27,500 therapy ses-
sions for hundreds of Jewish, Christian, Muslim, and Druze
children. And we did this in order to preserve and honor the
memory of a beautiful, sweet young woman who never reached
the age of sixteen. I am filled with hope by the stories of a society afflicted by terror that is learning to honor and respect the
memory of the human beings who have lost their lives. A society's correct answer to actions of hatred is actions that affirm
life and dignity, starting with the lives and dignity of the
victims."

Roth explains that the concept of *chesed* is different from
that of charity; it is a Hebrew word more similar to "love."
"When you perform an act of *chesed,* you know that you will
receive nothing in return from the person who benefits from it.
There will be no 'thank you.' People who do *chesed* do so
because they know that it is intrinsically good, and adds goodness to the world." One example is the preparation of the
corpse. "In every Jewish community, there are people who do
this for free, without being paid. It is clear that the deceased
person cannot offer any thanks. In Hebrew, this is called *chesed
shel emet,* true generosity. My daughter Malka knew this. And
she took great pleasure in the simple fact of helping other

people, especially children with problems. Her sister, Haya, is blind and does not communicate with the world, not even now, at the age of thirteen. Haya didn't know how to thank Malka when she picked her up. When we decided to remember Malka by creating a foundation bearing her name, it was because we wanted to honor her beauty and generosity. We wanted to emulate her values. This way she will not be forgotten. We wanted her memory to be respected. As I said at the funeral, her life was an act of beauty. The people who live on the other side of the security barrier, the Palestinians, are not worse than us. It is the values of our society that are different. By doing an act of *chesed,* we remind ourselves every day that our society is different from theirs. A person like Malka couldn't have been born in a society that produces murderers."

Arnold Roth was one of eighteen victims of terror from different countries who spoke at a symposium hosted by the United Nations in New York. "The challenge to individuals, to the victims who endure terrorism, is to find and adopt ways to survive the evil of the perpetrators of terrorism," he said. "To reaffirm our humanity, our dignity, our generosity, and our optimism."

Arnold has always felt that the life of his daughter was the continuation of another story cut short by barbarism sixty years earlier—that of Feige, his father's sister, who was killed by the Nazis in Europe. "Malka herself saw a strong connection with Feige. I live in Israel, and I have chosen to come here to be with my wife and my children. Although our life in Australia was certainly comfortable and good, we wanted more: a place where Jewish values would be at home. Malka, like me, grew up knowing that she was part of Jewish history. She seemed very similar to the aunt that I never met. Feige's upbringing was very similar to that of Malka; both of them prayed from the same book and mentioned Jerusalem in their prayers three times a day. Unlike Malka, who had the privilege of living in Jerusalem, Feige was murdered in the Nazi campaign of hatred that turned into something unimaginable on a vast scale."

Malka knew well what terrorism does. "She wept secretly for the victims; we found this out from what she had written. We found it out only after she was gone. Hers was a pain that was intimately connected with that of her people. She wept over the death of innocent Jews, and Malka's tears have become our tears. Her life was taken away just as the life of my father's family was torn from him, leaving him alone. It is therefore impossible for me to think about my daughter's death without it reflecting on the stunning number of Jewish victims over the course of history, especially the victims of the Holocaust. My parents, victims of the Holocaust in which they lost everyone, tried to live productive lives after the horrors of the Nazi extermination. In the same way, my wife and I are trying to help people and to express an optimistic perspective on life."

Israel is a country that has become all too accustomed to digging graves for its children. Is the Holocaust really over? Those killed at Sbarro also included two-year-old Hemda, four-year-old Avraham Yitzhak, fourteen-year-old Ra'aya, their mother, Tzira, and their father, Mordechai—five members of the Schijveschuurder family cut down in a single stroke. They had come from Holland, where their Jewish ancestors had lived for more than four centuries, since the time of Baruch Spinoza. The children's grandmother, who had survived the Holocaust, was called the next day to identify the bodies of her loved ones. "I had sworn that I would have another family after the war. Now Arafat is finishing what Hitler started," said Naomi Friedman. Born in Czechoslovakia, she had gone through the concentration camps of Ravensbruck and Bergen-Belsen, while her husband was in Theresienstadt. "We survived that hell, but we lost seven brothers and sisters. Here we have found worse murderers than the Nazis."

During the funeral, a woman ran away weeping: "This isn't a funeral, it's a holocaust." The chief rabbi, Yisrael Meir Lau, who had married the Schijveschuurders, turned to God: "How long will it last, O my God, how long? It's been three generations." Rabbi Lau himself is a survivor of Buchenwald, where he lost two of his brothers, while his father was killed in the gas chamber at Treblinka, where the Jews were exterminated in less than two hours.

Mordechai Schijveschuurder had decided to live "on the front line," in the Neria settlement. Shortly before he was killed, a friend asked him if he was fearful in driving that route every evening. Mordechai replied, "A bomb could kill me in Jerusalem, too." He was a man of faith who loved the Torah and had been the principal of a religious school. His wife, Tzira, had taken care of deaf children. After the explosion, before he died, Mordechai recited the first line of the ritual prayer *Shema Yisrael,* "Hear, O Israel." He died with those words on his lips.

At the funeral, a friend of the family remarked that "the angel of death can reach wherever he wants." Ten-year-old Leah wanted to take part in the ceremony for her parents and siblings. "I loved you so much, dearest," she said. "I am sorry for how naughty I was." The oldest child of the family, Ben-Zion, also spoke: "We will hold tight what you left us, love for one another. We love you. Watch over us from above, so we can remain united." Meir, another son, remarked, "The terrorists want to kill the free world, and America and Israel are the symbol of the free world." Grandma Naomi said, "Thanks to God, we had returned to the land of our dreams, to the land that symbolizes our freedom. Now that the bloody hands of our murderers have reached us, all of this is incomprehensible."

"To my father, Neria was a place to live like any other," says Ben-Zion. "He made the aliyah from Amsterdam, and in his mind Israel was Israel. It's not that Neria was a better place than Petah Tikva, where I was born. Israel was very important to him, but he never protested against the government because of the withdrawal from the Territories. He thought that Israel went from the bank of the Jordan to the Mediterranean." Ben remembers his father as a businessman first of all, "and then a *talmid hakham,* a person who studies the Bible. Photographs show him with his black kippah like the Haredim, but he always thought that unless one is a genius, one must work. And he was a genius: every morning he learned something before going to work. He brought books with him every time he traveled. I think that one of his dreams was to be a teacher, but he knew that he could do better in business. But I am grateful that after the death of my father, a school was named after him. Everyone talks about him, never about her, my mother, who was the true genius behind my father. She loved to stay in the background, but he always listened to her. The school wouldn't have existed without her. She loved her family, my father, and her job. The rest isn't so important. The others in my family, the ones who are gone now—well, I was in the army, and I didn't go back home often enough to talk with my sister."

Ben also talks about how it was possible to get over his mourning, to move forward. "My relationship with the State of Israel is not simply one of hope and strength. I live in Israel as the place of my birth, where my friends are. Those who have helped me have been the friends of the family and my personal friends, and also people on the street. Returning to normal life was very difficult, and at the same time very easy, because I had two sisters to think about. So you can't beat yourself up all day and feel sorry for yourself. But this deprived me of my own space to mourn. Nonetheless, I must say that I am happy with the way I chose. For a whole year after the death of our family, we went from one place to another without any plan, like a ship without a captain."

The story of the Schijveschuurders has influenced the education of all the family members. "My father's grandparents were killed during the Second World War," Ben explains. "In my father's mind, the fact that his family had survived the Holocaust and that he had chosen to live in Israel, well, this was a victory over the Nazis. My father visited the concentration camps, and I have a photograph showing him at the entrance to Auschwitz, making the victory sign. He is laughing. I think that he wanted to express his victory over the Nazis. I can also say that a few days before the start of my military service, we took a trip to Europe and visited a concentration camp in Munich, and he made the same victory gesture again. He raised us to be proud of being Jewish, and to believe that we will be survivors in spite of everything. The Holocaust is something that runs in our veins. My brother, my sister and I have also had our own little Holocaust. And this is also inside and part of us."

Haya Schijveschuurder, who suffered burns on 50 percent of her body, says, "Now my parents aren't alive anymore, but when the Messiah comes they will get up. Hashem knows what he's doing. He wants to tell us that we need to behave a little bit better and that soon the Messiah will come and then all the dead will rise again."

Marc Belzberg's family was vacationing in Palm Springs, Florida, and had been planning to throw a big party for his twelve-year-old daughter Michal's bat mitzvah upon their return to Israel. But after hearing of the attack at Sbarro, the family decided to cancel the party and donate the $100,000 planned for the event to victims of the attack. "It shook everybody," Belzberg said. "When kids your own age are getting murdered, how can you throw a party?" Out of this generosity, the One Family Fund was born. It has helped 3,500 Israeli families who have been affected by terrorism—families in mourning, or struggling to cope with the injuries, the fears and nightmares, the memories and anguish that have accompanied terrorism into their lives. One Family has set up a special fund to ensure that orphans get a fair start in life.

When Pope Benedict XVI made a historic visit to Israel in May 2009, representatives of One Family took part in an audience with the pope at the offices of the Chief Rabbinate of Israel. Benedict XVI was presented with a book listing the names of all the children who had been orphaned by terrorism in the previous ten years—the 32 children under age nineteen who had lost both parents, and the 931 who had lost either their father or their mother.

The One Family Fund is a major sign of Israel's triumph over Islamist destruction. "Israel is a country that has been built upon anguish and suffering," says Yehuda Poch, director of communications for One Family. "The modern State of Israel represents the return of the Jewish nation to its past glory after two thousand years of anguish and suffering, blood and pogroms. Israeli society is one of caring and compassion, where the fortunate help the unfortunate, and where there is always somewhere to turn. That is part of the Jewish culture, and it is especially ingrained in us after so many centuries of suffering throughout the world. Even in ancient times, the Jewish nation was formed out of the slavery of Egypt into a nation that was commanded to remember that we were once slaves, and therefore to have compassion on others."

The Bloodstained Utopia

Golan stands high and solitary in Galilee. Here began the legend of the socialist pioneer who founded the kibbutz in honor of his philosophy, as a bulwark of defense for the country and for Jewish humanism. The kibbutz was Israel the way it should be, secular and socialist. *Kibbutzniks* want an Israel that is secure, democratic, and Jewish. Thanks to its deep Jewish roots, Israel has in fact produced a type of person fit to be a democrat and a soldier. Four photographs taken by Robert Capa sum up the history of the kibbutz. In the first, a young fisherman is emptying a boat near a kibbutz in Galilee, holding up the traps full of fish. Then there's a girl driving a tractor with a rifle slung over her shoulder. In the third, a young woman, freckled and beautiful, with blue eyes and wavy hair, turns toward the camera in surprise as she cooks a communal meal. The best photo is the last: Konrad Adenauer and David Ben-Gurion stand at the window of a bare room, looking out onto the Negev desert, with two empty glasses on the table.

The nuclear physicist from Vienna, the Sephardic Jew from the Sahara, the Ethiopian descendant of Solomon, the wiry fellow from Poland, the Yankee from Brooklyn, the Jews from India and Morocco and Tripoli—all met in the kibbutzim. Speaking twenty different languages, they were not a racial or ethnic group, but a "metaphysical family" founded on remembrance, and on the principle of armed defense of their own future. The only definition on which Jews from all over the world agree is that of Israel as a refuge for the Jews. If the State of Israel had already existed during the time of the Shoah, millions of lives would have been saved. If the British blockade had not stopped those fleeing from Europe, if Israel had had embassies and consulates throughout the world, such evil could not have assumed the proportions of the extermination camps.

The first kibbutz, Degania, was founded forty years before Israel itself by a group of young pioneers: Russian Jews, Zionists and socialists who had worked in the marshes of Madeira. Born as a farming community based on collective property, the equality of all members, the rotation of duties and leadership responsibilities, and the exclusion of the use of money within the community, the kibbutz was the greatest and perhaps the only success of the socialist ideal in the twentieth century. But the kibbutzim gradually departed from their original configuration. Beginning in the 1970s, they went through a severe crisis caused by triple-digit inflation, the arrival of satellite TV, computers and electronic technology, telecommuting, commercial tourism. The history of the socialist pioneers seems like an irresolvable tension between the utopian project of a just and egalitarian society, and the concrete results—including the vital result of security on the borders through the Nahal, the army's agricultural units. The *kibbutzniks* considered themselves the defenders of what the Israeli foreign minister Abba Eban called "the borders of Auschwitz."

In 1882, Leon Pinsker urged the Jews to seek political emancipation as a solution to the problem of persecution, and subsequently many "societies of lovers of Zion" were founded in Odessa and Warsaw, while Ukrainian students went to create farming colonies in Palestine. The arrival of the Jews was followed by shipments of huge wooden crates to be used as tool sheds and temporary shelters. There was also heavy mahogany furniture, beautiful grand pianos, crystal and porcelain dishes, hand-embroidered pillows, lace hand towels, and tailored clothing. The kibbutz was the beginning of a magic, transformed world. The pioneers, tempered in Marxism or the Talmud, went to cultivate the dunes and swamps, and the atheist and socialist Jews discovered that the only map they really knew was that of King David, King Solomon, and the prophets. The lawyer became a ditch-digger, the student became a farmer, the art dealer who had sold paintings by Chagall and Soutine in Moscow would break stones in Jerusalem, the violinist became a rancher, the Talmud scholar from Krakow became a shepherd in Nazareth, the intellectuals were enlisted to improve the soil, the librarians' pale skin turned dark as they broke up rocks in Masada. It was a return to the tradition of the patriarch Yochanan ben Zakkai, who worked as a shoemaker; Rabbi Yehuda Hanassi, a baker; Rav Huna, a farmer; Baruch Spinoza, a lens grinder. The light of Judaism that was flickering out in Europe was being rekindled on Jewish soil, in the kibbutzim, in the moshavim (cooperative agricultural communities), on the farms, in the Nahal villages.

The kibbutzim have lost many of their children at the hands of Islamic terrorists, and these attacks are the more chilling in that many of the victims were peace activists, willing to give up land for the sake of coexistence with the Palestinians; they were idealists who believed in a moral, just, democratic, egalitarian, better Israel. Thus the suicide bombers have struck at the ethical ideal of earthly justice that has played such an important role in Jewish history.

Ofer Kenrick was a farmer like those in the 1920s who watered the desert with their sweat. He grew bananas and raised sheep together with his brother, who was also his business partner. Ofer loved the land and his family; his favorite pastime after work was watching sports on television. On the day he died, he was going to adjust the irrigation system in the fields. His son was supposed to celebrate his bar mitzvah three days later, and the whole family was busy with the preparations.

Yotam Gilboa was from Kibbutz Maoz Haim. His mother was a teacher in the kibbutz school, and Yotam always helped her organize events for children. They believed in the virtue of knowledge and education. This was an ideal characteristic of the Israeli republic, which immediately after its founding made education free and obligatory, established equality between men and women, abolished the death penalty, regulated working hours, gave every Jew a right of habeas corpus that sanctified the human person, separated the powers, and defended every human life, trying to rescue even the unburied remains of its own soldiers.

Sergeant Shlomo Adshina had immigrated from Nigeria when he was three years old. His adoptive parents of Kibbutz Tze'elim described him as "a simple young man with a big heart." His supervisor recalled the day that Shlomo joined the army: "I saw the tears in his eyes, and he said to me about the kibbutz: 'I have finally found a home.'" Erez Ashkenazi of Kibbutz Reshafim told his father that "often you go to battle and don't come back." He had just celebrated his twenty-first birthday. His brother had been killed in the Yom Kippur War—as countless other families have lost two children in different wars. "Erez fought like a lion," his commanding officer said. "He was always the first at the front." When three generations of pioneers gave him the final salute, it was as if those faces composed the timeless image of Israel. Erez believed in coexistence and was a member of Meretz, the party of peace. Such casualties on the side of compromise increase the significance of Israel's martyrdom.

Major Tamir Massad was buried in Kfar Masaryk, dedicated to one of the most important intellectuals and politicians of the twentieth century. Tamir's grandparents were among the founders of the community in 1944, when it welcomed Jews fleeing from Nazi Europe. Tamir's face was immortalized alongside that of Menachem Begin, the prime minister, in front of the Beaufort Castle in June 1982, after six Israeli soldiers had been killed there. "He was a fascinating man, not the kind of person one meets every day," said his brigade commander. "He was brilliant and courageous." The week before, Tamir had talked about how the brigade's objective was to return home safe and sound. "You forgot about yourself," the commander remarked.

It is unbearable even to read the number of Jewish mothers killed in recent years. In 1988, Rachel Weiss and her sons—Netanel, three; Rafael, two; and Efraim, nine months—were killed in a Palestinian firebomb attack on a bus. Her husband, Eliezer, was the only member of the family to survive. Yehudit Cohen was a math teacher with a seven-year-old son. Tuesday was the only day of the week when she finished work early enough to pick him up after school. "Destiny wanted the angel of death to be waiting for her on the way, on a Tuesday," her sister said. Her husband was an air conditioning technician, and the three had moved to the village of Shlomi, not far from the place of the attack, because they loved plants, nature, Galilee. Near her grave, her son said, "Dad, I want to stay here, by Mom. Can I?" Yehudit is commemorated with a plaque: "She knew how to make her light shine for those around her. She will be in our hearts forever."

The Yemeni matriarch Yaffa Ben-Shimol was overjoyed at the birth of another grandson, before she was killed by terrorists. She had taken care of the elderly and sick in the hospital wards. "It was an honor for her to take care of those in need." Mazal Afari's door was always open. She was born in a village in Yemen, where Jewish orphan children were often forcibly converted to Islam, and where a law had been passed prohibiting Jews from raising their voices in the presence of Muslims or building houses higher than theirs. Mazal had been abandoned by her father and mother, who fled from their village with the help of the Jewish Agency. In Israel, she had eight children. The members of the moshav always saw her reading the Psalms on her front porch. She liked to believe in the prophecy of Moses: "You will return to the country of your fathers on eagle's wings."

Sharon Ben-Shalom threw herself on top of her two daughters to shield them with her body. The police found her in the back seat of the car, shot in the back and in the neck, but the two girls were unharmed. Their father, Yaniv, also died—another family ruined, and two more orphans on the list. Michal Mor had three children of her own, but worked for a religious institution that cares for hundreds of children. Her brother said that she had a noble soul, and that their mother had asked her to take food to an orphan that day. Miri Ohana had immigrated from Spain and was taking care of her disabled daughter. They were murdered together in their moshav. Moranne Amit, born and raised in a kibbutz founded by her grandparents, was stabbed to death.

Esther Galia was an ultra-Orthodox Jew who worked at the Bank of Israel. Every day she commuted from the settlement of Kochav Hashachar in Jerusalem, and that's where she was killed. She had been among the pioneers of the community, which today numbers two hundred families. "She was a sober and rational woman who lived simply," one neighbor recalls. "She had faith in God; she said that whatever might happen, the Most High would give her strength." Aviel Atash was returning home to Beersheba with his mother, who had gone to buy diapers. They were blown up in the bus that defied fear every day in traveling its route. Aviel would have started school the next day. His father, who had to have him identified by DNA analysis, called him "a gift from God."

Batsheva Unterman was returning home with her six-month-old daughter, Efrat, when a bulldozer, with a cry of *"Allahu akhbar,"* tore through the center of Jerusalem, crushing everything in its path and killing three Israelis. Batsheva did what Jews learned to do during the Holocaust, and for two thousand years before that: make sure the children are safe, at any cost. She was able to drop her little daughter through the window just before the terrorist drove the bulldozer at her car, crushing it completely. Batsheva, the daughter of Dutch Jews, had married the grandson of the chief rabbi of Israel. Her daughter's name, Efrat, dates back to the story of the pharaoh who ordered the killing of all infant Hebrew males, telling the Hebrew midwives, "When you act as midwives for the Hebrew women and see them giving birth, if it is a boy, kill him; but if it is a girl, she may live." The midwives feared the wrath of God, however: "They did not do as the king of Egypt had ordered them, but let the boys live." One of the midwives, Miriam, was given the name Efrat, which comes from the expression *Pru u'revu,* "Be fruitful and multiply."

Tzipi and Gadi Shemesh had gone to downtown Jerusalem because Tzipi was pregnant and needed to get an ultrasound. They had just left the doctor's office. Everything was fine, and they were going back to pick up their two daughters, ages four and seven. The grandparents say that the girls were excited about the news they were going to receive. But as soon as they heard about the suicide attack on the radio, they started crying in terror, calling for their mother over and over. Their mother had died on the spot, with her little brother in her womb. Her husband died in the hospital soon afterward. He was a graphic artist and she was the accountant for a bookstore. They were ordinary people living on the outskirts of Jerusalem, "authentic presences" among so many others, who left behind a great void and two girls scarred for life.

Avital Wolanski had been talking with her mother and her husband, Avi, about how hard it was to see so many children orphaned by terrorism. Avital had two children and was six months pregnant with a third. She and Avi were content to live in a trailer; for them it was enough just to be in the land of Samaria. "This country is all we have," said Avital. She and her husband were killed on the way to their home in Eli. "A great sadness has taken hold of Israel," Avi's father said, while Rabbi Eliyahu Bakshi Doron asked, "How many more, O God? How many more?"

The dovish Kibbutz Metzer suffered one of the most horrific attacks. The irony is that it had long promoted coexistence with the surrounding Arab villages, and for nearly fifty years there had been good relations and frequent sharing of resources. Arab children came to Metzer to play basketball and use the swimming pool. Close relations with the Arabs "became a multi-generation tradition," in the words of one veteran member of the kibbutz. "These were our founding principles—tolerance and egalitarianism, a view of our neighbors as people and equals," said Dov Avital, who has lived in Metzer for twenty-one years. Yet this tradition did not shelter the kibbutz from the crime inflicted that horrible night in November 2002.

The terror squad broke into a home that was chosen at random and killed Revital Ohayon, along with her two sons, Matan, age five, and Noam, four. Avi Ohayon, who had maintained a close relationship with his ex-wife, heard the children cry out "Mommy" before the sound of gunfire. The little ones were shot in the head, murdered in their beds, dressed in their pajamas and hugging their teddy bears. They died in the arms of their mother, who was trying to protect them. In their little bedroom, spattered with blood, there were stuffed animals, toys, colored pictures. A dim light was shining on a book of fables.

"They killed a child with a pacifier!" Avi exclaimed, over and over, to those who tried to comfort him in the room where the horror had unfolded. "My God, help me, they killed a child with a pacifier in his mouth." Neighbors and friends put candles on a stepladder by the front door of the small, white house. Photos of the children were affixed to a wall near two little songbirds in a hanging cage. Avi said, "God looked from on high and said, 'I want them, no one is better than them. I want them to sit here beside me.' And now it is up to me to bury them. I'm all alone now." Their grandfather, Danny, commented that "they lived such short lives, they didn't know hatred. Learning from them is like continuing to live."

Two other people were murdered in Kibbutz Metzer that night, including Yitzhak Dori, who had arrived in 1976 with a group of pioneers from the youth movement Hashomer Hatzair. He taught in the community school. "He was a splendid person, a great organizer, a true leader," his neighbors said.

Home to 450 Israelis who farm the land, raise dairy cows and run a small fitted-pipe factory, Kibbutz Metzer became a symbol of random slaughter in Israel. When the Israeli army was about to clear an Arab olive grove to build the security wall, the *kibbutzniks* of Metzer suggested that the soldiers confiscate their own land so as to avoid sacrificing the Palestinians' olive trees. That's how they were, but not even the most diehard pacifism was able to prevent a massacre.

On March 5, 2003, a Palestinian suicide bomber blew himself up on a passenger bus approaching the University of Haifa, killing seventeen people and seriously injuring dozens more. If you take a bus in Haifa, the driver is likely to be Arab, and some of the passengers too. If you visit a hospital in Haifa, the doctors, nurses, and support staff, as well as the patients, are both Jewish and Arab. The University of Haifa has a high proportion from the Muslim and Christian communities among its thirteen thousand students and on its faculty. The attack killed two employees of the university and injured some students. To strike at a bus bringing such people to a university that is a symbol of coexistence, where future leaders of the Arab community are educated, was more than an expression of calculated hatred; like the attack on Kibbutz Metzer, it was intended to destroy the very idea of coexistence.

Or Shachar was killed in Lebanon the day before his twenty-first birthday in 2006. His grandfather had died defending the Yad Mordechai kibbutz, a community founded by the combatants of the Warsaw ghetto in honor of their commander, Mordechai Anielewicz, who took his own life. On May 19, 1948, the Egyptians attacked the tiny settlement, but they were forced to retreat by 150 Jews with nothing but a few light weapons. Afterward, this historic victory was defined as "the continuation of the battle begun five years earlier."

The Druze gave 249 of their sons for Israel in the War of Independence in 1948. Sayef Bisan, a Druze, was killed in Gaza in April 2008. His father had also served in the army. His uncle said that Sayef had grown up in a Zionist home, and that his parents are proud of having given a son for Israel. "That is how we were raised, to contribute to this country." Hundreds came to say goodbye at Sayef's casket. "He had wanted to join an elite unit since he was a child," said his uncle. "He had prepared himself physically and mentally." Sayef was known as "the handsome *kibbutznik*" because of his smile. Asked if he was afraid of being killed in Gaza, "he replied that he would rather die in Gaza or Lebanon than be stabbed to death in a pub or die in a car accident."

On March 12, 2002, on the road that connects Akko with Zfat, a squad of Palestinians fired wildly at the passing cars, killing six persons. They also shot the people who were trying to help the wounded. Lynne Livne and her daughter Atara lived in Kibbutz Hanita, on the border with Lebanon. They were going to visit a friend who lived a five-minute drive away. Born in England, Lynne had moved to Canada, where she met Tuvia and they fell in love. She followed him back to the kibbutz in Israel and never left, she loved it so much. Lynne became Jewish, married Tuvia, and raised four children.

"I have lost a wonderful wife and an incredible daughter," Tuvia would later say. "You two were so beautiful, like flowers. Atara, it seems like just yesterday that I was watching you being born. And today we have to bury you." Atara had left her inseparable notebook open on her desk, along with a book about Galilee during the War of Independence—as if life were to continue. Tuvia recalled that on the day of the attack, shortly before his wife was killed, he had gone to see her at the laundry of the kibbutz, which she managed. "She was relaxed and cheerful, and we hugged, certain we would see each other again for dinner. It was our last hug."

In Israel there are many women named Hanita, after the kibbutz whose construction and defense were one of the biggest Jewish projects before the birth of the State of Israel. Kibbutz Hanita is linked to the memory of Jakob Berger, who during the 1929 Arab massacre of Jews in Hebron took an Arab boy and told him to go back to his Muslim leaders with this message: "We do not kill children."

In Golan there are no Palestinians—only Jews and Druzes who have lived together in harmony. Some of the

Druzes are divided from relatives across the border in Syria, and often the families speak through megaphones asking for news of loved ones. Here you feel the strategic fragility of Israel. If Jerusalem ceded the Golan Heights to Damascus, the Syrians would turn their sights deep inside Israel; and what could happen if the Syrian government were in Islamist regime with genocidal ambitions?

Former Syrian bases are everywhere in Golan, now used by the Israelis. You can travel by car to the edge of Quneitra, a ghost town that the Syrians have kept as a memorial to the blow inflicted by Israel in 1967. Even the Israelis have left signs of mourning intact. There is the gaping mouth of a house gutted by bombs, with a plaque beside it memorializing a son killed at age twenty. A local artist has made sculptures from the remnants of missiles and tanks. There is a monument to the Egoz Brigade, and thirty bronze plaques engraved with the names of the fallen. The whole of Golan is a place of mourning.

The old city of Gamla overlooks a series of craters and valleys of basalt. At the bottom of the ravine are the ruins of a Jewish village conquered by the Romans after a tragic battle. The settlement of Katzrin is a pearl of modernity, but the red-roofed houses are cheap because their future is always uncertain. Trucks full of the famous Golan wine, boycotted by the anti-Israel activists, are going out all the time, and the "settlers" are planting new vines. Before the 1967 war, the Jewish state had built rows of trees along the roads to protect pedestrians from Syrian snipers. Those trees are still there, silent witnesses to a truce always under discussion.

Golan and its magnificent communities produced a young man named Gavriel Hoter. At age seventeen, he was completing his studies in the settlement of Otniel before joining the army. He was serving dinner to the other yeshiva students on December 27, 2002, when a terrorist killed the four who were on kitchen duty. Gavriel's parents kept a respectful silence, as

Yemeni tradition requires. His mother, Elaine, had been born in England and arrived in Israel when she was eighteen years old. At university she met Haim Hoter, the son of Yemeni Jews brought to Israel on the "Magic Carpet" of the airplane with the Star of David on it. The Hoters decided to move to the farming moshav of Alonei Habashan, the easternmost Israeli community, on the Syrian border of the Golan Heights. It's a communal life, rich in values, children, nature; there are night watches with rifle at the shoulder, as in the earliest kibbutzim.

"Five and a half years after Gavriel's death, it is hard to believe that he was taken away like that," says Elaine Hoter. "I have tried to accept it and find meaning for my life, and to keep something of Gavriel with me. Before he was killed, I thought that the only thing that mattered was the fact that this person would no longer be with us. That's not true; the way in which we lose someone has value. Gavriel was very religious and spent his life living the Torah. The fact that he died in a holy place on Shabbat is very significant."

For Elaine, just as for the hundreds of mothers of Israel struck by terrorism, there was no script for dealing with the loss. "Every morning when I open my eyes, I see Gavriel's smile, and this gives me the strength to get up. My four-year-old son needs attention, too. I have looked through Gavriel's books; I have collected material. For me, everything new is a challenge, and I have felt a sense of accomplishment every time. I have learned every day the goodness of those who have helped us. Going to work has given me a routine. It seemed to me that I was walking around with a weight on my heart, but this feeling left after a year. I couldn't sing anymore, not at all, for more than a year. Weeping had become part of the routine. I couldn't cook by myself anymore; it took me two years to do it." Did she ever lose trust in the people and the State of Israel? "Never, because this is a national tragedy."

The ancient Greek historian Thucydides observed that it is normal for children to bury their parents, but parents burying children contravenes the laws of nature and angers the gods. Avi Ohayon survived the murder of his wife and two children in Kibbutz Metzer. "I will have to say the prayer for the dead for two little kids."

Welcome, Messiah

Twenty years ago, an elderly Jewish man knocked on the door of Gershon Gera, a scholar and enthusiast of the land of Israel. The old man placed on the table a packet wrapped in tattered paper. "You will know what to do with them," the man said, refusing to explain where the contents came from. Inside were 111 photographs of corpses, Jewish victims of the 1929 massacre in Hebron, taken just after their death, as well as photos of the wounded. The name of each victim was written on the back. Seven years after Gera's death, his wife donated the photographs to Noam Arnon, a leader of the Jewish community in Hebron. Today they can be seen on the official website for Hebron, with the following disclaimer: "Warning, very graphic images."

The pogrom in Hebron began on August 23, 1929, when two Talmudists had their throats slit. They were not making political speeches; they were just searching for God. The next day it was the turn of about fifty Jews who had taken refuge in the Anglo-Palestine Bank. They were all together in one room; it didn't take long for the Arabs to find them. The Arabs hacked off feet, fingers, heads; they gouged out eyeballs; they burned severed heads on top of a stove. One rabbi was commending his fellow Jews to God when he was slaughtered. One by one, six students were placed on the lap of Mrs. Sokolov, who was still alive, and their throats were slit. The men were castrated. Girls, mothers, grandmothers were forced to dance in the blood and then were raped. Meanwhile, Rabbi Slonin had been taken to the hospital. "They have killed my wife, my children, my wife's family." There were tears in his eyes. "In 1492, the Jews who had been expelled from Spain brought a scroll of the Law to Hebron, a holy scroll, a divine Torah. The Arabs burned it."

If the Holocaust influences the mentality of even the most liberal Israelis, the Jews of Hebron are pickled in it. Haj Amin al-Husseini, the grand mufti of Jerusalem who instigated the Hebron massacre, would go on to become a collaborator in the Nazi final solution. The Arab leaders justified the pogrom: "You don't kill the people you want to kill; you kill the people who are there. Run everyone through with the sword, young and old." In the meantime, they were preparing another massacre in Safed, in Upper Galilee. The only people there were elderly Hasidic mystics who sang and danced in honor of the Lord. In 1929 there was no State of Israel, and the Jews of Hebron had not "occupied" anything. They were living in their homeland— in what had been their homeland since biblical times: "And Sarah died in Kiryat Arba, which is Hebron in the Land of Canaan. And Abraham came to eulogize Sarah and to weep over her" (Genesis 23:2).

Hebron is one of the four holy cities of Judaism, the mythical burial place of Abraham, Isaac, Jacob, and their spouses; it is a place of pilgrimage for all religious Jews, and for many it is even more significant than the Western Wall. On the other hand, Hebron is a densely populated Palestinian city, where every house and every room is hotly contested. No Jews are as reviled as the Jews of Hebron. Vilified as "zealots" and "fundamentalists," they are the Jews whom legions of critics love to hate.

The Cave of Machpelah in Hebron, where "Our Father Abraham" is buried, contains a secret of the human psyche and of Jewish history. Sanctity, madness, idealism, cruelty, magic, hatred, brotherhood: this is the essence of Hebron. Some 3,800 years ago, Abraham—the first Hebrew, the Jewish national patriarch—began his sojourn in *Eretz Yisrael*. After being commanded by God to "stand up and walk in the land, to its length and its breadth, for I shall give it to you" (Genesis 13:17), he chose Hebron as his first place of settlement. From the altar that he built there, Abraham disseminated monotheism, the belief in the One God. Hebron is also sacred to Muslims, who revere Abraham as a prophet.

Hebron is mentioned in the Bible more than eighty times, and is designated as a city of refuge and a priestly city. According to the biblical account, God instructed David to establish his kingdom at Hebron. It became an important administrative center for King Hezekiah in his eighth-century war against the Assyrians, and a crucial battleground during the Maccabean and Bar Kokhba uprisings. Through centuries of exile, the sanctity of Hebron remained undiminished. Despite the ascendancy of Jerusalem as the revered capital and site of the First and Second Temples, Hebron was irreplaceable in the construction of Jewish memory. Machpelah is the shrine of consolation and inspiration, the source of Jewish "sacred intimacy."

Even atheist and socialist Israelis like David Ben-Gurion, Moshe Dayan, and Golda Meir were marked by the stories and legends of King David and the prophets. In other words, their lives had been shaped by Hebron. They saw themselves in the heroes of the Bible, and they saw the land that would become *Eretz Yisrael* as the land that had been delineated by the patriarchs. This was the only map that the Jews knew after sixty years of wars, with boundaries that were still unclear and unrecognized. It is the map of religious memory that had permitted them to survive as a people during two thousand years of dispersion. And on that map, Hebron—the "sister of Jerusalem" according to Ben-Gurion, where the Cave of Machpelah houses the remains of Abraham and Sarah, Isaac and Rebecca, Jacob and Leah—plays a magical role.

Hebron was occupied by Greeks, Romans, Arabs, Franks, and Turks. The Jews had been denied access to the Tomb of the Patriarchs since 1266; they could only leave little slips of paper with prayers written on them in the crevices of a rock. In 1518, the Ottomans massacred many of the Jews, but a community of devout scholars of the Torah moved back to the city. There is almost no trace of the dominators anymore, but there are still some Israelis who stretch out, full of hope, to kiss the stones in the Cave of Abraham, and maybe there will be for a while longer.

The great English journalist Albert Londres visited the Jewish community of Hebron in 1929: "It is incredible what appears before the view. This ghetto is a mountain of homes, a genuine mountain, without even an inch of land, completely covered with houses. A thousand Jews live there. Not a thousand Tel Aviv toughs waving the white and blue flag. A thousand Jews who did not come to Palestine on a ship, but were born there, a thousand perennial Jews, always here, since the days of Abraham." There were many who had to pay for the right of the Jews to pray and live within those millennia-old walls.

That same year, four Jews, three men and a woman, made their way from Jerusalem to Hebron. The woman's name was Rachel Yanait. She later married Yitzhak Ben-Zvi, the second president of Israel. The group, armed with weapons, came to Hebron as Haganah representatives carrying a tragic message: the grand mufti of Jerusalem, Haj Amin al-Husseini, a future ally of Adolf Hitler in the war against Jews, was inciting a pogrom in Palestine. They offered the weapons to Hebron's Jewish community, just in case the rioting reached them. But the city's pious leadership was not worried. Hebron's Arabs and Jews lived together as one big family. There were Arabs who spoke Yiddish, and the Jews spoke Arabic. They attended each other's weddings and other festivities. Hebron's Jewish leadership refused to take the weapons, and the four fighters of the Haganah were sent back to Jerusalem.

Wrapped in prayer shawls, men began the morning service. They were interrupted by the pounding of bars and axes, while the screams of *"Shema Yisrael"* resounded through the building. In the Slonim house, the only object left intact was a picture of Theodor Herzl, the founding father of Zionism. Almost the whole Slonim family—Eliezer, Hannah, their son, his wife, and his father-in-law, who was the chief rabbi of Zichron Ya'akov—were among twenty-two persons who were stabbed to death and, in some cases, disemboweled. The Slonims' one-year-old son survived, having been hidden under dying Jews, a scene also seen during the Holocaust. Rabbi Hanoch Hasson was murdered, along with his family. The killings in Hebron went on for two hours, and the death toll reached sixty-seven Jews. The Arabs even ravaged the Hadassah medical clinic, which treated Jews and Arabs equally, and also slaughtered the pharmacist, Ben-Zion Gershon, who had served both Arabs and Jews. His eyes were gouged out before he was stabbed to death. Rabbis Meir Kastel and Tzvi Dabkin and five of their students were tortured and castrated before being murdered. One of the survivors, a student from Chicago, recounted that in Hebron he "had seen greater horrors than Dante in hell."

Here and there, in the midst of the terrible atrocities, there were glimmers of humanity. In one house where some twenty Jews had taken refuge, the Arab owner and his son blocked the doorway and prevented any of the rioters from entering. They stood there for hours until the police arrived and brought the Jews out.

Sarah Hamburger was one of the last survivors of the pogrom in Hebron and the widow of Rabbi Pinhas Hamburger, who was a founder of modern-day Jerusalem. She always used to say, "The land is ours; we have to live here." In 2002, while waiting for the bus in Jerusalem, she was killed by a Palestinian suicide bomber.

The remaining Jews were evacuated from Hebron in 1936. The Jordanians captured the city in 1948 and razed the ancient Jewish neighborhood to the ground. Where the Jewish holy places had stood, they built a market and public toilets. The ancient synagogue of Abraham was demolished and replaced with a pen for goats, sheep, and donkeys. The Jewish cemetery, with its stone commemorating the martyrs of 1929, was completely destroyed, and the gravestones were used to construct buildings and pave streets.

After the war in 1967, Rabbi Shlomo Goren, an army chaplain, was the first Jew to enter Hebron in thirty years, and the first Jew to pray at the Tomb of the Patriarchs in seven hundred years. The day before Passover in 1968, a group of families arrived at the Park Hotel in Hebron. The women and children slept in the rooms; the men and boys slept on the floor of the lobby. It was the first Jewish Passover in Hebron since 1936.

At age fourteen, Pinchas Lapid had tried to leave Lithuania by sneaking onto a foreign ship, but he was discovered. A champion swimmer, he tried over and over again to swim across the sea. He almost made it, reaching international waters, but fatigue and the waves put him back into the hands of the Russian coast guard. Despite these failures and two years in a Soviet prison, the brave refusenik kept repeating his request to emigrate to Israel. Finally Moscow allowed him to leave in 1968. Pinchas packed all his possessions into one small suitcase, leaving behind only his bedroom slippers, facing south toward *Eretz Yisrael*. In the Soviet Union he had been Mark Bloom of Riga; in Israel he became Pinchas Lapid of Hebron. In Hebrew, *lapid* means "torch."

With its white concrete block houses, guarded gates, and inaccessible entrances, Kiryat Arba is a Jewish fortress surrounded by Arab hatred. Mention the settlement to most Israelis inside the Green Line and the image conjured up is one of gun-toting, wild-eyed fanatics like Baruch Goldstein. Established on the outskirts of Hebron in 1968, Kiryat Arba is a community that feels itself very much under siege—by the world, the government, the media.

"Welcome, Messiah" reads the yellow banner that greets visitors at the gate of Kiryat Arba. It's a town with colorful gardens and clean streets, a supermarket, some restaurants, a museum of Hebron history, a medical center, schools and yeshivas. "This is more ours than Tel Aviv," says Meir Menachem, a teacher of history and Judaism in the settlement. "This is the land of the Bible, not Tel Aviv. This is our land, of Abraham, Isaac, and Jacob. We returned here after two thousand years, and we don't have any other place to go." Menachem has buried more than thirty friends since he moved here in 1979. "Until the Messiah comes," he says, "there will be no peace." The settlement of Kiryat Arba was founded with the blessing of the Labor Party, not Likud. People come from all over the world to live there. Donations come in from Christian Zionists, whose historic ties to the Jewish settlers are rooted in the belief that the Messiah will not return until Jews reclaim the land God gave to them. "The heart of their faith is the realization of the prophecies of the Old Testament, of our Bible," said Rabbi Eliezer Waldman.

Yet even the settler movement regards Kiryat Arba as a borderline case, a spiral of blood and violence. The city endured horrific trials in 1993. A girl raised there, Chava Waksberg, was murdered in February. The yeshiva student Erez Shmuel was murdered on his way to worship at the Tomb of the Patriarchs in May. Since then, the alley leading toward the tomb has carried his name. Igor Gorgol was murdered in August. On

December 6, Muslim terrorists gunned down Mordechai Lapid, one of Baruch Goldstein's closest friends, as he was driving out the town gate. Dr. Goldstein rushed to his friend and tried to revive him for forty minutes, long after it was medically hopeless. Mordechai's son Shalom also died that day.

During the week before the Purim holiday in February 1994, American tourists praying in Machpelah heard the terrifying shouts from nearby Arabs, *"Itbakh al-Yahud,"* "Kill the Jews." Reports of impending Arab violence circulated within local military circles. After their community had been obliterated and finally rebuilt, after dozens of their own had been killed and wounded, the Jews of Hebron did not take threats to their security and survival lightly. Nine military officers reported information about "an imminent Arab attack," expected to coincide with Purim. After so many attacks by Arabs already, Dr. Baruch Goldstein—a devout Jew from Brooklyn, a quiet family man who had treated all of the Hebron victims, Jew and Arab alike, who never hesitated to drive alone at any hour of the day or night to help someone in need of medical attention, who wore his beeper twenty-four hours a day, next to his pistol and the fringes of his prayer garment—on Purim morning, February 25, 1994, opened fire with an assault rifle on the Muslims praying in the Cave of Machpelah, killing twenty-nine of them. The uncharacteristic event touched off a global wave of shock.

A note was found in Goldstein's pocket: "With God's help. Text of a confession from the bridge of life. I thank you, oh Lord, our Father and the Father of our fathers, in whose hands are my health and my death, for the life and life's requirements. . . . I beseech you, make me well." It is the text of a religious prayer formulated centuries ago (attributed to Nahmanides) for use by terminally ill Jewish patients. The humane compassion for which Goldtsein was revered made his aberrational act all the more astonishing and confounding.

Goldstein's massacre was a dreadful exception to the normal, pious, harmless life in Jewish Hebron. "The exception is what an armed Israeli did in Hebron's mosque, the rule is why the Israelis have to arm themselves in the first place," wrote Jeff Jacoby in the *Boston Globe*. More importantly, Goldstein is almost universally regarded as an abomination to the Jewish faith.

Arab attacks against Hebron Jews continued after the "Zionist carnage," but without the same media attention. Two months after Goldstein's massacre, Shani-Sarit Prigal was murdered at the gate of Kiryat Arba. Dov Driben of Kiryat Arba was killed in April 1998. Rabbi Shlomo Ra'anan was murdered in August 1998, and Danny Vargas died in October 1998. The wave of violence continued on November 15, 2002, when Palestinians ambushed a group of Jews as they left the Tomb of the Patriarchs. The worshipers, accompanied by officers from Israel's Border Police, were going to make their ritual walk to Kiryat Arba after praying at the tomb. The "Sabbath Massacre" evoked a notorious ambush in Hebron that killed six Jews in 1980, also on a Sabbath eve. Those who died in the 2002 ambush were a microcosm of the Hebron community: a French Jew, an immigrant from Ukraine, two immigrants from Azerbaijan, a Druze officer, and the son of settlers from nearby Gush Etzion.

Lieutenant Dan Cohen was one of twelve killed that day. After his death, Dan's family received a box marked "secret, personal." It was his testament: "Dad, Mom, *shalom!* Does man have a job to do? The world exists for something that is still to come, that has yet to happen, and each of us is an integral and irreplaceable part of this great unfolding. If this is the case, then we have been called to do our best to be part of this puzzle, and for those who follow the path of the Jewish religion this means living out our values in the most effective way possible, in order to give life to generations better than our own through our influence on our children and those around us. Maybe I am one of those who will influence those around us, and you are among those who have influenced your children." Dan expressed his gratitude to the full. "Since something might happen, and since in my brief life experience I have seen that most of the people who suffer a breakdown after the loss of a child are those who feel a sense of guilt, and since I know you well (especially you, Mom), you might needlessly regret something you did or didn't do, something you said or didn't say. So I want you to know that you did everything right, that I, except for a few moments, have been satisfied with everything for more than twenty years, and I want to tell you, Mom and Dad, with all my heart, thank you! Dan."

Since the pogrom of 1929, the Jews have always tried to go back to Hebron, despite the prohibitions of the Jewish state. Even Menachem Begin, godfather of the right, drove them out until a series of murders of Jews by Palestinians convinced the government to allow Jewish settlements in Gush Etzion again. Fifty years after the pogrom, residents of Kiryat Arba decided that the time had come to return to Hebron itself. A week after Passover, at four o'clock in the morning, ten women, joined by thirty-five children, arrived by truck at the rear of Beit Hadassah, the former medical clinic in the heart of Hebron. They quietly climbed ladders, cut wires to the windows, and unloaded mattresses, cooking burners, gas canisters, water, a refrigerator, laundry lines, and a chemical toilet. Inside the dilapidated building, the excited children sang "V'shavu banim l'gvulam," God's promise that children would return to Zion. Hearing their voices, an Israeli soldier came to investigate. When he inquired how they had entered the building, a four-year-old girl answered: "Jacob, our forefather, built us a ladder and we came in."

In 1997, the hawkish right-wing prime minister Benjamin Netanyahu divided Hebron into two parts: sector H1, encompassing 80 percent of the city, was given to the Palestinian Authority; sector H2 was given to the Israelis. Today, there are about six hundred Jews living within Hebron—boys with sidelocks, and pregnant young women wearing kerchiefs on their heads, modest and determined. "It is important to be here and remember we were here first, because the struggle going on for Hebron is related to Jews being in Israel," said Mordechai Taub. "The symbolism of Hebron is larger than almost anywhere in the land of Israel." From Beit Hadassah and the neighboring buildings where the Jews of Hebron live, to the Tomb of the Patriarchs, there is nothing but a labyrinth of Arab streets.

More than forty Jews have been killed in Hebron since 1993: students like Erez Shmuel, fathers and sons like Mordechai and Shalom Lapid, converts from Christianity like Rafael Yairi and Margalit Shohat, young married couples like Efrat and Yaron Ungar, innocents like little Shalhevet Pass, great rabbis like Shlomo Ra'anan, or Elnatan Horowitz and his wife, Dina. A suicide terrorist murdered Gadi and Dina Levy in downtown Hebron in May 2003. Three young people from communities in the Hebron Hills were murdered in October 2005. Yossi Shok was killed near Hebron in December 2005. In addition, there are the soldiers who have died while guarding the little Jewish community.

The teenagers Avihai Levy and Aviad Mansour were killed at a hitchhiking station near Hebron in June 2005. Avihai was a member of the Zionist youth movement Bnei Akiva, whose slogan is: "The Jewish people in the land of Israel according to the Torah of Israel." One of Bnei Akiva's leaders, Eitan Yosef, said, "We have been abandoned to a great sadness. These young men cared about inhabiting the land and doing good. Their names symbolize the journey of their ancestors, and are linked with eternal life." Hava, Avihai's mother, said, "You have not gone to heaven in vain. I am paying the price for Israel because you completed your mission here on earth. I sent you to a religious school, now I am sending you to heaven. You were an emissary."

Beside the lifeless body of his wife, Matat, Yisrael Adler sang the same melody he had chanted at their wedding just two months earlier. Yisrael recalled that his wife did not want him to sing at their wedding: "You were so humble that you didn't want people to see you laugh or cry. Now it doesn't matter; now you are watching us." Her sister recalled that Matat always went to the Tomb of the Patriarchs to pray. "I don't know where you found your strength. We will be strong because that is what you would want from us if you were here today." Matat's father noted that both of her maternal grandparents had survived the Holocaust; they thought and believed that the State of Israel would prevent another massacre of Jews. "Grandpa Eli, we have not swerved an inch from your path; we have constructed a tradition and have defended it with our lives."

The Jews of Hebron have always refused special security measures. "Protective measures mean cowardice, and all they do is worsen the terror," says Noam Arnon, a Hebron spokesman. One example is the playground that sits in the line of fire of Abu Sneineh, the Palestinian hillside neighborhood three hundred yards away. The Israeli army offered to build a security roof over the playground to protect it from snipers, but the settlers of Hebron declined the offer. Subsequently, ten-month-old Shalhevet Pass was killed by a Palestinian sniper at the entrance to the playground. Many settlements near Nablus and Hebron turned down the offer of a perimeter security fence on principle. Danger is neutralized by ignoring it. Hebron's settlers even rejected a protective concrete wall for the seven mobile homes of Tel Rumeida. Elisheva Federman, the mother of a large family, tells her children not to be afraid during Arab attacks: "I teach them that the One, the Holy, the Blessed governs the world, and each time a miracle happens for us, and we come out unharmed. I tell them, 'Feel how much God loves you, feel it here, here, God is not far away, he is with us, feel his protection and love.'"

Only a mystery can explain the fierce determination of Jews to live in such a hostile and beleaguered place, where so many of their predecessors have been brutally slaughtered. "This is our home, where the kingdom of David was born, where the walls bear witness to the most ancient Jewish community on earth, where we lived throughout the centuries until we were driven out by an Arab pogrom," says David Wilder, spokesman for the Jews in Hebron. "Living in Hebron is like going back to the beginning," explains Shalev Ben Ya'akov, the most famous singer in the Jewish community of Hebron. Born to Catholic parents in the United States, he came to Israel in 1994 with a love of Judaism in his heart. "It is like having been here thousands of years ago. It is *dejà vu*. I have escaped numerous terrorist attacks, but I'm not moving from here. To me the Jews who died are holy people; they are like Rabbi Akiva. And we must be brave."

It was in thinking about Hebron that the American rabbi Shlomo Riskin, who today lives in the settlement of Efrat, wrote about the "ultimate sacrifice" that the Jews must be willing to pay out of fidelity to God: "Our Bible teaches that God does not want us to die for him, but to live for him. Our ideal is to serve God in life, but there are times when we must sanctify his name in death. Being Jewish means undertaking an exhilarating but dangerous profession. Sarah is a consummate mother, concerned not only about her son, but about all of her descendants. Her soul is also tormented by the terrible trials and executions that await her heirs."

Hebron is a fault line dividing Israeli society. For leftists, the city evokes revulsion and fanaticism, slaughter and vengeance. For the devout and people on the right, Hebron is the cherished birthplace of Jewish history. Hebron Jews, wrote the American author Maurice Samuel in 1929, are concerned only "with the remotest past and with the remotest future, with the beginning and the end of things." In Hebron the dead, the living, and the unborn are partners in the renewal of Jewish life. Leon Kass observes that "ancestral piety, burial and sacred memory" link the Jewish people to the Tomb of the Patriarchs. "Hebron was the burial place of the human agents of divine purpose," says Professor Jerold Auerbach, the author of *Hebron Jews: Memory and Conflict in the Land of Israel.*

The fascination of the city of Abraham is so great that many of the seven thousand members of the Indian tribe of Bnei Menashe, descendants of a Jewish tribe dispersed 2,700 years ago, now live in Hebron. They came from the Indian-Burmese jungle to Hebron, as in a second Exodus. Just a few years ago, they lived as Protestant Christians in the Indian state of Mizoram, along Burma's frontier. According to Rabbi Eliyahu Avichail, who has spent decades combing the continents for reliable evidence of the Jewish tribes scattered in the Diaspora, bringing the Lost Tribes back to Hebron means the fulfillment of the biblical prophecies of Isaiah and Ezekiel. It was 1979 when he received the first fragmentary information about the Bnei Menashe tribe. In addition to the name Menashe (from Manasseh, one of the tribes of Israel), their oral tradition contains other Hebrew-sounding names: Efram (Ephraim), Yassak (Isaac), Gakob (Jacob). Some of the elders described a journey made by their ancestors that mentioned Shiloh (a Jewish location near Jerusalem), Sinai, and the Red Sea. Other similarities involve a ceremony practiced on the males seven days after birth, a ban on eating meat containing blood, and a shawl that resembles the Jewish *tallit.*

The glory of Hebron is in the ancient past and perhaps the distant future. The present, for many of the settlers, is but the painful and necessary link between them. On one road leading to the city, known as the "alley of death," where dozens of

Israeli civilians and soldiers have been killed, a monument was erected with the inscription: "Land, do not be quiet, do not be silent and do not be mute anymore. Land, do not cover the blood of your children like water over your land."

In 2001, Shalhevet Pass became the Israeli symbol for the innocent victims of raging terrorist violence. A photograph of her cherubic face was circulated around the world by Israeli diplomats. Many Israelis have long regarded the settlers of Hebron as living in a world apart, but they rallied behind the community after Shalhevet was killed. Newspaper headlines referred to the killing of an "Israeli" baby rather than a "settler" baby. Shalhevet was simply "our murdered baby," mourned nationally.

Oriya and Yitzhak Pass were well known in the Jewish neighborhood of Hebron, wedged into the heart of Palestinian Hebron. Their love nest had sandbags in the windows. Their first child, Shalhevet, was born there. Oriya, wearing a long skirt and with her hair tied up in a kerchief, was pushing the stroller, while Yitzhak, with his long beard and skullcap, was walking beside her on March 26, 2001. A shot rang out, just one, and Oriya turned around. Yitzhak was lying on the ground. Oriya didn't even ask if he was okay; she just grabbed Shalhevet and started running. She didn't stop until the blood was running down her hands. There was a hole in her daughter's head. Oriya's father had almost been killed in 1993; her sister Orital was shot in the back near the city market; and her brother was shot in the leg while visiting the family.

Shalhevet's funeral began with the reading of Psalms at Machpelah. Her body was wrapped in a deep blue velvet cloth with the Star of David embroidered on it. To a mourner from Jerusalem, "she looked about the size of the Torah scroll taken out of the Ark for reading." The inhabitants of Hebron dedicated a march to Shalhevet some months after her death, going all the way to the Dolphinarium nightclub, where many teenagers of Russian origin had since been murdered, on June 1.

One of the cards sent to Yehudit Dasberg had an inscription made by her daughter Efrat a few years before her death: "May you be comforted by the lamentations of Zion." Efrat and Yaron Ungar lost their lives coming home from a wedding on June 9, 1996. Their nine-month-old son miraculously survived. Yaron was an idealist who had studied in a yeshiva on the Golan Heights. He had taught lessons on Judaism in Russia before finding work as a teacher in Hebron. Efrat came from a nearby settlement, Alon Shvut, where her parents still live today. The name of the settlement means "lone oak." After the destruction of Gush Etzion, following Ben-Gurion's declaration of the State of Israel, when the Arab fighters killed all the Jewish settlers, only one tree remained standing. Since then it has been known as the *alon shvut*.

"I feel that my mission is to explain to the world that even though we have a big army, we are an intimidated people," says Efrat's mother, Yehudit. "My daughter's case is typical. She was killed in the car, in her land, coming back from a wedding. Killed because she was a Jew. She had her child in her arms and was carrying another in her womb. The Jews are here because the right to live here was given to us by God, not by the UN. It is sad that we have forgotten the source of our legitimacy." The Dasbergs suffered greatly during the Holocaust. "My family is from Czechoslovakia. They went through the concentration camps; they concealed themselves and reached Israel in 1948. My husband's family is Dutch; his sisters were killed in Bergen-Belsen, and at the end of the war they took thirty Jewish orphans and brought them here."

Yehudit talks about the young couple: "Efrat and Yaron loved each other dearly. My daughter was a graphic artist, and she wrote satirical books. Love and honor were her values. As a teenager she was humble, she never told anyone what to do or not do. As a woman she was observant and humble, with a great sense of honor that did not take for granted what children wanted. One of her books talks about love for human beings. They had chosen to live in Hebron because they had found jobs there, and because the heart of the Jewish people is there. Religious Jews feel that it is a privilege to live in the historic cities where our biblical fathers lived. Hebron was the cradle of the Jewish kingdom, and Efrat had grown up with a deep awareness of the Bible. Jews treated Arabs for free at the Hadassah clinic until 1929. That year, sixty Jews were massacred and the city was purged, made *judenrein,* free of Jews. But we came back in 1967. Even today in Hebron, simple and idealistic people welcome children with learning problems from every part of Israel. They help everyone. My daughter went to live in a trailer. I live twenty miles from Hebron. There are three generations of Dasbergs here; I have twelve grandchildren, and I love this place so much."

The Jews killed in the 1929 pogrom included a couple named Shlomo and Nechama Ungar. Like the Ungars killed seventy years later, they left two orphans behind. It is the story of the Hebron Jews, which seems to repeat itself in an eternal cycle.

Dina Horowitz was born in Florida, where she left behind a life of comfort and luxury to go live in Kiryat Arba. She helped many Jews "return" to Orthodox practice. Dina was killed in her home, during the celebration of Shabbat, along with her husband, Elnatan (Eli), a rabbi. "I am a simple man, happy to be living in an independent state," Eli had written after witnessing an earlier terrorist attack. "I am a normal citizen who respects the law and loves music. I am in a difficult situation, but I laugh a lot. I love flowers and children." Eli had chosen to live in the most imperiled Jewish community in the world to be near the tomb of Abraham. "We know that God gives and God takes away," said his father, also a rabbi. "And we know that you, Eli, were a gift from God."

"My daughter Debbie, as we called her, had chosen to go to the Jewish school in Washington instead of the public school," says Dina's mother, Bernice Wolf. "She was a Zionist at heart and wanted to go to the Michlala, a famous religious school for women in Jerusalem. It was there that she met Eli, who had rebelled against religion even though his father was a famous rabbi. They got married, he started studying in the yeshiva, and they moved to Kiryat Arba. They loved the community because there were many Zionists there, and it was one of the settlements that represented the dream of Israel. Over the years, Eli was invited everywhere in Israel to teach lessons on the Bible, and he was popular with both the 'right' and the 'left.' Debbie was also very well known; she taught at the *ulpena,* a school for immigrants in Kiryat Arba, and the girls in Hebron vied to get into her class. Debbie played in the city orchestra, while her husband flew to the United States once a month to teach. They loved living in Hebron; they knew it down to the last pebble. Debbie believed in the Bible and lived according to the 613 mitzvoth of the Jewish faith. In addition to being a profound thinker and the author of numerous books, Eli loved working in the garden; he grew exquisite flowers that he gave before Shabbat to the people in the building next door. He planted fruit trees in the vineyard. They're still there."

Bernice Wolf arrived in Israel in 1984 with her husband, who had lost his uncles and cousins in the Holocaust. Debbie's father's family came from a little village in Ukraine twenty-five miles from the Polish city of Łodz. "I am now eighty-four years old, and I have cancer," says Bernice. "It is comforting for me to think that my daughter and her husband were so well loved. There were fifteen thousand people at their funeral. It was incredible, all of the streets were jammed with cars, and everyone was crying in a way I had never seen before. My greatest anger is with the part of the world that is against Israel. My Debbie never said anything bad about the Arabs. Then why was she killed? She talked only about beautiful things, and about peace. I want answers. Debbie hoped for peace between Jews and Arabs. I believe in it less. The Arabs may want it, but their leaders are stoking their hatred."

Debbie's decision to live in Hebron coincided with her awareness of the Holocaust, Bernice explains. "Debbie was not there during the Holocaust, and it was not taught in the schools when she was studying at the Jewish school. She had friends who had been through the Holocaust, and she felt that those children were different. She never asked any questions until she was an adult, when she became aware of the Holocaust and criticized me for never telling her about it. She was mad at me because the relative closest to her, one Debbie loved very much, had been the only member of the family to make it out of Europe alive."

Debbie's father, Emmanuel, died three months after making the aliyah in 1984. It was Israel's Independence Day, and Bernice was studying Hebrew, as every immigrant does upon arriving in Israel. "As soon as you start living in Israel it gets into your blood; you can't go anywhere else. When my daughter decided to move to Kiryat Arba, she knew that it was an important part of Israel. They thought they had a mission. I can say what Jerusalem means to me. Last winter I was in Florida for chemotherapy; I was very sick and all I wanted was to die. My daughter-in-law, Lynne, gave me strength and love, and the doctor told me, 'If you gain weight, you can go back to Israel.' I was back here after one month."

Eli and Debbie Horowitz were typical inhabitants of Kiryat Arba. "Their door was always open. Anyone who had a problem could go in and talk with them; they always had people in their home, or were on the phone with someone. My daughter taught at the local school and was also involved in the dormitory. The girls thought of Debbie like a mother and talked with her more than they did with their own families. Even after these girls graduated, got married, and had children, they frequently called her just to talk. Debbie made her clothing herself; it was very simple. The women here cover their heads after they get married so as not to attract other men, and the men almost always wear dark clothing—even at weddings. Everyone thought that Eli and Debbie were everyone's best friends. They loved and respected them. When they were killed, my doctor left his daughter's wedding to watch their funeral." Bernice died of cancer in early 2003.

We talk with one of Rabbi Horowitz's best friends, David Wilder, who is the spokesman of the Jews in Hebron. He lives wedged inside the Arab *suk,* with a Smith & Wesson pistol always at his right hand and a cell phone always at his left, keeping him updated on everything. For Wilder, being here is "both a duty and a privilege." He says that "Eli Horowitz and his wife Dina loved their community; they were humble and full of faith, tremendous faith. They were so much alive, it's hard for me to consider them dead. Eli was someone who risked his life for the Jewish people. Eli and Dina didn't *teach* the Torah, they *were* the Torah, living examples of a life of patience, understanding, wisdom, and fear of God. And of love, so much love—love for their children, for their family, for their friends. Dina also taught music, which was the essence of her soul. Eli loved nature, and together they walked among the flowers of the land of Israel. What I remember most about him is what he taught me: the need to listen, to feel, to absorb, in order to hear the voice of God. They were people of hope and prayer, optimism and values; they embodied what life should be. You can't live here without faith. It is a miracle to be here, and my faith has been strengthened by the suffering of seeing friends like Eli and Dina die."

Asked what makes a Jew from New Jersey move here, Wilder replies, "We are still fighting a war for independence; we are fighting for the right to live as Jews and as free men in our land. None of us wants to die, but we know that we have to be ready to pay this price." Wilder is emphatic on the future of Judaism. "There is no future for Judaism outside of Israel. In the diaspora, the Jews are decimated by assimilation and secularization. When I came to live here, I did it because I wanted to contribute to the battle for Israel. The people call us 'monsters' or 'heroes.' I think instead that we are normal people, normal Jews with a few ideals. We are not motivated by hunger for wealth, money, or vacations in Switzerland. We are idealists, not materialists." And this idealism is combined with Hebron's special character. "It is the first Jewish city in history. On Tel Hevron, the hill of Hebron commonly known as Tel Rumeida, remains have been found dating back to the time of Abraham, and also a royal seal from 2,700 years ago, with the word 'Hevron' inscribed on it in ancient Hebrew characters. To evacuate Hebron, the first Jewish city of *Eretz Yisrael,* would be the equivalent of evacuating Americans from Boston or Philadelphia following a terrorist attack—with the difference, obviously, that American history goes back only about 250 years, while Jewish history in Hebron dates back to more than 3,700 years ago. Hebron, the home of Abraham, is not only the place where Judaism had its beginning, it is also the origin of monotheism for all the peoples of the earth. Hebron is the heart of the Jewish people, the vital sap from which the Jewish people derives its sanctity."

Hebron was the home of Rabbi Shlomo Ra'anan, the grandson of the first chief rabbi of Israel, Avraham Yitzhak Kook, and a relative of the founder of the ultra-Orthodox Meah Shearim neighborhood in Jerusalem. His friends say that Shlomo, who was stabbed in the heart in August 1998, had "a Shabbat soul," pure and serene, and that he was made of "humility and holiness." Everyone in Hebron knows his name. It is synonymous with martyrdom. After the evacuation of Yamit—the city that had sprung up from nothing in Egyptian territory, from which the settlers were cleared in 1982 following the treaty that gave Sinai back to Egypt—Shlomo and his wife had gone to live in a mobile home, a trailer, in Hebron. They were married in the Cave of Machpelah, where the four Jewish patriarchs are buried. Shlomo was killed at night, in his own bed, and the rabbis promised to create a Torah study center on the site of the attack. It is called the "Light of Shlomo," the Ohr Shlomo Torah Study Center.

Shlomo Ra'anan's wife, Chaya, comments on the fact that the place where her husband was killed is now a school of religious studies: "It gives me life; otherwise I could not live for one minute. Every day, the people who come here literally give me life. This room where my husband was killed was our bedroom. I have heard Rav Ginzburg say that in Jewish homes, the rooms are laid out the same way as the Temple, and that the bedroom is the Holy of Holies, where the Ark of the Covenant was kept. So I thought to myself, now that it's not our bedroom anymore, let it be a Holy of Holies for studying the Torah and for prayer."

On the wall at the home of Chaya and Shlomo's daughter, Tzipi, there are three photographs. There is one of Shlomo; one of his father, Rabbi Tzvi Yehuda Kook; and one of *his* father, Rabbi Avraham Yitzhak Kook, who was the first Ashkenazi chief rabbi of Israel. Avraham Yitzhak was also the father of religious Zionism, the first to explain that returning to Zion was the decisive factor for the advent of the redemption, since the rebirth of the Jewish state permits the reassembly of the people of Israel (*Am Yisrael*) under the law of Israel (*Torath Yisrael*) in the land of Israel (*Eretz Yisrael*). Zionism, in spite of its secularism, was neither impious nor antireligious, but instead was the bearer of sanctity. Avraham Kook led hundreds of rabbis and students to this religious and political interpretation. His son

Tzvi Yehuda led the settlers' movement to return to ancient Judea and Samaria.

Thousands of people went to Shlomo Ra'anan's funeral, including Benjamin Netanyahu, the prime minister. The procession ended at the Mercaz Harav yeshiva, which was founded by Rabbi Avraham Yitzhak Kook in 1924 and remains the heart of religious Zionism. "I knew Shlomo for fifty years, and I never heard him speak a word of hatred against anyone," said the principal of the yeshiva, Rabbi Avraham Shapira.

"My father was a *talmid hakham,* a sage," says Tzipi, the mother of eleven children. "He was a man of the Torah. He didn't want to be important, but to respect the laws, to be a man of understanding. My father treated everyone as his equal, even children. He did not want to be spoken of as an important man, and he followed the Jewish saying 'do not speak evil of anyone.' The first time he came here to Hebron he was excited, but my mother was less so, because she knew that there had been attacks by Arabs. But my father knew that this was the city of David and the patriarchs. My grandmother had survived the pogrom of 1929. They have wanted to destroy us for many generations, so I must be strong, even though this is not easy. But we cannot and must not surrender."

After the death of her husband, Chaya said, "The terrorists have tried to drag us into the darkness, but this yeshiva has given light." Today the Ohr Shlomo Torah Study Center is directed by Tzipi's husband, Rabbi Yisrael Shlissel. "It is a great honor for me to lead this school," the rabbi tells us. "My father-in-law Shlomo was a wonderful, quiet man. He moved to Hebron because he wanted to be close to the Tomb of the Patriarchs. He and the others have died for the *Kiddush Hashem,* the sanctification of the name of God, in that they were killed because they were Jews. Shlomo often talked with the Arabs of the city; they did not kill him for personal reasons, but because he was a Jew."

Another inhabitant of Kiryat Arba is a French Jew named Uri Baruch. He was born in Nice to a Zionist family, and his father had been in the Nazi concentration camp in Buchenwald. At the age of eighteen, he left France by himself for Israel. Through the French-Israeli military accords, he carried out his military service as a paratrooper during the Six-Day War. He was sent to Belgium in 1970 to work with the young Zionists there. Then he married Francine and had three children. In 1981, he returned with his family to Israel, where his fourth child was born. His daughter Sarit was killed in 2001, nine days after the attack on the Twin Towers in New York.

Sarit was six years old when her parents decided to make the aliyah from France. In Kiryat Arba, she entered a religious school and joined the Bnei Akiva youth group. "In her free time, she read a lot and played the guitar," her father, Uri, tells us. "Sarit had a happy adolescence in Kiryat Arba. The community here is made up of idealists, people of religion and faith, simple people from all over the world—Russia, France, India, Ethiopia. This return of the exiles is part of the dream, after two thousand years of exile. Here there are teachers, doctors, engineers, rabbis. About 30 percent of the people are secularized; others are Jews who have become observant, or converts. While I was in school I took a trip to Poland to see the places of the Holocaust. I came back home saying that every Jew should go there during his lifetime, to see what happened to his people sixty years ago."

At age eighteen, Sarit became a volunteer in southern Israel, in the city of Yerucham, known for its high poverty rate. "Sarit worked at the day-care center and with the elderly; she loved to listen to their stories intently and with a big smile. After this she went to Saint Petersburg for two years. She talked to us about her experiences, and I believe that these travels affected how she viewed her Jewish identity and the opportunity to live in Israel. She and her husband moved to Nokdim, where they had three children."

Uri Baruch's story has its roots in Europe and in the disappearance of the Jewish people. "My family's history is an example of Zionism and of education in love of country. As the saying goes, 'From the Holocaust to the revival.' Sarit's grandparents had survived the Holocaust, the only ones in their family; the others were incinerated by the Nazis. They did not move to Israel; that was done by the next generation. We were the ones to live in a kibbutz, to learn Hebrew, to wear the paratrooper uniform, to take part in Israel's wars. Between the third generation, Sarit's, and the first, the Holocaust survivors, there is a clear historical link to the persecution of Jews because they are Jews. We do not regret deciding to come here to the city of the patriarchs, Hebron–Kiryat Arba, to a history that goes back thousands of years, and seeing that nothing has changed."

He continues: "I do not regret any of the choices that I have made, and even if I had known the price that I was to pay in the future, I would have decided to live my life with the same faith and happiness of the past years. Sarit's death is both similar to and different from the historical persecutions of the Jews. It is similar in its circumstances: Sarit was killed because she was a Jew and wanted to live as a free woman in her own country. It is similar in the motivations that drove the terrorists to aim their rifles at a mother and her children, to kill them all. But Sarit's death is different from the other stories because her family history is different, her circle of friends is different, the memories of her are different. The scenario of death repeats itself, the Jews killed in pogroms and so forth, but every Jew killed has his own story. Behind every person who is murdered—in our case Sarit as sister, daughter, and mother—there is a human story. Every personal story is full of nostalgia for the dead, with the children growing up and celebrating their birthdays without their mother and getting their diplomas without being able to show their mother; with the parents who do not sleep at night, they are so full of pain and sorrow, solitude and tears. Just as we say of the victims of the Holocaust that 'every Jew has a name,' the victims of terrorism also have a name and a family."

The story of Gad Marasha, who came to Kiryat Arba from Ethiopia, is emblematic of the Jewish melting pot. It is moving to see the pride of the parents, often illiterate and poor, when they visit the young, black Jews who, with a background of starvation and defenselessness, are now Israeli soldiers capable of defending themselves and their own homes. Captain Marasha was from an extremely ancient Jewish lineage, the original subjects of the Queen of Sheba at the time of King Solomon, who remained poignantly faithful to the Torah. They had simplified their rituals, but were fiercely and unequivocally devoted to the religion of Abraham and Moses. From time to time they would send a horseman from Addis Ababa to find out if the Messiah had arrived.

Gad lived in Kiryat Arba and intended to marry his fiancée in a few months, but their dream was shattered by a roadside bomb in December 2000. Hundreds of people accompanied him to his final resting place on Mount Herzl, in Jerusalem. "You really had such a big smile," his sister Rivka said. "You were my second father. Gad, your pure Jewish soul has returned to heaven, and your body is here in this coffin. Nonetheless, I can still feel you smiling from inside the coffin." Finishing her eulogy, she said, "Whisper it up there, that down here we won't give up even an inch of *Eretz Yisrael*."

His commanding officer, Pini Ganon, remarked in his eulogy, "You spent all of your military service in the region of Gaza. You knew every trail, every bush, every stone. You inspired trust in your men, and they admired you. They believed in you as their commander, and you were a friend to them. Only two weeks ago, you told me that you intended to get married next April. I congratulated you, and we even made plans for your wedding. I can't believe that, instead of celebrating to the sound of wedding music, I am here in front of a microphone to mourn you."

In the Israeli army, Gad had volunteered to serve in a tracker unit, where he was the only Jewish soldier among Bedouins. "During the fast in the month of Ramadan, Gad did not eat or drink in the presence of his men," his friends recalled. "Despite the fact that he had no obligation to do this during the Muslim holidays, he scrupulously respected them. The Bedouin soldiers admired him for this. During the night, he sat with them and made coffee. He was outstanding on the ground, able to create a relationship of mutual trust and respect with the Bedouin scouts." Gad's brother in arms, Ya'akov, said, "We constantly fight a war amid suffering, sorrow, and sadness, but when you realize what a great honor it is to die for God and for one's country, then sadness remains sadness, but faith is the true consolation."

Gad Marasha had completed a journey of a thousand years in Kiryat Arba, where a third or more of the residents are Russian or Ethiopian immigrants placed there by the Israeli government. Through Operation Moses in 1984 and then Operation Solomon in 1991, Israel saved thousands of Ethiopian Jews in danger of death. They disembarked from the planes at night; the airport lights had been turned down to be less intimidating. The immigrants were given Israeli flags to hold, and they knelt down to kiss the land that was welcoming them with such enthusiasm. Many were weeping. Hundreds of Israelis were on the tarmac to applaud and embrace them. Most of those Ethiopian Jews—tall and slender, full of ancient dignity—were dressed in white, the color of celebration, weddings, joy. They were about to marry Zion, to become Jews in every way, not having to hide or risk death as they did before Israel flew them out in a bold rescue operation. Many were sick with tuberculosis or malnourished; they had lived in huts with dirt floors, lacking electricity, gas, and running water. They knew only that they were Jews, the children of King Solomon and the Queen of Sheba. The IDF taught the young Ethiopian Jews to join a brotherhood, with a common identity, a religious and historical solidarity.

The attack that killed Gad Marasha in 2002 also took Major Yonatan Vermeulen, a Christian immigrant who was born in a little Dutch village. Yonatan had been the poster child for the Jewish National Fund's campaign to get donors to plant trees in Israel. After completing military service, he volunteered to join the antiterrorism unit. Asked why he risked so much, he always said, "This is my home." Yonatan was a blue-eyed young Dutchman; Gad was a black Ethiopian man; they had virtually nothing in common, not even religion, but they were united in giving their lives out of incredible love for Israel.

Rafael Yairi was killed in Hebron in 1994. He was a convert to Judaism who came from Holland, where his last name had been Klumfenbert. His wife, Chaya, still lives in Kiryat Arba and sells modest clothing for Jewish women. Rafael and Chaya had met in Amsterdam, at the start of his religious studies. Theirs may be the most heartbreaking story of Jewish Hebron. "Souls come into this world to repair what has been damaged," Chaya explains. "When God wrote the 'plan for this world,' the Torah, he gave every non-Jew the opportunity, not the requirement, to convert. Conversion is like a marriage with God. One can love even without converting, but if one does so one becomes closer to him. Rafael wanted this. It was a very beautiful thing for him, and God was happy about this, for him and for me. When he was killed, many questions occurred to me. But simple answers are not part of this world. That's why it's called faith. It was a great privilege to be married to Rafael, and

I would do the same things again even if I had to lose him once more."

Chaya, also a convert, does not regret anything. "Rafael was a man hungry for the truth, he was very happy and had found inner peace after his conversion. After we got married, he told me that he felt complete. I am a human being, so yes, sometimes I feel resentful toward God, Rafael, the Jewish people, but only for a few moments. In general the answer is no, thank God, no. I consider myself a fortunate and blessed person. My pain and anger have gone away; I have happy memories and I laugh often. I feel good when I think about Rafael. I still love him and he lives inside of my heart; he is part of me. Detached from its body, his soul is closer to me now. I am not a saint, but I know that God loves me, so I try to care for myself, too."

Why choose Hebron? "Hebron is a Jewish city," Chaya replies. "Rafael and I thought of Abraham and Sarah as our parents. Paradise began here, and Rafael rests here, until eternity. There is no place in the world to which Rafael and I felt closer. He died for this, but his soul lives on. In the Psalms it says that 'Even though I walk through the valley of the shadow of death, I fear no evil, for you are with me.' For me, these words have become a reality. We have to bring some light of hope and believe in this world."

So That God
May Smile Again

Decoding *the media bias and the war* against Israel begins where the effects of Islamic terrorism are concealed. That is what happened to the bodies hurled into the void from the Twin Towers, which immediately disappeared from the television screens and from the front pages of the newspapers.

Dizengoff Street, named after the first mayor of Tel Aviv, is the city's Broadway, a stretch of bars and cafes forming the heart of a city that likes to boast that it never sleeps. One day in October 1994, Dizengoff Street turned into a ribbon of horror. A bus full of poor devout Jews, Russians or Ethiopians who could not afford a car, became a smoking wreck dripping with blood, scattering gray matter on the windows of the homes nearby, leaving a hand lodged in the branches of a tree. There were clumps of long black hair smeared with diesel and studded with bits of glass. Noam Semel, director of the nearby Cameri Theater, heard the explosion and ran down the block to the scene. "I had a feeling that no one was alive. There was smoke and bodies—no screams, no panic, just silence." Pieces of human flesh landed on terraces and in trees. A hairdresser who had taken the bus to work and suffered blast injuries to her chest and back remembered "a woman without a face." A plaque hanging on a tree at the Dizengoff bombing site today says: "At this spot, murderers took the lives of twenty-two victims. Their memory will stand forever."

In May 1996, another suicide bomber blew himself up in a crosswalk outside the Dizengoff Center, surrounded by dozens of people including children in costume for the Jewish carnival. On the asphalt were the pulverized remains of a baby stroller. The intersection was covered with mutilated corpses, some of them on fire. In the air was the acrid odor of burned flesh and hair. All the advertising billboards were shredded—Benetton, Sbarro, the guitar of the Hard Rock Cafe—modern icons shattered by totalitarian hatred. At the moment of the explosion, the movie theaters, restaurants, and boutiques were all crowded. One woman screamed, "They're slaying us all! In a year there won't be a State of Israel anymore."

Working his way to a blood stain on the ceiling of Bank Leumi, a volunteer takes out a wad of cotton and delicately mops it up. The Alitalia office on the fourth floor is also devastated. "Only seven bodies have been identified. How will names be matched to the others? They have been reduced to a piteous state," say the devout emergency responders, who make the rounds like compassionate peacemakers, salvaging the wreckage. They are the guardians of fragments that may be insignificant in our eyes, but will mean everything to those who want to mourn one of the victims. A teenage boy, helped by his parents, climbs to the top of a tree, its bark and leaves burned by the explosion, and places a bouquet of flowers between two bare branches. At the foot of the tree, a mute witness to the horror, people light dozens of candles.

Dana Gutman, age fourteen, had come to Tel Aviv with three friends for a day of joy. Three of them were killed. They were always explaining to their friends how important the peace process was. Bat-Hen Shahak, fifteen, dressed up for Purim in her mother's wedding dress. At lunchtime, she called home and asked her father for permission to stay a few more hours. Later that day, he identified Bat-Hen's body at the forensic institute. Leah Mizrahi, sixty-one, had gone to Dizengoff Center to buy a present for a bar mitzvah. Dan Tversky, fifty-eight, was an economics editor at the liberal newspaper *Ha'aretz*. Tali Gordon, twenty-five, was politically active in support of the peace process.

On a quiet night in 2002, a bomber killed himself and fifteen others at the Sheffield Club, a billiards hall in Rishon Lezion, a working-class city near Tel Aviv. Popular with teenagers as well as middle-aged men and women, the club attracted Arab patrons from the nearby city of Jaffa. Amid the jingle of slot machines, the blare of rock music, and the crack of billiard balls, few patrons would have noticed the young Palestinian suicide bomber slipping into the nightspot. The blast catapulted bodies through windows and onto the cars parked three floors below. The attack was powerful enough to lift a refrigerator into the air and shear off the front and back walls of the club, leaving the third floor looking like a crumpled dollhouse with bodies trapped under the collapsed ceiling.

In front of the Diamond Exchange, in the heart of one of the business districts in Tel Aviv, among the skyscrapers for computer company offices, a terrorist detonated his bomb on a city bus. The explosion was so violent that it took the pathologists hours to piece the corpses together so they could be recognized. In Netanya, a suicide bomber blew himself up in front of the Hasharon Mall, which Israelis now call "the gate of death." One passerby spoke of seeing "an elderly woman sitting on the pavement, her clothing and hair on fire. She was doing nothing, absolutely nothing. It was like she was in a trance." That woman is the symbol of a country subjected to the most horrifying terrorist campaign in living memory. And who remembers that man who tried to cover the corpses with a jacket, as if he wanted to protect what remained of them, of their broken dignity? Who remembers the teenage boy, an

immigrant from Georgia, who ran to the restaurant of the
Sharon brothers after it was bombed for the second time? He
wanted to know who was responsible for collecting body parts.
"I found some bits of flesh, who deals with flesh?" And who will
commemorate the father who passed in front of the Dizengoff
Center, holding his little daughter's hand, just two minutes
before the explosion? Or Shimon, who embraced the remains
of his son when the emergency workers arrived, whispering,
"Don't die, don't die, your father loves you so much."

The worst bus carnage happened in 1978 along Israel's main
coastal highway from Haifa to Tel Aviv. Slipping ashore from the
Mediterranean on the afternoon of Shabbat, the terrorists
hijacked two buses filled with tourists and sightseers, took them
on a wild ride down the road toward Tel Aviv, shooting at everyone in sight along the way, and destroyed one bus in "an orgy of
fire and death." Official statistics put the number of dead at 37
(among them 10 children), with 76 wounded—a toll that
exceeded the 1972 Munich massacre (11 dead) and the slaughter at a Ma'alot school in 1974 (26 killed). It was the worst terrorist attack in Israel's history. The terrorists' only purpose was
to kill as many Israelis as possible. David Halevy, a correspondent for *Time* who was the only journalist on the scene, reported
that "the highway looked like a slaughterhouse." A city square in
Ramallah was recently named after Dalal Mughrabi, the lead
terrorist in the Coastal Road massacre.

In 1989, a bearded Palestinian man shouting *"Allahu
Akbar"* seized the steering wheel of a Jerusalem-bound No. 405
Egged bus from Tel Aviv and sent it crashing over a steep
precipice, killing fourteen passengers.

In 1997, a suicide bomber blew himself up amid the tables
at Cafe Apropos in Tel Aviv. A twenty-eight-year-old Palestinian walked into the cafe but couldn't find an empty table inside,
so the waitress showed him to a place on the terrace. Beneath
his shirt he wore a belt, eight inches wide, with six loops for the

six sticks of dynamite. A wire was threaded through his pants to the control switch. Moments after he sat down, he pushed the button to detonate the bomb. Three women were killed. One image was replayed again and again on television: a distraught policewoman cradling an injured baby outside the ravaged cafe. She was six months old and her mother had died in the explosion. There were dozens of children in costume for Purim. The white umbrellas were covered with blood and bits of brain, and two infants were injured by the shrapnel.

Jaffa Road is one of the main arterial roads in Jerusalem, running alongside the plaza of the modern city hall, the general headquarters of Bank Leumi, the post office, the building that used to house the Assicurazioni Generali, and then the shops, emporiums, Jewish craft stores, bookstores, cafes, restaurants, pizzerias, and pharmacies. Jaffa Road is also the "street of terror." There was a morbid joke going around: a man who is about to get on a bus asks the driver, "Excuse me, does this go to the end of Jaffa Road?" The driver answers, "Don't you think that's a little too optimistic?" The bus's route is called "the line of life," because the number of the bus is 18, and the tenth and eighth letters of the Jewish alphabet form the word *chai*, "life." At the station of departure, a sign warns the drivers, "Be alert! Check everything." It is like driving through a minefield, except the bombs have not been hidden on the roadsides, as in Iraq, but behind the hand paying the four-shekel fare.

The bus was blown up in front of the big Klal Center, a few dozen yards from the King George Street intersection—where two years earlier another attack had massacred the clients of the Sbarro pizzeria. The explosion was terrifying. It split the bus in two and blasted open the driver's cabin. The injured and dead flew out into the street. "Amid the wreckage, people burned and bleeding were jumping down from the sides," witnesses recounted. The surrounding shops, cafes, and terraces were devastated by the shrapnel.

And then there was the massacre of children at the gates of Meah Shearim, the most important ultra-Orthodox neighborhood in Jerusalem. The roof was blown off. The bodies of children flew out over the heads of their parents and fell onto the pavement. The scene was "full of terrified children, injured and covered in blood."

The remains of victims end up in a commemorative cemetery in Kiryat Ata, along with the carcasses of blown-up buses. Next to the buses are the objects never claimed by the victims' relatives: school notebooks, military berets, books, tennis shoes, videocassettes, kippot of every color, T-shirts, officers' insignia. Looking at these paltry remains brings to mind the ones preserved at the extermination camps: worn-out shoes, bottles with labels from Warsaw and Krakow, baby's bottles, dentures, prayer books, documents, family photos, eyeglasses, dolls without arms or heads.

There are survivors of attacks who struggle even to get rid of the stench of death. Talia Sapir survived the attack on Cafe Moment in Jerusalem. On television, Talia saw that two Palestinian attackers had opened fire in a hotel in the coastal city of Netanya, killing two Israelis. "Don't go out," her mother told her. But Talia thought, "They've done their thing for today, there won't be another." She put on her pale green jacket, her favorite, over her black slacks and pullover, and then went to the Cafe Moment with her husband, by car. Talia wanted to sit inside. Her husband preferred to stay outside on the terrace, smoking. After the explosion, Talia wanted to go home to see her little daughter and "to get rid of all those clothes as soon as possible." Getting out of the taxi, she took off the green jacket, a souvenir from a trip to France, and her husband quickly stuffed it into a trash bin. Many Jews are scrupulous about burying all human remains according to religious precepts, but Talia felt no remorse in throwing away that clothing, since the blood on it was not from Jews; it was from the Muslim bomber.

While she was lying on the floor in the cafe, Talia had seen his head nearby.

On March 2, 2002, in the Beit Yisrael neighborhood in Jerusalem, Grandma Hannah Nehmad lost seven members of her large family: a son, a daughter-in-law, and five grandchildren between fifteen months and fifteen years old. The entire Nehmad clan, an ultra-Orthodox family from Rishon Lezion, had come to Jerusalem for a bar mitzvah celebration for one of the offspring of Hannah's eight children.

Afterward, the Nehmads stopped to talk outside the synagogue and the modest hotel where the party had been held. Dozens of children were hanging around the women's long skirts. The men, dressed in black, with wide-brimmed hats and long sidelocks in honor of the Eternal, were preparing for the Havdalah, the ceremony that separates Shabbat from the profane days. It was the hour when the first three stars appeared in the sky, formally closing *Shabbes,* as the devout call it in Yiddish. Then everyone goes out together: young people go to the pubs, older adults go to restaurants, the devout leave the temple and stay to chat and wish each other *"Shavuah tov,"* a good week. In the devout neighborhood of Beit Yisrael, the Jews live as they did in eighteenth-century Poland: no movies, no television, no entertainment, no compulsory military service, no cafes.

Shabbat, as the famous theologian Abraham Heschel used to say, brings us out of the tyranny of the material, bringing man into harmony with the sanctity of time and with God. That is why it's an attractive time for terror to strike. Shaul Nehmad, fifteen years old, was rushing back with the wine to be blessed and drunk at the Havdalah ceremony. Then came the explosion, and Shaul was killed on the spot. On that day, *Shabbes* was desecrated.

Eleven-year-old Lidor Ilan also died, along with his sister Oriah, one and a half. Their mother, Ronit, had gone with her six-year-old daughter Linoi to change clothes before returning home. Lidor was sitting in the car when his father, Shimon, asked him to bring the keys to open the trunk. Shimon saw Oriah fly out of his arms, thrown dozens of yards. Ronit came running down the stairs and embraced the bodies of her two dead children with her eyes, as if to protect them. Linoi asked in shock, "Mom, am I the oldest now?" Also killed were Ronit's brother Shlomo Nehmad, her sister-in-law Gafnit, their daughters, Shiraz and Liran, in addition to a nephew, Shaul, who had studied in a yeshiva and loved the Torah. They called him a *talmid hakham,* the honorary title reserved for the most talented students. The pious students who founded a democratic theocracy and rebelled against Egypt, the most terrible autocratic monarchy of the time, were *talmid hakham.*

The victims at Beit Yisrael also included Tzofia Ya'arit Eliyahu, twenty-three, and her son, Ya'akov Avraham, five months old. The child had started crying and Tzofia bent over the stroller to pick him up. Her sister, Livnat, kept walking; she was about ten yards away when she heard the explosion and turned around. There was no trace left of Tzofia or the stroller. That's how life ended, on a walk at the end of Shabbat, for a five-month-old child and his mother, a Jew who had decided to "return to the answer," to become Orthodox, out of love for her husband. Livnat recalls that the couple had left notes for each other on the refrigerator: "My husband, have a good day. Take with you the respect and love of your wife."

A tenth victim, Avi Hazan, died two days later from his injuries. Avi was an accountant who had moved to a settlement because "he liked the atmosphere," as his friends recalled. With the passing of time, he had become a dedicated supporter of the settlement policy and had also "returned to the answer." But the situation had ruined his morale. "He cried like a baby every time a funeral was broadcast on television," his wife explained. "But he wanted Ariel Sharon to pay the terrorists back in kind." Avi had gone with his seven-year-old son to a nephew's bar mitzvah, while his wife stayed at home with their infant. On television, she saw relatives and friends who had been injured by the explosion. Her son saw his father sink in his own blood.

The eleventh victim to die of his injuries from the terrorist attack in Beit Yisrael—and the sixth grandchild that Hannah Nehmad lost—was Avraham Eliahu Nehmad, seventeen years old. "He was a wonderful young man, a student full of happiness, and with the virtues of ethics and justice," said the rabbi of his yeshiva in Bnei Brak. "He was noble and simple."

The No. 2 bus was full of the faithful returning from the Wailing Wall on August 19, 2003. They were ultra-Orthodox Jews, the Haredim. Many lived in Meah Shearim, where one can find the remnants of the tribes from European Bessarabia: the Belzers, with their fur-trimmed hats; the Jerusalem-born Yerushalmi, with gold-colored jackets tight around their waists; the Satmars, in Zouave-style pants and white socks; the Lubavitchers, who offer phylacteries to passersby in order to hasten the coming of the Messiah. Some of those on the bus had come to visit the sacred places of Jerusalem from Safed, the city of the Kabbalah; or from Bnei Brak, the city that looks like a Polish *shtetl* where only ultra-Orthodox Jews live. These people were part of the least known and least understood segment of the Israeli population. Twenty-three of them died that day.

In its own way, bus No. 2 was a sacred bus. For many of the victims, going to the Wall was a source of immense joy. The Wall is, first, a tall barrier that constituted the western defense of the Second Temple, built in around 600 BCE and demolished by the Romans in 70 CE. The Temple was a marvelous, immense building made of huge stones, cedar wood, marble, all the precious materials available at that time. The Sancta Sanctorum (Holy of Holies) was there, containing the words of the Law inscribed on the tablets that God gave to Moses on Mount Sinai, and transported in the Ark of the Covenant, which found its final resting place in Jerusalem. For centuries, the Wall was the only physical fragment of a Jewish identity to link the Jews with Israel. Soldiers swear their oath of loyalty to the state and are given a Bible beneath those great stones. The devout dance in a circle, dressed all in black and clutching the scrolls of the sacred scriptures. The victims on bus No. 2 were cut from the same cloth.

The social workers and doctors were not prepared for what they would find that August day. All the victims were ultra-Orthodox Jews, recognizable by their long black caftans and sidelocks. Instead of shouting for vengeance, they responded with an eerie silence. They were big families, with six, seven, eight, even ten children. There were many children and infants among the dead and injured, in some cases several children from the same family. The genocidal strike has come to be called "the children's attack" due to the large number of young victims. "It is important for people to understand that the children who died and were injured were specifically targeted by the suicide bomber who saw them," said Dore Gold, a spokesman for the Israeli government. It was Elul, the month of penance. "Forgive us, father of the Universe," the prayer goes, "in the name of the infants who have not sinned against you."

When the men of Zaka started to clear away the bodies, they heard the whimpering of an infant, but they couldn't see where it was coming from. Then they realized that the infant was beneath those bodies. The dead had shielded him from the explosion. There were many stories of infants waiting in emergency rooms for a possible survivor to claim them. The X-rays of some tiny bodies were labeled with numbers because their names were unknown. A wounded month-old infant was identified as Elhanan Cohen when a CT scan revealed that he had only one kidney; he lay in bed with no relatives to comfort him because his parents, also wounded, were in another hospital. One fatally injured older woman was identified by an orthopedic surgeon because of a hip fracture that he had once treated.

When Matanya and Chana Nathanson ushered their three little girls onto bus No. 2, they were returning to Chana's mother's house in Jerusalem. Tehilla Nathanson, age three, was killed. Chana suffered a broken jaw and leg, injuries to her spleen, and shrapnel wounds over her entire body. In Hebrew, Tehilla means "praise." And the Nathansons' faith remained strong. "God acts only out of *rachamim,* mercy," Matanya said. "We can't understand his ways, but the Almighty knows exactly what is right to do." Matanya sees his family tragedy in the larger framework of the Jewish people. "The suffering of one Jew lessens that of another. We are all here for each other." Chana's mother, Bracha Toporowitch, said, "I don't want to put the focus of my energies toward hating my enemies. I am not going to live with hate. Let's work on bringing the Messiah— not only to relieve our personal pain, but so that ultimately truth will reign over the world and everyone will recognize the reality of God."

Rabbi Eliezer Weisfish came from one of the most famous Hasidic families in Israel. He had just been to Ukraine to honor his ancestor Rabbi Nachman of Braslav, one of the greatest Hasidic masters of all time, spoken of in the books of Martin Buber. That day, Eliezer was returning from the bar mitzvah of a friend's son. "We have lost a precious flower," said a Hasidic friend. His neighbors recalled that Rabbi Weisfish "gave everything without asking for anything in return." He had told his wife, Rivka, "When I die, bury me with my two suit-cases." They contained his favorite books.

Feiga Dushinksi went to pray every morning at what remains of the Temple of Solomon. The terrorists killed her as she was returning home. "She was a saint. Every Shabbat she fed a hundred children at her home," said her brother, a rabbi. The Jewish mothers remember the wives of the patriarchs, the prophetesses Miriam and Deborah, Naomi and her daughter-in-law Ruth the Moabite, Michal the daughter of Saul, Abigail, Bathsheba, and many more. These women embody all the ten-derness of the earth, the goodnight kiss, the hand that caresses children and comforts them. They are real and true Vestal Vir-gins of the Jewish presence in the Middle East. Lilach Kardi, twenty-two, was in her eighth month of pregnancy when she was killed. "She was full of life," her husband said. "She was a simple woman. I have lost Lilach, and our son has lost his mother." Lilach had given birth to her first child a year earlier.

Mordechai Reinitz, from one of the most ancient families of the Sanz community in Netanya, had gone to the Wailing Wall with two of his children, nine-year-old Yisachar and eleven-year-old Mendel. Yisachar was killed along with his father. Both of them loved life, and were mourned by hundreds. Ya'akov Binder left behind seven children and many grandchil-dren. "He gave his children an excellent education, ensuring that they would become better every day, that they would pray and provide for their wives and children."

Liba Schwartz left behind five children and a husband who works as a judge on the rabbinical court. "Every time my mother had a problem, she went to the Wall," said her son Yoel. "The fact that she died on the way back from the Wall makes me think that she was at peace with herself." She would have survived if she hadn't stayed so long at the Wall to recite the Psalms, but she couldn't give up—not for anything in the world. "It's as if she had completed her mission in the world, and she died sanctifying the name of God."

The ultra-Orthodox student Menachem Leibel was still dressed in black and wearing his prayer shawl after going to the Wall. "He was about to get married, and continued to study the Torah," a friend explains. His family said, "We are not looking for revenge; everything comes from heaven." Avraham Bar-Or was preparing for his bar mitzvah and was returning from the Western Wall with his parents when he died. Hanoch Segal was a teacher at the Talmud Torah in Bnei Brak, a cantor at the synagogue, and the son of Holocaust survivors. He left behind five children, twenty grandchildren, and two great-grandchildren.

Shmuel Taubenfeld, three months old, had come from New York to Israel with his parents and a sister to attend a wedding. He died along with his mother, Goldie, coming back from the Wall. "Now you are an angel protecting us all," the rabbi said at his funeral. Shmuel Zargari was only eleven months old when he died in his mother's arms. "We think that the Lord granted him to us for a year," one of his relatives said. "He will be a saint in heaven; he was a tiny innocent soul."

Malka Dishi, from Givat Shaul, was on the bus with her four-year-old grandson Netanel. All of a sudden, everything went dark. "As soon as I could see again, my first instinct was to look for Netanel. I saw him standing among the corpses. He was covered with blood and bits of human flesh. He wasn't crying. He was looking for his religious head covering."

A loudspeaker blares from a car: "Israel's blood runs like water." It is announcing a penitential prayer assembly with the most prominent rabbis at five in the afternoon. The Haredim live with an acute sense of Jewish tragedy; the destruction of the Temple, the mass pogrom of Chmielnicki, and the Holocaust are physically in their lives as survivors. For this reason, the names of Arafat and Sharon were not mentioned at the funerals; nor were there any calls for vengeance. The relatives of the victims repeated that "no one knows the plans of God." Almost all of them refused any public aid; the community would take care of their needs. An infinite compassion, concealed in a wrapping of mistrust and fear, is the beauty of the Haredim communities.

"O Most Holy, may you be blessed, we love you," the Haredim sing, holding hands and dancing in a circle, laughing and embracing after a failed attack in their neighborhood. "We are the only truly secure bunker in Israel." They say that it is the Torah that protects them.

The men of Zaka work through the night, looking into the cracks and crevices in the walls of adjacent buildings, where bits of human flesh may have lodged. People call Zaka "angels on two wheels," because their scooters arrive on the scene even before the ambulances do. They are ultra-Orthodox Jews, with beards and sidelocks; their pant legs are tucked into their boots, and the *tzitzit,* the fringes of the *tallit,* the prayer shawl, stick out through the sleeves of their white shirts. Wearing yellow vests with reflective stripes, they move through the smoke, through the fire, among the dismembered bodies. Their aim is to reassemble the remains of the dead, even the smallest fragment. The most mysterious figures of Israel's resistance against terrorism, they are called to undo the suicide bomber's work of fragmentation. Photographs show them intent on preserving every scattered remnant of the dead. "Saving those who can be saved; honoring those who cannot" is their motto.

Thanks to Yehuda Meshi-Zahav, a founder of Zaka, the relatives of the victims have had a body over which to weep. "In 1989, a bus of the line 405 was knocked off a cliff, a little outside of Jerusalem, by a Palestinian terrorist," Meshi-Zahav recalls.

About twenty people were killed. "I rushed to the spot with my coworkers to help in the recovery of the bodies, smashed against the rocks, but we weren't prepared, and it was a shock. Only faith in God and the awareness that we were fulfilling the mitzvah of 'true kindness' sustained us in that first moment and afterward. These terrible scenes brought our minds back to the Holocaust." Meshi-Zahav, who for fifty years has lived in Jerusalem's pious Meah Shearim neighborhood, says "we must stand beside others, in the streets, in their suffering."

His men enter into the intimacy of death: "It is difficult to look at what an eighteen-year-old kid had in his pocket, or what was in a baby stroller: until just a moment before, they had their entire life ahead of them. Many of us weep as we work. Sometimes we pull children from the lifeless bodies of their mothers, or the dead infant from the arms of his mother. In the morning, we see smiling pictures of those we have gathered up in pieces. And then we confront unspeakable horrors with our hands, with our bodies. I don't think I could do it if I didn't believe in God." Israel has learned to understand better and better these devout men who used to live in segregated communities. They are called "soldiers of piety" and "the holy servants."

Yossi Landau, a Hasidic Jew who used to be a New York ambulance volunteer, talks about "the sanctity of human flesh." The men of Zaka treat the body as if it were alive, and believe that "if you don't respect dead people, you don't respect living people." Zaka doesn't even look to see if the victim is a Jew or not. The volunteers can come from any segment of the Haredim, but they must be married. Their wives help out by hosting bereaved families, and have set up their own support group called "Zaka Wives." During the Intifada, one of the most popular Purim costumes for Haredi kids was the Zaka volunteer with the yellow vest. This is their best definition: "Somebody who is spontaneous, who is always ready to go, day or night, like a combat soldier."

Zaka's main office is located in the garage of a little apartment building, near the Jerusalem bus station. The organization was called to work amid the rubble of the Twin Towers and the wreckage of the Space Shuttle *Columbia*. They were in New Orleans after Hurricane Katrina, in Indonesia after the tsunami, in Mumbai after the terrorist attack—wherever Jews have been killed, Zaka is there. Meshi-Zahav has even gone to Rome to identify the Jewish catacombs. "In the tunnels of Villa Torlonia, I touched the skulls of men who had been connected to the Second Temple, a cosmic emotion," he said. In case of disaster, like the attack on the Mahane Yehuda marketplace, the rabbis permit Zaka to operate on Shabbat.

After the bomb squad searches the scene and the ambulances evacuate the wounded, Zaka's men go to work, their white prayer fringes swaying as they carry away corpses. Sometimes they are called back to the scene later. The morning after the Jerusalem mall bombing, a shopkeeper phoned to say he had found a couple of fingers. When they had finished their work in the Chabad House in Mumbai, where Islamic terrorists killed many Jews in December 2008, the volunteers sat on the floor and sang and cried. It's probably the most difficult job in the world. A survivor in the Mahane Yehuda marketplace bombing described that scene: "The streets littered with overturned boxes of fruit and vegetables, splattered with blood. The smell of death, charred bodies, and burnt blood filled the air." Someone else said that "there was a smell you'll never forget."

The men of Zaka follow the commandment of *kevod hamet,* to honor the dead. Respect for the dead is absolute, "because one can ask nothing in return from the deceased." It is true compassion. According to Nurit Stadler, who studied the world of Zaka, the organization has accomplished a "resacralization" of Israeli society.

"When you see a person who only a minute ago left his family, his social circle, his work, who just left everything that surrounds a man and suddenly, in the blink of an eye, it is all fin-ished, you try with all your will to reconstruct this person," explains Elazar Gelbstein, one of Zaka's founders. "You cannot get into this person's spiritual side, but you try to reconstruct the physical side, the body of the man. You try to find every-thing that belongs to him."

Meshi-Zahav says that his work is done "to make God smile." He is dressed like a typical God-fearing Jew, with side-locks and a black kippah on his head. "Zaka's work is inspired by two religious principles: to honor the living, and honor the dead," he explains. "Honor for the living means that after a terrible thing has happened to a family, they cannot be at peace until it is certain that all of the remains have been buried. Honor for the dead means that, according to the Jewish religion, every human being has been created in the image of God, and every human being has done some good work. We believe that persons are not like animals, which, when they die, are left on the ground with no one to care for them. According to Jewish principles, the last honor for the dead is that of bringing their bodies to burial."

After thousands of deaths and injuries from terrorism, Meshi-Zahav has established a relationship with the victims. "When the volunteers of Zaka take care of a body, they learn everything that can be learned about a person in a short time—his story, his family. An empathy with this person is created. The most difficult moment is the following day, when you see this same person smiling in the newspapers, and you remember the situation in which you took care of his body." The pictures show smiling brides, graduations—and he recalls how he last saw them, burned and shriveled, like "human confetti." It is painful, but Yehuda can't quit. He is doing a holy job. Any Jew, he says, who is killed simply because he is a Jew automatically gets a seat in heaven. For him, heaven offers no carnal delights. "In paradise, you study the Bible. It is a spiritual place where you sit with wise people and learn."

Yehuda explains the strong link between the terrorist attacks and the Holocaust: "It is an obvious connection when we talk about the attacks in Israel; you see that Jewish people are being murdered. They remind me of the scenes of the Holocaust, when you understand that these people are being killed simply because they are Jews, and that there is no political or other sort of justification for murdering people going to work, or children going to school. When you find yourself facing surreal scenes and you see the injured in agony, you understand that once again, here in Israel, these people are being killed because they are Jewish, while the 'intelligent world' speaks of political justifications for the terrorist attacks. And it is incomprehensible."

The horror has been great, but Yehuda has not lost his faith. "The terror raises many questions for you. About faith in God, I mean. Why did these people deserve such an end? But our strength and our faith come from the Holocaust, when a people that had suffered through a horrible war for five years stood firm on their principles, without ever losing them. The goal of our enemies is to destroy our faith and kill the idea that human beings are created in the image of God. And when you remember this, then you know that you can never give up."

The men and rabbis of Zaka often compare the bodies devastated in the attacks to scrolls of the Torah in flames. A volunteer named Avraham says, "If a copy is burning, a Jew will rush to save it, with all his soul." And that is how Zaka intervenes to take care of a body. "The soul is the strength that guides the body," another volunteer explains. "From the first instant in which God gave a soul to the body, it became divine. When the soul leaves the body, the body becomes a sacred receptacle." At first, the rabbis had seen the organization as sinful and heretical because it was taking students away from the yeshiva. Now they speak of the Zaka volunteers as "holy servants," or as the "angels of God." It is one of Israel's most beautiful faces.

In one of their most recent operations, in Mumbai, the volunteers of Zaka spent the entire Shabbat in the building that had been ripped apart by the terrorists in December 2008. They worked in the dark, without eating or sleeping, watching over the bodies to prevent autopsies from being performed on them, as the local police wanted to do. The bodies of the Jews tortured and killed by the Muslim terrorists had to be brought back to Israel intact.

In Mumbai, the Jews were the first target of the Islamic terrorist brigade that came to the seaside city to carry out a massacre, which killed two hundred in the end. The Jews of Chabad House were tortured before they were killed. "The Israeli victims bore the maximum torture marks," one doctor said. "It was very strange. I have seen so many dead bodies in my life, and yet I was traumatized. A bomb blast victim's body might have been torn apart and could be a very disturbing sight. But the bodies of the victims in this attack bore such signs of violent urban warfare that I am still unable to put my thoughts into words." Another doctor explicitly called it an "execution." Rabbi Gavriel Holtzberg and his wife, Rivka, were killed along with four other Israelis. Photographs taken after the shootout in Mumbai give a vivid picture of the brutality unleashed on the Holtzbergs. The rabbi's legs had been tied together with a belt. Rivka, who was five months pregnant, was found covered with a *tallit,* the religious shawl that her husband spread over her disfigured body before he was cut down in his turn, as if he wanted to protect it. Alongside him was a copy of the Torah, still open.

The argument made in some quarters about a distinction between anti-Zionism and anti-Semitism looks threadbare after the attack in Mumbai. While the Chabad House provided a refuge to Israeli travelers passing through India's commercial hub, it was an outpost of traditional Judaism, not Zionism. The Chabad House offered business people and backpackers a kosher place to eat; a place to visit, put on phylacteries, hear a sermon, or receive a blessing from the rabbi.

The attack on the Chabad House swept away all the clichés about the distinction between "Jewish" and "Israeli." Historically, the Lubavitchers, the group to which the Holtzbergs belonged, were against the State of Israel. Rabbi Holtzberg was one of the *shluchim,* the emissaries of the movement that takes its name from the Belarussian "city of love," Lubavitch, which became the center of the group at the end of the eighteenth century. They are also known by the name of Chabad, which comes from three words of the Kabbalah: *chokhmah, binah,* and *da'at,* meaning wisdom, understanding, and knowledge. The Lubavitchers experienced the most terrible persecutions during the twentieth century, and not only in the Holocaust. Under the Stalinist tyranny and through the repression of Jews in Russia even after Stalin's death, the Lubavitchers were the ones who worked the hardest and most heroically for the survival of Judaism. They built yeshivas, clandestine synagogues, and underground ritual baths, and they organized the emigration and escape of many Jews. Today in the territories of the former Soviet Union, the presence of the Chabad-Lubavitchers is so strong that the term Chabad is becoming a synonym for Judaism.

The head of the Chabad in Rome, Itzchak Hazan, speaks of *mesirut nefesh,* Hebrew for "self-sacrifice," when he recalls the Holtzbergs, slain in the Jewish center of Mumbai. "A Jew killed because he is Jewish has died sanctifying the name of God; he is called *Kiddush Hashem.* It is the highest level of Jewish sanctity. They are very holy men and women, like those murdered in the Holocaust."

In the Eastern Parkway neighborhood in New York, the world center of the Lubavitchers, Rabbi Holtzberg is remembered as "a modest and simple servant." Gavriel and Rivka had left Brooklyn for Mumbai. "We have joined the rabbi's army," Rabbi Holtzberg would explain. "Gavriel and Rivky left Western comfort to spread Jewish pride to every corner of the world," said Rabbi Moshe Kotlarsky. "Their altruistic love will live in the people they knew." Gavriel had been a star student. A video shows Rabbi Menachem Mendel Schneerson, the great Lubavitch leader and founder of the emissary movement, giving him a dollar after teaching him about a passage from the scriptures. "You must give it in charity," Rabbi Schneerson told him. Gavriel was educated according to the idea that "every person is a vehicle for the observance of the precepts" and can become a *tzadik,* a just person. In his pictures, Gavriel Holtzberg is always smiling, maybe because his first rule was "obey God joyfully." A course in Judaism has been inaugurated in memory of this couple martyred far from home.

A Torah scroll damaged by the terrorists' gunfire was discovered when officials examined the Chabad House. A bullet had torn through Leviticus 16:1, which reads: "The Almighty spoke to Moses after the death of Aaron's two sons...." It refers to Nadav and Avihu, the sons of the high priest Aaron who died when they performed an offering that was not commanded by God. The oldest son of Rivka and Gavriel had died at the age of three from a rare genetic disorder. Their youngest son, Moshe, was saved from murder when his Indian nanny Sandra snatched him and fled the terror-infested building.

Thousands of Israelis, secular and religious, came from every part of the country to attend the funeral for Gavriel and Rivka. "They were massacred with a copy of the Torah and phylacteries still in their hands," said Mordechai Shmuel Ashkenazi, the rabbi of Kfar Chabad. Rabbi Kotlarsky addressed little

Moshe: "You no longer have a father and a mother to hold you in their arms; you no longer have parents who can kiss you and embrace you. But remember, you will be the son of the entire nation of Israel." President Shimon Peres also had comforting words for him: "The whole world, in particular the Jewish world, owes an answer to this two-year-old child. He must understand why his mother has been killed. . . . The world will not know peace until Moshe has been given an answer."

The leading Chabad rabbi said, "The death of Gavriel and Rivka will be avenged not with rifles or hand grenades, but through the spread of our emissaries, who will go throughout the world and return to Mumbai, where they will rebuild the Jewish center and make it even more splendid." Rabbi Kotlarsky added, "The answer to terror will not be grenades and tanks, but the spreading of the light. We will fight the terrorists not with AK-47s, but with torches." The torches of the Torah. The Holtzbergs were bound and mutilated, and they emerged as immortals in the calamitous tree of Jewish memory. Their names will inspire other people in acts of kindness and love.

His Music Lives On

In answer to the murder of two of their friends, Eli Pressman and David Rosenfeld, a handful of Jewish settlers from Tekoa set up a tiny trailer park in the desert of Judea in 1982. It was where Amos had preached and tended his sheep—Amos, the author of one of the most gut-wrenching books of prophecy in the Hebrew Bible. The new community, built over the rubble of the home where one of Rosenfeld's murderers had lived, was known as El-David at first, and later renamed Nokdim, because Amos is said to have come from a place called Nokdim. The settlement's website displays a photo of Ariel Sharon visiting it.

One inhabitant of Nokdim, Aryeh Tapper, recalls that David Rosenfeld had graduated *cum laude* from Georgetown University with a degree in history, and had decided to make the aliyah, "led by the two-thousand-year-old dream of returning to the land of our fathers." So David and his wife, Dorit, left the United States for Israel. "A little while later they decided to go live in Tekoa, which at the time was the very spartan home of thirty-five families." David knew it was the region where Amos had lived. The Bible says about Tekoa: "the plowman shall overtake the reaper, and the vintager, him who sows the seed; the juice of grapes shall drip down the mountains, and all the hills shall run with it."

Another friend, Mohammed Hassan, explained that "David was attracted by the silence of the place. His heart was pure; he had never harmed anyone." David and Mohammed had struck an agreement: David would work at the Herodion archaeological museum on Fridays, the Islamic holy day; Mohammed would work on Saturdays, the Jewish holy day. "David was killed on a Friday, stabbed a hundred times," said Aryeh Tapper. "The murderers knew that he would be alone." The murderers were two of David's employees. Shortly before his death, Rosenfeld had written a letter to his father saying, "I'm not surprised that other peoples, who have not gone through what the Jews have gone through, are not capable of understanding the violence experienced by the Israelis. We abhor it; we have been victims for centuries. And we still are today."

At the beginning of the al-Aqsa Intifada, two Jewish teenagers, Yossi Ishran and Kobi Mandel, were barbarously killed in that area. Their hometown of Tekoa, a few miles from Bethlehem, stands at the gates of the Judean desert, amid rocky hills and golden sand. Yossi and Kobi lived in a row of trailers on the hillside. Kobi's parents had come from the tranquility of Maryland to make the Zionist dream a reality. They overcame the uncertainty of their situation with the conviction that they had a mission to fulfill. At age fourteen, Yossi and Kobi were old enough to understand the dangers around them, but they didn't think that a hike in the canyon could harbor such threats. They were immobilized and stoned to death, and their bodies were hidden in a cave. The terrorists soaked their hands in the boys' blood and smeared the walls of the cave with red.

Edoardo Recanati, who also lives in Tekoa, doesn't like to be called a "settler." He explains, "We came to the desert of Judea, to the land of the Jews, more than thirty years ago—not to steal the land, but to make it like it was in the time of Amos, with vineyards and sheep." Born in Italy in the mid 1930s, Edoardo and his family took refuge in Tunis to escape the

Fascist persecution. After returning to Italy he studied law and joined the far left politically. In 1978, deciding to make the aliyah, he moved to Tel Aviv. His wife runs a factory that makes hats for women. Edoardo always takes a pistol with him when he goes out at night. "There are twenty languages spoken in Tekoa; it's a unique place. Some live in houses, some live in trailers. There are the devout who wanted to live like Amos, and there are the nationalists who came out of patriotism. It's a little piece of heaven here. No one ever wanted to live in this land. Only us Jews."

If you tell him that he's running a risk, watch out. "Look, four years ago in the war against Hezbollah, all of northern Israel was paralyzed, and I accommodated many friends in my home. Then it was the south's turn, with the rockets of Hamas, and then we hosted many families from the south. Most of the victims of the suicide attacks have been in Jerusalem, Haifa, and Tel Aviv, inside the Green Line, in the heart of Israel. There has been a diabolical campaign against us. The people thought that if we gave the settlements to the Arabs, everything would be fine. And Gaza is still there, with its magnificent greenhouses turned into military camps by Hamas, showing us that land is not the solution. The Arabs have been slaughtering us since the 1920s, and there were no settlements back then. Just like the Nazis and the Communists slaughtered us. The conflict here is religious. Islam does not tolerate a Jewish presence."

Edoardo knew Kobi and Yossi, the teenagers from Tekoa who were murdered in a cave. "They were stoned so badly that their parents didn't recognize them; the doctors had to identify them by their fingerprints. That day my son, who was in the army, called and told me they were digging the graves. Then the terrorists murdered a Russian painter, Mordechai Lipkin, a good person, extremely kind. They choose their victims carefully, always people far from the military stereotype."

Nokdim saw its saddest day in 2002, when the settlers were returning home after a day's work in Jerusalem. Their cars were riddled with gunfire. Avraham Fish was killed after he stopped his car on the roadside as a last attempt to protect his five-year-old granddaughter and his daughter, who was nine months pregnant. He had come from Russia nine years earlier and had established himself decisively in Nokdim, buying plots of land to allow his two daughters to follow in his footsteps. One of them later moved to Tel Aviv, while the other stayed in the settlement.

That day, Tamara was with her father, returning from her job as a nurse in Jerusalem. She was shot badly in the stomach and was rushed to the hospital while her little daughter, covered in blood but unharmed, was taken up in the arms of a neighbor. With a double surgery, a Caesarean section and the extraction of the bullets, the lives of both mother and infant were miraculously saved. The gynecologist said that the amniotic sack had saved Tamara's life; otherwise her vital organs would have been hit. This is the image of Israel, where death is always hovering over the innocent, but a remnant of life resists the devastation. In one moment Tamara was left without a father, and in the next she became the mother of a daughter who had just saved her life.

Avraham Fish's wife, Galina, talks about him: "My husband's family came from Ukraine; his parents were very devout. His mother taught Hebrew in a school there, and his father was a public servant. Like many others, they did not make it through the Stalinist repressions unharmed, and in 1932 they were exiled to the city of Krasnoyarsk. They lived a simple, humble life. He ran a newsstand, and she took care of the house. They had a cow and a few chickens. Avraham was born there in 1937. "At that time, few families raised their children as observant Jews. The Fishes were no different. They were afraid that the Bolsheviks would accuse them of 'Zionist propaganda.' The Fishes secretly practiced their faith their whole lives, but Avraham and his sister grew up like all the other children. My husband wanted to become a pilot, but at the time, Jews were not permitted to practice such professions; so after he got a degree in physics, Avraham worked as a schoolteacher. He was an industrious man, the author of about twenty inventions and scientific dissertations."

Then everything in their lives changed. "It was 1990. Avraham was on a business trip in Vilna and went into a synagogue. At the time, he was a secularized man, and Israel wasn't on his mind at all. In the synagogue he met an Israeli rabbi who gave him a copy of the Torah. He went back home and started reading it, and the more he read, the more religious he became."

The Fishes started thinking about the aliyah. "We both had good positions at the research institute, and then I presented my dissertation. Our daughters were in medical school, at a time when it was not easy for a Jew to be admitted. Avraham was fifty-three years old, and I was forty-six, not an easy age for such an abrupt change. But Avraham always said that the most important thing was for our grandchildren to be born in our homeland, Israel. So we left behind everything we had—friends, apartments, jobs—for Israel, where we had nothing and knew no one. Avraham was overjoyed. He was a very devout man; he started covering his head and keeping kosher. After renting a place in Jerusalem, Avraham said that we should move to a settlement to preserve the Jewish character of Israel, and because we hadn't done anything for the country yet. That's how we came here to Nokdim. My daughters and I never became devout, but we always tried to make sure Avraham had what he needed."

Along with Avraham, Aharon Gurov was also killed. He was returning home from his job at the Ministry of Education, in the department that handles the integration of new immi-grants. Aharon had arrived from Russia a few years earlier. His wife worked in the Knesset for the party Yisrael BaAliyah ("Israel, Up"), the political force led by the former Russian dis-sident Natan Sharansky, five feet two inches of heroism and Zionist devotion. That day, Aharon had asked for permission to go home early because he had to play for Purim, when people dress in costumes, and joy and laughter reign everywhere. His boss happily granted it: "This year it's more important than ever, and more difficult, to have a little fun. Hurry home and get out the accordion," he said. Aharon left behind four chil-dren between two and eight years old.

On January 29, 1997, Natan Sharansky returned as the Israeli trade minister to the country that had imprisoned him, the Soviet Union. "When I was in prison," he recalled, "I comforted myself by dreaming about landing in Israel aboard an El Al flight, with my wife Avital waiting for me at the airport. I had never dared to dream about going the opposite way." When his father died, Natan was in prison, and he told his mother what to write on the gravestone: "May his soul rest in peace, and his descendants inherit the land of Israel." Aharon Gurov and Avraham Fish were two of the spiritual children of Sharansky and the other Jewish dissidents. Aharon was follow-ing their example when he went to Israel. In Russia, Sharansky had decorated his home with photos of Jewish Palestine. His uncle was arrested by Stalin's thugs for "Zionist activities," the same accusation they would use against Natan.

One week before Natan Sharansky came into the world, the great Jewish director Solomon Mikhoels was murdered by the Soviet police. The famous Yiddish poet Itzik Solomonovich Feffer, a colonel in the Red Army, was also executed along with about twenty Jewish intellectuals. At the Lubyanka, the infamous Moscow prison, August 12, 1952 was the "Night of the Murdered Poets." But in spite of the horrific tortures inflicted on these Jews, the majority of them refused to confess. That was the year in which every famous Jew who was proud of his Jewish name ended up in front of a firing squad or in the Siberian gulag.

Eight years went by before the Western intelligentsia took to the streets on behalf of the Russian Jews and against the Soviet tyranny. On September 15, 1960, dozens of intellectuals met in Paris to ask Moscow to allow emigration to Israel. Great humanists and writers contributed their support, like Martin Buber, François Mauriac, Reinhold Niebuhr, and Albert Schweitzer. It was the first demonstration of dissent against the anti-Semitic oppression that reigned in the Soviet Union. Eighteen Jewish families from Georgia wrote a beautiful letter: "We are not asking for much; we only want to go to the land of our ancestors."

The first refusenik to be arrested was Boris Kochubievski, while he was mourning the Jewish dead at Babi Yar, the deep ravine in Ukraine where the Nazis had killed more than thirty thousand Jews within two days. That day in 1968, Boris mounted the stage during the ceremony and said, "I am Jewish, I want to live in Israel, I want my children to learn Hebrew, I want to read Hebrew newspapers, to go to a Hebrew theater. What is my crime?" He was sentenced to three years.

There was also Arkady Timor, who as a colonel in the Red Army had been among the first to enter a ghostly, gutted Berlin. He knew that the Nazis had incinerated his entire family, from his two-year-old sister to his ninety-year-old grandfather. After the war he organized a center to care for orphans, which he always called "my revenge." Arkady was sentenced to seven years of forced labor for "Judaism." His crime was that he had told the Jewish Soviet officials that their homeland was in

Palestine. He was set free after five years and would fight heroically in the Israeli war of 1967. Boris Yeltsin was the first Russian head of state to give him a medal, but Arkady refused it,
saying "there are five hundred thousand other Jews who
deserve it."

Another champion of the dissidents was Yechezkel Avi
Shabi Maor. His family had been split apart for thirteen years
because of the exile imposed by Stalin under the accusation of
"Zionism." "My music is mute, but still alive," Yechezkel wrote
during his imprisonment in Siberia. The Russian refusenik
singer Nechama Lifshitz recalled that "Yechezkel went from
school to school, from one army unit to the next, talking about
resurrection and faith." The Israeli army would play the music
he composed in prison—notes full of hope and freedom.

Three colonels in the Red Army wrote to the leaders of the
Communist Party: "Long live the Jewish people." They were all
arrested. Yosef Begun also wound up in prison for helping some
intellectuals organize a strike in protest against the emigration
restrictions. Yosef would later recall, "even when we were in the
Soviet prisons, we felt like Israeli citizens." In those army
colonels—as in Aharon Gurov and Avraham Fish—echoed the
ancient and immemorial voice of the prophet Jonah: "I am a
Jew."

Six months after Israel's victory in the war of 1967, Natan
Sharansky celebrated his twentieth birthday; it was also the
year of his "return" to Judaism. He met Vladimir Slepak, son of
an expert in Judaism who had fought in the Red Army against
the Nazis. Slepak's apartment on Gorky Street, in the heart of
Moscow, became the headquarters of the Jewish resistance.
Sharansky also became close to Ida Nudel, a young woman
who had lost her whole family in the concentration camps, and
who hung a sign from her balcony saying: "KGB, give me a
visa." She was called a "guardian angel" because of her
painstaking care for the refuseniks. Sharansky decided to learn

Hebrew, along with Natalya Stiglitz, who would soon become his wife and change her name to Avital. She obtained a visa, and for eleven years she waited in Israel for her husband.

The Jewish musicians who had asked for permission to leave the country were driven out of the orchestras. Books that were written in Hebrew, discussed Judaism, or mentioned Israel were banned from the Soviet Union. Zionism was branded "pornography" in the state-run media, and the devout were called "parasites," just like drunks and druggies. Russian state television described the refuseniks as "soul traffickers." But Sharansky and his associates organized an underground network that kept Jewish thought alive; secret courses were held in Jewish history and the Hebrew language. The struggle of the Jews was linked to the great scientist Andrei Sakharov.

The KGB arrested Sharansky in 1977 under the accusation of espionage. Ida Nudel was sentenced to four years, and Vladimir Slepak was sent to the border with China. Sharansky told the judge that "the world has not yet accepted the fact that the Jewish people will not disappear from the face of the earth." He was sentenced to thirteen years. Outside the courthouse, dozens of Jews sang the national anthem of Israel, the *Hatikvah,* "Hope." In prison, Sharansky was forced to clean the toilets. On the feast of Hanukkah, he would light candles as a sign of protest and to tell the world that there was still light, still hope. Each time, he was punished. He became seriously ill, near death, and the books in Hebrew that Avital sent him secretly from Jerusalem were confiscated. From New York, the great physicist Edward Teller called him one of the "martyrs" of the twentieth century.

In February 1986, Sharansky was exchanged for some spies in American custody on the Glienicke Bridge in Berlin. With this gesture, the United States emphasized to the world that the cause of Israel was also the cause of the Americans. No other country had done so much for Judaism since the time of

Cyrus the Great. When six million Jews were shot to death, gassed, cremated, incinerated, only two centers of Judaism were left standing: Jerusalem and New York. "Every American star is a star of hope," Simon Wiesenthal wrote about the American flag that he saw in the concentration camp when it was liberated. For their part, the Americans have never forgotten that one and a half million Jews stood side by side with them in the liberation of Europe.

As soon as Sharansky set foot in the airport of Tel Aviv, the first thing he said to his wife, Avital, was, "Sorry I'm late." Symbolically, thousands of other Jews were late, too. Then he asked if he could pray at the Wailing Wall. The *Hatikvah* was sung, as it had been outside the courthouse years earlier. In 1997, Natan knocked at the door of the Lefortovo prison, displaying his Italian passport, and asked to visit the cell where the KGB had kept him confined. He asked Avital, who had accompanied him on the trip, "Do you recognize the cell? You were always here with me."

During the Second World War, Aharon Gurov's father, Chaim, had run away from home to join the partisans. He acted as the go-between for the resistance and the Minsk ghetto. "His father had blond hair and green eyes; he didn't look like a Jew," says Gurov's wife, Miriam, who still lives in Nokdim. "He was given a Russian name, Gurov, to mask his more Jewish name, Gurvich. At the age of seventeen, Chaim joined the Red Army. At the end of the war, he was in Berlin. My father-in-law kept his Russian name because it was the one he had when he was decorated and received all those medals. In Israel, Aharon would find out that his real name was Gurvich. When he was asked if he wanted his original name, Aharon said, 'No, it is my *shem gvurah,* the heroic name of my father.'"

Aharon Gurov's mother was a chemist. Aharon graduated from the Minsk Conservatory, and in 1980 he became a member of the prestigious Composers' Union of the USSR. "They were all stunned, because he was only twenty-three years old, and at the time there was a tacit anti-Semitism. But Aharon had an amazing talent; he had composed symphonies, quartets, cantatas, vocal compositions, and music for the movies. Aharon was also interested in Jewish philosophy. He started to study Hebrew, which was forbidden at the time, and in the end he also came to respect religious tradition. He became a *gabbay*, an important role in the life of a synagogue. Aharon also had a great influence on me and on my views of Judaism. He became my Torah teacher. Aharon had no other dream than to live in *Eretz Yisrael*."

At first, the Gurovs moved to Gush Etzion, south of Jerusalem. "Then we bought a little house in Nokdim. Aharon loved its special atmosphere. He loved visiting the archaeological excavations and had many friends among the archaeologists. We were one big family, and since the attack I have not been alone for a moment. Almost everyone here has a university degree; it is a place with a very high level of culture. In the synagogue you can hear people speaking Russian, French, Spanish, and Italian."

It was not easy for Aharon at first. "He was forced to start over from nothing, but he never lost hope. He taught music to the children. He was humble to the point of accepting even the most menial jobs. In 1993, he was commissioned to compose a symphony for the klezmer festival in Zefat. It was a great success, and even today the symphony is performed in Israel, Russia, and Ukraine." Meanwhile, they had two boys and two girls. "Love and happiness reigned in our home. Aharon loved his family and was a great support for all of us," says Miriam. "We have built these homes in a beautiful land; we have turned a plot of Judean desert into a cozy home; every tree was planted by us. My husband, the father of my children, died here. But it is here that our children were born. We will never leave this place."

When Aharon was killed by terrorists, his son Haim, named after his grandfather, was ten years old, Hanna-Bella was nine, Ben-Zion four, and Shoshana two. "After the tragedy, I never hated Israel," says Miriam, "only those Arab terrorists who killed my husband, a peaceful man who even in the Soviet army had been enlisted as a musician in the main orchestra. He was never admitted by the Israeli army, and Aharon was pained that he couldn't serve in the reserve like his friends. He was a musician, a philosopher, a humanist."

Miriam hasn't forgotten about the day of the attack. "Aharon phoned me at home, we were getting ready for the feast of Purim, and there was a dessert in the oven already. Since then, we have never again celebrated Purim at home. All I wanted to do was pick up an M16 and do to those terrorists what they had done to him. My responsibility for the children stopped me, they needed me, but for a long time it was difficult for me to enter an Arab village—it seemed to me that there was a terrorist behind every window. It took me two years to work up the courage to get a driver's license. We still live in Nokdim, and I'm not afraid anymore of driving down the road where my husband was killed. My sons go to a religious school, they wear the kippah and love Israel. We observe Shabbat and the Jewish holidays just like we did when Aharon was here. In 2005, we produced a CD with his compositions. My husband was a musician with a Jewish soul, a man of great faith. He was killed, but his music lives on."

The Last Meal

66 **T***here is a saying in Hebrew,* 'Only I can take care of me.'" Yossi Zur lost his son Asaf to a Palestinian suicide bomber. Since then, he has led a campaign to get the State of Israel to recognize not only military but also civilian victims of terrorism as "war casualties." He doesn't want his son to be a second-class casualty. "It's a long process. Since 1948, wider and wider segments of the population have been declared 'Israeli war dead,'" Yossi tells us. "It goes back to 1860, when the Jews left the walls of Jerusalem behind to establish themselves in Israel. Even to the absurdity of Jews recruited by the Turkish or English armies, and who may have fought against each other in Gaza or Beersheba. Today the absurdity is that a soldier and a civilian may be sitting in the same bus and be killed. A soldier who dies in a car crash has 'fallen in the battles of Israel,' but the civilian killed by a terrorist hasn't. Our request is very simple: We want the civilian victims of terrorism to be declared 'fallen' as well, because they have been killed by an enemy in battle. They must be part of the ethos of the state, and of the meaning of Memorial Day."

For those who want to see the locations of the attacks in Israel, the website "A People Remembers" (www.ezy.co.il) presents an amazing project of photographic documentation run by Yossi. "It was important for the collective memory to be well documented and available to all. There are memorials that no one has ever seen, and I wanted the whole world to see the places where Jews have been murdered since the beginning of the twentieth century."

Ron Kehrmann and Alexander Katsman lost their daughters in the same attack. Ron's grandfather went to Israel from Germany in 1934, fleeing the Nazis. "After March 5, 2003, I had two choices," Ron says. "I could mourn my daughter Tal or try to construct a different life—not new, but different. So I chose the second possibility, and I told Tal's story. I have been strengthened by the care of my family and by the memory of Tal." In spite of so much violence, Ron has not lost trust. "The people of Israel and people abroad have shown me their support and affection by visiting Tal's memorial on the internet. It's private individuals who are giving aid, not the government."

Ron wants to explain to the world how significant it is for entire families to be destroyed, as happens in Israel. "The war in the Middle East is part of a global battle among cultures. The Western world and the Islamic world. Reality can change in an instant, as happened to me. Tal was killed because she was an Israeli and because she was Jewish. A citizen of the State of Israel who lived here—this is what our enemies would like to change. The terrorist did not want to kill Tal Kehrmann, but as many Jews as possible, in order to purge the land of Jews. This war started at the beginning of the nineteenth century, and it's not over yet. Tal is a victim of Israel's war for its own independence. The killing of Tal is part of Israel's battle to be a free country and a democratic society. An event that the State of Israel was unable to prevent, but could have done if it had had a policy of protecting its citizens. The problem is that Israel uses its citizens in senseless experiments in order to reach peace with groups that say they want to eliminate us."

Tal was killed together with her friend Elizabeth Katsman, who had immigrated with her family from the Soviet Union twelve years earlier. She had marvelous green eyes, pale white skin, and black hair. Her classmates nicknamed her "Snow White." Just before the attack, Liz and her friends had been auditioning for a play. Two months earlier, she had sung at her sister's wedding. "It is impossible to rebuild our lives as they were before. Everything has been destroyed," explains her father, Alexander. "Our life now is more precisely an 'existence.' We have found the strength to go on every day in the memory of Liz. We believe that a person continues to exist and to influence the world as long as people remember him. So we do everything we can to keep the memory of Liz alive." A film about her was made for television. Her school has dedicated a garden to her, and there are exhibitions of art and photography in her memory, in addition to a website. "It was impossible for us to imagine and accept that Liz, so kind, a gift full of life, could stop living. We are not religious people, but we believe that life continues after death. We want to believe. And now we receive many letters and phone calls from people who have been touched by the film or the website." Liz's parents have another reason to go on living: "Our oldest daughter, Marina. She's thirty years old and married, and we hope to become grandparents very soon."

During the Second World War, the Katsmans lived in Odessa, and one of Liz's great-grandfathers was killed in the Stalinist repression, along with two of his brothers. Her grandfather fought against the Nazis and was disabled. After making the aliyah with his children, his wife, Elena, and his parents, Alexander got a job as a physicist at the Technion-Israel Institute of Technology in Haifa. "Elena is an electronic engineer, but after the attack she stopped working. She couldn't encourage people to build a better and happier life anymore. We have received help from hundreds of people, but thousands and millions have remained indifferent; it wasn't their life. They think it can't happen to them. They're wrong. Fanatics have to be stopped all over the world. Israel was the first country attacked by Muslim fanatics. But then came New York, Madrid, London ... If Israel is destroyed, all of modern civilization will be destroyed. This is another reason why we made the film about Liz. Maybe people can compare the way we raise our children, who want to shine brilliantly, with the Palestinian training of the terrorists, the *shahid,* who kill."

Alex explains how the attack took away not just one life, but his entire family: "Liz was the 'heart' of our family, the personification of our most authentic values, education and culture, our view of life and happiness. She lived seventeen years, three months, and nine days, and was killed by a Muslim Palestinian commanded by Hamas, who was on a bus to Haifa with seventeen other people, most of them children. Our life has been destroyed; we were killed together with Liz. All of our goals, intentions, and desires have lost their meaning. We were a young family, happy, healthy, rich, and we have become old and infirm. For three years we were helped by psychologists and psychiatrists. Elena has had heart and digestive problems, severe headaches, and insomnia. I have suspended my scientific activity. Before the tragedy, I wrote fifteen publications and participated in international conferences. Elena can't see other people or talk with them; the doctors have diagnosed her with severe depression."

Commemorating the Holocaust has failed. Politicians pay homage at Yad Vashem, attend diaspora memorials for the six million, and feel themselves inoculated as philo-Semites. This enables them, the morning after, to say that Israel practices apartheid, or declare themselves able to understand the motivation of suicide bombers. What they fail to acknowledge is that the massacres in Haifa were a result of Islamists calling for the extermination of Jews—in the same way that the Holo-caust occurred because of incitement to hatred.

Just as the Nazi newspaper *Der Stürmer* showed Jews as vermin, snakes, and spiders, Hamas in many of its publications describes the Jews such as "bloodsuckers," "brothers of apes," "killers of the prophets," "human pigs," "descendants of treach-ery and deceit," and "butchers." They are "a cancer expanding" in Palestine, "threatening the entire Islamic world." They are "spreading corruption" in the land of Islam. "Deceit and usury are stamped in their nature," and they are all "thieves, monop-olists, and usurers." Repeated reference to Jews as despised beasts provides justification for their destruction. Thus the Hamas Covenant calls for the extermination of all Jews.

Islamists are committed not merely to the political goal of expelling Jews from the land of Israel, but to what they believe is a sacred goal of exterminating Jews everywhere. They envi-sion a struggle "between truth and falsehood," between good personified by the Muslims as the party of God, and "evil incar-nated" in "the party of Satan," represented by the Jews. Sheikh Muhammad Sayyid Tantawi, the highest-ranking cleric in the Sunni Muslim world, called Jews "the enemies of Allah, descen-dants of apes and pigs." In one of his sermons, Sheikh Abd al-Rahman al-Sudayyis, imam of the al-Haram Mosque, the most important in Mecca, beseeched Allah to annihilate the Jews because they are "the scum of the human race, the rats of the world, the violators of pacts and agreements, the murderers of the prophets, and the offspring of apes and pigs." In Khomein-ist Iran, Israel is characterized as a "filthy germ," a "stain of disgrace," a "stinking corpse" populated by "blood-thirsty bar-barians."

Indoctrination in hatred of Jews begins early. Palestinian toddlers are dressed up as suicide murderers, with fake bomb belts strapped around their little bodies. Official Palestinian tel-evision and schools have saturated young children with hatred of Israel and glorification of warfare and martyrdom. Many Palestinian parents have proudly shared the hope that their children will die fighting Israel. A Syrian schoolbook for the tenth grade teaches that Jews are to be "exterminated." Hate language is a predictor, initiator, catalyst, and promoter of slaughter in Israel.

Rosh Ha'ir is a kosher fast-food stand in Tel Aviv, famous for its traditional Israeli shawarma sandwiches and falafel. It was struck twice by suicide bombers from Palestinian Islamic Jihad in 2006. The first time, in January, the restaurant was devastated and many people in the vicinity were injured, but only the suicide bomber died. After a lot of hesitation, Pini and Aryeh Sharon, the brothers who own Rosh Ha'ir, decided to rebuild it, adding a fence and a security guard. The second time, the explosion at the entrance to the eatery was more powerful, killing eleven and injuring more than sixty. A mother was killed next to her husband and children. "The father was in shock," a witness said. "He threw himself onto his children to protect them, while they were crying and screaming, 'Mommy, Mommy!' But she didn't answer. She was already dead." Islamic Jihad intended to sway public opinion by bloodying the same place once again. Pini Sharon commented, "Last time we had a miracle, but there is no second time. Now it's a lot harder, especially when you see all the dead. That was the worst sight."

Whole families have been devastated by terror attacks in Haifa. On March 31, 2002, a suicide bomber killed fifteen people in the Matza restaurant for the Passover holiday. The only member of the Ron family to survive the blast was the mother, Carmit, who was almost unscathed. She hasn't been able to clean the rooms of the house yet; they have remained just as they were seven years ago. And she constantly asks herself how her family could have been obliterated. "I can't stop asking myself idiotic questions, like: Why did I sit in that exact seat, and not insist on changing tables? Why didn't I listen to the fear that I felt inside, and at least convince them to seat us in the corner? I continue to believe that I'm about to wake up from a nightmare, that I'll go to check and find all three of them sleeping in their beds. But it doesn't happen. And I'm the one who has to go on living. I don't know why, but I feel that somehow I owe it to them, to Aviel, to Anat, to Ofer. And I will go on." Speaking at the funeral, Aviel's brother said, "We are a strong family, but no one prepared us to accompany three caskets in a single day. None of us believes in the power of revenge, so we don't know what to do with our hands now. They're not even any good for pointing out who's to blame. Whether it's the attacker, or God, or we ourselves ... what use is it to know that?"

Aviel was a man of action; he had insisted on taking his family to the restaurant in spite of his wife's apprehension and the recent spate of attacks. But Aviel wasn't afraid, and he knew that Jews must be brave, at least in their own country. He had been an engineer in the military for years, and had helped perfect the armed and armored vehicles. After his retirement, he directed the mapping center at the Ministry of Defense for a few years. He was athletic and liked playing basketball, but more than anything else he loved cycling. He had a group of friends with whom he went on long rides up and down Mount Carmel, the coastal mountain that looms over Haifa.

Anat, his daughter, was a gorgeous young woman who had recently finished serving in a key military post, and immediately afterward had gone to the United States to work in a center for handicapped children. She had decided to return to school so she could continue working in the same field in Israel. Ofer, Aviel's son, was finishing high school and preparing to study

architecture after he completed his military service in the elite
Golani unit. He had planned to go running on the beach that
day, but the bad weather convinced him to go instead to the
restaurant with his parents. He wanted to see a movie later that
evening, recalled his friend Eldar, who talked with him on the
phone a few minutes before the explosion.

The Korens were described as a united and happy family
who continued to find time to spend together. The mother,
Rachel, had decided to stay home the night of the attack at the
Matza restaurant. Her husband, Shimon, was a manager at a
big maritime shipping company. The son of a Holocaust survivor, he was known for his optimism, his love of life, and his
sense of humor. Ran Koren was in his last year of high school;
he was a great athlete and everyone remembers him with his
inseparable skateboard, on which he whizzed down the steep
streets of Haifa. His younger brother, Gal, was in middle school.
After the attack, his school would be reopened during the
Passover holiday so his classmates could mourn together and
get over the shock a little. His friend Adam recalls that Gal was
a music and movie buff, who didn't understand how his classmates sometimes let their fearful mothers persuade them to give
up some form of entertainment "because of the situation."

Danielle Manchel had gone to the Matza restaurant after
math class; she was studying to improve her grades because she
wanted to get into the university. "She was experiencing one of
the most wonderful stages of life," her mother said. "She was
studying, she was working, she was deeply in love. What can I
say about her? She was wonderful. We loved her madly." In
order to pay for the apartment she had rented with her
boyfriend, Danielle worked in a bar on the beach of Haifa. Her
parents were concerned about the possibility of an attack there,
but that day they knew she was in class, so they were calm.
Danielle had grown up in Rome until she was ten years old,
while her father was studying there. She spoke Italian fluently

and dreamed of returning for a while to the streets of her childhood. Her father was a businessman and her mother owned an alternative medicine clinic; in addition to Danielle, they were raising three younger children, between the ages of eight and fifteen. They all got along well.

Ya'akov Shani managed a high-tech company, and loved the city and the ocean. His wife, Dalia, a well-known pharmacist in Haifa, had recently been helping her seriously ill mother. Ya'akov ate nearly every day at the Matza restaurant, where he felt at home and knew almost all the other regulars. That day, he had gone to meet his wife at her mother's house to adjust a rug, and then tried to persuade her to go eat with him, but she didn't want to leave her mother alone. They intended to go to the theater that evening, but Dalia started getting puzzled when Ya'akov didn't answer his cell phone. "I suddenly understood what might have happened. I ran there and saw his car. My heart sank."

Moshe Levin, a lawyer, had stopped at Matza to food to take home. His daughter Anat, fifteen, had preferred to wait in the car. Their house was so close that the rice and falafel would still be hot when they got home. Anat was watching when her father was blown up. Moshe worked as a lawyer for the real estate registry of Haifa. He loved his work, he loved Haifa, and he tried to defend it from excessive industrialization. He enjoyed nature, landscapes, hiking. His coworkers remember his seriousness and humanity. In addition to Anat, Moshe left a wife and a son behind.

Orly Ofir was sixteen years old. "We all got out of the restaurant alive, Orly, me, Mom, and Ilanit," her sister Roni recounts amid tears, "and afterward I said, 'How lucky we were to have chosen that exact corner.'" But Orly was seriously wounded in the abdomen and was taken to the hospital, still conscious. She died on the operating table. Orly was a good student, very joyful, and a member of the Maccabi Haifa girls' soccer team. Her family were also regulars at Matza, where they felt safe and at home.

Seventeen-year-old Adi Shiran loved to sing; she was a member of the high school choir, and her friends describe her as a "musical soul." She composed songs and wrote poetry. Her dream was to be in the army's music corps, the springboard for launching a career in Israeli pop music. Her older brother and sister, Eyal and Einat, said, "Now we need to take care of our parents. We can't do anything for Adi anymore."

A handsome man with his thick hair combed back, Carlos Wegman had come from Argentina in 1973. He was a civil engineer with a thriving consulting business, and he had refused to let the threat of terrorism keep him at home. The evening before the attack, at dinner with friends, he had insisted on his right to enjoy himself, saying, "We can't let ourselves be buried alive." Carlos was going to get married the following summer. He had two daughters, ages twenty-three and twenty-one, from a previous marriage. From her home in Eilat, one of his daughters saw images of the Matza attack on television and recognized her father's car. "I was immediately sure that he was there, because there was a bumper sticker on his car that I had put there."

Carlos Yerushalmi was eating at Matza with his close friend Carlos Wegman. They had known each other since their days in Buenos Aires and had decided to move to Israel at the same time. They died together, too. A television producer with a big, stocky body, Carlos Yerushalmi battled between life and death for five days before giving in. His wife had been called to the morgue immediately after the attack, because his documents had ended up there by mistake. Unable to find his body there, she had rushed to the hospital full of hope, and had found her injured husband there. The couple had a son and a daughter in Israel.

Another victim of the attack was Suheil Adawi, the father of a four-year-old boy. "His wife and son were his whole world," said his friends. Suheil was a member of the Arab Israeli family that owned the Matza restaurant.

Haifa was severely tested again in October 2003, when the Maxim restaurant was devastated on the eve of Yom Kippur. Attached to a gas station, with big windows facing the ocean, it was simple but renowned for its Middle Eastern cuisine. In addition to being the hangout of the Maccabi Haifa soccer team, Maxim had been known for decades as a place of encounter among Jews, Christians, and Muslims. Yigal Allon, an Israeli general and politician, called it a symbol of Arab-Jewish coexistence. Israel is the only Middle Eastern country in which an Arab member of parliament or minister in the current government can openly criticize his prime minister without risking a thing.

It was a beautiful, sunny day and the shore was crowded with the last beachgoers of the season; the heat and the Shabbat holiday had brought many families to Haifa, which has extensive beach areas and also sits near the forests of Mount Carmel. Hanadi Jaradat left her home in Jenin, in the West Bank, passed the Barta'a checkpoint, and went to Maxim with an Arab Israeli. The presence of the young Palestinian at the restaurant didn't raise any suspicion. The explosive belt was ready to sow death, but Hanadi wanted to savor every additional moment of her vengeance. An Arab waiter brought her a menu and took her order. The terrorist ate calmly, watching the Israeli families unaware that they were eating their last meal and taking their last breaths. Then she blew herself up.

All that remained of nineteen people—including five children, along with fathers and mothers and grandparents—was a pile of indistinguishable body parts. Witnesses described a wreckage of burning bodies and jumbled furniture. One woman bent over a wounded son, beside the broken bodies of her husband and another child. Sinjana Wakid, a Russian immigrant married to an Israeli Arab, emerged from the restroom, where she had been tending to her two-year-old daughter, and saw "a man with a cigarette, but no head at all." When the men of Zaka arrived, they found that the ponytailed head of the terrorist had rolled out onto the sidewalk in front, where it got tangled up in some electrical wires.

"We are receiving congratulations from people," said Hanadi's brother Thaher. "Why should we cry? It is like her wedding today, the happiest day for her." Hamas ignored the presence of Israeli Arabs in the restaurant and celebrated the bomber for exploding "her pure body in a crowd of the thieves of our homeland."

"Our restaurant symbolized Arab-Jewish coexistence," said one of the owners, Sharbal Matar, an Arab Christian who lost an uncle and two other relatives in the attack. He would reopen the restaurant after only a couple of months. The fact that the blood of Jews and Arabs was shed in the same attack magnified its meaning. Entire families were destroyed. Among the victims was Mark Biano, a journalist who often followed the news coverage of terrorist attacks. He was there with his wife, Naomi. Zvi Bahat was killed while he was waiting to pay the bill after having lunch with his wife and their two children. Osama Najar died because he loved the restaurant where he had worked as a cook.

The Zer-Aviv family was decimated in an instant at Maxim. Bruria, her son Bezalel, daughter-in-law Keren, grandson Liran, and granddaughter Noya were having lunch when they were annihilated by the explosion. Freddy Zer-Aviv, a Jew from Algeria who worked as an orthopedist at the Bnei Tzion Hospital in Haifa, had met his future wife Bruria at work. When Bezalel was born, they decided to go live in France. Sophie and Gabi were born in Nice. Ten years later, they returned to Israel to live in a kibbutz. They loved rural life. "If a person dies, you must face the problem of what to do," one of their neighbors said. "When an entire family is exterminated, you feel all five of them in your heart." Liran had just celebrated his fourth birthday. Noya was one year old. Another neighbor of the Zer-Avivs recalled, "When I saw the slaughtered children I recognized Noya's bottle, because those who are familiar with life in the kibbutz know that the name is marked on the bottle."

Ze'ev Almog, seventy-one years old, had been a pioneer of the Israeli navy and was a "great man," according to his granddaughter. Before he was killed, he had met with his entire family, a clan of 184 persons, telling them that "it is impossible to know what is waiting for us around every corner." Ze'ev had gone to the beach with his wife, Ruth, and had decided to have lunch at Maxim. Both were killed along with their son, Moshe, and two grandchildren, Tomer and Assaf. Speaking in the name of the Almog family at the funeral, Uri Sagi said, "May you finish your last meal in paradise." Oren Almog, age ten, was blinded by the attack that killed his younger brother. "There are things it is better not to see," Oren comments.

The Best and
Brightest Youth

I t was a time when the air of Jerusalem trembled with
unusual vibrations. To walk in the streets was already a
challenge, and to send children to school an act of heroism
and audacity. The world capital of suicide attacks seemed to be
designed not to host human beings, but dead men walking.
Islamic terrorism mowed down dozens of people gathered in
bars and cafes, in buses, cinemas, clinics, pizzerias. Death lived
everywhere.

One evening in September 2003, in the residential area of
West Jerusalem, five miles from the city center and not far from
the Museum for Islamic Art, a suicide bomber demolished
Cafe Hillel, which had been open for only a few months. The
terrorist was smiling faintly when he entered. After the attack,
one young man was unable to speak Hebrew anymore and
asked for help in Russian, his native language. "Who speaks
Russian?" shouted a volunteer paramedic. An elderly woman,
also a Russian immigrant, came to comfort the injured young
man while he wept.

One year earlier, on March 9, 2002, at Cafe Moment in
Jerusalem, the Jewish young people had been sitting at the bar,
a few dozen yards from the residence of the prime minister. It
was a favorite hangout for university students, concealed in the

tranquility of Rehavia, the beautiful neighborhood that has been home to many illustrious intellectuals, beginning with the philosopher Hans Jonas. Cafe Moment was a perfect target, often so crowded that people waited in line just to enjoy coffee and a croissant on the small, shaded patio. There was a line outside that day, and the terrorist blew himself up as soon as he crossed the threshold. Eleven were killed and dozens wounded, many of them mutilated for life. All of the victims were young.

Dan Imani was born in Iran to a family of rug merchants. In the early 1980s, they fled the persecutions of the ayatollah Khomeini, who had vowed to destroy Israel and had identified the Jewish people as one of the roots of evil in the world. Dan's oldest brother had already been killed in Lebanon, in 1984, while his father was still in Tehran and could only visit his son at his grave. Nir Borochov was sitting with Dan at Cafe Moment. After two of his cousins had been killed in military operations on the Lebanese border, Nir insisted on enlisting in a combat unit. To pay for his studies, he worked as a mechanic at the Subaru dealership. Also with Dan and Nir that evening was Livnat Dvash, who had just undergone surgery for a tumor. Her last name means "honey," and in fact everyone describes her as being very sweet. She thought that Cafe Moment, so close to the prime minister's residence, was the safest place in the world.

Danit Dagan and Uri Felix were saving money to buy a house, and were about to get married. Everything was ready— the dress, the car, the dinner menu, the guest list. While he studied environmental planning, Uri earned a living as a courthouse security guard. With his broad shoulders, he stood in the way of the bearers of death. "His presence alone brought us security," one judge said at his funeral. "He made us feel well protected." Danit worked at a travel agency. The newspaper printed the recollections of the children who lived in her building; Danit had been their babysitter since her early teens. "We were just waiting for our parents to leave so that you would come. You were the first person we told our secrets to; you were the one who was able to get us into bed with a smile on our faces. When you chose Uri, it was clear that he was the best of all: so big, so tall."

"Now you will be together for eternity," said Maya before the remains of her sister Danit. The family members formed a circle around the two slaughtered bodies. Wrapped in a traditional prayer shawl, Uri was laid next to Danit, who was covered in a blue cloth with verses from the Psalms embroidered on it. The rabbi who would have married the couple in two months gave the eulogy. Guy Levy, one of Uri's coworkers as a security guard at the Jerusalem courts, remembered his friend as a real live wire. "You have been killed with the love of your life," he said. "We will never forget." Uri's father, sitting in a wheelchair, recited the Kaddish, the Jewish prayer of mourning.

Orit Ozerov had a splendid face, like a child's, and her best friend remembers her as "a flower that had just opened." She was famous for her voice; everyone loved to hear her sing. Because Orit had worked at the Ministry of Foreign Affairs, President Shimon Peres spoke at her funeral: "Her physical beauty was equal to her inner beauty. She worked with the dedication of those who have a purpose beyond earning a living. Orit believed in what she did." Six of Orit's coworkers were also at Cafe Moment that evening. "We are used to feeling threatened when we are on mission abroad," said Ghidon Meir, "but to feel concretely that the danger even follows us home has shocked us." Orit was always cheerful and had great willpower, spurring everyone forward. "To those who asked her if she was afraid to go to the pub at night, she said that she wouldn't let anything or anyone prevent her from doing the things she liked."

It was Tali Eliyahu's first night on the job at Cafe Moment, where she was being trained by an experienced coworker. Pub

work is an old standby for Israeli students. For Tali, the decision had even greater meaning: she was one of eleven children
from a devout Orthodox family, and she had decided to abandon her religion and her plan to become a kindergarten
teacher, one of the few professions allowed for devout women.
Tali wanted to study the history of the Middle East and work in
a cafe, to live in the secular and modern Israel. Her father had
made a journey in the opposite direction: from secular to
Orthodox. A former Mossad employee, he is now a famous
scholar of the Kabbalah. Tali had narrowly escaped death earlier, and temporarily lost her hearing, when a Palestinian
woman detonated a bomb on a bustling shopping street in
Jerusalem. Tali had called her parents and told them she had
blood all over herself but didn't know if it was hers or someone
else's. "My sister wasn't scared by anything," said Ayelet, who
recalled Tali saying, "It's my country—I can go where I want."
Ayelet added, "She was proud to live in Israel." Tali's violent
death was the second in the family: an older sister had lost her
husband in Israel's war with Lebanon in 1996. "My sister died
because she was Jewish. She was murdered because she was
Jewish."

Another victim at Cafe Moment, Baruch Lerner, loved to
say that "it is beautiful to die for one's country." He lived with
his parents in Eli, a West Bank settlement among Arabs, in
order to assert the historical right of the Jews to live in Judea
and Samaria, and as a necessary means of defense for Israel.
He worked as a security guard in the Jewish neighborhood of
Jerusalem's Old City, but his dream was to set up a horse
breeding farm in the Gaza Strip. His grandfather, also named
Baruch, had died at the same age while fighting the Nazis in
France. Recently, Baruch had written an open letter to Ariel
Sharon: "In your latest speech, you called upon the people to
demonstrate the capacity for self-control. Yes, so according to
you, while they are killing us with terrorist attacks, we should

stand there twiddling our thumbs and watching how they grad- ually improve their techniques?"

When Avi Rahamim's father arrived at the hospital to see if his son had been hurt, he breathed a sigh of relief. His son was in the hallway, crying, and came forward to embrace him. "Dad, it's me, Yaron. Avi is dead." Avi and Yaron were identical twins. Avi had called him shortly before the blast to persuade him to come to Cafe Moment. "He insisted. I told him, 'Come home, it's not the night for it; there's just been an attack in Netanya.' I didn't convince him. He told me not to worry, to stop being paranoid. When I got to the hospital, the doctor who saw me in the hallway almost fainted. She had just finished writing 'my' death certificate. We were always together; we talked on the phone two or three times a day. It's like I've had part of my body ripped off."

Natanel Kochavi had been the head of the students' union at Bar-Ilan University, and he was finishing his apprenticeship at an important law firm in Jerusalem. Cafe Moment was like his second home. Two days before the attack, his mood had suddenly turned grim and he said, "The next one will blow him- self up here." But he didn't stop going to his favorite place. A member of a large family, Natanel had been a corporal in the Givati Brigade, an elite combat unit, and was regarded as an excellent soldier. "If he had wanted to, he could have made it his career," said his commanding officer, "but he wanted to go to college."

Limor Ben-Shoham had just celebrated her twenty-seventh birthday at the Cafe Moment. Her best friend had gone to the restroom, and so escaped the blast.

The best and brightest of Israel's youth were massacred in a cafeteria at the Hebrew University of Jerusalem on July 31,

2002. The Frank Sinatra Cafeteria is a very popular spot at the university, a few yards away from the administrative offices where students go to withdraw scholarship funds and sign up for classes. The suicide bomber knew he would find dozens of students in line at the cafeteria, along with professors and foreign visitors—all blown sky high. "Those who were here will never forget the sound of the explosion and the silence that followed, the sign that everything was over," said Efrat Pinhasi, a student representative. On the sidewalk in front of the cafeteria were bottles of water, fragments of food mixed with the remains of shredded bodies, tableware, broken glass, a charred pair of shoes, scraps of clothing used as makeshift bandages by emergency workers. Many hours later, the benches near the cafeteria were still stained with blood.

The Hebrew University was not a random target, but a great symbol of Zionist culture. Where the emperor Titus had ordered the destruction of Jerusalem, the Jewish pioneers had laid the first bricks of the famous Hebrew academy. "The university was born even before the State of Israel. Ben-Gurion wanted it to be built before the houses, before the banks and the hospitals," said the president of the university, Menachem Magidor, standing in front of the shattered windows not far from a human torso not yet removed by the devout. Before attaining national sovereignty, Israel established libraries, of which there are now thousands in a country of seven million inhabitants. It gave birth to publishing houses well before 1948. Its ideological schools of thought were already clashing in dozens of newspapers written in various languages.

In Israel, culture came before the state: the Israel Institute of Technology was inaugurated in 1924, the Hebrew University in 1925, the Habima Theater in 1931, the Weizmann Institute of Science in 1934, the Palestine Orchestra in 1936. Arturo Toscanini conducted the first concert of the orchestra, which in 1948 became the Israel Philharmonic Orchestra. A few years later, the Mann Auditorium was built as a home for the Philharmonic; today it is still one of the most intriguing concert venues in the world. Since 1968, a great non-Jewish soul, Zubin Mehta from India, has directed the orchestra—even under Saddam Hussein's missiles in 1991 and through many suicide attacks. Proportionally, Israel allocates a larger budget to research, both applied and basic, than any other country in the world. There are seven Israeli Nobel Prize winners, a number sharply disproportionate to the population.

The desire to found a Jewish university was an integral part of the Zionist vision. Construction began in 1918 with the acquisition of the land on top of Mount Scopus and the laying of the first stone. Seven years later, on April 1, 1925, the university was inaugurated with a ceremony attended by international Jewish leaders and important British figures including Lord Balfour, Viscount Allenby, and Sir Herbert Samuel. "From now on, we will no longer need to hope for the birth of the Third Jewish Temple," said Chaim Weizmann, the first president of Israel, at the ceremony. The Hebrew University became a place of refuge for Jewish intellectuals and students who had been rejected by European universities because of anti-Semitism. They fled from a threat of massacre spit through the fangs of Arab terrorism. Albert Einstein came to Jerusalem to give the first lesson, speaking on the theory of relativity.

On April 13, 1948, thirty-five professors and students of the university, in addition to doctors and nurses of the nearby Hadassah Hospital, were executed in an Arab attack on a convoy of vehicles trying to get from West Jerusalem to Mount Scopus. The convoy included two trucks loaded with materials for building water tanks for the hospital, two ambulances carrying patients and medical personnel, two buses filled with hospital and university staff, and escort vehicles. Forced out of the vehicles by the fire and smoke, the passengers were shot while they were rolling on the ground to put out the flames. The dead included the mother of David Cassuto, who later became an architect and had a substantial part in rebuilding the Jewish quarter in the Old City of Jerusalem. David's parents had been deported to Auschwitz; his mother survived and brought her children to Israel after the war, when David was seven. Also killed was Chaim Yassky, the medical administrator of Hadassah. Knowing that he was about to die, Yassky said *"Shalom"* to his wife and coworkers, and passed away a few minutes later.

The war of 1948 left Hebrew University isolated from the rest of the city, the part defended by the Israelis. The university was forced to look for another location. With the reunification of Jerusalem after the Six-Day War in 1967, the long exile of Mount Scopus ended.

From Melchizedek, who blessed Abraham, to Noah, Enoch, Abimelech, and Balaam, Jewish history is marked by the presence and words of non-Jews. Ruth, one of the ancestors of the Messiah, was not a Jew, but a Moabite. Almost all the sons of Jacob, except for Benjamin, were born in modern-day Iraq or Syria, and therefore outside of the Promised Land. Moses, the boy who survived the extermination of male children, was saved by the pharaoh's daughter, Bythia. Some of those killed in the attack on Hebrew University in July 2002 were foreigners, and some were converts—from Pennsylvania, California, New York, Massachusetts. Three were in Jerusalem on study-abroad programs, one was escorting new students, and one was working as a university librarian. They had in common their belief in Judaism and commitment to Israel. In the United States, a Torah scroll was dedicated to the victims of Mount Scopus.

David Gritz was a young man who had grown up in Paris, but had dual American-French citizenship and spent summers with his parents in Massachusetts. He had come to Jerusalem to study Jewish philosophy. His friends recalled, "He was so happy to be here, in spite of the danger. He wanted to learn, he wanted to live here."

Twenty-four-year-old Marla Bennett, from San Diego, was in Israel to complete a course of studies. Shortly before she died, she had written: "My friends and my family keep telling me how dangerous it is to be here. But I am part of the struggle for Israel's survival." In his eulogy for Marla, Rabbi Martin Lawson called her "a martyr of Israel." Marla had once said, "I am not a tourist, I am part of Israel, in the joy and suffering of every single day. I love it. Life here is magical. I am afraid for Israel, but there is no other place in the world where I would rather be at this moment." One of her friends remarked, "Marla gave me the Jewish hope of someone who always goes beyond herself." In the words of one of Marla's teachers in San Diego, "it took four thousand years of Judaism to produce such a person."

Dina Carter had come to Israel from the United States after converting to Judaism and had dual American-Israeli citizenship. She worked as an archivist at the university and had just passed her Hebrew proficiency exam. She was thirty-six years old.

Janis Ruth Coulter, a Boston native, had just brought a group of American graduate students to Jerusalem. Born an Episcopalian, she had converted to Judaism after being inspired by the memoirs of the Holocaust survivor Elie Wiesel. She chose the Hebrew name Yonit, which means "little dove," a symbol of peace. "Janis Ruth was a wonderful, loving, caring person. Her faith, to which she converted, was at the core of her being," the family said. A colleague of Coulter's, Jonathan Rulnick, recalled, "Janis loved Israel and her job was involved in sharing her love for Israel. The thing that makes it so difficult for a lot of people here and a lot of my colleagues is that here we are, trying to get people to share our love for Israel, and here's a group of people taking that away."

For Eliad Moreh, the fact of having survived the bombing of the cafeteria has taken on religious significance. "I emigrated alone to Israel from France in 1993," she said. "I was eighteen years old, and I was happy because I knew I was doing the right thing. Now I am more determined than ever. No, the terrorists will never make me go back to Paris. I will stay here and help the Jews to live in their land." She was a researcher at the university's Center for Jewish Art and was having lunch with her close friend David "Diego" Ladowski that day.

Born in Argentina, Diego had emigrated to Israel in 1992 and was an "old-school Zionist," according to his friends. He worked for Israel's Ministry of Foreign Affairs and was about to take an important post at the embassy in Lima, Peru. Diego did not survive. His brother, Gabi, comments that "if you lose a loved one because of an illness, you try to prepare yourself for the worst before the moment arrives. If you lose him in a catastrophe or an accident, you curse fate. But when the death comes as the result of hatred, it is difficult to justify and comprehend."

Gabi remembers his idealistic brother in a traditionally Jewish way: "We Jews put life before everything else, and we honor the deceased by celebrating their lives, their memory. We find the strength to go on in the depths of our hearts, in the memory of their lives and their legacies. David, 'Diego,' dedicated his life to helping others and improving their lives. Not only Jews, but also Palestinians. He put others before himself. So we can't sit around and cry, or just live remembering him." They needed to continue his work as well, so they created the David Diego Ladowski Memorial Foundation. "Destruction will never be the way of education, progress, peace and understanding. The Israeli leadership is far from perfect, but it does not incite the killing of one's neighbors, it does not kidnap, it does not throw stones or shoot at passersby. The people of Israel have a long history of victory over destruction, hatred, annihilation and persecution. The right way is love of life, good works and education, and doing good for humanity."

Gabi remembers that his father, his uncles, and his other relatives were able to leave Poland before the Nazis started gassing the Jews. But other family members stayed behind. Two of his father's brothers, Faibel and Yosef, were from Kielce, where there was an infamous pogrom after the war. They were gassed in the extermination camp of Treblinka. "I can't describe what went on inside of me when I found out that my brother had been killed in the cafeteria of the Jewish university in Jerusalem. My family was destroyed, just like the cafeteria. Every time we hear that people have been killed by terrorism, we always feel that same emotion again. We Jews honor life, so there is no symbolism in death. We honor the dead for their lives. The word 'martyr' has a different meaning for us than for the suicide attackers. The death of David, 'Diego,' was an enormous loss, not only for us but for the whole world. He was the personification of goodness. By killing him, the terrorists have deprived this world of what it needs most. But his legacy lives on in the foundation, and his memory remains in the hearts of those who had the opportunity to know him."

Five Empty Seats

When the time came for him to leave the community of Katif, in the bloc of Jewish settlements
in the Gaza Strip, David Hatuel put five chairs out
on his porch and placed a candle on each of them, in memory
of his four daughters and his wife, murdered a year earlier by
Palestinian terrorists. On the chair in the middle was the reflective green jacket of his wife, Tali. She had done volunteer work
for the settlement, which was dismantled in the summer of
2005 by Ariel Sharon. As the sorrowful farewell ritual for Katif
began, Hatuel was approached by an Israeli official. Then
another. Ten or fifteen minutes later, they came out together.
Meanwhile, men and women were leaving their homes and
gathering together in the synagogue. They prayed for two
hours, gathered around the sacred scroll of the Torah. David
was with them; then he returned home, removed the five chairs
from the porch, closed the door, and left. Yitzhak Rabin, the
Labor Party leader, had personally placed the first mezuzoth
there, the boxes containing the sacred scrolls and fastened to
every door frame in the house as a divine blessing.

David Hatuel was the principal of a middle school, and Tali
was a social worker who also took care of victims of terrorism in
the Gaza Strip. She was thirty-four years old when she met her
death during the protests by settlers against Sharon's plan for

withdrawal. A terrorist squad opened fire on her car, and Tali died on the spot. Then her four daughters were murdered with a shot to the head at point-blank range. It was an execution.

The people of Gush Katif built a little memorial for Tali Hatuel and her daughters, which tells us: "Hila, the oldest, was sensitive and quiet, and had a good heart. She always spoke wisely, and she had a warm smile. Hadar, the second daughter, was a responsible child. She was creative. She always had an expression of curiosity and a bottomless smile. Roni, the third, loved everything connected to holiness, and showed this in her innocent and pure prayers. Merav, even though she was the youngest, was a born leader. She was full of innocence and grace, energy and happiness." Tali was also eight months pregnant with a fifth child. The *Calgary Herald* in Canada asked, "Why does the world remain silent in the face of the killing of a woman eight months pregnant, and of her four daughters?"

Tali and David Hatuel lived in the same settlement bloc as Rabbi Yitzhak Arama, who was killed in 2002 while he was driving to a religious celebration. His neighbors describe him as "the heart and soul" of the community of Netzer Hazani. Others speak of him as a unique combination of "humility and knowledge of the Torah." Rabbi Arama had made a living by farming fish and growing plants in greenhouses in Netzer Hazani. Originally created in 1973 as a Nahal outpost, Netzer Hazani was refounded as a civilian moshav by twelve devout families. The community grew a wide variety of herbs for export. Yitzhak Rabin had been among those who presided at the birth of Netzer Hazani, saying, "It is a great day for the country. This settlement symbolizes the strength of our presence in the area, which has become an integral part of the state and its security."

Israel would later cede those lands, which had been hallowed by every Israeli politician, both on the right and especially on the left. In the heartrending withdrawal from Gaza, 42 day care centers, 36 kindergartens, 7 elementary schools, and 3 high schools were closed; more than 5,000 students were placed in other schools; 38 synagogues were dismantled; 166 Israeli farming operations were shut down, with a loss of employment that included the jobs of 5,000 Palestinians; finally, the 48 graves in the Jewish cemetery of Gush Katif, including those of 6 inhabitants killed by terrorists, were dug up and moved. While the bulldozer advanced through Netzer Hazani, a prayerful group of Jews wearing the *tallit* called out, *"Adonai, Adonai."* The dream ended in summer 2005 with the sound of guitars from makeshift camps set up around the trailers.

"Inhabitants of the Gaza Strip," said Sharon in evacuating those communities, "this day marks the end of a glorious chapter in Israel's history, a central chapter in the history of your lives as pioneers, as the achievers of a dream who have borne the burden of security and settlement for all of us. Your suffering and tears are an inseparable part of the history of this country."

He could have been talking about the tears of Hannah Barat, who was holding her daughter Hodiya in her lap when she was paralyzed in a terror attack in 2002. Hodiya's father, Eliezer, was driving. Hannah felt the bullet go through her shoulder and saw Hodiya bleeding. She has kept her daughter's bloodstained sweater. "Whoever drives me away from here will remember for the rest of his life what he has done," Hannah said before she was evacuated from the settlement of Kfar Darom in Gush Katif. "The soldier who drags me away from this house will never forgive himself for having displaced an invalid, for having forced me and my children to live in a prefabricated home. Whoever looks us in the eyes will not forget our expression, he will not forget our suffering, and one day he will curse those who made him do it. There will be no violence, there will be no acts of hostility; our only reply to those Jews will be that they condemned other Jews to deportation."

According to Ramadan Shallah, the leader of Palestinian Islamic Jihad who claimed responsibility for the attack on the Hatuel family, the murderers have earned admission to the paradise of Allah. Killing Jewish women and children is permissible, Shallah claims, "because they decided spontaneously to go live in a war zone." But Tali Hatuel was not a "fanatic," as she was described in the Western media; she was one of many modern Orthodox Jewish women who are not willing to give up their land. They are people who, in memory of an ancient Promised Land, sought redemption there from the life of oppression they had suffered in Arab or Communist countries, from which an overwhelming majority of them came.

When Cyrus permitted the Jews to return to Israel, few of them did so, preferring their exile in Babylonia, the native land of Abraham. Still today, half of the Jewish population prefers "to live out in the cold," as George Steiner put it, in the far-flung offshoots of the diaspora. One can continue to live in Crown Heights, in Golders Green, or in Grünewald, the neighborhood in Berlin once inhabited by the rich Jewish middle class that was wiped out in Majdanek and Birkenau. One can do this because, with the existence of Israel, the Jews can choose in complete freedom whether to live in the communities that have hosted them, and they are morally free to leave them. Their choice, to leave or to stay, is no longer imposed, but an authentic choice. After their unique experience of abandonment during the Second World War, which went beyond even the Christian Passion, the Jews of Israel are once again at the center of humanity's religious history, reestablishing the connection between biblical and historical Israel.

"The Book of Books has been our most faithful and instructive guide, and has established in our hearts the sense of universal redemption," said David Ben-Gurion. "If we continue to act according to its light, the nations and their governors will be able to attain the good." But election also comes with a grave duty: "It implies an extra burden, an added responsibility to live according to conscience, listening to what the prophet Elijah would later call 'the still small voice.'" And the Hatuels knew this all too well.

From Brooklyn, Jews go to live in Beit El, where Jacob dreamed about the angel; to Shiloh, where a tabernacle was erected; or to Bet Shemesh, where the kings of Judea and Israel met. They go there because that's where the history of Israel unfolded, and they go there knowing that it means risking their lives. Israeli Judaism has accepted the danger. Within the State of Israel, in the little seeds that are scattered in the desert, people who have accepted and glorified the danger of being Jewish set down roots. Like the heroes of rural legend all over the world, the Gaza settlers dreamed that by cultivating the land with the sweat of their brows, they would make it their own. Because they are Jews, this outcome has been withheld from them. Still, their story is a heroic tale of work, dedication, and hope. They have had to abandon the homes they built, the fields they cultivated, like caravans of sharecroppers forced to move on by the inflexible laws of farmland ownership. History and its contradictions require this, although it need not compromise their indomitable dignity. Even Ehud Barak, the Labor Party leader and Zionist who had offered almost all of the West Bank to Yasser Arafat, once said, "On the extreme right, I sense a combination of profound fatalism, of diasporic anxiety and messianism, wrapped in fierce nationalist rhetoric. There is a great contradiction in this. But in these emotions, I feel close to them."

Children in Gush Katif grew up with a strong connection to the land in which they were born, where their grandparents and parents began their activities more than thirty years before, helped by government subsidies. They were large families, some with as many as ten children; they were used to living together and helping each other. Everyone knew everyone else, and they all kept their doors unlocked.

The story of the Hatuel family is emblematic of the Jews expelled from Gush Katif—the farmers of Atzmona, Katif, Netzer Hazani, Kfar Darom, and Netzarim, the fishermen of Shirat Hayam, the Torah scholars of Neveh Dekalim, and the mothers of Gadid. The Hatuels were a living image of the fertility of Gush Katif. While the average age in Israel is very low, about twenty-five, the population of the settlements is even younger. The students from Netzarim marching out of their synagogue behind the menorah, the soldiers shutting down the communities of Katif and Atzmona—these are images that will be forever impressed on Israel's history, along with the names of the many children of Gush Katif who were killed in terrorist attacks or in battle.

Sergeant Israel Lutatu of Neveh Dekalim had done volunteer work since he was thirteen. His father knew that the government was going to dismantle the communities in Gaza over the next year, but he decided nonetheless to have Israel buried in the land where he had grown up. "He lived here, he fought here, he will rest here." A year before his death, Sergeant Amsa Meshulami's family had been among those forced to leave Gush Katif. Amsa was an Orthodox Jew who "wanted to take part in the resettlement of his land; he was not afraid of dying, and he said he was ready to fight." His wife was expecting a child when Amsa was killed in Lebanon.

Corporal Elkana Gubi was proud of the red beret he wore as a paratrooper. He had been returning to the military base with his brother, still dressed for Shabbat in white shirt, ritual vestments, and black jacket, when he saw that a few Israeli automobiles were under Palestinian fire. Elkana stopped his car and started shooting at the terrorists, who retreated. But the crew of an Israeli jeep mistook him for a terrorist and killed him. His family, which is extremely devout, believes that he died for the *Kiddush Hashem,* the sanctification of the Name. "For us, it is Memorial Day 365 days a year," said his mother,

Miri. Corporal Gubi was buried in the settlement of Neveh Dekalim. He had carved these words onto the door frame of his house: "We are here for eternity."

Ariel Sharon designated the land to be abandoned in Gaza, the barracks to be torn down, the greenhouses to be buried, the Jews to be transferred. And then, house by house, Jew by Jew, he evacuated the same lands that Israel had conquered in battle. It was an exile without precedent: Jews forcibly removing other Jews, dragging them away by the legs, stunning images of the inconceivable.

It is the story of farmers like Assaf Assif, known as "king of the geraniums," who from his company in Ganei Tal, a little settlement of moderate religious Jews, exported almost twenty million geraniums to Europe each year. He had created the company from nothing in 1982, after losing a leg to a landmine in Sinai while serving his country as a soldier. "Back then, it was desert here," he recalls. "The Palestinians didn't want to live here; they called it badlands, cursed land. It's sand, and they thought nothing could be grown here. We found water, thirty meters down." In 2001, one of his forty Palestinian employees placed a bomb under the seat of Assaf's car. Miraculously, it didn't explode. Assaf moved his company to the south of Ashkelon, but the Palestinians continue to lob rockets at him from the Gaza Strip.

An elderly Gaza settler told the young soldier who came to clear out the graves, "I care about you—you could be my son; but think about how many friends I have lost to Palestinian fire in order to remain in this village, and for your sake, too." They had stayed there for the sake of all Israelis. That land was the only thing worth bartering in exchange for a little peace, and they had defended it at the cost of much blood. In Neveh

Dekalim, the settlers used the Torah scrolls as a shield. They hoped that the soldiers and policemen would not dare break into the temple to stop the protest against the evacuation. These scenes resembled the first, chaotic Israeli withdrawal from Yamit, the settlement in Sinai that was given back to Egypt in 1982. Ayelet, who had enlisted in the border guard, found herself face to face with her sister, Shulamit. The two had been born and raised in Neveh Dekalim, but after their parents had decided to leave Gush Katif, Shulamit had chosen to stay and "do something," while Ayelet returned twenty-four hours later in uniform to fulfill her military service.

Many of those settlers had in mind the historic words that Rabbi Tzvi Yehuda Kook said to Yona Efrat, a government representative, on the occasion of a visit in 1974 to the first Jewish settlements. Efrat told the venerable teacher, "I ordered all of you to evacuate." Kook replied, "There are orders one simply does not obey." In the summer of 2005, the Israelis of Gaza ripped off their shirts in a Jewish gesture of mourning, while others kissed the scroll of the Bible on the threshold of the synagogue.

On Independence Day in 1967, Rabbi Kook had asked, "Where is our Hebron, our Shechem, our Jericho?" The victory in the Six-Day War a few weeks later, with the conquest of biblical Israel, made the whole country delirious with joy. The settlers were an expression of this metaphysical and political return to the lands named in the Bible. So in Gaza, the settlers wrote on their homes, in the sand, on the walls of the synagogue: "This is the Cohen family's tree," "This beach belongs to Israel," "This fortress will last a thousand years." A letter from the Hebrew alphabet was written in black on the wall of every house marked for destruction in Gush Katif. On the wall of a little house in Pe'at Sadeh was written, "We love you, dear house."

With the gates barricaded and the houses enveloped in the smoke of burning blankets and trash, as if the Gaza settlements were battlefields, the soldiers arrived without weapons or helmets, with nothing but the menorah and Star of David on their vests. They came to the front door of each home with great respect: "Good morning, we're very sorry, but it's time for you to leave. I know that it's difficult. I ask you to help us do our work with dignity." Rabbi Yom Tov said to the soldiers, who had protected them for so many years, "You are also heroes. You have held up in such hard times that no one can blame you. One day, we will all live together again." The employees of the demolition companies, paid by the Ministry of Defense, preferred to remain anonymous because, they said, "we don't want to be remembered as the destroyers of the homes of Gush Katif."

The mother of a boy who had been killed by terrorists locked herself in her bedroom with canisters of gasoline, threatening to set them on fire. A family whose son had been killed in Lebanon while serving in a navy attack unit was ready to do anything rather than leave. House after house, teams of soldiers listened patiently while the settlement families, weeping and tearing their clothing, begged the soldiers to change their minds and let them stay. Female soldiers played with children in tears, telling them stories and embracing them. Everyone was embracing.

"Bible lesson, Bible lesson," said the voice from the loudspeaker in the little square in front of the synagogue in the settlement of Morag, the southernmost settlement in the Gaza Strip, wedged in between Rafah and Khan Yunis, between Egypt and the Palestinians, the target of constant attacks during the al-Aqsa Intifada, with Qassam missile strikes and terrorist incursions on a routine basis.

Some of the lawns had holes where plants used to grow; the settlers even took the plants away with them. In Netzer Hazani, words from a popular song were written on the wall of one home: "We have no other country, even if my land should burn." Underneath was an outline of the State of Israel. On another wall was a drawing of a palm tree, like the ones that grow on the beach nearby; next to it were the lyrics of a song by the Israeli singer and icon Naomi Shemer: "Do not uproot the trees, do not forget hope, take me back to that land."

One of the harshest tests was the evacuation of the synagogue of Badolah, where the settlers were granted an extra hour for prayer before their departure. The soldiers found the settlers clinging to the benches and the Torah ark, or writhing on the floor. The rabbi, insisting on the need for a final gesture and final words, asked for permission to speak to the soldiers. The commanding officer granted it. So five hundred soldiers stood at attention with a hundred settlers, with Israeli flags waving around them, while the rabbi talked about the importance of channeling suffering into the creation of a more loving and ethical society. "We are still a people, a state," he said. Together, the displaced and those who had evicted them sang the *Hatikvah,* the national anthem, "Hope."

While Pope Benedict XVI was visiting the synagogue of Cologne, which had been destroyed in 1938 during the Nazi persecution, the Israeli army was entering the synagogue of Gadid in the Gaza Strip, where about ninety settlers had barricaded themselves in defiance of an evacuation order from Jerusalem. In the synagogue that almost seventy years earlier had suffered the start of increasingly horrific persecutions, the atmosphere was serene. In the other one, situated in Palestinian territory, there was strife among brothers, then desperation and weeping, shared by those who were driven out and those who had the unwelcome task of expelling them.

A particularly heartbreaking moment was the evacuation of the forty-eight graves of Gush Katif, where everything had been built upon an extremely strong sense of Jewish solidarity. The graves were silent testaments to the settlers' claim on land they see as a biblical birthright. Relocating the Gush Katif cemetery has set a symbolic precedent for a Jewish state that is still struggling with its identity. When Israel demolished the Sinai settlement bloc of Yamit in 1982 under a peace deal with Egypt, there were no graves to be removed.

"These dead represent all of Gush Katif, as if the whole nation of Israel went with them to their eternal rest," said the chief rabbi, Yisrael Meir Lau. "If the dead could walk on the streets, if their bones could come back to life, they would say that we are all brothers, descendants of the same person." Those forty-eight graves bore words of mercy: "My love, my husband, our brother, our son"; "Your love and your memory will never leave us"; "A man who loved life and sought justice"; "Lover of Israel"; and "Young woman of pity and kindness."

The Hillberg family had to dig up the body of a son killed in the war in Lebanon. When the soldiers came to evacuate his mother, Broide, she said, "How can you come here to drive us out of our homes wearing the same Israeli flag on your uniforms that we placed on Jonathon's grave?" A young officer told them, "I only want to assure you that I love this country no less than you do. Please believe me. My friends and I serve in the best army units, just like you son, about whom I have heard so much. We are fighting the terrorists just like he did. And I am here to try to overcome the divisions that exist between us today; we can't allow it. Please, let me help you bring your luggage outside."

The exhumed graves also included that of a woman who had survived Auschwitz. Her daughter said goodbye to the land that she had loved and defended while clinging to the tragic dream of being Jewish in a sea of Arabs. There was the grave of Elkana Gubi, who believed in the right of the Jews to live in Gaza. His grandfather was a Holocaust survivor, the only one of his family. And there were the graves of Tali Hatuel and her young daughters, Hila, Merav, Hadar, and Roni. Shortly before they were killed, the girls had written to their father, David, who was protesting in Jerusalem on behalf of the Jewish communities of Gaza: "Daddy, we are proud of what you are doing to save the house we were born in."

David Hatuel, originally from Morocco, went to mourn for his exterminated family in the Kiryat Sanz neighborhood in Netanya. Kiryat Sanz is a living memorial of the Holocaust, where almost all the elderly are people who escaped the extermination—like the devout Pole whom the Nazis had punished by immersing his hands in icy water because he had tried to follow the precept of washing one's hands before meals. There were Jews who had performed incredible acts of spiritual resistance in the Nazi concentration camps: a *shofar* hidden in a camp, *tefilim* passed from barracks to barracks, Hanukkah candles secretly lit in the middle of the night. One rabbi started dancing and singing when he was taken to the gas chamber. Others asked if they should recite the *Viduy,* the confession before death. One picked up a pouch of liquor and shared it with his friends, shouting *"l'chaim,"* "to life." A rabbi yelled at an SS officer, "You will not succeed in exterminating the Jewish people. Don't even think it!" He put his hat on and said the *Shema Yisrael.* And then there was the mother who hid her son in her arms; the father who risked his life to put aside a piece of bread for his daughters; and those who courageously brought comfort to the dying.

Kiryat Sanz was founded more than half a century ago by the great rabbi Yekutiel Yehuda Halberstam, the genius of Klausenberg, in Romania, who lost his wife and eleven children in the gas chambers. There is a story about General Dwight Eisenhower's visit to the Red Cross camps for survivors on September 17, 1945. At the camp of Feldafing, Eisenhower knew there was a great rabbi among the survivors and asked to meet him. Rabbi Halberstam told the general to wait until he had finished praying. "I was praying before the General of generals, the King of kings, the Holy One, blessed may he be," the rabbi recounted. "The general of the earth would have to wait."

After the war, the few Hasidim of Klausenberg moved to Netanya, in Israel, and started building from the ground up: hospitals, yeshivas, kindergartens, cultural centers. Rabbi Halberstam, who emerged from the ashes of the Holocaust as one of the most profound figures of the twentieth century, remarried in Israel and had seven more children. He lived like a saint, and personally cared for young women who had survived the Holocaust; he urged them to rest, to start a new life, and not to withdraw from religion. He founded the Laniado Hospital in Kiryat Sanz, which one survivor, Edith Lieberman, called "a promise to the Most High built on the ashes of the Holocaust, a living legacy to keep the Jewish nation alive for the generations to come." The hospital has treated more than five hundred victims of terrorism, and it has brought thousands of children into the world. Among them is the son of Vadim Norzich, an Israeli reserve soldier who was lynched in Ramallah during the first weeks of the al-Aqsa Intifada. The benefactors of the hospital include Renee Korall, who lost all her relatives in the Holocaust, and the Neiman family of Chicago, who donated a million dollars for a pavilion dedicated to the memory of one and a half million murdered Jewish children.

In Kiryat Sanz, David Hatuel found the strength to start life over again. "Over the past eighteen months of my life," he says, "my private family tragedy has expanded to the national tragedy, because in the end I even had to leave my home in Gush Katif to the murderers of my wife and daughters." David saw two ways out of the tragedy that was consuming his own life and that of the nation: "The way of death, of mourning, and of self-pity, a way without hope, with a daily descent into the depths of suffering. The second way brought me back to life. The continuation of my life, of my work in public education, and also in the building up of *Eretz Yisrael* and of my spiritual life with God."

Eventually, David got married again. "It is the continuity of life," he explains. "My wife and my children have not disappeared, they live inside of me, they are part of my life. They are like a tree that has had its branches cut off, and is now starting to grow again. Instead of focusing on the horrific way in which my family was taken away, I dwell instead over the twelve wonderful years that God gave me. I have to believe that God has a plan." David met Limor through a mutual friend who among other things took care of terrorism victims. In announcing his decision to marry Limor, he quoted Psalm 30:11, "You changed my mourning into dancing; you took off my sackcloth and clothed me with gladness." Today, David lives in the coastal city of Ashkelon, where he works as a school principal. "Without the help of God, I never could have done it, but the Almighty has called us to life, even if it is not easy for us." He now has a daughter named Tachiya, "rebirth."

"I am one of those who have experienced tremendous suffering, and I can say that it is very difficult, maybe the most difficult thing that a person can do, to start life over after such a tragedy," says this teacher who in many ways is a symbol of those wounded by terrorism. David has served as president of the One Family Fund, which cares for the victims of terrorism. "When someone suffers that kind of loss, the pain never goes away. It is always there, and often it becomes even worse over time. Living with this pain, seeking to rebuild in the midst of all this, is incredibly difficult. So the people working at the One Family Fund are true heroes. They are the ones who refuse to allow terrorism and tragedy to sweep life away, so they rebuild.

They need our help to rebuild, but our help works only if people want to rebuild. And this desire to rebuild, this desire to continue, is pure heroism in my eyes."

In spite of so much violence and pain, David has never lost his faith in Israel. "The Jewish nation has survived things much more terrible than the terrorism and hatred that Israel now faces. We survived thanks to our faith in God and in justice; we survived thanks to our intelligence and our resources. The Jewish nation will survive terrorism. Although the power of our leaders is self-referential, and in spite of the many challenges facing the Jewish nation, we see the existence of the State of Israel as the beginning of the nation's salvation, and our faith in salvation is unshaken."

David sees volunteers and the charitable as those who bear the weight of the salvation of the Jews as a people and a nation. "These are the people who can truly lead and change the world. One hundred years ago, these people carried the nation out of exile and dispersion, and created the state with all its institutions. Today, these people are creating aid organizations. Day after day they continue to change the lives of the people, and to bring hope to millions of us. The leaders of one hundred years ago worked against tyranny, oppression, and hatred. The leaders of today, with their vision and their desire to improve everyday life, are working against hatred and inhumanity, poverty and depression. It is my privilege to work with such a group."

David Hatuel has written a sort of breviary of Gush Katif, with the emblematic title *Faith, the Everyday, Hope, and Brotherhood.* The faith that drives him to believe that "Tali and my daughters are in the highest place, together with all the other martyrs killed sanctifying God and the Holy Land." The everyday that "gives the strength to go on, and keeps the spirit from crumbling." The hope that "the Messiah will soon bring complete redemption." The brotherhood that constitutes Israel's strongest sinew. The hope and optimism written on Hatuel's face are the most beautiful image of Israel. David says he has seen with his own eyes God's words and acts of love for Israel, as written in Ezekiel (16:6), "Then I [God] passed by and saw you weltering in your blood. I said to you, 'Live!' Yes, I said to you as you lay in your blood, 'Live!'"

Dead Souls

*S*derot is like Guernica, the Basque town* that was bombed by Nazi planes during the Spanish Civil War. Sderot is the Israeli town that has suffered the most rocket attacks; but unlike Guernica, it has not had its Picasso. It was first populated by North African Jews who emigrated to the young Jewish state in the 1950s. In the last decade, the town has filled with immigrants from the former Soviet Union and Ethiopia, living in apartment buildings that are old and crumbling. The siege of Sderot involves much more than one poor community: it represents the moral clarity of the Jewish people, the courage and resistance of Israel, and it reveals the rest of the world's indifference to the genocidal hatred of Islamism. "We're still fighting the War of Independence," said Sderot's former mayor Eli Moyal, a proud Israeli of Moroccan descent.

The nightmare of this city in the Negev desert, a few miles from the Gaza Strip, began on the cameras of the American television network CBS. On January 24, 2002, the *60 Minutes* program broadcast an interview with a leader of Hamas, Moussa Abu Marzouk, who threatened to use Qassam rockets to strike Israeli cities. The name Qassam comes from a fundamentalist imam who incited pogroms against the Jews during the 1920s. In June 2004, a rocket hit an elementary school,

killing a man and a child. They were the first in a long series of
Israeli victims in Sderot, the "most bombed city in the world."

Twelve thousand Palestinian rockets have fallen on Sderot
and Ashkelon. Every day for nine years, Israelis have awakened
to hear two news bulletins on the radio: the weather forecast
and the rocket strikes in Sderot. Children in the city have been
sent to stay with relatives and friends elsewhere; sporting
events have been postponed; the sense of death has pervaded
the empty streets, the shops, the market, everything. Death has
fallen from the sky without warning. Even today, if you are driving in Sderot it's a good idea to keep the window down at all
times, your seat belt unfastened, and the radio off so you can
hear the siren. There have been times when the population
thought the warning siren was broken because it didn't stop
sounding for hours on end.

The Tzeva Adom (Color Red) alert starts with the click of a
loudspeaker, and then a calm female voice repeats *"Tzeva
Adom, Tzeva Adom."* In Sderot, the only place in a Western
democracy that has been plagued with rocket fire for many
years, you are always within fifteen or twenty seconds of a shelter. When a Tzeva Adom alarm would sound, children tended
to start crying, so a song called "Color Red" was created, along
with breathing exercises, to help keep the children calm while
they run for shelter. Ten years ago, in the early days of Qassam
rocket attacks on Sderot, Arab terrorists would fire the missiles
in the morning when children were on their way to school and
had no protection. The words that the anonymous woman
repeated then were *Shachar Adom,* meaning "Red Dawn." But a
little girl named Shachar, "Dawn," told officials it was painful to
hear her own name being used as a death warning, so they
changed the word to *Tzeva,* "color."

After an attack in Sderot, children are screaming and doctors are pulling shrapnel out of the bodies of Jews. Many Holocaust survivors have suffered because they can't run to a

neighborhood shelter. These are people like Sara Herskowitz, age ninety, who last saw her mother and sister when they were pulled out of the line at Auschwitz. Several Holocaust survivors in Sderot take antidepressants because of the Qassams, say volunteers for Amcha, an organization that provides social services to Holocaust survivors.

It's a daily war to destroy the Israeli population. "There is only one example in history in which thousands of rockets have been fired on a civilian population," said Benjamin Netanyahu, the prime minister, at the United Nations. "It was when the Nazis launched rockets on English cities during the Second World War. In that war, the Allies razed German cities to the ground, leaving hundreds of thousands dead. Israel decided to behave differently."

We are in the triangle of fear: Ashkelon-Sderot-Netivot. These civilian towns are well inside Israel proper and are still assaulted by rockets. Some of Sderot's residents have moved to Netivot and Ashkelon in recent years, renting or purchasing apartments there, only to discover that the rockets continue to chase them. For many of them, the only shelter is the kitchen table. The rocket attacks have created a new reality in which nearly one million Israeli residents (about 15 percent of the entire population) are at risk.

Sderot is a sick city. Economic life is a disaster; businesses are closing one after another; the schools, the hospitals, the transportation, all of public life has been immersed in misery and clinical shock. Property damage remains uncalculated, as does the psychological damage suffered by the inhabitants— men, women, and children—who have endured the daily onslaught. Independent medical investigations suggest that one out of every two inhabitants suffers from psychological problems.

Every day, dozens of people knock at the doors of the Sderot Trauma Center, which offers psychological help to those who suffer the trauma of the bombings. The director is Dr. Adriana Katz, who has spent years alleviating psychological suffering in Sderot. "This is a country of living dead," Dr. Katz remarks as she counts the latest attacks by Hamas. "In nine years, I have treated six thousand victims of rocket strikes." The people in Sderot are not suffering from PTSD, post-traumatic stress disorder; the symptoms are the same—insomnia, anxiety, apathy, psychosomatic pain—but in Sderot the "post" never comes.

"Seventy-nine percent of the population of Sderot is psychologically handicapped," says Batya Katar, the leader of the Sderot Parents' Association. "Every day, for nine years, we have had attacks by Hamas. My son has slept with me for five years because he is afraid of rocket attacks. We have twenty seconds to get to a shelter. It is with this thought that the people of Sderot live: we could die at any moment. Here children sleep with their parents, and when they go to the bathroom they wake everyone up, because the children are afraid of going alone."

Noam Bedein, director of the Sderot Media Center, notes that "Sderot is the only city in the world where terrorism strikes the civilian population in the twenty-first century day after day, without interruption." Bedein was a witness before the United Nations commission on the war in Gaza. "You can't count on the fingers of both hands how many times rockets have exploded a few meters away from a kindergarten. What other democracy would tolerate even a single rocket fired at the civilians of its territory? Do we have to wait for a kindergarten to be hit dead center for Israel to obtain international support to do what is necessary to protect its own people?"

Sderot's children—five thousand in the local area—live as prisoners in their own homes, unable to play outside, swim in a pool, ride a bike, or kick a football. "What I hate most is the impossibility of communicating the disability of the soul and the mind, because this cannot be photographed, it cannot be broadcast on television," says Dr. Katz, a Romanian who came to Israel with her husband after spending sixteen years in Italy. In case of an attack, Adriana always gets going, even at night. She is always on call. "My problem is that I can't communicate what is happening here. During the war in Gaza, the Israeli foreign minister wanted to send me to the European Parliament to talk about Sderot. I refused, because there was no way for me to express the gravity and the tragedy of the people of Sderot. Those who don't experience it can't understand it," Adriana explains between one cigarette and the next. It is said that Sderot is the worst place in the world to quit smoking.

"We have been unable to heal all of these tormented souls, who for the most part do not continue to function as they did before—families destroyed, children with all the effects of posttraumatic disorder, because there are rocket alarms almost every day. These rockets seem like toys compared with Katyusha rockets. But when we realized that this 'toy' kills, when a child was killed, then a grandfather, and then when a woman lost her legs, we started to understand. They have not stopped firing Qassams for even a single day, in spite of the ceasefire. You Europeans need to live here for a week. We have had people killed and disabled, homes destroyed. It's like Russian roulette: you never know who's next. Normal life is gone. Life has been shattered. You leave your home and you never know if you will get to where you're going. The alarm sounds and you have to lie down on the ground—it's humiliating. It is a tremendous trauma. People are watching television or eating when all of a sudden comes the 'Color Red.' As a psychiatrist, I know that fear has no taste or color or smell, but here in Sderot fear is 'Color Red.'" Dr. Katz adds, "There is a poor seller of melons who can no longer shout through a megaphone to sell his wares because it sounds too similar to '*Tzeva Adom,*' and it made someone pass out."

Adriana Katz is proud of her leftist credentials and proud of being on the side of compromise. "I am against war, I come from Europe, but when you live here you see things a different way. There are disabled children in Sderot, without legs, adults too, but most of all it is a population exposed to fear, uprooted from its own normal life. So many people have stopped working and don't leave their homes; so many older children still wet the bed. Nothing seems the way it was before. Panic attacks over loud noises become a source of terror. It is a disabled society. I wonder if it is less serious than the bombing of Gaza. The trauma does not diminish, it is not temporary, it is a chronic disease. We don't make any plans. It is a gloomy life, without enthusiasm. People may have children, but it's always with fear. It is not a healthy population. For Holocaust survivors, it brings all of their sufferings back. With the children, we have a 'Qassam generation.' The children of Sderot are like elderly survivors of the Holocaust—they don't play outside, they're afraid, the playgrounds are bomb shelters. It's a horrible feeling. The children are born and raised with terror; they are afraid of going out in the daylight, afraid of sleeping alone, some of them are in total regression, they can't detach themselves from their parents. There's a feeling in the air that everything is about to explode. Every day there's a rocket strike in Sderot. I have no hope. The really sad thing is that the world doesn't understand what's happening here. I love my job; I studied medicine to become a psychiatrist, but in recent years it has become too difficult. What does the United Nations know about the thousands of Israeli victims of trauma, whose lives have become a hell on earth? Who will help the four thousand children get back to a normal life? Years and years of rehabilitation await the population that lives here. It is no longer the work of a psychiatrist. How much mental fortitude does it take to continue treating people without thinking about your own home, wondering if it is still standing?"

A poster on the Hamas website shows Israeli children in Sderot huddling in a shelter during a barrage of Palestinian

Qassam rockets. The caption reads, "Zionists, hide yourselves well." There are parks for children in Sderot, but they have remained empty for months. The children have been in the bomb shelters. A spokesman for the Ezzedeen al-Qassam Brigades, the armed branch of Hamas, had these words for the inhabitants of the city: "Prepare many buses! We will not stop firing until Sderot is empty." Each of the bus stops in Sderot has been equipped with a bomb shelter that has a single reinforced window. In the elementary schools, the children often learn math by counting how many of them are still at their desks.

A bomb-proof playing field was opened in March 2009. "Today we are bringing childhood back to the children of Sderot, and we're letting them live like other children all over the world," said the mayor, David Buskila. Costumed children can celebrate the feast of Purim, they can jump on an inflatable trampoline, they can play soccer; the girls can play with dolls. Everything seems normal, but they are inside a bunker. The children of Sderot under a reinforced roof, with their mothers looking at the ceiling when the siren starts to wail, as if they are waiting for death, are one of the most terrible images of this war against the Israeli civilian population.

Dr. Dalia Yosef is a former director of the Sderot Resilience Center, which specializes in caring for children. "Children of every age, from one year to eighteen, present extremely severe traumas," Dalia explains. "Many of them have nightmares, don't eat well, don't go outside alone, don't want their mothers to go to work, don't play, have lots of problems at school. Many of these children were born under the Qassam fire. They have never known anything different. It is not like losing a family member in a car accident; in Sderot there is collective trauma. Two weeks after the end of the operations in Gaza, they started firing again. In Sderot, the children react to any loud noise as if it's a Qassam alarm. Seventy percent of the children in the

Negev show symptoms of trauma, and these statistics are the result of independent research. Thousands of children also have physical disabilities from Palestinian bombs. There are children who want to stay inside the bunkers, or in the safe rooms of their homes. There are children who don't get out of bed anymore. We don't know what will become of this generation born and raised under the Qassams."

The Palestinian bombs have often hit the Israeli hospitals where Jewish doctors save the lives of Palestinians, such as the Barzilai Medical Center in Ashkelon, where the wounded were taken during the war in Gaza in January 2009. On the ground, all the patients of Barzilai are the same—Arabs and Jews, Israelis and Palestinians. The Israeli doctors do not ask for identification cards; they operate on everyone. If a Qassam were to hit the hospital, the "triumph" would be celebrated in Gaza without consideration for the Palestinians being treated there. Haula Fadlallah, a Palestinian from Gaza, has given birth to two boys and two girls with the assistance of Israeli doctors. Barzilai coordinates the transfer of patients with the health services in Gaza; it is a dialogue that has never been interrupted, even when a hundred rockets a day were falling on Sderot and Ashkelon. The Barzilai hospital is an island of life in a lake of death. A few minutes away, imams and terrorist leaders are inciting the extermination of Jews. "Send these children of monkeys and pigs to hell on the wings of Qassam rockets," said the Egyptian imam Safwat Higazi on al-Aqsa TV, run by Hamas, on December 31, 2008.

Dr. Ron Lobel, the longstanding head of Israeli health services in Gaza and also the deputy director of Barzilai, explains that "we have been taking care of hundreds of injured Arabs for years. We have always been the hospital of reference for the Palestinians. I myself worked for many years in Gaza. And ever since then there has been an excellent professional relationship. We trained Palestinian doctors and nurses before the Hamas monster grew out of all proportion. In Khan Yunis, we built an intensive care unit. And even after Hamas took power, every day we have had ten or fifteen Palestinian patients from Gaza. Blood is blood. For us, it is a privilege to be a doctor. Every patient who asks for care receives it." Dr. Lobel knows what it means to live under the threat of the rockets. "It is difficult to work like that, but when the injured come, we think only of the emergency. Then come the thoughts about family, children, home. I live in a farming community, Netiv Ha'asara. The distance between my house and the Palestinian border is only three hundred meters. The Israeli army says that I am lucky, the rockets pass over my head."

Dr. Adriana Katz remembers the first Qassam well. "It was 2001 when the rockets started raining in the south. We had no idea what they were, even though I had experienced the sirens in 1991 when Saddam Hussein fired Scuds at Israel during the Gulf War. The news programs filmed what was happening; they showed how these homemade rockets were made. We laughed— there was no sense of danger. The people in the greatest danger were the Israelis living in the Palestinian Territories. I thought, 'They should leave; there's nothing left for them there.' One day, I went to work in Sderot and there was a kind of alarm with a human voice saying *'shachar adom,'* red dawn." Adriana recalls, "It didn't seem right to me, and in the beginning I was strongly opposed to it—I was convinced that the alarm itself caused more panic. Also, I come from Europe, and I fell into a world that I didn't know."

Dr. Katz, who now must combat diabetes caused by stress, has a few bouquets of artificial flowers at the clinic. "I received them each year from a good man who had a brother in therapy. He brought flowers every Mother's Day. To tell the truth, I never liked them and I couldn't wait to get rid of them, but I was never able to. One morning I arrived in Sderot and heard *'Tzeva Adom.'* We all ran to the place of the explosion, and at that very moment I was horrified to realize that bombs made in a kitchen can kill. The first to be killed were a child with his grandfather, the man who loved to bring me a bouquet of flowers every year. I can still picture Mordechai Yosefov. The boy who was killed was four years old. For a long time, we treated the girl who worked in the kindergarten near where the tragedy took place." These first fatalities from a Qassam attack occurred in June 2004. Today there is a park in Sderot named after Afik Zahavi-Ohayon, the child who was the city's first victim of Hamas.

Adriana Katz tells the story of Batsheva. "They filmed her while she was yelling at Arafat, 'If you are a brave man, step forward, I'll show you myself what it means to terrorize an entire population.' She was a strong woman, a teacher full of energy. But a short time later, while she was hanging her laundry up to dry, a rocket hit her home, a few meters away from her. Batsheva has been in therapy since that day. She has never been the same; she doesn't teach, she doesn't work, she's a shadow of her former self." Adriana asks, "Can you really imagine how it feels to be driving the car with the windows down when you suddenly hear that damned alarm, and you have to stop where you are, get out and lie down in the middle of the street, summer or winter, rain or shine—can you imagine how it feels? It has happened to me more than once, but I couldn't obey the orders from the army; it's too humiliating."

Dr. Mirela Siderer is a symbol of Israeli suffering under bombardment by Hamas. "I heard something like a ball of fire whirling around inside me, and all of my teeth were knocked out. I still have a piece of shrapnel four centimeters long buried in the left side of my back, too close to my spinal column to be removed." Dr. Siderer was injured by a Palestinian rocket that hit her clinic in Ashkelon, where the bus stops are cement shields and the playgrounds are equipped with alarm bells. She flew to Geneva to speak in front of the UN commission on

Gaza. With her was Noam Shalit, the father of the soldier kidnapped by Hamas.

"My entire peaceful life was turned upside down in a second when, without any warning, a rocket hit my clinic," Siderer says. "In a fraction of a second, the place was completely destroyed. I found myself beneath the rubble, seriously injured, but I continued to talk to the patient I was treating, who was also seriously injured: her stomach was torn open, with her entrails hanging out. What was my crime? That I am a Jew who lives in Ashkelon? I studied medicine in order to help people all over the world, and I have also helped many women from Gaza. I am a simple civilian who has never had anything to do with any act of war. For you to understand better Israel's war against terrorism, I would first like to explain the notion of terrorism. Terrorism is the regime of violence on the part of an organized group with varying membership, varying political and religious aims, which directs its violence at a civilian population with no possibility of defending itself. There is a big difference between the wars that take place between two countries and terrorist attacks. I was injured during such an attack, while I was doing my work as a doctor."

Dr. Siderer continues, "In 2005, Israel withdrew from the Gaza Strip, so it can't be called occupied territory, but this conflict has become religious as well as geopolitical. With great displeasure, I realize that these are Islamic fundamentalists who are doing nothing other than provoking the State of Israel and the Jewish people. In southern Israel, we have been living in terror for more than nine years. Imagine living in any Italian city that is bombed every day for nine years. Could you carry on that way?"

Few can better understand the plight of Sderot's residents than their counterparts in Kiryat Shmona, a Galilee town near the border with Lebanon that suffered from rocket attacks and terrorist infiltration for decades. More than four thousand

Katyusha rockets, which have a longer range and carry a bigger payload than Qassams, fell on Kiryat Shmona from 1968 until May 2000, when the IDF withdrew from Lebanon in compliance with UN Security Council Resolution 425. Today in Sderot, the courtyard of the police station has become a storage place for the remains of missiles: the red ones launched by Hamas and the yellow ones by Palestinian Islamic Jihad. A few miles away is Havat Shikmim, the ranch of Ariel Sharon. Once fortified and protected, it is now neglected. Rockets have fallen near the grave of Sharon's wife, Lily, and the flowers named by the general were burned by Islamist hatred. Hamas claims Havat Shikmim as its own.

And yet Sderot is not a "ghost town," as it is often described. The number of inhabitants has never gone down. There are those who sleep with their clothes on, with the windows open a crack, and who talk quietly, out of fear that the emergency signal might escape their attention. But the Israelis have never left their city. Sderot lives.

The Lord's Spouses

The blood of *Eyal Sorek and Yael Kandel* was smeared on the front of their trailer in the Tzur Shalem outpost many hours after the attack. Residents of the Carmei Tzur settlement, the most isolated village in the Gush Etzion region, didn't permit the site to be cleaned until after Shabbat ended at sundown. Carmei Tzur people are young, many of them teachers and academics, in a community where religion is taken seriously. Eyal and Yael belonged to the "Hilltop Youth," the children of the first settlers sent by the Israeli government to "make the desert bloom" in the territories disputed after the Six-Day War in 1967. Thousands of Jews, many of them fresh from the aliyah, began to move into what they knew as Judea and Samaria. There are now about three hundred thousand settlers in all, and the American president Barack Obama, in his Cairo speech, called them the main obstacle on the road to peace between "two peoples and two states."

The settlers were certain that they would be vindicated by history, by God, and by their own country. For three-fourths of them, the difficulties do not appear to be insurmountable. They live not far from the Green Line of the old armistice between Israel and Jordan, east of Jerusalem and in the big settlements of Ariel, Gush Etzion, Ma'aleh Adumim, and Givat Ze'ev, covering no more than 5 percent of the disputed territories, and negotiable. And then there are the others, the fifty thousand who live in small or tiny settlements—a few hundred or a few dozen inhabitants—in the most inaccessible places. The ideological core of the settler movement is digging roots ever deeper into the rocky hills.

The first wave of outposts began in 1996, the year Benjamin Netanyahu rose to power as prime minister. There were even government ministers who came to the foundation-laying ceremonies of some outposts. The Israeli governments in power over the years have generated a great deal of confusion by oscillating between regarding those lands as a currency of exchange for peace with the Palestinians, and considering them to be freed land that could give Israel security and protection as well as historic memories. There are all kinds of settlers: religious and not religious, ideologues and simple people, hippies and those leading an austere life, men and women and many children. Almost all the settlers have the motivations of people who have built their homes with their bare hands and who risk their lives every night when they come home.

A hilltop settlement is a dangerous place—exposed, rocky, almost uninhabitable. There are about one hundred of these outposts. Bible in hand and rifle on shoulder, the young settlers, like Yael and Eyal in Tzur Shalem, spend their days in spartan hilltop encampments deep in the big-sky territory of the far northern West Bank, sleeping rough among their sheep and goats. Most outpost residents were born in settlements. They don't have a memory, as their parents do, of moving onto disputed territory. To them, the West Bank is simply home. They conceive of themselves as part of a work in progress: *Israel*. Their parents were satisfied to populate comfortable, suburban-style communities that lie close to Israel proper. Some of those settlements have tidy brick sidewalks and grocery stores, schools and universities. Others have dirt roads and no running water. In the outposts, electricity comes from a generator and the only way to communicate with the outside is via cell phone. The synagogues are often made of baked clay.

Mothers stroll their toddlers a few dozen feet from their front doorsteps and set out coffee in the house-trailer synagogue each evening for the Israeli soldiers who patrol the community. Husbands take turns patrolling at night with M16s or Uzis slung over their shoulders, pistols on their hips. They live a stone's throw from the Arabs. They are called "hippies on the hill," with their long, scraggly hair and beard, oversized kippah and wanderer's scarf blowing in the cold wind. They get around by horse or donkey. The women wear the *mitpahat,* the Jewish equivalent of the Islamic chador, but less concealing and more delicate.

It is a new generation imbued with the pioneering ethos of the secular kibbutz, a mystical nationalism combined with an ascetic spirit and an oriental sense of fatalism; it rejects the consumerism of the big cities on the coast, and lives by ideology, faith, and zeal. In many outposts, the young couples construct a giant Star of David so the Jews in nearby settlements and the Palestinians can see it. "It's the only thing Arabs understand," said Tamar Tzur. "The only thing that will stop the Arabs is a Jewish star on every hilltop." Tamar was in a car outside the settlement of Beit El when Palestinians fired on them in 1996, killing her mother and youngest brother. Prime Minister Netanyahu praised Jewish settlers as "heroes" and "pioneers" after Etta Tzur and her son were killed. "The Jewish people are rooted in the land of Beit El," he said. "These roots not only will not be uprooted, they will be deepened."

For the settlement generation, the Jewish resurgence comes, as it did at the beginning of the twentieth century, through a toe-to-toe confrontation with the Arabs. They feel like rebels from the time of Judas Maccabeus, who challenged the Romans to the death. They are edgy young people, their heads full of biblical history, who don't want to convince anyone and will not be convinced. The rules of the "peace process" do not seem to hold any weight with them. The Israeli soldiers, whose brigades and uniform the settlers share, have to drag them away by force when the evacuation order comes from Jerusalem. No one should think that the outposts are a phenomenon of the extreme right, a category that has no meaning in Israel. With Sharon as prime minister, forty-four outposts were created. Another thirty-nine, according to the data of Peace Now, were built under Rabin, Peres, and Barak, the participants in the Oslo peace negotiations. They range from simple containers placed at the top of a hill, or a few rows of barracks, to genuine settlements made with the kind of prefabricated buildings that are used to rebuild after an earthquake. Ra'anan Gissin, who was a senior adviser to Sharon, claims that many outposts serve as strategic lookouts and provide a first line of defense against Arab attacks on more established settlements. Hundreds of settlers have been killed in the Territories, and the outposts, Gissin argues, are "a justifiable response."

The memory of the many who paid with their lives is almost everywhere. The Mitzpe Danny outpost was named after Danny Frei, who was killed by a terrorist in 1995. The Judean desert lies to the east, Jerusalem to the southwest. The area is surrounded by brown hills that, to paraphrase one of the Psalms, "skip like rams, leap like lambs." Beit Haggai is a settlement in the Hebron Hills that was founded by a handful of Jewish seminary students and their families in 1984. They set up mobile homes on twin hilltops just south of Hebron, and named their community with an acronym of the names of three friends who had been killed in Hebron in 1980. Money donated by Christians in the United States helped equip the settlement. There is no fence or wall around Beit Haggai. In the synagogue, the young people doing reserve duty, among them many commanders, show determination and self-confidence. Their stern faces radiate inner calm. There are prayer books and Psalm books on the tables, and weapons nearby.

Shevut Rachel, "the Return of Rachel," is named after a young mother, Rachel Druck, who was killed in a terrorist attack on a bus in 1991 just before the peace conference in Madrid. "Jewish life grows again in this place," the first settlers had declared. David Druck decided to bury his wife's body at Shiloh. Hers was the first grave since the settlement was founded thirteen years earlier. "A grave is stronger than a house," David noted. "A house you can move. A grave you can't move. This is my answer to the killers." Mrs. Livyatan, a neighbor of Mr. Druck, said, "Wherever there is blood, we will build new life."

Sara Klein lives in an outpost near Eli. She is the wife of Roi Klein, who threw himself on a grenade during the war in Lebanon to protect his soldiers. In his last seconds of life, Roi mustered the strength to shout the *Shema Yisrael,* the prayer declared by Jewish martyrs through the generations. A stone plaque describing his heroism stands at the Hayovel outpost, in front of a park built by private donations from the United States. The perimeter of the settlement is patrolled night and day by residents with rifles slung on their shoulders. Hayovel was built to mark the fiftieth anniversary of the founding of the State of Israel. Aside from the Kleins, the outpost was also home to Avi Wolanski and his wife, Avital, who was in an advanced stage of pregnancy when both of them were killed by a Palestinian sniper as their car neared the settlement.

During the past three years, Eli has been on the frontlines of the violent conflict with the Palestinians. Bustling with both religious and seculars, the settlement overlooks rolling hills speckled with grazing goats. In the distance, the Palestinian village of Luban is visible. The beauty and quiet conjure up images of peace, but the tranquility of the landscape is deceptive. Farther along Route 60, deeper into the West Bank, those images of peacefulness are shattered by the reality of bullet-proof bus windows and drivers wearing ceramic vests.

Below Eli, you cross through a bottleneck where a Palestinian sharpshooter eliminated ten people, one by one, with an old rifle. A week after the Jewish settler Meir Chai was shot dead in December 2009, hundreds of residents set up a new outpost on a hill overlooking the site of the murder, and established a "regional Torah center" to be dedicated in Chai's name. Daniel Bin-Nun built an outpost with his own hands in memory of Harel, his brother who was killed. The outpost contains a therapeutic horse stable where Daniel treats a hundred children from all over Israel.

Rabbi Netanel Ozeri and his family, including five children, were enjoying a Shabbat meal with friends in their home on Hilltop 26 outside Hebron when they heard a knock on the door. Suspicious, Ozeri opened the door with a cocked pistol, but two Palestinian terrorists immediately shot him dead. Ozeri's friends fired back, killing one of the assailants and wounding the other, who was later killed by the army. The two friends and Ozeri's five-year-old daughter were also wounded. As founder of the Next Generation hilltop encampment movement, Ozeri moved out of Kiryat Arba to settle the hills around the city. "We believe that Jews should live in the land of Israel," he said. "It's a matter of sanctifying God's name, as opposed to desecrating it." Ozeri's house was surrounded by Arab houses several meters away. He lived there without electricity or running water. His wife, Livnat, said at his grave, "I had the honor of living with a holy man. He was both a scholar and a warrior. He sacrificed his life for the nation and the land of Israel."

Itay Zar lives in Havat Gilad, an outpost named after his brother, who was shot to death through the windshield of his car. Gilad refused to drive with a bulletproof vest and turned down the army's offer of a bulletproof car, saying it wasn't right for him to have one when other settlers didn't. In Havat Gilad there are twenty families, a dozen metal boxes, forty children, and a corral for the horses. "We didn't come here to have fun," Itay remarked. "This was desert; today the land is blooming." The spiritual leader of the outpost, Arie Lipo, said that their job is to build "little paradises." Netanel Valis, who belongs to one of Jerusalem's oldest families—Israelis from eleven generations—said, "We have a wonderful life in Havat Gilad. I wake up every day at 4:30 to study Torah." To reinforce the outpost's spiritual mission, Itay Zar erected a yeshiva that houses thirty-five young men. Yehuda Shimon, whose parents came from Poland and Yemen, comments, "We say 'God is the King,' or as in the dollar 'In God we trust.' It's not an easy life; we don't have water or electricity if we don't bring it here. I came here because I felt that my soul should be closer to God. Now I am happy. When someone is killed, like Gilad Zar, our immediate reaction is to build in his name. If you don't build, your spirit is dying."

Maoz Esther, an outpost of seven corrugated metal barracks and five families not far from Ramallah, has been removed three times—and always rebuilt. The leader of the community, Avraham Sandack, came to this hill straight from one of the settlements in Gaza that was dismantled by Ariel Sharon. He is studying to become a rabbi, and in the meantime he does the cleaning at a synagogue. "Our spirit is the same as that of our fathers," Avraham tells us. "Two years ago on the feast of Hanukkah, we left a nearby settlement and built a stone house. One mother, alone with her three little daughters, moved to the hillside for two months. They had no electricity or water. But they knew that they belonged to the land of Israel. In the Bible, this land is spoken of in the prophecies about the kingdom of God. That gives us strength to continue forward. Here we are able to be at peace with our souls. There is something metaphysical here. God is not in heaven or somewhere else. God is part of us; he is in our whole life."

"The idea is that of a life antithetical to the materialism of the cities," says Arieh Eldad, "a life in which TV is no more important than going for a walk in the desert or sitting down, all of the generations together, to talk." Arieh is a reserve general and an illustrious plastic surgeon whose experience with the attacks in recent years has been decisive in saving hundreds of lives, including Arab lives. "Those who persist in living here do so in the name of security for Israel, and of an understanding of the world."

That was the conviction of Yael Kandel, a young woman of Italian origin, the daughter of beekeepers, who was nine months pregnant when she and her husband, Eyal Sorek, were murdered along with a soldier who had tried to defend them. The Soreks were educated and religious people, but they didn't wear black—they dressed in colorful hippie-style clothing. They loved the land, and their lives were full of prayer, tradition, patriotism. They lived in a tiny settlement, just a few trailers, on a barren hill of stones and brambles in the middle of the desert.

The settlement was born one night in 1985, when two hundred Israelis arrived with prayer shawls, an electrical generator, and blocks for making steps up to the mobile homes, arranged in a rectangle. They named the community Carmei Tzur, after Etta Tzur and her son Efraim, killed near Beit El. They built, organized, and set up supplies of water and electricity. The men formed a Bible study group; they danced in a circle to religious songs, while the women took care of the children. The families were very young, and they all wore the clothing of religious pioneers, checkered shirts and crocheted kippot.

The residents of Carmei Tzur have become "frontline soldiers" in the conflict between Israelis and Palestinians. Carmei Tzur, a collection of red-roofed houses, sits amid Arab villages about four miles north of Hebron. Flanked by vineyards, it is home to about a hundred Jewish families. After morning prayers the men vanish to their jobs as career army officers, policemen, teachers, and lawyers in the State of Israel. The women stay at home, or work part time. Children roam freely, seemingly looking after each other. It is a haven, once you have passed through the security checkpoints. On the Israeli-built highway that is their main conduit to other Jewish communities in the region and to Jerusalem, the settlers of Carmei Tzur must traverse a battlefield of roadside bombs, drive-by shootings, rocks flung at windshields, and sniper fire from hostile neighbors.

Yael Kandel was a modest young woman who even refused to dance with the soldiers at her wedding. Her father, Yehuda, learned about the attack on the way out of the synagogue of Kfar Pines, a moshav where they had lived for many years. He decided not to say anything to his wife, Elisheva, or to his other two children, because "there's no crying on Shabbat." The Kandel family is a symbol of Greater Israel. They are everywhere—one son in Haifa, another in Carmei Tzur, one in the Old City of Jerusalem, yet another in Hebron. Kfar Pines is near Hadera, one of the greenest and most fertile areas of Israel. Little moshavim, flowers, bungalows, the environmental and religious spirit all combine in a unique blend. The Kandels are also the embodiment of religious Zionism. "If I forget you, O Jerusalem, may my right hand wither," said Yehuda, a hero of the Six-Day War, in front of his daughter's casket. "When a person is forced to bury his child, it is as if the world suddenly comes to a stop," said Eyal Sorek's father, Hanan, one of the founders of a program for foreign volunteers in the army. Yehuda recalled that Yael was a humble woman, "but now you are warriors."

The association Ayalim, created in honor of Yael and Eyal, is their legacy, the child they never had. Through Ayalim, university students from all over Israel, full of idealism, are establishing themselves in the north and south of the country, to strengthen these regions. These pioneers live in poor areas, border cities, and historic centers, making themselves available to the local communities and working to improve the lives of the inhabitants in material, educational, and social terms. In desert and rural areas, the students are building villages with their own hands, turning barren and sterile places into centers full of life. Most of the villages are tiny settlements in the Negev or in Galilee, where the students live in temporary trailers and work on humanitarian projects. "People think that this country was founded in 1948, but we are still founding it now," say the leaders of Ayalim.

Yael's mother, Elisheva Kandel, says, "We were never afraid for our children, maybe because of what our family had suffered and the way we brought them up. My husband's family, all of them, were killed in Auschwitz by the Nazis. Only Yehuda's father survived. My husband is a decorated hero of the war of 1967, and he was injured in the war of 1973. We wanted all of our children to study the Torah, to be true Jews to the end. Yael was an idealistic young woman, a special woman. She had volunteered in Eilat to teach immigrant women, many of whom were Ethiopian. She wanted to bring about the Jewish ideal." Yael didn't think of the settlement of Carmei Tzur as a place different from Jerusalem. "For her, living there was the right thing to do. She was the kind of woman who comes to the house one day and tells us, 'I'm getting married, here's my husband.' And she introduced Eyal to us. They thought that Carmei Tzur was the most beautiful place in the world. It is written in the Bible, this land is holy, and no one can change that."

Shai Kandel, a beekeeper, remembers his sister Yael this way: "She was a young woman who wanted to learn the Torah and live as a religious woman. She was an idealist. Her friends say that when she decided to do something, she did it immediately. She loved the land of Israel, as she had been taught by the writings of Rabbi Kook. But knowing wasn't enough for her, she wanted to experience the land. At the time, I was living in Carmei Tzur with my wife and six children; we arrived in 1995. One day Yael called her husband, Eyal, and said, 'I have seen the most beautiful sunset in the world.' They were married after the seven days of mourning for Dr. Gillis, who had been killed by terrorists. And they started their life in a trailer."

Carmei Tzur is on the outskirts of Gush Etzion and particularly exposed to danger. "My parents taught us that the Jews have the right to live where they want, just like in Italy you Italians can choose to live where you want," says Shai. "For us it is the same with *Eretz Yisrael*. And also, the homes of Carmei Tzur are not built on the private land of Palestinians, but on state property." In order to defend his dream, however, Shai has to carry a pistol with him. "Going out without one is dangerous, especially at night." It is extraordinary how much Elisheva, daughter of an Italian family who still has relatives in Rome, exudes Israeli pride. "My husband Yehuda is a *moshavnik*; nature and the land are everything to him. We are a family of beekeepers—that's how we raised our children. One of my sons lives in the Muslim quarter of Jerusalem, because he thinks that a Jew should live near the holy places. And it is a dangerous life. Yael lived a life in which every minute was precious, a life made up of Shabbats, of love and moments of great beauty. Knowledge was everything to Yael; she wanted to learn and learn, to get inside Judaism and fulfill the mitzvoth. Yael believed that Israel, her people, and the Torah were one and the same thing. It is the nation that is holy. And you must be ready to fight for it. I am proud of having raised children like these."

Eyal Sorek was born in Sinai, in the settlement of Yamit. Where the white dunes of the desert trail off into the sea, various Jewish settlements arose between 1967 and 1979, for a total of 600 homes and 2,500 settlers. Today the Egyptians mainly grow apples, figs, and peaches here, having returned following the signing of the peace accords with Israel. After almost thirty years, the ruins and remains of the Israeli residences of Yamit are still in place: broken bits of cement, walls knocked over. On what is left of some walls, there is writing in Hebrew. Weeds and colorful bougainvilleas grow among the chunks of cement. Amid white rubble stands the synagogue, a large, squat building, just one story. Inside is more writing on walls, mostly people's names. There are only a few political statements or religious references: someone has written "Hamas"; someone else, "The light of Islam."

Few in Israel today remember the futurism of Yamit, the dazzlingly white city on the sea with its downtown off-limits to automobiles. The great majority of Israelis were immersed in everyday modernity, sheltered from nationalist and religious fervor. And then there was Yamit, the first extraterritorial Jewish settlement, a sort of Jewish Arcadia. "It was a magical place, like a dream, a new city on the sea, with fascinating new architecture and no cars," explained Dudu Noiman, one of the first settlers of Yamit.

The settlers considered themselves a bit like the first Zionist pioneers in Palestine: as a wall of defense against the enemy armies and the incarnation of Israeli optimism. They were intellectually and physically exuberant, fondly attached to this "lost paradise" in Egyptian territory. At first they lived like Bedouins, and then, from nothing, they built the "pearl of the desert," with schools, streets, homes, shopping centers, synagogues. The Israeli government's brochure said, "Come to Yamit; it will be a model city." The project also foresaw a port, a university open to all, and a prestigious yeshiva. "We saw ourselves as the vanguard of the paradise on the sea," said Gary Mazal, a librarian who immigrated from America, dreaming of Yamit. A newspaper was started, called *Yamiton*. Mazal's wife worked there after quitting her job as a secretary for *Time* magazine. Relations with the Arabs were excellent; Egyptians and Palestinians knew that the Jewish presence meant jobs, economic benefits, and prosperity.

After news arrived of the agreement between Begin and Sadat at Camp David, desperation took hold of the settlement. There were suicides and divorces among the inhabitants. Some of the rabbis compared Yamit to Masada, the fortified city on a spur of rock in the desert in which zealous Jews committed collective suicide to avoid being captured alive by the Roman legionaries who had come to quell the revolt. The destruction of the little village of fishermen, farmers, and pioneers was a genuine disaster for many families. Many had invested everything they had there. Most of the Jewish settlers agreed to return inside the Green Line, while others decided to settle a little ways past it, near Gaza. Geula Cohen, one of the last settlers to leave Yamit on April 26, 1982, said, "The taste of that sacrifice is still in our mouths."

Rina Sorek had been one of the first to move to Yamit. At the time, she could never have imagined that the leader of the Israeli right, Menachem Begin, their idol, would have traded Yamit for peace with Egypt. Rina's family was from Vienna, and those who didn't flee to Israel before the war were slaughtered in the concentration camps. Her husband, Hanan, has Yugoslav origins, and many of his family members also were exterminated by the Nazis and the Fascist legionaries; only two of his cousins were saved. Eyal Sorek was one of Rina and Hanan's four children.

The Soreks lived in the Ogda moshav near Yamit; it was the third Jewish community in Sinai. At the time, all of the communities were secular, with no trace of the religious messianism that dominated in Judea and Samaria. The settlers were in Yamit because of the ideology of the land, and for security reasons. In case of an Egyptian attack, the settlements would be a protective cushion for Israel.

"We had splendid relations with the Arabs," Rina tells us. "I myself got my driver's license in Rafah, something that would be unimaginable today. We had a wonderful life in Yamit, a simple life, centered on work and family. We lived in humble little houses. For us the community was everything. The moshav began with five families, and we grew to fifty-seven after seven years. We were young couples, mostly farmers and tomato producers. We thought of ourselves as 'pioneers,' and there was great consensus between right and left in living in Yamit. Eyal's birth was a great joy, impossible to describe. Our son was born during the Camp David process, and we knew that Yamit was in danger. Eyal was a fascinating child, full of light; he filled the house with joy and from the first moment we knew that he was special. We left Yamit when he was three and a half years old. During the evacuation, even though he was so young, Eyal realized what was going on, and he would be influenced by it for the rest of his life."

For two years, the Soreks were emissaries of the aliyah in New York. In Hebrew they are called *shlichim,* the standard bearers of Zionism in the world. "In those two years, we realized that Israel was stronger than anyone. In the meantime, Eyal became a teenager, and then a man, handsome, intelligent, sensitive, loved by all. He was a consultant for the youth movement, he loved to go on walks, and we also went on frequent outings to get to know every place. Eyal loved farming and sheep."

When Eyal was thirteen, the Soreks moved to Kfar Adumim, a half-religious, half-secular settlement. "We arrived here as secularized Jews with a passion for the devout life. There are all kinds of people in Kfar Adumim—devout, secular, young, old, on the right and on the left. They are tolerant people. There are doctors, lawyers, teachers, police officers, psychologists and social workers. Life in Kfar Adumim fills you with questions: What is a Jew? What is a devout Jew? And a secularized Jew?

These questions were the subject of discussions in our home. Eyal felt the immediacy of the question of faith, of God and of how to live. He had gone to a secular school and had all kinds of friends. After high school, he decided to try a religious yeshiva, in Atzmona, which at the time was part of Gush Katif in Gaza. He was the first secularized student to be admitted to the school. Eyal began to establish a very strong faith; he discovered love and spiritual tranquility."

Then came enlistment in the army special forces. "Military service was very important to Eyal. He was in a secret unit, and we heard very little about him. After his death, we discovered so many stories about him, about his courage and good relations with everyone, soldiers and commanding officers." During his third year in uniform, Eyal announced that he wanted to get married. "He and Yael planned a new life in Carmei Tzur, and after that they wanted to go live in the Old City of Jerusalem. Their community was made up of idealists who love the land."

Eyal's brutal death has not destroyed Rina Sorek's ideals. "Our faith in the people and in the State of Israel has not been diminished by it. On the contrary, it has come out stronger. Our pain and our loss have received a greater significance, reinvigorating our faith and our right to live in Israel. We do not understand the ways of God, but we know that we are part of these in good and in bad."

You can see Jerusalem from atop the arid hill where Psagot sits. In a field just outside one of Psagot's gates, the biblical hero Joshua won a critical battle that helped open the door for the Israelites to settle these same hills some four thousand years ago. The residents of Psagot calculated that 120,000 bullets were fired at the village within the first year of the Second

Intifada. Almost every house has bullet holes in it. The windows are often barricaded with sandbags, and the families have to sleep on the floor. Between this tiny Jewish settlement and the first Arab house is less than a hundred yards—child's play for a precision rifle. In Psagot, life and death are one and the same. This is where Yosef and Hannah Dickstein lived with their ten children, between two and twenty years old. Yosef was a well-known rabbi who had been trained in the yeshiva of Rabbi Kook, the father of religious Zionism. He was murdered on July 26, 2002, near Hebron, along with his wife and their nine-year-old son, Shuvel Zion.

"He was pure and never hurt anyone. He loved to read; he was smart," said Tzvi Yehuda about his little brother Shuvel. In eulogizing his parents, Tzvi Yehuda said they had found their place in Psagot and taught their children to love the land. "Everything that you built was looking to the future. We recognize the price that you paid for your dreams." He noted that his grandfather was a Holocaust survivor, and that his family was willing to make a sacrifice for freedom. His parents were killed "because they were Jews who lived freely in their own land." A plaque was dedicated to the Dickstein family, saying: "This place is sanctified by the blood of martyrs." Samaria—as the settlers call it, by its biblical name—has paid a very high price.

Just a few minutes before the attack, Yosef Dickstein's mother had urged him not to travel to another West Bank settlement to spend Shabbat with friends, but he just said, "Have a peaceful Shabbat" before hanging up. One of his sons, Shlomo, was shot in the arm. He climbed out of the car and searched for the cell phone that his mother usually carried. Seeing that she had been shot repeatedly in the head, he went to his father, who was lying on the ground, still alive. His father said that everything would be okay. Shlomo used the phone to call the army. "The terrorists looked us in the eyes and shot at us," say the children who survived the massacre.

"Yosef and Hannah were optimistic people, full of joy, their eyes full of light," recalls one of their neighbors. "They built their home in Psagot with their whole heart and soul, in spite of the difficulties." One week before he was killed, Rabbi Dickstein looked at his house and said, "We were dreamers, and now we possess the land of the Bible." The Dickstein's second child, their daughter Tzofia, worked as an obstetrician in the most important hospital in Jerusalem, the Hadassah. "My father was a person who loved the people of Israel and his land with his whole heart," she says. "He took the family on walks a lot. He was a happy man; he gave a lot to charity even though he wasn't rich. He provided hospitality in our home for many poor people, and he made them happy. He followed our Bible's rules about joy and happiness. My parents taught me to see life as something that opens up to me from heaven, and that everything is good. I will always remember the blessings of my father, that he loved observing the mitzvoth and giving hospitality."

Tzofia explains how her family had been marked by the Holocaust. "My paternal grandfather came from Poland and went through the Holocaust. My mother's family was rich; they came from Austria, and they left all of their property there just to come to Israel. My parents went to live in Psagot when the Palestinians were firing on it. They wanted to give hope to the people and make them feel stronger about living in *Eretz Yisrael*. Any Israeli could end up like my father. Terror is not only here in Samaria, it is everywhere." Tzofia feels ambivalent: "Angry that my parents left me alone, and grateful to God for leaving my brothers and sisters with me. I miss them a lot." The attack has not extinguished her faith: "Not at all; if anything my faith is even stronger. I love my country. I do not hate the Arabs, I even help them at the hospital to give birth to their children, and hoping that they will not act like my parents' killers. I believe that God only gives a challenge to someone who can face it."

Tzvi Nussbaum commented on the massacre from Rock-
land County, New York. He had been the same age as Shuvel
Dickstein when he was photographed, arms raised in surrender
and wearing a large beret on his head, while the Nazis were
rounding people up in front of the Polsky Hotel in Warsaw. The
photo was published all over the world. "Israel must emerge
victorious—it has to," said Nussbaum. "There is nothing to be
done with those who are willing to sacrifice their own lives in
order to kill us. And I do not believe that it will be different
between the two generations."

It was evening on the feast of Hanukkah and, in observance
of tradition, the ritual candles had been lit behind many of the
windows in the settlement of Emmanuel. Three Hamas militants
with automatic weapons and hand grenades attacked the
No. 189 Egged bus from Tel Aviv. The Tzarfati family was decimated. "They were believers; they never hurt anyone," said Udi
Lieberman, one of the leaders of the Samarian settlements. That
day, David Tzarfati, his brother Hananya, and their father
Ya'akov were killed. "When they heard an explosion nearby, my
sons crouched over me; they shielded me with their bodies," said
Dvora, weeping over the death of her husband and sons. "A few
moments later, the terrorists approached and rained down blows
on us, without any pity." Sylvia Shilon lost her son Gal and her
granddaughter Sarah. "What have they done to my children?" she
kept asking at the funeral. Grandma Kashi said, "Don't bury her,
she was such a happy child. Dear Sarah, you didn't have enough
time to see the world." Ayelet was pregnant when Gal, her husband, was killed. The chief rabbi of Israel, Yisrael Meir Lau,
recited the prayer of Tisha B'Av, the day that commemorates the
destruction of the Temple: "This house will not burn; the children
will heal and comfort their mother and their grandparents." A
rabbi from Emmanuel added, "It is as if the Temple had burned
right before our eyes." Galila Ades also died in the attack. Her
brother said of her, "You are like the martyrs who were killed

sanctifying the name of God in the course of Jewish history." The history of the villages of Samaria is steeped in these words.

Didi Yitzhak, who was killed in Ofra, had immigrated from France twenty years before. One of his uncles said he was an idealist who "loved Israel. Many of us came here thanks to him. He went to Jerusalem every day, and he wasn't afraid of anything." Yitzhak had a handsome, serene face. There is a sign at the entrance to the Ofra settlement: "After the shock of the Yom Kippur War, a group of young people knocked down the Israeli army checkpoint on Mount Hatzor, on the north side of the hill. On April 20, 1975, they didn't go back to Jerusalem. They slept in the 'abandoned base of the Jordanian army' that since then has been known as Ofra."

After the Six-Day War, Israel had found that it had to use an army made up mostly of reservists to control territories stretching from Sharm el-Sheikh (Sinai) to Mount Hermon (Golan Heights), so it seemed like a good idea to plant cells of settlers and adventurous young people along the border. Their job was to stop infiltrations by Palestinian fedayeen, or to watch strategically important corridors so as to prevent surprise attacks. On the steep slopes of the Jordan Valley, a unit of battle-hardened veterans armed with antitank rockets could stall a column of armored enemy vehicles for hours, giving the army precious time to organize its own battle lines.

Ofra has no defensive purpose; it is not close to the Green Line. It is an ideological settlement with the mandate of keeping the territory Jewish, with no guarantee that it will be included in future accords. Many have sacrificed their lives for that tragic dream, like Arieh Hershkovitz, who was shot to death while coming home from work. Some of the people in Ofra are third-generation residents, maybe the grandchildren of someone whom Shimon Peres asked to go live in the West Bank, calling it by its historical name of Judea or Samaria, and asking them to take "civilization and prosperity" there.

Among those people were the parents of Hadas Turgeman and Linoy Saroussi, two fourteen-year-old girls killed in the settlement of Hermesh. "A murderer has killed two flowers," said Asher Ohana, the minister for religious affairs. Udi Lieberman added that "dozens of people were killed in recent years because they wanted to live as free Jews in Samaria." A friend recalled, "Hadas always helped everyone. She wanted to be a model, she was so beautiful. She laughed a lot, and she dreamed of being famous."

Pinchas Gerber lives in the settlement of Karnei Shomron, and for many years he has worked with the victims of terrorism as a social worker. "We must not lose this battle by doing nothing," he tells us. "We must anchor ourselves in the land of the Bible, Samaria, through our religious and ethical values, taking care of our people." Gerber sees the terrorist campaign as another chapter in the history of Jewish suffering. "The Roman Empire killed millions of Jews during its rule of this area. The impact of these events on our national psychology has never been forgotten: it is part of the commemoration of Tisha B'Av. We 'celebrate' the destruction of the Temple through prayer." Those who have survived terror attacks demonstrate a mysterious capacity for recovery. "I have seen people die, I have seen their body parts scattered on the streets and in the buses, and I have had to tell children that their parents have been killed, or husbands that their wives were dead. It is important to understand that many are unable to recover. There are people who are afraid to leave their homes. The children sleep with the lights on and the windows closed. Their trauma is constant, it never goes away. Many survivors say they can't forget the smell of burned flesh. Many of them have eating disorders, problems with sleep and concentration."

Jews from North America, Europe, and the former Soviet Union live in Karnei Shomron, which in Hebrew means "the horns of Samaria." On February 16, 2002, the shopping center was reopening at the end of the Shabbat rest. That evening, a young Palestinian wearing a black sweater went to the middle of the pizzeria. There were two electric wires sticking out of the explosive belt. He was there to bring death. Nehemia Amar, fifteen years old, went to school in an armored bus and wasn't easily distracted; he knew he was "at war." That evening he had convinced his older brother, Moshe, to go with him to the mall. Moshe lost sight of Nehemia for a moment, and that was when the explosion came. Moshe found his little brother dead, in the middle of the pizzeria.

Keren Shatsky was also fifteen years old, the youngest of six children. Everyone loved her. Keren's parents had come to Israel from the United States. Her mother taught English at the school for girls that Keren attended in a nearby settlement. Her father worked at an electronics company. That evening, their daughter had gone out with a dozen or so classmates. She would never come back home. It had been Moriah's idea to go out, and from her hospital bed she kept asking all her friends to forgive her. "I beg you, I beg you, forgive me. If it hadn't been for me, we would all still be alive and well." At the funeral, the rabbi said, "We raised you here because we are convinced that we have every right to do so. Seeing you so united, so supportive and able to control your frustration, we, your teachers, are very proud of you." While the students were saying their last goodbyes to Keren, they were already working to repair the damage at the settlement.

This is how Steve Shatsky remembers his daughter: "Keren was our youngest daughter, and we and the five older children adored her. She was everyone's little princess, delicate, gracious, and kind. Her appearance reflected what was inside her. She laughed easily, and she was always ready to do good. She didn't need us to discipline her, and we heard her friends talk about her loyalty. She seemed pure and innocent in a way that is so rare today. Maybe her soul was too noble for this world. She was the sweetest daughter that any parent could wish for. I am thankful for all of the time we were given with her."

Steve says, "The Jewish faith demands that we try to live in the land of Israel. Because most of those who have lived here did not choose it, it is a privilege for me to be able to do so. It is an honor to be one of those the world calls 'settlers'; they are the finest people I know, they live according to the highest ideals, they are fighting for the return of the Jews to their own ancient land, laying the groundwork for later spiritual development. My faith has helped me to overcome our loss. I am talking about the survival of the soul, about the last judgment of God and the resurrection of the dead." But Steve does not trust the state as it has been structured in recent years. "Our government, the legal system, military, and media have become post-Zionist. The faith and hope that I foster are found only in our Creator. The most firm believers among us compare themselves to the Lord's spouse, and it is this marriage to which we are faithful. Our hope is in his redemption."

One of the Shatskys' neighbors is Sondra Oster Baras, a Cleveland native and a leader in the dialogue between Israel and Christian groups. She was one of the very first Americans to move here. "Karnei Shomron is a beautiful community from a geographical, social, and spiritual point of view. The first time I came here was in 1982, and there were only a few trailers on the hillside. I slept in a tent with some friends. It was January and I was freezing, but I came away from it full of love. My husband and I lived in the United States, but we planned our aliyah, and in 1984 the dream became a reality. The hill was deserted, except for a few trees. We fell in love with the place: the mountains, the fresh air, and awareness of our ancestors. This is the heart of biblical Samaria. On our first Shabbat, we were at the home of some friends, and our children became friends immediately. The people here take care of everyone; no one is anonymous."

This is also the reaction when there is a terrorist attack. "When someone is killed or injured in an attack, his neighbor cleans his house, cooks for him, takes care of his children. We are a mixed community, religious, traditional, and secularized; there is a lot of respect for the various lifestyles. When terrorism strikes we react like a family, because these people were killed for the reason that they were Jews. It could have been my family. They hadn't hurt anyone, they had only tried to develop this land and to live in peace with their neighbors. I think that someday there will be peace in all the land of Israel, but I don't have much hope for an agreement in the immediate future. The Arabs have instilled tremendous hatred in their children, and it will take generations for the damage to be repaired. I raised five children here, and now they are all over the world studying. I hope they will get married and settle down in Samaria and Judea, or in some other place in Israel. I raised my children to be productive members of society and to construct a wonderful life for themselves and for future generations."

Several months earlier, in August 2001, Steve Bloomberg of Karnei Shomron lost his wife to sniper fire; she was five months pregnant. Steve is now in a wheelchair, like his daughter Tzipora. He had made the aliyah from London in 1978 and served as a medic in the Israeli army. It was the fulfillment of a dream. Then he met Tehiya, a nurse from Netanya, and they were married. They moved to Neveh Tzuf, and later to Ginot Shomron, which was close to Steve's work as an engineer at Israel Aircraft Industries, and is now part of Karnei Shomron. Tehiya worked in the community clinic and also in Emmanuel. "She kept an assortment of first aid products at home and even had a blood pressure gauge, and was always willing to assist and treat people in her home at any hour, even on Shabbat," recalls Rina

Gruber, a friend of the Bloomberg family. "Yet she never gave anyone the impression that they were imposing or disturbing her. No matter how busy she was, she always welcomed people calmly and with a big smile on her face."

Steve remains strong, determined, and deeply committed to Israel. "I grew up in England. In school I learned the Bible and felt that I belonged to this land," he recounts. "For me, the places mentioned in the Bible, like Beit El and Hebron, where I studied for a short time, mean much more than modern Israel, like Tel Aviv. I was happy to build a house for myself in the hills of Samaria. After my wife was killed and I was seriously injured, while I was in the hospital, a journalist asked me if I was going to leave Samaria. My first reaction, without thinking about it, was that our murderers wanted to drive us out, so I was staying here. Since then, I have stayed in Samaria, and every day I pass near the place where they attacked us. Staying here and rebuilding my life is the only response to terrorism."

This determination to rebuild is part of the Jewish character. "There is a will to continue this battle that is not new; it did not begin sixty years ago with the Jewish state, because the Jewish people have been fighting to return to their own land for two thousand years," Bloomberg continues. "This is the force that has guided me here in Israel. With a family of five children, with my oldest daughter and I in a wheelchair, I remarried with a woman who has five children of her own, so now we are a happy family with ten children. I believe that with the help of God, we must look at the positive things that he has given us. I use the part of my body that still works, and I feel like a complete person." Steve says that he was literally yanked out of the solitude of death and suffering. "I was in rehabilitation for six months, and I learned to live in a wheelchair. For a long time I didn't want to talk to the media. When I returned home, I received amazing help from the community and from my friends, who allowed me to combat solitude."

In spite of all the violence, Steve has not lost faith in his people and his country: "I always try to look at the whole picture, not at the individual incident. For two thousand years we have been oppressed, and we have defended ourselves with only one state and one army. We waited for two thousand years to return to our land, and during the Holocaust we saw what happens to our people in a foreign country. For this reason, it is essential for us to live here even at the expense of our life if necessary, in order to defend the land in such a way that our children and future generations can live in safety. Even if we don't agree politically with our government, having a state of our own is always better than the alternative. It's enough for us to think about the Second World War to understand what has been done to the Jewish people when it hasn't been able to defend itself."

One year after leaving the hospital, Steve Bloomberg brought a lawsuit against the European Union because its funds indirectly financed Palestinian terrorism. "Most of that money didn't go to the needs of the people, but to building up the terrorist infrastructure. We found it unjust that European taxes should go to the terrorists. Although the lawsuit never had a direct effect, the EU decided with an internal vote to increase supervision of the money. We are still fighting terrorism."

Everyone here remembers what happened to the Shabo family of Itamar, near Nablus. Rachel was killed along with three of her children, Avishai, Zvika, and Neria. Their father, Boaz, was in another house in Itamar, and in the distance saw his own home burning until it was completely devastated. "When we arrived, they were taking away the bodies. Boaz and I started to count them," said one of the boys, Meir. "Nothing in the house remained intact. The only thing that wasn't devoured by the flames was the cabinet where the Jewish sacred texts were kept." The children here grow up reading the story of the ten martyrs of the Talmud: The Romans found Rabbi Haninah ben Tardion with a copy of the Torah in his arms. They wrapped him in it and burned him. His students asked him, "Master, what do you see?" He answered, "The parchment burning, the letters flying in the air."

Thousands attended the funeral for the Shabos. Five years later, Boaz would go to Sderot to help the citizens of the community hardest hit by the rockets of Hamas and Islamic Jihad. "Helping others gives me strength," he says. "I tell my children that their father goes wherever he is needed, and they are happy for me."

Boaz Shabo feels as if he is living through a "mini Holocaust." He explains, "The Holocaust was the destruction of a people; entire communities were destroyed and whole families wiped out. The destruction this time is smaller in scale, the community will survive and so will the state, but there is destruction, and just like in those terrible days, whole families are again being wiped out and the only motive for killing them is their Judaism, not where they live. The Jewish presence here is what disturbs them." Boaz says that the attack was a blow to his faith. "I find myself often talking to the Holy One Blessed Be He and asking him: why did you take the kids, the wife? What bad did they do in the world you created? My faith wavered. When I pray each morning, it's more for Rachel and the kids. But on second thought, I said to myself, 'Boaz, the Holy One Blessed Be He saved you because you were delayed at work and decided that your remaining kids will have a father; because if you had been there, you might also have been killed."

Itamar is in an unusual location in Samaria, with a view of biblical Shechem and the mountains of Gerizim and Ebal. The mayor's wife, Leah Goldsmith, says that "everything you see

here is imbued with biblical grandeur and Jewish nobleness."
Leah is convinced that God created these mountains to be "the
arms of the land of Israel." The Israelis who live there talk about
the "martyrs of Itamar." One of them is the writing teacher and
Holocaust survivor Binyamin Herling, who was killed when
Palestinians opened fire on dozens of Israelis who were going
to see the remains of Joshua's altar on Mount Ebal in October
2002. His son called on his friends not to avenge the death.
Some of the people in Itamar call him a *tzadik,* the righteous
man of Jewish tradition, or a "herald of the Torah." Three years
after his death, a beautiful Torah scroll was dedicated to him.
Herling was one of the many soldier-scholars who had emerged
from the Kerem B'Yavneh yeshiva, whose graduates follow the
motto of Poland's Shraga Schmeidler: "Exile yourself in some
place of the Torah." Shraga had left the security of Tel Aviv to
go live "on the front."

A Palestinian gunman killed three yeshiva students in Itamar on May 28, 2002. One of the victims, Netanel Riachi, was
the first native-born Jew in the community of Kochav Ya'akov
in Samaria. He was very devoted to his family, and he loved
Jewish history. Gilad Stiglitz, fourteen years old, was playing
basketball outside the school when he was shot. He wrote letters to the stars of the Maccabi Tel-Aviv basketball team. Avraham Siton lived in Shiloh, and he believed in the dream of
Moshe Dayan: "We have returned to Shiloh and Anathot, never
to leave them again." Avraham was known for his incredible
sense of humor; he respected everyone and was always ready to
help others. His parents were immigrants from Argentina,
where they had distinguished themselves as leaders of the large
Jewish community.

A teenage boy who lived in Itamar, Eliyahu Asheri, was kidnapped and killed by terrorists from Hamas while hitchhiking
back home from Jerusalem in 2006. His story resembles that of
Daniel Pearl, the reporter for the *Wall Street Journal* who was

kidnapped and killed in Pakistan because he was a Jew. "We know that the sun sets in the evening, but you, Eliyahu, you shone like the sun and yet you set in mid-afternoon," his grandfather said at his funeral. His mother, Miriam, said, "Dear Eliyahu, you ascended to heaven just like the prophet Elijah," referring to the Jewish tradition according to which Elijah "ascended into heaven in a whirlwind" and was admitted into paradise without having died. "We ask you now to intercede with the Almighty Lord on behalf of the Jewish people." Eliyahu's father, Yitro Asheri, appeared on television and said, "The fact that my son was kidnapped could be called a command from on high. It is as if God wanted my son in heaven to defend the people of Israel." The whole country was touched by how calm he was.

Yitro had been an electrician in Australia, named Cliff Harris, before he converted to Judaism. He was a man of "all-consuming faith" in the protection of God, according to Yossi Engel, the rabbi who presides at the synagogue in Adelaide where he converted. Cliff had done volunteer work in New Guinea and then had gone to an Israeli collective community, the secular Kibbutz Hatzerim. "There I witnessed the simple morality of the kibbutz members, who were not religious but had a deep moral way about them," he says. "I began asking people where Jewish morality comes from and was eventually given a copy of the *Ethics of Our Fathers* (a Mishnaic tract recording lessons in ethics from the foremost conveyors of Torah throughout the generations). It was like water for a thirsty heart." He began studying Judaism back in Adelaide, but was encouraged by members of the small Jewish community to return to Israel as soon as possible to learn more. Six months after embracing Judaism, he made the aliyah to Israel.

There, Yitro fell in love with the profession of Torah copyist. The scribe, the *sofer,* is not merely a copyist or calligrapher. On Sinai, Moses, who had no pen or paper, carved the Lord's words on tablets of stone. The scribe who dedicates himself to creating a Torah scroll destined to be used in the liturgy at the synagogue must do perfect work: just a stroke too many or too few and the whole is ruined, the scroll loses value. Hebrew writing is a form of art. The Hebrew alphabet is not a simple representation, it is the code for accessing the divine reality. "The scrolls of the Torah are the community," explains Raiah Harnik, whose son Guni was killed in the Lebanon War in 1982. "Synagogues have been abandoned and destroyed, but the Torah was saved from the synagogues that were burning in my city, Berlin. The Jewish quarter of Jerusalem was abandoned during the War of Independence, but the evacuees tried to save the scrolls of the Torah. Even when they were forced to leave behind their weapons and the dead. The scroll of the Torah is 'us'; it is eternal." This is the mission of Yitro Asheri.

"My job is to transcribe the sacred Scriptures," Yitro explains, interrupting his painstaking work. "I started after I converted to Judaism, when I learned to separate the clean from the unclean. The copyist recreates sanctity through the sanctification of the Name of God, letter by letter." The community of Itamar, which welcomed him as a brother, commissioned him to do a Sefer Torah after the death of his son Eliyahu. "One of the most holy things in Judaism is the scroll of the Torah. The memory of my son is not on a stone or a monument, but in this, something that is alive," says Yitro.

Despair has never conquered the heart of this man who seems to come from another time, with his long white beard and spartan life among the hills of Samaria. "We have our suffering, but we know that God has a job for Eliyahu, that he needs him for something more important," Yitro says. "We must accept the bad just as we thank him for the good. It's a terrible price to pay, but it's God's will. And the people must understand what a gift God's gift is, the land of Israel. The people need love, and they need to be educated." Referring to the many who have died in terrorist attacks, he says, "God chose them at that exact moment. In the scriptures it says that God judges among the nations. I have never lost hope, because in the Talmud it says, 'I want to live at this time.'" Yitro Asheri says he has never lost his faith in Israel.

Arieh Agranionic died defending Itamar in 2001. When asked why there was no one else with Arieh when terrorists attacked him, the settlement's chief of security, Yossi Levite, replied, "Would you volunteer here?" Arieh's son Oren recalls, "My father came from Brazil at the age of twenty-two. In 1978, he was the first to go to Ariel. When the community began to prosper, he decided to move to a more isolated settlement in Samaria. He was looking for peace and quiet. His objective was to keep the land in Jewish hands. I will carry my father's dream with me."

Meir Lixenberg also lived in Itamar. "Meir, Abba and Ima have always instilled in us the values of love for the people, love for the land," said his sister Gila. "Love in the way of our fathers. Meir, you loved being close to the holy people, so humble but also so great."

All over Itamar, the people are strong, welcoming, determined to stay in spite of the bombs and the sneak attacks, in spite of the clear contradictions posed by the peace process. On a clear day you can see Mount Hermon as well as the towers of Shalom Center in Tel Aviv. Almost twenty-five years ago, Itamar consisted of two tiny blocks of matchbox houses. The glorious hills surrounding the settlement seemed to mystify the newcomers. The homes had no telephones. A generator supplied electricity. When it shut down, the silence could be heard to the end of the world. The community of Itamar is one of the most frequently targeted sites in the Territories. But the attacks have not yet taken a visible toll on the stoic, unflinching settlers.

According to Itamar's mayor, Moshe Goldsmith, who immigrated from the United States, "Those who gave their lives to construct the land of Israel and settle here are among the most righteous persons walking this earth. I'm talking about their determination to attain their dreams and objectives in spite of the risks involved in this clear testimony of total devotion to the Jewish nation. Obviously, they would have preferred to stay alive and reach the same goals. We do not aspire to pay the price of blood, but we are not afraid of the danger if there is no alternative. Judaism values life more than anything else in the world. Through the sanctification of this world we will earn the redemption of all humanity and the world that is to come. Those who give their own lives are martyrs, and they will be seated in the highest places in the world to come, even if a Jew does not choose martyrdom, but life. It is God who decides which individuals will be martyred; the answers lie with him."

Goldsmith's wife is the daughter of a Holocaust survivor—the only survivor among the eleven members of his family. "After terrorism, we rebuild our lives in the footsteps of those who have given their lives for the land of Israel," Moshe continues. "By doing this, we sanctify those who pay that price. It doesn't matter how difficult it is, we will never lose our hope and our faith in our people."

The chief rabbi of the army, Avichai Ronzki, is also from Itamar. He "came back" to his faith while fighting under the command of Ariel Sharon on the Egyptian front. "We were supposed to be a nation of priests, a holy nation. We are here to be a light among the nations."

Since the arrival of the first pioneers in 1882, the idea of building has motivated the Jews in Israel. "It will be the settlers, the farmers, and not the soldiers and politicians, who will create the State of Israel," said David Ben-Gurion. That was practically the motto of Ido Zoldan's family. In November 2007,

Ido was murdered at age twenty-nine while returning to his home in the settlement of Shavei Shomron, in Samaria. His body, covered with his inseparable religious *tallit,* was accompanied by his wife and two children, his parents, three brothers, two sisters, and his grandfather who had survived the Holocaust.

Ido always described himself as "a simple working man." He was a man of modest habits, even an ascetic, immersed in the Jewish tradition and the sense of community. He followed the rule that every seventh year, in the year called *shmita,* the land must be allowed to rest, and whatever it produces is infinitely holy. "He loved the land and the people of Israel," his friends say. "He was always happy, faithful to the Golani Brigade and to the land, a Jewish laborer 'from head to toe.' He was always ready to take on dangerous tasks, without thinking about himself. A generous friend, smiling, who spoke little and did a lot." Ido had helped young Ethiopian immigrants in the Bnei Akiva movement, born in the bosom of religious Zionism. He also studied at the yeshiva in Beit El, center stage of biblical history.

It was in thinking of Beit El that Ariel Sharon described Israel as "the only place in the world where the Jews have the right and the power to defend themselves on their own." And it was he, Sharon, who designated Beit El, a minuscule settlement in the West Bank, as the first to be evacuated. Not even the Labor Party leader Ehud Barak, the most decorated man in Israel's history, had gone so far in the offer he made to Yasser Arafat in 2000.

The six thousand citizens are proud that their address is in the Bible. Countless synagogues and churches in the United States have taken their name from Beit El, or Bethel, one of the pivotal landmarks of biblical history. The traditional hymn "We Are Climbing Jacob's Ladder" is an integral part of the American Sunday school heritage. It was on these rocky hills, the Hebrew Bible says, that Jacob dreamed about a ladder reaching to heaven, on which angels descended, and God told him, "The ground whereon thou liest to thee I will give it, and to thy seed." The next morning, Jacob set a stone for a pillar, poured oil on it and called the place Beit El. Its biblical topography also suggests a defensive use.

On top of the hill, the settlers have built a self-contained community of parks and walkways, synagogues, shops, gymnasiums and swimming pools. Nearby is Ba'al Hatzor, the highest point in the West Bank and today the site of a large Israeli military base. Beit El is also a few miles from Ramallah, the center of recruitment for Palestinian suicide bombers. Sitting shivah, the traditional period of mourning, is not rare in Beit El. They have buried many of their own who have been killed by terrorists. Beit El has the dubious distinction of sustaining the first serious casualty of the Intifada. In December 1987, Dov Kalmanovitz had a petrol bomb hurled into his car. He was horrendously burned, but survived. Haim Mizrahi was not so lucky. A yeshiva student, he supplemented his income by buying eggs from Arabs and selling them in the settlement. Five masked men seized him, stabbed him repeatedly, and burned his body in his own car. The killers belonged to the Fatah organization, headed by Yasser Arafat. Today, most settlers travel in armor-plated buses to avoid falling victim to the frequent ambushes by Palestinian gunmen.

It takes a kind of courage to live in Beit El. It takes a kind of madness as well. What can possibly be the future here? For Yoel Tzur, the Jews of Beit El are the instruments of a sacred cause. His wife and youngest son were killed by Arabs in a drive-by shooting near Beit El in 1996. "The killer can kill the body, but not the spirit," said Yoel, the son of Jews who came from Vienna in 1936. "Religion is constantly getting stronger in a way unparalleled in the history of the Jewish people. The Jewish land of Israel will be a light unto the nations, spreading morality and justice through all the world."

Ido Zoldan chose to study in Beit El because it is the House of God, where Abraham pitched his tent and built an altar for the Lord; where his grandson Jacob, fleeing from Esau, dreamed about the ladder and the angels. During the Babylonian captivity, the elders sent a priest to Beit El to teach the people who had been left without any guidance. It is like Hebron.

"In 2003, we decided to move to Homesh," says Ido's wife, Tehila. Homesh boasts a spectacular view of Samaria and Galilee. The village, especially the older part built in 1977 by secularist pioneers, has the modest and poetic charm of the first settlements; it was expanded in 1987 when a group of artists, sculptors, painters, and poets turned it into an artists' commune and a permanent exhibition among the olive trees. "We loved that place; it is the highest point in Samaria. We loved our friends there. We all wanted to strengthen Homesh, and we believed in the importance of rooting ourselves in the places of *Eretz Yisrael*. Our first child, Aharon, was born in Homesh, and he was circumcised there, an exciting moment for our family." The village was fenced in, and you could enter only after the gate was opened and you presented identification. Soldiers were stationed all around for the residents' protection. Without those soldiers, the Jewish inhabitants would have been massacred by their neighbors. In all of Samaria, there was hardly another settlement so isolated and so tightly surrounded by hostile villages: Silat al-Dahar, Bazariyah, Ramin, Burqa, al-Fandaqumiyah, Beit Imrin. Homesh was a place eroded by despair and struck by death.

In 2005, Sharon evacuated Homesh, along with other West Bank settlements. The Zoldans tried to resist. "Ido felt betrayed by the government and by those who had founded Homesh twenty-five years before. He tried by every legal means possible to oppose the withdrawal. Our second child, Rachel, was born in Shavei Shomron. Through the window we could see the mountain of Homesh. We never gave up on the possibility of living in peace with our Arab neighbors, but in the end we understood that their only objective was to drive us away from here." Finally, Tehila talks about her husband: "He was a happy man, optimistic, a head of his family who prized it above everything else. He had very strong principles, and he lived for these. His faith had been firm since he was a child; he lived the Torah without compromise. He was devout, but he was also admired and loved by all of his friends."

His family recalls that Ido believed in the idea of Jewish labor "to establish a holy and perfect nation," and that "he woke up every morning with a smile. He enjoyed the sensation of direct contact with the earth. Ido mocked the contractors who humiliated the Arab laborers." He referred to his work clothes as "my uniform." His mother says, "Ido taught us a rare lesson, not only about how to combine the sacred and profane, but about how to live a wonderful life. He came into the world pure, and nothing disfigured his sanctity. He was a *hasid,* a *tzadik,* the Torah was his life and the memory of his soul." A few months before he was killed, Ido had built a turret from which he could look out on the ruins of Homesh—to which the Israelis would return for a few hours in the spring of 2008, to celebrate the sixtieth anniversary of the founding of their state.

The sky was gray at Ido Zoldan's funeral. The most important leaders of the Jewish communities in the Palestinian Territories were there. Rabbi Daniel Shiloh said, "If you were here with us, you would say, 'Don't weep—build, protect the project and continue forward.' But forgive us, it is difficult not to weep over the best of our sons." Another rabbi, Menachem Felix, called Ido a *tzadik* who worked the land with his ten fingers.

As the first day of Passover was coming to an end in 2002, the Gavish family gathered at their home in Elon Moreh.

"Not one, but a hundred Elon Morehs," Menachem Begin had stressed during the 1977 electoral campaign that would bring Likud to power for the first time. "We were granted our right to exist by the God of our fathers at the glimmer of the dawn of human civilization four thousand years ago," Begin said. "And for this inalienable right, which has been sanctified in Jewish blood from generation to generation, we have paid a price unexampled in the annals of nations."

Elon Moreh, like other settlements around Nablus—such as Bracha, Yitzhar, and Itamar—is both geographically and ide-ologically detached from much of Israeli society. Most Israelis do not know where Elon Moreh is, and those who do would never dream of visiting, even in a bullet-proof bus. Elon Moreh is a leper colony.

But Elon Moreh is also in the heart of biblical Samaria. It is the place where the Lord made a covenant with Abraham, to give this territory to him and to his descendants forever. In the account of Genesis, the Lord promises Abraham's descendants the territory from the river of Egypt to the Euphrates. Today, Elon Moreh is inhabited by people like Reuven Berger, a Mes-sianic shepherd who works and prays for reconciliation be -tween Jews and Arabs. "The scripture speaks of the promise of this territory to the people of Israel, and of a restoration that God will bring about physically and spiritually. God has a plan. He has a plan of blessing. He has a plan of peace. And Israel cannot be ignored. Israel is at the center of the plan. This is the reason why the nations, with their hatred for Israel, are depriv-ing themselves of the blessings that God has for them."

After the war of 1967, the State of Israel did not allow its citizens to stay there for more than twenty-four hours. "From Jerusalem to Afula, there was no Jewish presence," said Rabbi Menachem Felix. The army had removed many clandestine tents, before Yitzhak Rabin permitted the construction of the first core of the settlement. The isolation of Elon Moreh forced the community to be self-sufficient, with its famous rabbinical college, its school for copying the Torah, its alternative medicine and biblical tourism.

Everything changed for the community in 1981 when Adam Zertal, an archaeologist at Haifa University, discovered a structure on nearby Mount Ebal. Between 1869 and 1922, French and British archaeological expeditions had explored the summit in vain, looking for the altar built by Joshua on instructions from Moses, according to the biblical account, after the Israelites had crossed into Canaan. Zertal believes that he found the altar, and that it proves the Israelites crossed the Jordan and entered Canaan just as the Bible says they did. This is where Joshua allotted the Promised Land among the twelve tribes, he says, and where the Israelites "became a people," as the Bible puts it.

A sign at the settlement of Elon Moreh quotes Jeremiah 31:5, "Again you shall plant vineyards on the mountains of Samaria." Menachem Brody, who immigrated from Maine twenty-eight years ago and raised a family in Elon Moreh, runs archaeology tours supporting a literal interpretation of the Hebrew Bible. On one such tour, passing through numerous army checkpoints in the occupied West Bank, he traces the Way of the Patriarchs, the road traveled by Abraham according to Genesis.

Elon Moreh is also unique for its large number of Christian converts to Judaism. Most of them are Peruvians, who have changed their names from Maria Teresa to Miriam, from Humberto to Yosef, from Segundo to Zerubavel. The driving force behind their aliyah was Rabbi Eliyahu Avichail, the leading authority on the Lost Tribes of Israel, the communities presumed to be of Jewish origin that have preserved Jewish traditions while assimilating in part to the surrounding environment and culture.

David and Rachel Gavish were part of the initial group of settlers in Elon Moreh, the Gush Emunim (Bloc of the

Faithful), those most convinced of the ideological and religious mandate of the settlements. The Gavishes were chatting in their living room on March 28, 2002, with five of their seven children, their daughter-in-law, a granddaughter, and Rachel's father, Yitzhak Kanner. The terrorist let loose with a hail of gunfire, killing Rachel and Yitzhak instantly. Rachel's son Avraham, who "knew every hill in Samaria and went walking without a map," died soon afterward. David later died under the surgeon's knife. Avraham's pregnant wife, Na'ama, was in the next room with their two-year-old daughter, Daria. Hearing the gunshots, Na'ama immediately jumped under the kitchen table, clamping a hand hard over the mouth of her daughter, who had started to cry. The terrorist, blinded by homicidal fury, entered the room but didn't see them. Na'ama was able to flee through the side door with her daughter in her arms, while neighbors who had arrived within seconds returned fire on the terrorist. The other children—ages 19, 18, 16, and 14—were on the second floor, and escaped through the window with the help of neighbors who brought an improvised ladder. If it hadn't been for their quick response, the massacre would have been even more terrible. As it was, four Jews died.

David had worked as a teacher at the yeshiva of Karnei Shomron. "It will be difficult to think of this place without David," said the school's director. "Thousands of families are grateful to him for the education of their children." His wife Rachel, fifty, was an adviser at the women's college of Elon Moreh. She had also spent some time directing the school for all the female students in the area. They were a very close couple; David's sister Bela said that they never could have survived without each other, and that the only bitter consolation is that they died together. Rachel's father, Yitzhak, lived inside the Green Line. He often went to visit his daughter's family, and he had great respect for their decision to live in a place that was so dangerous but so important to them.

Their son Avraham was on leave from the army, where he was a career officer in an elite unit. That day his weapon was not within reach. After he had been mortally wounded, he crawled toward the stairs and shouted to his brother to bring down his weapon, but he was shot again and killed. At the funeral his wife, Na'ama, said: "Avraham, love of my life, I know that it's not considered proper for women to speak at funerals, but I can't stay silent. I have to tell you that I will be a mother, a father, a grandfather to all of your brothers and sisters who have been left without their big brother. And know that I will watch over our daughter, and over the child to be born. You always told me that you trusted me, that in dangerous situations I would be able to defend them. You've seen, I didn't disappoint you, I saved her even if I almost had to suffocate her to keep her from crying."

One of the other children, Menashe, explains: "Living in Elon Moreh means proclaiming the right to settle in the land of Israel, and in particular where the Jewish history of the nation of Israel unfolds. When our father Abraham entered the land of Israel, he came here to Elon Moreh in answer to the call of God. It is well known that Joseph, the son of Jacob, is buried near here, in Shechem. The settlement is called Elon Moreh, as is written in the Bible: 'Abraham crossed the country to the place of Shechem, to the oak of Moreh.' My father and mother were among the founders of Elon Moreh, and more generally among the first settlers of Samaria. They took part in all eight attempts to settle here. The Bible prescribes the obligation of settling in the places of Jewish history, which is why my parents were so determined to put up a fight where Abraham, the father of the Jewish nation, had sojourned. My parents taught us in the way of Abraham, and that is why they named their oldest son Avraham. My parents and my brother fought their entire lives to live in the land of Israel, and to allow other generations to live here. It is our Promised Land. It is for these

reasons that my father, my mother, my brother, and my grandfather fought and died, as Jews in Israel. May God avenge their
blood."

Menashe describes his father, David Gavish, as a genuine
man of the Torah. "His family came here from Germany in
1934. They were very Zionist and contributed to founding Kibbutz Afikim on the Jordan. My grandfather's sister had been
killed by the Nazis. My father was a teacher who had adopted
the way of the Bible after his military service, after getting a
degree in economics and studying for eight years in the yeshiva.
It was natural to him to follow the rules of the Torah, to settle in
Israel and declare that Israel was for the Jewish people. He had
taught in many schools, and always tried to instill the way of
the Torah in his students. He always demanded a lot from himself, even in the most difficult things—that was how he lived
and died. We are part of the war to revive the land and the people of Israel. Enemies have fought us in every decade, and even
when we left every part of the world to found this little independent state, no longer in foreign hands, they fought us. In all
this, the settlers are strong and devoted people, they are believers and ideologues, good people with strong motivations, who
have not chosen the easy life, but a life of faith, and their
strength drove them on without a moment of weakness."

His mother, Rachel, was a *sabra,* a woman born in Israel.
She was the daughter of Holocaust survivors—her mother from
Bergen-Belsen, her father from the labor camps in Siberia.
"Rachel was raised in a home where there was a sense of having
lost everything, where education and knowledge were revered,"
says Menashe. "Her mother, Leah, had seen her whole family
die, and after the war she was taken in by the Bet Halutzot in
Haifa, where orphans were taken. Rachel had many talents: she
was an excellent writer, and she loved dancing, singing, acting,
volunteering. She played the piano every day." After her military service, Rachel studied anthropology and literature, and

then worked as a teacher and librarian. "She wanted to learn as much as possible; she wanted to study the human soul. After years of teaching, she got a job in a nursing home and then as the manager of Elon Moreh College. She was always full of joy, and as the daughter of survivors she didn't want to miss anything in life. Her heart was sensitive to pain and sadness."

Menashe Gavish recounts how he was able to go on after the massacre of his family. "I found myself alone to fight. I had to survive, without time or energy for my personal growth. There are moments of desperation, because the system doesn't take care of us, even though there are many who have helped us. Living in Elon Moreh isn't easy; you have to go work in the nearby cities, and there's always the fear and stress of driving on the streets, especially at night. But it is a special place, magical and pastoral, it gives you calm and serenity, things you can't find in the city. The people of Elon Moreh sacrifice their own lives for Israel. They live far from the cities; they are connected to the land. I get my strength today from my wife and my two children, from the teaching of my parents and from the unity of my relatives. My parents taught me excellence, persistence, hard work, personal love and attention. They taught us to love Israel, to offer ourselves voluntarily. Our home was the combination of my father's determination and my mother's inner peace."

What happened to the Gavishes brings to mind Smadar Haran, not a settler but a secular Israeli mother. On April 22, 1979, the terrorist Samir Kuntar led a group of four guerrillas who, leaving from Tyre aboard a raft, landed at around midnight on the beach of Nahariya, an Israeli city about seven miles south of the Israel-Lebanon border. The four came across an Israeli police officer and killed him on the spot. Next they entered a building at No. 61 Jabotinski Street, and broke into the Haran family's apartment before police reinforcements could arrive. The terrorists took Danny hostage, together with his four-year-old daughter, Einat. Her mother, Smadar, was able to hide in a loft with her two-year-old daughter, Yael, and a neighbor. "I will never forget," Smadar recounts, "the joy and the hatred in the voices of Kuntar's men while they were going around the house looking for us, firing assault rifles and throwing grenades. I knew that if they heard Yael crying, they would throw a grenade into our hiding place and kill us all. So I put my hand over her mouth to keep her from shouting. Huddled in there, I thought of my mother's stories about when she hid from the Nazis during the Holocaust." Tragically, in the stress and confusion Smadar accidentally smothered her daughter Yael to death, realizing too late what had happened. In the meantime, Kuntar and his men dragged Danny and little Einat to the beach, where a shootout with Israeli policemen and soldiers began. Then Samir Kuntar shot Danny in the back at point-blank range, in front of his daughter, submerging him in the ocean to make sure he was dead. Immediately afterward, Kuntar was seen killing the little girl by smashing her skull open against the rocks with the butt of his rifle. He has always proudly defended the "mission" carried out in 1979 in Nahariya. Today Samir Kuntar is a free man in Lebanon.

Rabbi Hillel Lieberman had lived next door to the Gavishes in Elon Moreh. When he heard news of an attack at Joseph's Tomb in 2000, he left the village on foot, although his wife and children tried to stop him. "I have to save the books of the Torah," he said. He never made it back home. His mutilated body was found in Nablus. As in times past, what stirred up the anti-Semites was the sight of the long robe, the beard, the sidelocks.

In the Ukrainian city of Berdychiv, on January 4, 1919, militants stopped children who were studying the Torah, asking,

"Jew?" And then shot them in the forehead. Others made them march singing the *Ma Yafith,* the ancient song of Shabbat, and then shot them one by one. To those who offered money, they said, "We want your life!" The Aryan horde flung itself against the rabbis and great scholars of the Torah with spectacular dedication. During the Holocaust, it was the mistake of the Jewish councils to think that the Jews would be "useful," that the Germans would need watchmakers, dentists, and tailors. In Vilnius, where all the dentists were Jewish, they were the first to be killed. The "Jerusalem of the North," the city in which the most valuable editions of the Babylonian Talmud were printed, was purged of all its Jews. A few years earlier, the Cossacks had cut out their tongues to keep them from chanting the Psalms, and gouged out their eyes. They shaved the men and forced them to eat their own beards. They stripped the men and forced them to hold hands before shooting them.

Joseph's Tomb is a tiny, half-derelict stone compound in the heart of a residential district in Shechem (Nablus). Many Jews believe it to be the final burial place of the son of the biblical patriarch Jacob; it is one of the most hallowed sites of the Jewish people. Shechem, the first place that Abraham stopped after entering the Holy Land, is where God promised him: "I will give this land to your offspring" (Genesis 12:7). Jacob, settling outside Shechem upon his return to the Holy Land from Haran, bought a field adjoining the city (Genesis 33:18–19), and in that plot the remains of his son Joseph were interred after Joshua and the Israelites conquered the land (Joshua 24:32). It was Joseph who was sold into slavery in Egypt by his jealous brothers and then rose to the heights of power among the Egyptians by interpreting the pharaoh's dreams and presiding over Egypt's success in confronting seven years of famine.

Joseph's Tomb is iconic of the fate of Jewish holy sites. With the withdrawal of Israeli troops from much of the West Bank in 1995, the Jewish tombs were transformed into isolated enclaves, rooted in religious fervor but languishing in hostile territory. Every pilgrimage has the feel of a military mission, and it's a major struggle to get in safely—and get out. In the Jewish religion, pilgrims repeat as a mantra, "The soul of the prophets still remains in the places where they are buried." In these places, the Israeli-Palestinian conflict is boiled down to its essence of competing territorial, national, and religious claims.

Six Israeli soldiers were shot and burned to death at Joseph's Tomb in 1996 when an Arab mob turned on them, backed up by Palestinian security forces. On October 7, 2000, a mob of Palestinians ransacked the millennia-old holy site and devastated it in a matter of hours. Muslims declared the tomb an Islamic holy site and painted the dome green, the color of Islam. Since Israel forfeited the site, the Palestinians have continued to desecrate the tomb, using it as a garbage dump and sometimes burning tires inside. Jewish pilgrims have visited sporadically, stealing into Nablus alone in the dark. Boarding a bulletproof minibus, they arrive after the army has secured the tomb in advance and military vehicles are stationed at every junction along the route. The women cradle babies and toddlers in their arms.

Rabbi Hillel Lieberman was one of the founders of the yeshiva of Joseph's Tomb, and taught Torah classes daily for students who came from all over to study with him. He died trying to save the Torah scrolls from the vandals that day in October 2000. "Hillel was unarmed, and was wearing a *tallit*," witnesses say. "He was killed by our enemies, who want to wipe us out of existence." What happened to Hillel stunned America, too, which would see so many of its Jewish children die in Israel. His second cousin is Senator Joe Lieberman, a former candidate for vice president.

Hillel Lieberman was "a man far from anger" who was "kind to everyone," said one of his friends, Noam Livnat. "No one showed rabbis as much appreciation as did Hillel," he added. "In every action he fulfilled Psalm 34:15, 'Do good.'" The son of an Orthodox rabbi in Brooklyn, Hillel was a real Zionist. He graduated from the Jewish University of Manhattan, and then left America "to answer the call of God and of our history." As soon as he came to Israel, he studied and taught at Joseph's Tomb. Later he transferred to the synagogue of Elon Moreh.

His father, Rabbi Sidney Zvulun Lieberman, recalls, "My son was a very religious man, strong in faith in *Eretz Yisrael,* devoted to the teaching of the Torah and the performance of the mitzvoth. He was Hillel the honest, the just, the kind. He had chosen Elon Moreh because that was Abraham's first stop in Israel, so what happened to him was God's will. Hillel died for the *Kiddush Hashem,* the sanctification of the name of God. We don't choose martyrdom, it is God who chooses us for it. I loved my son, and now I love his memory."

One of his American friends remarked that "Hillel went beyond courage; he lived what he believed; he came to Israel to start over." He was proud to be one of the "settlers," a group loathed in the West and left to itself in Israel. Hillel loved the mystical profundity of the desert, with its constant reminder of human limitations and therefore of God's sovereignty over everything. The settlers build among the stones, and delight in the beauty of the vast sunsets; they live among purple bougainvilleas, flower beds and tendrils of vines; they live with a minimum of food and clothing, as if in a Soviet kolkhoz with features of California. The settlers say that when they go out, they leave their souls on the seat next to them, and take them up again after they've passed the checkpoint. Living there means challenging death.

The former mayor of Shiloh, David Rubin, also an American, was one of Lieberman's best friends. "It is always a privilege to live here, in a place with such historical-spiritual significance," he says. "The fact that we have had so many victims strengthens my resolve to stay here. If the Muslim terrorists don't want us here, it is because they recognize the significance of the return of the Jews to the biblical land of God. Every Jew who is killed as a result of this struggle is a holy martyr. But unlike the Muslims, we don't rejoice in the death of our children. The Muslim terrorists who are killed are not like our kids who are killed while playing basketball, going to school, or cooking for Shabbat. Each of our victims is a symbol of our determination to continue our lives, in spite of the pain, the terror. And we're getting stronger and stronger."

A picture of Avraham Gavish adorns the dignified walls of the Bnei David yeshiva in the settlement of Eli. For the rabbi of Eli, Israel is "the vehicle for the return of the exiles." Israel's history is in the hills of Samaria and Judea. Tel Aviv, Netanya, Herzliya, and Haifa find their reason for being in the home of the first Israelites—and in the dead of Eli. Zvi Goldstein was killed on the way to Jerusalem with his wife and his parents, who had just come from New York to celebrate the marriage of their grandson. "He was so happy, he danced even though he has had problems walking since he suffered polio as a child," said a friend who attended the wedding. "He was a man of peace, and he was murdered by the people of war."

The Bnei David yeshiva has given up many of its children in the wars of recent years. Yossi Ohana "loved simplicity; he always demanded perfection of himself, and the State of Israel was his highest priority." Ezra Asher was named after his brother who had been killed in battle. In his last letter, he wrote, "I have great responsibilities in my current military operation. I am leading soldiers on difficult missions, and my decisions will determine their fate." Alongside Avraham Gavish on the wall is Moshe Harush, who spoke of the need to use "the language of the people." One day before leaving with his unit, he had written to his sister Tali, "All of us have to learn the faith; I don't know how I would survive without it. I base myself on my faith and my ideas about the nation, the land and the Torah of Israel." Yitzhak Weinstock was a born volunteer. He had offered to go on many missions, like farming in Gush Katif and taking care packages to soldiers. On the day of his departure with his unit, he decided to stop to help a driver in difficulty. He was killed by a sniper.

Today there are about twenty religious military prep schools, and a new generation of Israeli soldiers has emerged from them. In 1967 there were no devout officers; today, 40 percent of officers are very devout. If the Palmach of David Ben-Gurion had a "Russian" character, the Israeli army of tomorrow will be led by God-fearing Jews, and made up mainly of immigrants. It is no longer the army of the Ashkenazi, but of Africans and Sephardim who see a religious motivation in the birth and existence of the State of Israel. Religious Zionism is now the torchbearer of Jewish tradition. During the war in Gaza in January 2009, eleven Israeli soldiers were killed; four of them came from the movement of religious Zionism. The idea that "the devout are the *kibbutzniks* of today" keeps getting stronger.

Another picture on the wall at the Bnei David yeshiva is a photograph of Benji Hillman, the twenty-six-year-old son of English Jews, who had insisted on going back into battle with his companions although he had gotten married three weeks earlier. He lost his life in Bint Jbail, fighting Hezbollah terrorists. In burying him, his father said that "this is the final step of the aliyah, entrusting him again to *Eretz Hadokesh*, the Holy Land." Benji was a *bitzuist,* a man of action. His parents have created a foundation for soldiers without parents in Israel. "Benji was very charming," said one of his friends and classmates, Shlomo Mirvis. "His joie de vivre was contagious; he supported his soldiers down to the last detail; he motivated people and was very accessible. He was tolerant and patient, without arrogance, in spite of his rank and professionalism, and his bond with the State of Israel made him very special."

Emanuel Moreno's face is not to be found on the wall at Bnei David, because Moreno was a member of the Sayeret Matkal, the Israelis who work undercover. He was known for his Zionism and his humility. Moreno's friends said on television that "he was one of the best fighters we have ever had in this country." Moreno lived in Moshav Tlamim, whose name means "furrows," from Psalm 65: "You water its ridges abundantly, you settle its furrows." He had three children, Aviyah, Neriah, and Noam. "He never thought of himself," a fellow soldier said, "but only of the group. His modesty was simply unbelievable." In giving his posthumous prize to his family after Moreno was killed in 2006, the Begin Heritage Center commented, "He was a warrior who saw his military service as an important mission to which he totally dedicated himself—and was also a passionate student who used every spare minute for Torah study and acts of kindness to others." The year before he was killed, Moreno brought food every night to his brother David, who had barricaded himself in Gush Katif when the communities there received evacuation orders. Emanuel never wore his uniform with its medals inside the moshav, because he didn't want to show off his military achievements; he wasn't looking for glory.

"At first sight, you would think that Emanuel was an ordinary person, nothing special," said Shlomo Mirvis. "But Emanuel was unique for the charisma, the charm, and the faith that made him a unit commander in the army. He was a great warrior whose creative vision brought success to his unit's operations. He is the only soldier decorated not for a specific action, but for how much he did as an officer. Emanuel believed in the Torah, the basis of everything in life, of our values, our morality, and our way of thinking."

The local rabbi dedicated a Torah scroll to the memory of Yonaton "Yoni" Netanyahu and of Emanuel Moreno, calling him "a modern Yoni." On every continent, from San Antonio to Jerusalem, there are schools that bear the name of Yoni Netanyahu. The great writer Chaim Potok said that Yoni's name is synonymous with "miracle," because it was a miracle that the Jewish people went "from Auschwitz to Entebbe in a single generation." The memory of Entebbe lights up the night in Gaza when the Israeli army goes in to search for its kidnapped soldiers. In the thirty years that have gone by since a few dozen Israeli commandos freed 104 hostages at a remote Ugandan airport, the name of Entebbe has become synonymous with a risk worth taking. Bypassing negotiations, Israel sent an elite unit to a country two thousand miles away, catching the terrorists by surprise with a combination of ingenuity and overpowering force. It was a heroic story of Hollywood proportions. Colonel Yoni Netanyahu commanded the raid, but paid for its success with his life.

Apart from the French flight crew, all the passengers of the hijacked plane were Jews, from Israel and other countries. They had been kidnapped as Jews, and they were set free as such. The impact of Operation Yonatan, as it is sometimes called, was felt far outside the borders of Israel. Natan Sharansky said that the rescue mission had immense symbolic importance for Russian Jews imprisoned in the Soviet gulags. "When I was in prison, when I heard the engine of some airplane, I immediately was thinking of Entebbe, and it gave me confidence that one day I would be released. . . . So the image of Israel as a society that is built to be concerned about the saving of Jews, that every Jew who is in danger will be saved by Israel, had a very symbolic and powerful meaning."

The devout soldier Jonathan (Yoni) Jesner also got his name from Colonel Netanyahu. On September 20, 2002, he was one of the six victims on a bus that was blown up on Allenby Street in Tel Aviv. Born and raised in Scotland, Yoni was a student at a yeshiva in Gush Etzion. "It was your love for Israel and Judaism that brought you here," said his brother Ari. "You were a model for me; you taught me love, Judaism, compassion and understanding." One of Yoni's kidneys saved the life of a seven-year-old Palestinian girl.

In 1980, a twelve-year-old Arab girl received a kidney transplanted from the body of a Jewish student who was murdered in the Arab market of Hebron. Jesper Jehoshua Sloma had immigrated from Denmark. His family was not very religious, but he became devout in Israel, wore a yarmulke, and combined his service in the army with religious studies in Kiryat Arba. Walking alone through the twisting alleys of the Kasbah in Hebron, he was shot twice in the head and died at age twenty.

Shiloh is a neighboring town of Eli. The first modern settlers came in mobile homes and got electricity from a generator and water from trucks. After Shiloh was founded in 1978, President Carter demanded that Menachem Begin remove the tiny village. The prime minister replied, "You, Mr. President, have in the United States a number of places with names like Bethlehem, Shiloh and Hebron, and you haven't the right to tell prospective residents in those places that they are forbidden to live there." There are sixty-five towns named Shiloh in the United States.

Shiloh appears in many passages of the Bible. The Jews first arrived there after the Exodus from Egypt. It is the place from which Joshua ben Nun, a descendant of Moses, launched his conquest of the land and distributed it among the tribal chiefs. The sons of Israel brought the Tabernacle here, to the territory of the tribe of Ephraim, making Shiloh the religious center of the Israelites before Jerusalem. Here, Hannah prayed to the Lord to give her a child, because she was sterile. She gave birth to Samuel, who heard God speaking to him in Shiloh. It was the capital of the Jewish nation for nearly four centuries, until it was ravaged by the Philistines. Jesus passed through its streets on his way from Galilee to Jerusalem.

In 1838, the archaeologist Edward Robinson first identified the ancient remains of Shiloh. In 2006, Israeli scholars uncovered an early church built on the place where the Ark of the Covenant is believed to have been kept. The settlers of Shiloh today conceive of themselves as a living reminder of Jewish history, the sacredness of Jewish land, and the theological significance of a Jewish presence. This biblical village sits atop a steep hill, surrounded by six Arab villages and overlooking bean fields that spread out like a green-and-brown checkerboard below. By climbing up a water tower in the center of Shiloh on a clear day, one can make out the Mediterranean coast to the west and the Jordan Valley to the east. In short, one can see from one side of Israel to the other.

"Then the whole community of the Israelites assembled at Shiloh," says Joshua 18:1. After the war of 1967, eight Israeli families returned here, with the government's permission to develop about one million acres not being used by the Palestinians and to carry out archaeological excavations. The great rabbi Tzvi Yehuda Kook, despite his age and the rigors of the trip, had a jeep take him to Shiloh to see the rebirth of the community of the Tabernacle and the nation of priests. One of the settlement's founders, Meir Stein, recalls that "several of the women were pregnant during those first few months. My wife was pregnant with twins, but nobody was too concerned. We were optimists and we felt that everything would work out for the best. Our parents and everyone else thought we were crazy to give up our comfortable lives in the cities to settle the heartland, but the truth is, we didn't care what anyone thought about us—the world, our parents, the government, or the media."

An elderly immigrant from Russia, a former officer in the Soviet army named Zechariah Begun, used to volunteer his impressive gardening skills for different families in Shiloh and would never take money for his services. When offered payment, the energetic eighty-year-old responded, "How can I take money for planting in the land of Israel?" The settlers have built homes, schools, yeshivas, synagogues, a library, playing fields, medical clinics, and a small farm producing oil, wine, and honey. Where at first there was only a group of trailers, today there is a flourishing village, and the homes look more like they belong in Denver or Phoenix than in the Middle East that we know.

Since Jimmy Carter asked for the removal of the modern settlement, Shiloh has been one of the hottest fronts in the Middle East conflict. It's not just Jordan out there past Shiloh; beyond it are Iraq, Syria, and then Iran. In 1991, there was a terror attack on a bus returning from Tel Aviv. Among the many Shiloh residents on that bus was a woman named Rachel Druck, the mother of seven children, who became the first terror victim from Shiloh. Today, some of the settlers sleep with machine guns under their beds and carry pistols when they travel. The bus has been reinforced underneath, as protection against landmines; the windows are thick and bulletproof except for the upper parts, which have ordinary panes to allow passengers to shoot out. But the people in the community seem to live as they always have, and are not afraid of having to leave. They are sure that peace will come through Shiloh. They say that the Hebrew words *yavo Shiloh,* "until Shiloh comes," represent the numeric value of the Messiah.

Yossi and Pirhiya Apter live in Shiloh; both of them lost various family members to the Holocaust. Yossi's parents immigrated from Germany between 1935 and 1938, starting a new life as Zionist farmers. His wife's parents came from Hungary, arriving on the shore of Tel Aviv in 1949; both of them had passed through the gates of Auschwitz. Their son Noam attended the yeshiva in the settlement of Otniel, south of Hebron.

On a Friday night, December 27, 2002, a group of terrorists broke into the school in Otniel to massacre Jews celebrating Shabbat. Four teenagers were cooking in the kitchen, while dozens more were dancing in the dining hall. When he heard the first shots, Sergeant Noam Apter locked himself in the kitchen with the terrorists, blocking access to the dining hall and saving over a hundred lives. His action cost him his own life. The other three on kitchen duty were also killed: Gavriel Hoter, Yehuda Bamberger, and Zvi Ziman, who used to tell his friends in moments of mourning and difficulty, "We survived the pharaoh, we'll get through this too."

Noam Apter was not merely one of the "four Israelis killed in the West Bank," as newspapers all over the world reported the day after the attack on the yeshiva. In Israel, his name is surrounded by a halo of greatness. Noam wanted to leave the army in order to study the Torah and dedicate himself to his community in Otniel. One day he prevented a soldier on his base from going out on Shabbat. It led to a fight.

Noam handed out phylacteries to passersby, as some Messianic Jews do in order to hasten the coming of the Messiah. "Every Friday, Noam and his friends went to the central bus station in Beersheba to distribute *tefilim* and Shabbat candles," his father tells us. "They would stop people and ask them to put them on and recite the *Shema Yisrael,* as a gesture of intimate connection with the Jewish tradition. He felt that this was his mission. Noam wanted to teach the Jewish tradition to the many nonreligious people in Israel." He often volunteered on weekends for On Wheels, an organization that takes care of disabled children. "Noam decided to dedicate part of his time to helping those most in need," Yossi says. "He loved the atmosphere; there were religious and nonreligious people."

There are some days of the year when Noam's absence is especially painful for the Apters. "During the holidays, when he isn't at our table, the day of his death, Memorial Day, and his birthday. On those days we are very sad, we cry, we don't have the strength to work. We miss Noam very much," says his father, Yossi. "Thanks to God, I went back to work a few days after the mourning of the shivah. For me and my wife, Noam's death, in that way and on a Friday, was like the completion of a life, for him who was born on a Friday and at the same time at night. His heroism in closing the doors to save his friends, giving up his own life, gives us strength and inspires admiration." In Israel, heroism is a family affair, not a military one. The incredible chain of heroism that has left the history of the Jewish state strewn with dead and wounded is celebrated without exaggeration or rhetoric.

All over the world, Noam's name is synonymous with heroism and lust for life. "They love us even if they don't know us personally," says Yossi. "Our religious faith has given us a lot of strength to go on living after Noam's tragedy. In Israel, many students who go to religious schools before entering the army have come to my home to hear Noam's story. The attack has reinforced my faith in God, because he controls everything, I feel that he is very close."

Their son's death has not in any way discouraged the Apters from continuing to live in Shiloh, one of the oldest and most historic Jewish settlements. "We believe in God and in his Torah, but also in the Zionist movement," Yossi explains. "This leads us to follow the laws of the Torah and to be involved in Zionist activities like the army, to live in settlements, to help the state. I decided to live in Shiloh because this is the place where our nation began to be independent 3,500 years ago. Even today, one can smell the 'holy air.' At the time, the U.S. secretary of state, Cyrus Vance, said that the Jews would no longer be able to live in the Territories. So after graduating from university, while we were living near Tel Aviv, I told my wife, 'It's time to go live there; later will be too late.' And today no one remembers who Vance was, but everyone knows about Shiloh. We lived in a trailer for three years. There was an extremely rich atmosphere, a small family-oriented community. We had excellent relations with the Arabs. My wife and I knew we were part of the history of Israel. Here there were only rocks, rocks, and more rocks; today there are trees and flowers and families. Thanks to God, there are three hundred of us."

Every Tuesday morning, Sara Blaustein went to guard a little two-room building that is believed to be the tomb of Rachel, situated between Jerusalem and Bethlehem, a few yards from the line that divides Israel from the Palestinian Territories. Rachel is a kind of Jewish Blessed Mother, the protector of sanctified maternity. The wife of Jacob, she gave birth to two of the patriarch's twelve sons, Joseph and Benjamin, the ones most dear to their father and to the history of the Jewish people. But she died in giving birth to Benjamin. The prophet Jeremiah uses the imagery of Rachel's death as a metaphor for God's promise to return the people of Israel from exile in Babylonia to the land of Zion. Among the four biblical Jewish matriarchs—Rachel, Rebecca, Sarah, and Leah—Rachel is the most revered. Jeremiah said, "In Ramah is heard the sound of moaning, of bitter weeping. Rachel mourns her children, she refuses to be consoled because her children are no more." In the Jewish tradition, Rachel Imenu, "Our Mother Rachel," is the mother of sorrows who weeps in prayer over the Jewish people.

"Rachel's weeping for her children represents the infinite compassion and the boundless hope that a mother can feel for her children," wrote Eetta Prince-Gibson.

The figure of Rachel has been a source of eternal admiration and identification for Jewish women throughout history. Her tomb is one of the three most important holy sites, next to the Western Wall and the Tomb of the Patriarchs in Hebron. In the small white room, women pray silently, they weep quietly, burying their faces in their Psalm books. Mothers in distress come here for consolation. Women who want to have children pray for help; they wrap the tomb in long white threads, several times around. It is said that miracles of fertility happen here.

Crusaders built part of the structure, and Ottoman Turks made additions six hundred years later. Until the 1800s, Rachel's Tomb was a simple domed building. In 1841, the British philanthropist Sir Moses Montefiore renovated the structure and enclosed the dome over the grave. The Jordanians who ruled the West Bank after Israel gained independence forbade Jews to worship there. That changed when Israel captured the West Bank in the Six-Day War and gained control over many Jewish holy sites. Although Bethlehem was handed over to the Palestinian Authority in 1995, Israel retained control of Rachel's Tomb, which is now placed within Jerusalem's boundaries by a security barrier along the city's southern perimeter. It is flanked on three sides by a Muslim cemetery.

Rachel's Tomb no longer resembles the romantic pictures of medieval pilgrims or early Zionist artists. It is a fortress with a twelve-foot-high wall, two guard towers, a maze of concrete barriers and a thicket of barbed wire, designed to protect Jewish visitors from Arab sharpshooters and stone throwers. A military outpost is just up the street, and soldiers are everywhere. During the al-Aqsa Intifada, shooting battles broke out around the compound almost every night. Bulletproof vehicles must travel the road to the tomb in single-file procession. Still, Jews come from all over the world to pray at Rachel's Tomb, to venerate this shrine as a fountain of Judaism and touch the sarcophagus, draped in black velvet, that contains the bones of the matriarch who died on the way to Hebron thousands of years ago. In front of the tombstone is a large menorah with an "eternal light," dedicated to "the souls of tens of thousands of Jewish martyrs who were destroyed by the cursed evildoers, may their names be erased, during the years 1939–1945."

Sara Blaustein had left her safe, comfortable, happy life in New York to live in Israel. But not just anywhere—she had chosen Efrat, a settlement in Gush Etzion. If it were not for Gush Etzion, if it were not for this little plot of ground within sight of Jerusalem, attacks in the capital would multiply and the rockets would rain down like they do from Gaza on Sderot. "If there is a Jewish Jerusalem, we owe it to the defenders of Gush Etzion," David Ben-Gurion remarked. Zevulun Hammer, who has served as minister of education and as minister of religious affairs, called the dead of Gush Etzion "our saints." The mayor of Gush Etzion, Shaul Goldstein, spoke of his father, who fought in the battle for Gush Etzion: "I remember him telling me that there was no alternative but to fight. Not winning meant another Shoah."

The first of four attempts to populate the area in modern times began in 1927, but harsh physical conditions forced the pioneers to abandon their settlement. The second effort was made by Shmuel Holtzman, who founded the village of Kfar Etzion in 1935. The name comes from *etz*, "tree," corresponding to the German *Holz*, "wood." Repeated Arab attacks drove away the pioneers. The third attempt, in April 1943, coincided with the Warsaw ghetto uprising. The pioneers, many of whom had escaped Nazi Europe and had lost family members there, were not deterred by such challenges as rocky terrain, water shortages, bitterly cold winters, and security risks. They founded a kibbutz on the site of Kfar Etzion.

The UN resolution of November 29, 1947, calling for a Jewish state alongside an Arab one, triggered the Arabs' siege of Gush Etzion. Traveling to the area was dangerous. Armed convoys bringing supplies were ambushed. Children and mothers were evacuated in January 1948. By May, Gush Etzion was under attack by the Jordanian Arab Legion and thousands of local Arabs. The day before Israel declared its independence, the Jewish soldiers surrendered. Gathered in the center of Kfar Etzion, they were suddenly fired upon. In the ensuing desperate struggle, 127 defenders were slaughtered; only four survived. Kfar Etzion was pillaged and destroyed. "The queen has fallen": these code words informed the army command that the kibbutz had fallen into Jordanian hands. The legendary settler Hanan Porat was born in Gush Etzion shortly before the Arab squad killed the Jewish inhabitants. Just after the war of 1967, all the children of Gush Etzion gathered at the graves of the heroes who had fought twenty years earlier. Porat concluded the service: "We told our parents, weeping, that we were going back home." Gush Etzion is now home to 50,000 Israelis.

Before she was killed by terrorists on May 29, 2001, Sara Blaustein divided her time between studying the Torah and praying at the Tomb of the Patriarchs in Hebron or at Rachel's Tomb. Her husband, Norman, recalls that she had visited Rachel's Tomb on that morning and had "prayed for the salvation of *Am Yisrael,* the people of Israel. Every night we studied a chapter of the Tanakh, the Pentateuch. We were talking about Samson in the car. She always carried money for the poor. I loved her so much." Her son Yoni said, "What drew her here was love, not hatred or revenge, only love of the land." He remarked that his mother "died as she had lived, in an act of *chesed,* of generosity."

Norman Blaustein tells us, "My wife was born in Brooklyn, in a modern and Orthodox family in which Zionism played a fundamental role in the approach to life. When we married in

1987, we first lived in Staten Island and were just like every other couple trying to make it. Then in 1991 we moved to Lawrence, New York, and everything changed. We started our own business and then agreed that we were going to live in Israel. We wanted our daughter, Atara, to have a better quality of life, which Israel could provide. We made a plan and a budget, and did not talk to anybody about our future plans. Every year during the Thanksgiving holiday we would go to Israel for ten days. Each year we were getting closer and closer to our goals. Our business was booming. In fact, our income was in the top 2 percent in America. In 2000 we reached our objectives, and announced at Atara's twelfth birthday party that we were moving to Israel in the summer. The whole room was in shock—some of our closest friends fell off their seats."

They established themselves in Efrat for many reasons, Norman explains. "Sara's younger brother David lived there with his family; the community spoke English (I speak only English); the level of religion was perfect for us; and the schools were great for our daughter. Sara and I used to say that living in Efrat was just like living in Long Island. Children played in the street all the time and everyone always had a smile on their face. The standard of living was very high, with most families having two cars and living in private homes. Efrat has all the stores to make it self-supporting. It is only fifteen minutes from Jerusalem."

Efrat was built in 1981 through the initiative of Shlomo Riskin, the former rabbi of the synagogue in the Lincoln Square neighborhood of New York. Riskin noted that "Efrat is halfway between Hebron, where Jewish history began, and Jerusalem, where we hope to set out toward redemption and peace." It is a settlement with moderate views on the Arabs; it is religious but not Messianic, conservative but not ultranationalist. At the funerals there, few talk about revenge or hatred of the Arabs. Efrat is a bedroom community meant to be a satellite of Jerusalem. Here it is politically correct to settle the land for Israel and to own a villa too. Populated mainly with self-described modern Orthodox Jews, the town boasts good schools, clean streets, landscaped roads—in short, a great quality of life.

Norman Blaustein says, "I would go back to New York every month for a couple of weeks. Sara immediately got involve in Jewish studies and charity work. She had a smile on her face that went from ear to ear. She loved living in Israel very much, and all who saw her said she would light up any room she entered. She was always saying how happy she was."

In the meantime, Norman explains, the Israeli government was talking with the Palestinians about giving up land without receiving anything in exchange. "Sara and some other women moved into a tent near the tomb of Rachel, to assert its Jewish character. She would go every Tuesday morning to do her shift. She asked me every month to bring bags of candy back from the United States for the soldiers, and she would give the candy out every Tuesday at the end of her shift. This went on for many months." One evening they were having dinner with friends. "At this dinner there was a bitter young man who had just finished his army requirement. He got into an argument with Sara and me about why we were living in Israel, and said that we should move back to New York. Sara let him have it between the eyes. She said how lucky he was to serve in the Israeli army and live in Israel, how before the creation of the state every Jew would have given their right hand to live here. All the other people there agreed with Sara. That night Sara and I spoke about what would happen if one of us was killed in this Arab trouble. We never thought it would be Sara. We decided to become spokespersons for Israel and tell everyone to move here."

The next day, Sara went with her mother and Norman to pray at the Tomb of the Patriarchs in Hebron. "We stopped at the Jewish cemetery, and the guide told us about the women buried there and their acts of bravery. We went back to Efrat in a private car, and this was very dangerous. The next morning, Sara awoke and went to the tomb of Rachel to ride the buses, and at the end of a tour she gave out candy to the soldiers and returned to our home. We decided to buy a large Torah to give as a charitable donation at the Western Wall.

"A few days later we were on the road to Jerusalem, and I noticed that a very large truck was stopping us from passing it on the road, while behind us was a white car speeding toward us. At some point the white car tried to pass us and the truck at the same time. I heard a noise that sounded like firecrackers, and my glasses fell off my face. I stopped the car and saw Sara smiling at me. I did not know she had been shot twice and was dead."

At the funeral, everyone asked Atara where she wanted to live, in New York or in Efrat. "Atara said. 'Israel!' Not only did Atara stay in Israel, but her brother Yoni Berg and her sister Adena Mark came to live in Israel with her family," says Norman. "Adena has six children now, with the last one having Sara's name. Sara's mother also made Israel her home until she died this year. As for me, the morning after Sara's murder, I was lying in bed with the feeling that I was in a grave and had to make a decision what to do. I decided to clear away the dirt and start my life again, and to do what Sara and I agreed to do if one of us was killed."

Joyful Flowers

J ewish children have always been a favorite target
for Islamic terrorism, ever since the first attacks on Israeli
society. As representatives of the various terrorist organizations in the Middle East have said, Jewish children are the
adults of tomorrow who must be killed according to the anti-
Semitic projects of Hamas, of the al-Aqsa Martyrs' Brigades, of
Palestinian Islamic Jihad, of Hezbollah and Iran. Israel has a
birthrate much higher than those of European countries and
the United States. As the Arabs' determination to destroy
Israel has become more and more explicit, having children has
increasingly become a silent ethical choice even among the secular. Israel is a Jewish state in which about 30 percent of its citizens are not Jewish (Arabs constitute a little more than 20
percent), and it must preserve a Jewish majority in order to
maintain its national identity.

So far, 128 Jewish children have been killed, 9 of them less
than a year old; 9 pregnant women have been murdered; 886
children have lost one parent and 31 have lost both. The
youngest victim of terror was just one day old. In the spring of
2009, a thirteen-year-old boy, Shlomo Nativ, was killed with an
ax. It is the massacres of Jewish children that reveal the nature
of the terrorism that Israel has faced for more than half a

century. Israel fights this war without hatred, remaining one of the greatest democracies in the world.

The bloody ending of the siege at the school in Beslan, in southern Russia, shocked the entire civilized world in September 2004. The attack was but the replay of a ghastly reality with which the Jews in Israel have had to contend for years. Thirty years earlier, on May 15, 1974—Israel's Independence Day—terrorists had struck at a school in Ma'alot. It was not chosen at random. Founded by Jews who had fled from North Africa, Ma'alot was one of the many seeds of Jewish freedom, a symbol of Zionism. A group of students from the high school of Safed, a thriving center for Talmudic studies, was on a field trip on the Golan plateau. They spread their sleeping bags on the floor of the schoolhouse in Ma'alot, sang late into the night, and then went to sleep. Meanwhile, the terrorists crossed the Lebanese border and attacked. Some of the students got away through a window, but the others were held hostage. It was the first time that Jews had ever been taken hostage in Israel, two years after the slaughter of the athletes in Munich.

Fifteen minutes before the deadline of the terrorists' ultimatum, the Golani Brigade stormed the school building. The students were hiding under the desks, wailing, while the terrorists began to find them and slaughter them like animals. Before Yasser Arafat's thugs were killed, they had murdered twenty-one Israeli high school students and three of their teachers, and wounded dozens more. In Beirut, the terrorist Naif Hawatmeh organized demonstrations in honor of the fallen fedayeen, the "noble martyrs." It was one of the first times that terrorists had prepared themselves for suicide, by scattering bombs around the building in case it was attacked—exactly as others would do in Beslan thirty years later.

Shortly before the Ma'alot attack, on April 11, 1974, there was a massacre in Kiryat Shmona, where three terrorists entered an apartment complex and killed eighteen Israelis, including nine children. A few years earlier was the massacre of Avivim, a community founded by Moroccan Jews. It was May 8, 1970, when terrorists attacked an Israeli school bus, killing nine children between the ages of six and nine. Thirty-five years later, Hezbollah's rockets would fall on the survivors of that massacre.

Ma'alot and Avivim would come back to mind in 1997 with the slaughter of seven Jewish girls, ages twelve to fourteen. They went to a religious school in Bet Shemesh and were on a field trip to the "Island of Peace," at the confluence of the Jordan and Yarmuk rivers along the border with Jordan. This is where, decades earlier, a dream had come true for Pinhas Rutenberg and Moshe Novomeysky, two Russian Jews who wanted to harness the water to produce electricity, and unite Arabs and Jews in a shared project. The girls had come to the top of the hill where a turret stood, with a large Jordanian flag waving in the wind. Rosa Heemi, one of the two teachers accompanying the girls, recounted what happened: "We got off the bus and gathered around our guide to hear her explanations, when suddenly I heard the gunshots. I started looking around to see where they were coming from, how we needed to protect ourselves, and I saw a Jordanian soldier shooting at us from the top of the tower. The girls started running, and some of them hid behind the bushes, but the soldier had come down from his spot and was following them, still shooting. When he had emptied the magazine, he stopped and tried to load another, but it wouldn't work." At this point his fellow soldiers grabbed him. Another survivor, Rifka, recalled, "Everyone was crying, screaming for help, fleeing in every direction. I saw Ivri, my best friend, shot in the shoulder, rolling around on the grass in a pool of blood. Then she stopped breathing."

Yehuda Shoham was just five months old when he was struck in the head by a rock while his parents were driving home to Shiloh in June 2001. His mother, Batsheva, a kindergarten teacher from Detroit, lunged to give him CPR. "This is our land, these are our roads," said his father, Benny. "If we are afraid of driving here, we will also be afraid in Tel Aviv and Netanya. The Jews are in danger everywhere in the State of Israel." Yehuda clung to life for a week on a respirator. His parents gave him a second name, Chaim, "life," hoping in a miracle that did not come. Ariel Sharon, the prime minister, spoke at his funeral: "I am not here to make a speech, but to weep, to weep together with you. May the memory of Yehuda be blessed." One of Yehuda's cousins remarked that "he was just a baby, without any blame or enemies, killed for only one reason: he was a Jew at home in *Eretz Yisrael.*" His parents are collecting donations for dormitories built in his memory at the yeshiva in Shiloh.

Danielle Shefi, five years old, was one of four victims in an attack at the settlement of Adora, near Hebron, in April 2002. The terrorists shot her while she was playing in her parents' bedroom together with her two younger brothers. It was just after 9 A.M., and many of Adora's fifty-two families were either attending Shabbat prayers or spending time with their children, or sleeping late. Most people, in line with the settlement's emergency procedures, locked themselves in bathrooms and lay on the floor, trying to shield their children with their own bodies, as homes were sprayed with bullets. "Danielle, who never hurt anyone and was taught to love everyone, Jew or Arab, was killed in her parents' bed—which should have been the safest place," said her father, Ya'akov, a policeman. "She was beautiful, and very intelligent. Despite her young age, she understood the gravity of the situation, and often asked questions about various attacks." Danielle's mother has not stopped mourning for her "pure and innocent" daughter. Her grandfather escaped the pogrom in Hebron in 1929.

On March 9, 2002, in Netanya, two terrorists entered a hotel lobby, shooting wildly and throwing grenades. Avia Malka was nine months old, "always laughing, with a beautiful smile." She was hit by a burst of fire from an assault rifle, and then with a hand grenade while her father was trying to unbuckle the strap of the stroller. He was seriously wounded and couldn't go to Avia's funeral. Her mother, who was in another part of the lobby, secured her other four children in the bathroom before running to her daughter and husband. She was shot in the leg. The Malkas had come to Israel from Johannesburg, where Avia's father was a manager for El Al airline, to attend a relative's wedding. Grandparents, aunts, uncles, cousins met Avia for the first time. The Malkas were planning to return to South Africa the next day. Israel Yihye also died in the attack. He was staying at the hotel for a weekend of study organized by his yeshiva. In addition to studying the Torah, Israel was a volunteer for Magen David Adom. As soon as he heard the shots, he started running toward the injured, as he had always done. His cousin remarked that he "found death while seeking to save a life"—as the Talmud says to do.

Shaked Avraham, a seven-month-old girl from Negohot, to the south of Hebron, was killed by a terrorist who had penetrated the community enclosure while the inhabitants were celebrating Rosh Hashanah, the Jewish new year, in 2003. Shaked had just started walking. A center for the children of Negohot now bears her name. The road leading to Negohot (from the Hebrew word *noga,* which means "splendor") branches westward off the Hebron-Beersheba highway and goes past the Adorayim army base. The settlement, sprawled on a hilltop, commands a panoramic view of the area: on a clear day, one can see as far south as Beersheba and westward to the Mediterranean.

Yuval Abebah and Dorit Benisian were Ethiopian children who had gone to visit their grandmother, in September 2004. They were playing under an olive tree outside her home in Sderot when they were hit dead center by a rocket launched from the Gaza Strip. "My son was playing," his mother said.

"He was having fun. Suddenly there was an explosion." They knew it was a Qassam rocket; they were all screaming. "I looked for my Yuval. Then I saw him; his body was mutilated. Yuval was everything to me." The rockets of Hamas fall on Sderot almost every day. In spite of the 3,500 Qassam rockets that have been fired at this city and its surroundings, the number of inhabitants has grown steadily since 2002. It is the Israeli response to the killing of children.

On May 27, 2002, Chen and Lior Keinan had gone with their daughter, Sinai, or "Bubu" as they called her, to a shopping center in Petah Tikva. They were having ice cream at an outdoor cafe, a joyful place full of children with their parents. "Save the children!" the mothers shouted when they heard the battle cry of the attacker, *"Allahu Akbar!"* An eyewitness said, "When I arrived, I saw a child with half of his face normal and half bloody flesh." Dozens were injured. Sinai Keinan, just over a year old, was killed, along with her grandmother Ruth Peled. There were four generations to say their last goodbyes to Ruth: her mother, her husband, her brother, her children and grandchildren. "Only one is missing, Sinai, 'Bubu,' your granddaughter, because she's with you," her husband said. "She was so beautiful, and she gave us so much happiness," Sinai's mother said. Her father, Lior, pledged that Sinai will not become just another statistic, that the world must be told about the murder of innocent children.

Pnina and Isaac Eisenman had their first daughter in 1997 and named her Gal, "ocean wave." Pnina had been born in Jerusalem in 1967, during the Six-Day War. Her parents were Lithuanian, and were devout pioneers. On June 19, 2002, Pnina's mother, Noa Alon, had invited them all to a children's performance that she had organized at the kindergarten in Ofra where she worked. Gal and her grandmother were among the seven victims of the bomb detonated by a suicide terrorist of the al-Aqsa Martyrs' Brigades, a group connected to Arafat, at the French

Hill bus stop in northern Jerusalem. The police found Gal's little brother Sagi sitting on the ground among the mangled and bleeding bodies. Pnina and Isaac did not allow themselves to be overwhelmed by death; they had another daughter and named her Noga, "a combination of Noa and Gal, the names of my mother and my daughter," Pnina explained. She has also found the strength to write a children's book, *Poems for Gal.*

Then there was the massacre of Jewish children in Taba, a few square kilometers on the border with Egypt, under the control of the Egyptian government but traditionally a free zone for Israelis. The heart of this little enclave is the Hilton Taba, a hotel built by an entrepreneur from Jerusalem when Sinai was occupied by the Israelis. Al-Qaeda's second-in-command, the Egyptian doctor Ayman al-Zawahiri, had called upon "the combatants of Islam" to strike "Israeli, American, and Western allied" targets. On October 7, 2004, two truck bombs exploded at the entrance of the Hilton Taba. Shortly afterward, to the south, there were two simultaneous car-bomb attacks on beach camps in the Ras al-Satan area, popular with young Israelis. There were ten thousand Israelis on vacation in the area. Many were celebrating the last day of Sukkoth, the Feast of Booths, which commemorates the departure of the Hebrews from Egypt—and what the terrorists were seeking was a new Jewish exodus from Egypt, the destruction of that "impure" city.

The vehicles that exploded in front of the Hilton Taba contained more than two hundred pounds of explosives, and produced an enormous crater. The lobby looked like a dark cave, a frightening open space. There were cables, pieces of iron, light fixtures hanging from the ceiling. "Do you see that wall? I saw the most atrocious scene there: a girl of five or six impaled on an iron bar," an Israeli soldier said. But paradoxically, not a spot of blood can be seen in the entire lobby. "It is always like that," one worker explained. "It is as if, amid this rubble, everything human were eliminated."

Many Israelis lost their lives at the Hilton: a lawyer married to a woman who had converted to Judaism, a computer engineer with a passion for the cinema, a beautiful former army officer who worked in the Prime Minister's Office, a young woman who played the guitar in the nightclubs of Tel Aviv. Tzila Niv died with her young sons, Gilad and Lior, when the explosion brought the ceiling down on top of them. Her husband, Zohar, survived with moderate injuries while their twin daughters were unharmed. The only possession of the family's that survived the blast was a little white book of Psalms. Tzila taught Arabic and had served in the army even though she had lost the use of an eye to glaucoma. Zohar explains that "the thing I miss most is when I would fall asleep in bed with Lior, when he would rest his head on Tzila and his legs on me." Lior was three years old. Gilad, eleven years, "wanted to participate in everything," his teacher said. "When I met him on the street, he always asked me how I was. When I asked him, he answered, 'Great!'"

On Ben Yehuda, a busy street in downtown Jerusalem, two explosions a dozen yards apart killed eleven young people on December 1, 2001. An engineering student, Gideon, was drinking a beer with his girlfriend in a cafe when the explosion blew away tables and patrons. "I got up, I felt myself, I realized that my fiancée and I were miraculously unharmed," Gideon recalled, "and then I saw around me people without arms or without legs. I saw a woman with her innards spilling out. I saw a child breathe his last breath." Not satisfied with having sent two of their number to sacrifice themselves among innocent Jews, the terrorists had also planted a car bomb; they wanted to kill the emergency workers, too.

That evening, Ben Yehuda Street was no longer part of the world—it was an antiworld. There were people running around aimlessly. Other were sitting on the sidewalk, dazed. A young woman walked back and forth on the sidewalk like a robot. Someone was holding a human limb. A black plume of smoke rose into the air. "I saw people who had lost arms," recounted Yossi Mirzai, one of the first to arrive on the scene together with the emergency workers. "I saw a young woman eviscerated. I saw a ten-year-old boy die. A couple of volunteers were working strenuously over a crumpled body: 'Come on, come on ...' A soldier with a kippah and an assault rifle slung around his shoulder spread a shroud over unrecognizable remains."

The two locations were soon covered with candles and flowers and farewell cards: "We think about you always"; "We will never forget you." A poster says, "Your death has changed our lives." The victims included Yosef El-Ezra. "He was an angel; I was proud of him," his mother said. "Now he is an angel among the angels." Also there that evening were Assaf Avitan and Golan Turgeman, both fifteen years old and inseparable friends. Assaf planned to go bowling. Their parents went looking for them in the hospitals all over Jerusalem; it was late in the night when they discovered that Assaf and Golan were among the victims. Their friends remember them as "the neighborhood clowns," who made everyone laugh. Another victim, Nir Haftzadi, had been selected by his military unit as an "excellent soldier." His family described him as "a ray of sunshine." Ido Cohen, who died of his injuries a week later, had a beautiful voice. "We loved to hear him sing," his parents said. "His face was so handsome," his brother commented, with a sad smile.

Vladimir Korganov, an inhabitant of Ma'aleh Adumim, had lost his wife, Isabella, to cancer a year before his only son, Yoni, was killed in the attack on Ben Yehuda Street. "They were buried together, side by side," Vladimir says. "Yoni was very attached to his mother; he loved her so much and assisted her during her illness. Now they are together again. He wasn't even supposed to be downtown. That evening, he had gone to a friend's house. When I heard the sirens and watched the news, I didn't imagine for a moment that Yoni might be there too. After midnight, I received a telephone call that changed my life instantly. The brother of Yoni's friend was on the line; he was calling from an ambulance, and he told me that his brother and Yoni had been downtown and had been injured. I was stunned for a moment, but I recovered immediately. I knew that I had to go and look for him. I went to the Shaare Zedek Hospital, where Yoni's friend had been taken, but I didn't find my son. I scanned the list of the injured like a crazy man: I knew that there couldn't be any problem of identification, because he always carried his identity card with him. His cell phone was unreachable, and I started feeling worse and worse by the moment. I realized that if he wasn't on the list, there were no other possibilities. I laid my last strands of hope on an uniden-tified injured person who was at the Hadassah Hospital in Ein Kerem. I went there, but it wasn't him. So then I went to Abu Kabir (the Institute of Forensic Medicine) and identified him there."

The Korganov family had immigrated from Ukraine twelve years earlier. After only a few weeks in Israel, Isabella was diag-nosed with cancer, which she fought for many years, undergo-ing numerous medical treatments. When she felt better, she worked at the post office, but in 2000 the illness exhausted her. His mother's death made a deep mark on Yoni. "She was every-thing to him," his father says. "He cared for her during her entire illness, never leaving her. When she died, the light went out of his eyes. He changed, he became more sad, and it was only recently that he was becoming himself again." After his mother died, Yoni was given an early discharge from the army. He was planning to finish his university entrance exams, and also travel to East Asia. "He immediately got a job at a matzo factory," Vladimir recalls. "He refused to stay at home twiddling his thumbs. He went to work every day, but he didn't even live long enough to get his first paycheck. He dreamed of working with people, of studying to be a social worker or something like that. It was a good fit for him, for his heart, for his love of humanity." Yoni Korganov was just one of many young people from the former Soviet Union who have lost their lives to terrorism in Israel.

At the beginning of the 1970s, there were 2.2 million Jews in the Soviet Union; today there are fewer than 400,000 in the countries that used to make up the Communist behemoth. The prayer "Let my people go" has been answered. The majority of those who have left the USSR—more than a million women, men, and children—are in Israel. The first small wave was made up of immigrants involved in Zionist activities and resistance against the Soviet regime. When the Iron Curtain finally collapsed on itself, it set off a mass exodus of Jews. These people were not fleeing from persecution; they had not suffered in the cells of the KGB before emigrating. They had not secretly studied Hebrew, and perhaps they hadn't even listened to Kol Yisrael la-Golah, the Israeli radio station that broadcast to the diaspora. Over the course of a decade starting in 1991, almost a million emigrated to Israel, the proportional equivalent of fifty million immigrants streaming into the United States. In an incredible show of solidarity, every Israeli family could "adopt" a Russian. And for their part, the Russians in Israel have fought and died to rediscover their Jewish roots, which decades of Communism had tried to obliterate.

"It is tragic," admits Salai Meridor, the president of the Jewish Agency for Israel, "but the pact of blood that has been established among us over the past three years has made the new *olim* [immigrants] feel closer to the lived reality of the country." Dr. Eliezer Feldman, a statistician for the Mutagim polling firm and an expert on Russian affairs, confirms that the Intifada has created "a new spirit of cohesion and a high level of identification with Israeli society. I have visited dozens of families of *olim* who have lost loved ones to acts of terrorism, and I have been struck by the noble way in which they suffer and accept the pain of their tragedy. I always leave with the feeling that with every passing day we must thank these people for being here with us. I have never heard any of them say, 'Why did we ever come to live in Israel?'"

Gary Tauzniaski was from Odessa, where he had survived the Second World War by hiding in an apartment with his mother when the city was being searched by the Nazis. He was killed in 2002 while waiting for the bus in Rishon Lezion. In October 2005 there was a massacre of Soviet immigrants in Hadera. One of the victims was Michael Kaufman, who had come from Uzbekistan twelve years earlier. His wife did not speak at the funeral; she had suffered a breakdown. "Kaufman's family was annihilated in the Holocaust," one of his friends said. "The deaths of the victims of terror require us to fight for our right to live in safety and peace." The terrorist attacks in Hadera, at the Megiddo junction, at the market in Netanya, at the Park Hotel, on the bus on Allenby Street, at the Dolphinarium—these are like bloody thumbtacks on the map of immigration. The Russians who have suffered do not have the privilege of longstanding friendships, which sometimes predate the foundation of the state. They do not have a support group on the part of the army or the neighborhood. Many of them do not even know how to behave during the first seven days of strict mourning. Because of this, their pain has the added value of the effort and struggle for integration.

The young people swept away forever at the Dolphinarium on June 1, 2001, were the progeny of Natan Sharansky. While he was fighting against the killing of Jews in the Soviet gulags and struggling to get Russia to open its borders for the Jews who wanted to live in Israel, the parents of the young people murdered at the seaside in Tel Aviv were still unfamiliar with their Judaism; they had been taught to be atheist and without nationality, to view their Jewish past as a form of alienation contrary to the Communist spirit. Yet Karl Marx's own daughter Eleanor, speaking at a rally in London's Hyde Park, had proudly proclaimed, "I am a Jew!" Eleanor's cry was echoed along the beach of Tel Aviv that night in 2001.

The attack in Tel Aviv was devastating to the Jewish adventure of "returning to freedom," as the rabbis define it. The Dolphinarium was named for a dolphin tank that once stood there; nearby were the big hotels of Tel Aviv—the InterContinental David, the Dan Panorama. That evening, dozens of Russian high school students were waiting to get into the disco for an evening of dancing, relaxation, and friendship. Their graduation exams were coming up in a few days, and they wanted to have a little fun on a warm summer night and forget about the stress of studying for a few hours. Some of them were the only children of families that had decided to move to Israel so they could live in a Jewish state. They were proud and happy to be free in the land they had spent so much effort to reach. In a few more months they would be enlisted in the army. But Roman, Irina, Mariana, Alexei, and their friends would never finish school, never wear the uniform.

When they saw the terrorist, thinking that he was a member of the band, some of the young people asked him what instrument he played. "The drums," he answered. And then a place of happiness and freedom was turned into a slaughterhouse—young people with hands blown off and faces reduced to a pulp, a hail of blood, corpses, torsos. The parking lot in front of the Infinity nightclub was covered in blood, and the cars were littered with body parts. Many witnesses described a Dante-esque scene in which survivors waded through large pools of blood, navigating around arms and legs. The bloody clothing was left on the ground for hours, along with the purses of young women who had been killed, the wallets with money and documents still inside. At four o'clock in the morning, the city workers and firefighters were still trying to clean up all the blood.

"I am very happy and proud of what my son did and I hope all the men of Palestine and Jordan would do the same," said Hassan Hotary, whose son Saeed blew himself up at the entrance of the disco. Saeed Hotary was born to a Palestinian family in the Jordanian community of Zarqa, the hometown of Abu Musab al-Zarqawi, the slain leader of al-Qaeda in Iraq.

That night, Natan Sharansky wept for a long time and then went to bring comfort to the devastated families: "No one yet knows the names of our dead, but I am a family member of this little world that understands and speaks Hebrew poorly, that eats and listens to music and reads poetry in Russian." The mayor of Tel Aviv, Ron Huldai, told the wounded, "We can endure, because we are stronger than them." Stronger than the terrorists.

On the day of the attack, seventeen-year-old Simona Rudina from Vilnius was overjoyed because "she had just passed her literature exam with the highest grade in her class," her mother said. "We left the house together. She told me that she would call two hours later. She never did." Mariana Medvedenko, sixteen years old, wanted to work with computers. Irina Osadchaya had celebrated her eighteenth birthday the previous week. "I hope that God exists," said her mother, Bronislava. "My hopes lie in him, that he will allow me to see her in the next life." When Anya Kasachkova went out, her mother, Anna, needed to study for her medical license. Late in the night, she opened her pharmacology textbook and found some old photographs of her daughter inside. "There she was as a little child, then as a student. They calmed me down. She will be home tomorrow, I thought. Then I went to sleep." Anya did not return that night.

Diaz Nurmanov had enlisted in the army. Ilya Gutman came from a little town in Kazakhstan and had been exempted from military service so he could take care of his disabled brother. "Are you going to the nightclub?" asked his mother, Larissa. "I won't stay long," Ilya replied. Then he turned around and gave her a look full of love and tenderness. "He wasn't afraid of anything," Larissa remarked. Roman Djanashvili was the youngest son of a family from Tbilisi. "He helped me make dinner for Shabbat. He loved the entire ritual," said his mother. "He always asked me, 'What are we eating for the Shabbat dinner?'"

Liana Sakiyan was born in Moscow and had been in Israel for a year and a half, studying art in Tel Aviv. Her mother recalled that "before going out, she asked me how she looked. 'You're beautiful,' I told her. As she closed the door, I told her, 'Be careful.' I said that every evening." Irina Nepomneschi loved music. Her mother, Raissa, asked her that evening, "Why are you going out tonight? Didn't you say you were studying?" Irina replied, "I didn't want to, but my friends insisted." She didn't take her keys or her passport with her. "Good night, Mom." Raissa said, "If God exists, I ask him that my daughter may be an angel in heaven, and that she may be better off than when she was on earth."

Yulia Sklyanik had been in Israel for eleven years. Her mother, Irina, consoles herself with the last goodbye at the hospital, where Yulia died the day after the attack: "It may be blasphemy, but we were the lucky ones. Seventeen young people died, many were dismembered, and their parents went to identify them at the morgue. We had the fortune of saying goodbye to Yulia, of taking care of her, even though she couldn't hear us. But I think she heard me."

Maria Tagiltseva came from the Ural region, and she had chosen the Dolphi because ladies got in free that evening. One year after the attack, her mother gave birth to a child. With Maria was Raissa Nemirovskaya. It was her first time in Tel Aviv. "In college, I was an atheist," said her mother, Ljubov. "When I arrived in Israel, something inside of me changed. But God has taken innocent people before their time."

Fourteen-year-old Yevgenia Dorfman had come from Tashkent with her mother seven years earlier. "My instincts are usually good," says her mother, Faina, "but not this time. Not a ping inside." She recalled that her daughter had seemed nervous lately. "I remember once when Zhenya was getting ready for a school concert. We had to buy tights, ballet slippers, things like that. 'Let's go to the Dizengoff Center of Tel Aviv,' I said. 'Don't you understand?' she replied. 'I'm afraid.' . . . I often had to go to Jerusalem on business, and she always cautioned me: 'Where do you think you're going? Don't you know the situation in the country?'" Faina Dorfman's grandfather, a famous rabbi, was killed by the Nazis in the Russian region of Smolensk. "The Nazis killed him because he was a Jew," she says. "I brought my daughter here so that she could be at home, and now a Palestinian has killed her for the same reason."

In many ways, Faina represents the wounded mothers of Israel. Seven years after the attack, Faina reflects, "She was my only daughter, she was my world, my everything. After what happened, I decided to dedicate my time to telling Zhenya's story to the world. I still can't understand where I found the strength to do all of this. We have traveled all over the world to tell the stories of our children. We have gone to Germany, to the Czech Republic, to Moldova, to Ukraine, and to many other countries, and we have realized that the people don't understand what happened to our children. I have worked with the survivors of the attack, I have sat down with them, I have gone with them to the rehabilitation centers, I have given them support. Today these young people call me the 'Iron Mama.' I was the one who collected so much material, poetry, paintings, and creations of these lost young people in order to show them to the world and explain their beauty, talents, hopes and dreams that were brutally taken away from us and snatched from the world." It is as if Faina wanted to shake the indifference of those who don't understand. "It was not only the twenty-one children who were killed, their worlds were destroyed. Their grandparents have become ill and have died of heart attacks. Their parents have become ill. Their brothers and sisters have suffered psychologically. When they killed my daughter, in that moment they also killed me. They have killed us physically and psychologically. This truth must be repeated to every child who comes into the world."

Faina talks about her return to reality after the explosion that cut down her only flower. "At first, I didn't cry. I had to act. The battle was still going on. Zhenya's best friend, Sonya, was injured. Zhenya died from her injuries on Sonya's birthday. So I tried to dispel the pain and loneliness, in order to live, in order to survive. I didn't have the luxury of taking a break. I had to keep Zhenya's memory alive." Faina Dorfman hasn't lost her faith in Israel. "There's an expression in Hebrew to say that everything will be fine, *'Yihye besseder.'* I remember hearing my grandfather and other people saying it when we emigrated. We believe that; it's part of who we are as a people. We want to believe in a better tomorrow, to go on living in spite of our pain."

Yulia and Yelena Nelimov were sixteen and eighteen years old. "They were so beautiful," says their mother, Alla. The family had arrived in Israel in 1995, from Ekaterinenburg in the Urals. For the first month, they had no idea what was happening around them. Near their home was a community center, where the children spent all their time. They lived modestly, but they had a home, food, and clothing. "The children were full of the joy of living," their mother says. "They were always smiling; they even did their homework with their earphones on. It was like they had been born here." Yelena and Yulia loved music and dancing. "Even at the bus stop, if they heard music, they started dancing. They loved going to parties and seeing their friends." Yulia, the younger one, dreamed of becoming a hairdresser. "Ever since she was a little girl, she loved playing with hair, and she was always giving her dolls new hairstyles." Yelena wanted to study accounting. "She dreamed of enlisting in the army and studying. She spoke English well, and had learned to speak Hebrew in three months. She hoped that in the future she would be able to study in London or Paris." They worked as waitresses at a restaurant. "When we walked together, I only came up to their shoulders, and I would think to myself, 'Look at the children I have brought up!'"

The day of the attack, Yelena and Yulia had gone shopping for new outfits to wear that evening. "They put on their makeup together in front of the mirror, while my mother and I watched them. Lena had painted her fingernails green, and I had done Yulia's hair in pigtails." At the Institute of Forensic Medicine, they identified the girls by the green fingernail polish and the pigtails. "I saw them through a window. I should have gone in and touched them."

Alexei Lupalo helped his parents financially and wanted to be a lawyer. When they heard about the attack on the radio, his parents called him on his cell phone. He didn't answer, and they thought he was helping the injured, as he always did. Jan Blum was a security guard at the nightclub. He had already bought tickets for a flight to Ukraine so he could visit his parents along with his wife, Irina. That evening, he left his cell phone at home. "See you tomorrow," he told Irina, smiling. Marina Berkovskaya never went anywhere without her necklace. That's how her mother recognized her at the morgue, stretched out on the cold, clinical table. Before going out that evening, Marina had said to her mother, "Go to bed, and when I ring, come to the door but don't open your eyes—that way you won't wake up."

Alena Shaportova survived the blast, but she left the Dolphinarium with two pieces of metal in her brain, too risky to be operated on. She struggled to learn to talk, read, and write again. The shrapnel from the suicide attacker has left her physically and mentally disabled. Her father, Igor, speaks little Hebrew, but he makes an effort to explain: "She lost consciousness; the shrapnel from the bomb removed a piece of her brain." Irina Karp was also at the Dolphi that evening, and later said that she would rather have lost consciousness than see all that horror. Malka Chernyakov worked at the nightclub, and for years she has felt the heavy responsibility of having invited many of the young women who were there that night. She was saved only because she had entered the building just a few seconds before the blast.

A series of specially chartered buses took hundreds of students from the Shevah Mofet science high school in Tel Aviv to the funerals for their five classmates killed at the nightclub. At Shevah Mofet, 90 percent of the students are immigrants from the former Soviet Union; the school is like a second home for Russian Jews. The soldiers Ari Babich and Leon Davidov, who had graduated three months before the attack, left their respective bases to attend the funeral for Yelena and Yulia Nelimov. Avi Benbenisti, the school's principal, spoke at the funeral: "As head of the school, my job should be to accompany my students to the conclusion of their studies. But in the reality of Israel, my job now consists too much in accompanying my students to the grave." There was also a delegation from the Ministry of Education, including the minister himself; the girls' mother works at the ministry as a cleaning woman. One of their teachers said, "You were smiling and radiant. What will we do without your joy?" Marina Shniper, a cousin of the Nelimov sisters, said, "They loved life so much. I never saw them cry; they were always laughing."

Mariana Medvedenko was given a secular burial in the cemetery of the Givat Brenner kibbutz. She had come to Israel two and a half years earlier from Yakutsk, in northern Russia, along with her parents, Viktor and Tatiana, and her three younger siblings. Mariana was buried in a white dress, according to the tradition in her native country. It was symbolic of all the victims: pure and innocent, like the flowers of Israel.

"For three years, we have been haunted by the terrorist attack in which our companions had their lives extinguished in half a second, while others were crippled and will never have a normal life again," said a letter from students who survived the massacre. "Still today, it is hard for us to enter the classroom where the slain students studied, and look into the eyes of those continuing along their way. But we cannot give up. Terrorism must make us stronger."

Yulia and Yelena's mother wrote, "May all our names be written in the Book of Life." It was the most beautiful answer to the carpet of human remains at the Dolphinarium.

The Just Soldiers

S *ince the beginning of the Second Intifada,* 452 soldiers and police officers have been murdered in the uniform of the Jewish state. During the hours of Yom Hazikaron, the Israeli Memorial Day, one by one the young people of Israel are remembered on radio, on TV, in the newspapers. Seeing the hundreds of young faces, you want to get to know each one of them, but they no longer exist, except in the memories of their loved ones. All these young lives are briefly summarized, celebrating the many instances of self-sacrifice in order to save their friends. There are the idealists, the immigrants, the devout, the reservists. They are always celebrated in life, not in death. We couldn't tell all of their stories, so we chose a few of great heroism and humanity. These young people, with their olive green uniforms and fiery expressions, are a fundamental part of Israel's history.

Liran Sa'adia came from one of the oldest families in Kiryat Shmona. His parents have dedicated a memorial to him on the mountain above the city where he was born. "We are all walking behind him and in his shadow," said his father, Tzion. Liran's mother wanted the memorial to bear an inscription giving the meaning of each letter of the name "Liran": *lamed* for "lekhidut" (unity), *yod* for "yosher" (honesty), *resh* for "re'ut" (friendship), and *nun* for "netinah" (to give). One of Liran's teachers described him as a "pure soul" who planned to adopt a handicapped child.

According to his commanding officer, Itzik Grobas, "Liran was the man of innocence. He was not devout, but he put on the *tefilim* and prayed every day."

Sergeant Liran Banai was the voice of his parents, Guy and Gila, who were deaf and mute. During the Gulf War, when Saddam's missiles were falling on Israel, Liran had to let his parents know when the siren was sounding. He could have been exempted from military service because of his family situation, but he insisted on going. "Everything you did came from the heart," his mother said in sign language at the funeral. "What remains is our love for you. We love you." At Sergeant Kiril Golenshin's funeral, a friend said about him, "You were wide-eyed, a warrior on the front, and you died while you were doing what you loved most. We envy you for that." Yonatan Ankonina "saw protecting his country as a positive commandment, and knew that his service was like a mission." Before leaving for Lebanon, he told his parents that if he died, it would "sanctify the name of God, who protects his people."

According to Yossi Klein Halevi, "the greatest and most enduring psychological transformation of the Zionist revolution was the militarization of the Jew. If the dream of the Jewish worker has faded, the reality of the Jewish combatant persists." Israel's militarism is not a glorification of death but an offering to life, in the self-defense of a people in a democracy that fights without hatred. It is a sanctification of life, day after day, starting before the dawn of history and continuing through the antifascist uprisings in the ghettos and extermination camps. As Major Roi Klein said before being killed in Lebanon, the Israeli army is dominated by the idea that "the heroism shown in war is an act of such great benevolence that all other acts of benevolence vanish in comparison."

Israel is the only country in the world where there is no monument to the unknown soldier, because each of those fallen in battle is a hero in Israel, and his name lives on like a flaming brand in the nation's history. It took sixty years for Menachem Math, one of the Jewish volunteers in the War of Independence, to receive burial. But in the end, he was given his last goodbye. There are more than nine hundred memorials in Israel, one for every seventeen soldiers killed, compared with one for every ten thousand in other countries.

The Israeli army was created in 1948 with an obsession for being connected with the people; Moshe Dayan, the greatest of all the chiefs of staff, had a mystical idea of fusing the people and the army. The Israeli army was intended to be egalitarian, intelligent, moral, humane. It is the smallest, toughest, most unusual, and most talked-about army in the world, and the only army whose statutes include a clause that obliges the soldier to disobey an inhumane order. Israel's military laws embody an effort, without parallel in any other modern country, to teach moral behavior on the battlefield. The Israeli soldier, at the moment he is no longer fighting another soldier in a uniform or carrying a flag but rather an armed boy in blue jeans, must know very well when to open fire and what are the rules of combat. It would be easy for Israel to use its security forces without moral compunction; instead, these forces follow certain rules that, while intended to spare the civilian population, always tie one hand behind the backs of the fighters. The Israeli army, holding firm to the categorical imperative of defense, is still structured in such a way as to heed the underlying doctrine of international law and the humanistic inspiration of Zionism.

The requirement of three years' military service (two for women) beginning at the age of eighteen means that everyone must defend the country. Even your father is with you in the army when he is called up from the reserve one month a year. David Ben-Gurion spent a long time fighting with Mapam, the socialist party, to impose general conscription. At first, Israel preferred a military elite supported by a militia of haphazardly armed farmers, laborers, and fathers backing the ranks of heroes: soldiers in the morning, scholars at noon, and farmers in the evening, hoeing the ground. And in essence, that is how it's always been.

The army illustrates the difficult effort to blend the various Israeli tribes—Russian and Yemeni, Ukrainian and Ethiopian, religious and secular, Moroccan and American, Polish and Tunisian—until cultural and class divisions are broken down. Although the devout in Israel have succeeded in imposing a few rules, like substantial observance of Shabbat and dietary rules, and exclusively religious birth, marriage, and death ceremonies, there was an unwritten agreement to preserve harmony. That is the choice Ben-Gurion made when he decided not to write any constitution, and to leave the coexistence between secular and religious, between the kibbutz and the Torah, to the political battle. And that is why most of the rabbis did not order the devout soldiers to disobey the evacuation of Gaza, because doing so would have shattered the most sacred form of solidarity that Israel has instituted: the pact for life and death. The soldiers who evacuate the Territories are the same ones who are under orders to defend the settlers from terrorist attacks.

The IDF (the Zahal) is sacred, and this has always saved the country. "We are willing to accept hundreds of deaths in auto accidents or from suicide attacks," Sima Kadmon wrote in the newspaper *Yedioth Aharonot*. "When the victims are soldiers, it's a different story. If the young people on the stretchers are wearing the olive green uniform, your heart stops. And it's understandable. We have all had, have, or will have children in the military." In their photos, they look like teenagers in their third year of high school. They are Moroccan, Russian, Iranian, Ukrainian, or *sabra* born in Israel.

In the New Testament book of Revelation, it is Megiddo—Armageddon—that is the setting of the world's final battle. A few miles to the west is Caesarea, the port city founded by Herod, governor of Roman Judea; to the north is Nazareth, the town of the Annunciation and of Jesus' childhood. It was in Megiddo that a Palestinian suicide bomber decided to wipe out the lives of seventeen Israelis on June 5, 2002. Bus No. 830 runs from Tel Aviv to Tiberias, visiting the places of the Bible. It was approaching the Megiddo junction at around 7:15 in the morning when a speeding Renault full of TNT rammed into it. The bus burned for an hour. Everything inside was melted. Responsibility for the attack was claimed by Palestinian Islamic Jihad.

The bus was blown up next to the biggest Israeli military prison, where hundreds of Palestinian militants were kept. They rejoiced in front of the young Israelis torn to pieces and burned alive, while the guards helplessly watched the massacre from their towers. Many of those on the bus were soldiers returning to their bases. The driver, Mickey Harel, had already survived three suicide attacks, and now he lived through another. The only ones to survive were those who had been thrown clear, while those trapped inside the bus found themselves in a fiery inferno. Two charred corpses, a man and a woman, embraced amid the twisted metal. One of those responsible for recovering the corpses said with dismay, "Many of the bodies are unrecognizable. I'm afraid that we will have to bury them in a common grave."

David Stanislavsky had immigrated from Ukraine a year earlier and had bought a plane ticket to bring his fiancée, Victoria. Adi Dahan lived in Afula; her mother calls her "my beautiful, my intelligent Adi." Violetta Hizgayev, twenty years old, was a technician in the military. Liron Avitan, nineteen, "was like a mother to her younger sisters and brothers." Sivan Wiener was also nineteen; her older brother had accompanied her to the bus stop, and then called after half an hour to see if everything was okay; Sivan had reassured him. Ygal Nedipur was in the army and worked as a waiter because his family had serious financial problems. His sister says that now she is afraid, because "he protected all of us." The last Israeli victim of the attack by Palestinian Islamic Jihad at Megiddo was identified several months later. On the presumption that it was a foreign manual laborer, the body had been buried at the edge of a cemetery. But instead it turned out to be Eliyahu Timsit, from Sderot. His mother died from the grief of her loss.

Several years earlier, on January 22, 1995, a single suicide bombing had killed the most Israeli troops in one day since the war in Lebanon. The attack at the Beit Lid junction near Netanya mostly killed and maimed teenagers doing their three-year national service. A man wearing a uniform exploded the first bomb outside the snack bar. When soldiers rushed to see what happened, the second bomb detonated. An hour later, the smell of burned flesh was still heavy in the air, and the tattered bodies were still lying in the space between a soda vending machine and the bus shelter. Kitbags, jackets, and the red berets of the elite paratrooper unit—many of them blood-stained—were scattered amid broken glass and other debris. The men called in to recover the bodies had to root around among the shreds of military uniforms and gutted backpacks. The next morning, Israelis woke to newspapers with nineteen young faces framed in black. "The Children Who Won't Return," tolled one headline. "Tears of Rage," said another. The suicide bomber struck on the day when Israel was commemorating the fiftieth anniversary of the liberation of Auschwitz. "Never again like then" was the tearful prayer of the three thousand survivors who were gathered at Yad Vashem that day.

Attacks on places where officers and recruits are gathered thrust before our eyes the shared fate of civilians and soldiers in Israel. On February 14, 2001, seven young soldiers and one civilian were killed when a bus plowed into a waiting crowd at the Azor junction, south of Tel Aviv. Among them was Sergeant Julie Weiner, a French Jew who was going to fulfill her dream of serving as an officer in the army, and was waiting for the bus to take her to the base for training. She had not seen her parents in a long time and didn't want to visit them until she had become an officer. Julie was buried in Jerusalem after her father and mother arrived from France. Staff Sergeant Ofir Magidish and Sergeant David Iluz lived in the same building in Kiryat Malachi, and served on the same base. They had missed the transporter to the base by a couple of minutes, and had taken a bus to the Azor junction, where they were killed. Ofir's family said, "We did everything we could to get Ofir out of Lebanon, and we never thought that we would lose him right in the middle of our own country." Corporal Yasmin Karisi had also dreamed of becoming an officer. She was the firstborn and the pride of her family. Her father laments, "I have nothing more to live for." Corporal Alexander Minevich was an only child whose family had come to Israel from the Soviet Union. His parents were divorced, and his mother had raised him alone since he was a year old. "He was my only hope, a wonderful young man, who succeeded in everything." Alexander was preparing to finish his university entrance exams before the end of his military service.

Sergeant Rachel Levy worked in the logistics division at the base in Tel Hashomer and had signed a three-year extension of her army service. Her father said, "Adi, my oldest daughter, told me that the attack had taken place at the intersection where Rachel went every day. We called her on her cell phone, but she didn't answer. We called her commanding officer, and he told us that she hadn't arrived. Then we called the hospital, and they told us that she was not among the injured. We asked about her neighbor and dear friend, Sigal Yunsi, and were told she had been seriously injured. My knees buckled. We didn't know what was happening. Then came the officers with the terrible news."

Then, in October 2002, came the massacre that killed fourteen people on a bus, including three "sentries of suffering" who served at the Border Police Memorial in Wadi Ara. The units deployed at the monument are small, intimate teams of six border guards whose job is to provide information for visitors and take care of maintenance. "There were six of us in our unit; now there are only three," said Ivak Tahauko, commander of the unit serving at the memorial. "Half of our team doesn't exist anymore. I don't know how you get over something like this. I go from one family to another. I feel like I've lost three children." Aiman Sharuf had served in Hebron. Following an auto accident, he was transferred to the Wadi Ara unit just a week before he was killed in the explosion. Liat Ben-Ami, who had also been a combat soldier, had just started working as a guide at the Border Police Memorial because of a medical problem. Esther (Etti) Pesachov had been serving there the longest. She was responsible for contacts with the families of the fallen soldiers whose names are carved on the monument.

"Every morning, we met at the bus station in Hadera," recalls Etti's best friend, Liran. "We rode the bus together to the monument, and we returned in the afternoon. I wasn't there on the day of the attack—I had to have some tests done—and that saved my life. Because hitchhiking is prohibited, we took the bus, and this is what happened to my three companions. We served together for six months. She was so dedicated to her work. She visited grief-stricken families; she understood what they needed. She was an angel in uniform." Etti Pesachov knew the meaning of loss personally: her cousin Shoshana Reiss had been killed two years earlier in Hadera. About three weeks before her death, Etti had gone to visit the Franco family, whose daughter had been killed in a terrorist attack. "She was so lovely," Yochi Franco says, in tears. "She gave us so much courage. A woman that young needs a lot of inner strength to do that kind of job. She was truly a special person, and now her parents will have to go through this hell." Liran, also in tears, adds, "She liked this memorial so much, and now she and my other two companions will have to have their names inscribed here on this wall."

Speaking of Liat Ben-Ami, Liran says, "She made us laugh. Because our base is not large, we were always together. When Aiman Sharuf arrived, we did everything we could to make him feel at ease, so that he wouldn't feel like the new kid on the block. We told him everything, to bring him up to speed with the situation there." Liat had enlisted in the Border Police in July of 2001; she had completed her training on base with honors, and was assigned to the north. She was transferred to the monument unit two months before the attack. "The saddest thing of all," says Liran, "is that she had served as a combat soldier for a long time; she had been involved in various operations in Jenin, and then she paid with her life after she was transferred to the monuments unit."

In Hebrew they are called miluim, and they are a symbol of Israeli self-sacrifice. They are army reservists, between the ages of 25 and 50, and the older ones can be recognized by the fact that they have gained weight over the years. While the 120,000 soldiers (one-third of them women) on active duty are crucial, it is the 400,000 "old guys" ready to rush off in times of danger to wherever their country needs them, even at the risk of their business interests, who enable the Jewish nation to mobilize for every war. Some who are exempt from service since they have passed the age of 50 ask to be allowed to return to the combat corps; the older volunteers join other units. They are the real secret weapon of the Israeli army. In 1973, during the famous concentric attack on Yom Kippur, it was only after the reserves were mobilized that Israel could respond to the shock.

One of the first, terrible images of the Intifada was the lynching of two Israeli reservists who, on an October day in 2000, went the wrong way and ended up in Ramallah, where they were apprehended by Yasser Arafat's men. A frenzied crowd of Palestinians gathered at the police station, shouting as in a pogrom: "Give them to us! We want them! If you don't give them to us, we'll come get them!" The two soldiers were tortured and torn to pieces; one young Palestinian broke a window and hacked at the bodies with a shard of glass. The Palestinians appeared at the windows waving their hands ecstatically to the crowd outside, showing everyone the blood of the Jews. Then they burned the bodies in the town square, as in the time of the Inquisition. An Italian television crew filmed the profanation. The doctors would be able to assign names to those pitiful bodies only through fingerprints and dental records.

One of the two Israeli soldiers, Vadim Norzich, had immigrated from Russia and had just married Irina, who would soon give birth to his son. The other, Yosef Avrahami, sold toys. His wife, Hani, tried to call him on his cell phone that day. One ring, then two, then three. Hani had heard that something terrible had happened in Ramallah. A man answered the phone, a Palestinian, and asked her in Hebrew, "Who are you looking for?" Hani: "My husband, Yosef." And the Arab: "I just killed him."

Irina Norzich had come from Kazakhstan in 1995, after visiting Israel the year before. "I saw that the flowers here grow even in the winter, and that you could go to the beach year-round. I knew that this was the place for me." Irina and Vadim still lived at their parents' home, waiting until they could afford an apartment. Vadim had just been called to reserve service, so they decided to postpone their honeymoon and the purchase of their new marriage bed until he got back.

On the evening of February 25, 2005, a group of reservists gathered for a celebration at the Stage Club in Tel Aviv. Most of them had done their military service in the elite units, and they had met in a reserve unit eight years earlier. It had been the beginning of a friendship, the birth of a little secondary family. They had come to Tel Aviv from all over—from the Jordan Valley, from Tiberias, from Galilee, from Kfar Saba, from the Negev—to attend a surprise birthday party for Yaron Grayevsky, one of their group. "This is a proud friendship, started in the reserve and continued in civilian life," said Grayevsky, who at the moment of the explosion was with his wife, Revital, in a hotel nearby. "When we received the calls for our month of *miluim,* it was a joy for all of us. And then, after the reserve, we continued to get together at least once a month. At least two or three times, during the summer, we went camping near Lake Tiberias, or met at a hotel in Eilat. There was no big event for any of us that went uncelebrated."

The party was supposed to be the opportunity for a second surprise. Ofir Gonen, who in civilian life was a computer engineer in Kfar Saba, had arrived at the party with his fiancée, Yael Orbach. After her service in a combat unit, Yael had studied law and theater, dreaming of becoming an actress. At the party, she and Ofir were planning to hand out invitations to their wedding in three weeks. Yael was hit full force by the explosion. Ofir, who had let go of her hand for a moment, sustained a serious injury to his eyes.

Also killed that evening was Yitzhak Buzaglo, a farmer in the Mishmar Hayarden moshav who cherished the dream of building a home for his family on a little farm in the Jordan Valley. For years he had worked doggedly to raise his four brothers and two sisters, and finally he had a glimpse of hope in his future with his wife and their two children. At Yitzhak's funeral in the moshav, the commanding officer of his company, Eran Cohen, sang the praises of a "simple hero" who had finished his reserve service but continued to volunteer. His wife, Linda, was hospitalized with serious injuries. Yitzhak Buzaglo is remembered by his wife and children with a plaque: "He knew and loved the paths of Israel, and was killed in the land that he loved."

Then there was Aryeh (Arik) Nagar, the most joyful member of the group, who "at the age of thirty-six had the simplicity and freshness of an eighteen-year-old," Yaron Grayevsky recalled. Ronen Reubenov, who helped organize the party, "wasn't afraid of anything," said his sister, Orly. "He served in the most dangerous places, in Gaza and Lebanon. He was full of life, always smiling." One of the survivors revealed how a strange destiny united the victims: "A few years ago, some of them had miraculously escaped an attack by a Palestinian suicide bomber in the Territories—only to go and die in Tel Aviv, on a night that should have been a celebration."

Israel thought back to the *miluim* at the Stage Club a year later when a Hezbollah missile wiped out another group of reservists in an instant near the Kfar Giladi kibbutz in Upper Galilee. A century before, the mountains of the area had been patrolled by the "great-grandparents" of the IDF soldiers—the men and women who had decided to form the Hashomer, "the Guard," to protect the settlements of the first Jewish pioneers. "Guardian of Israel" reads the grave of Alexander Zeid, born in Siberia to a Zionist father of the very first generation who had been exiled by the tsarist police. After the pogroms, Alexander decided to found a militia to defend the Jews. He emigrated to Israel, where together with other pioneers he organized a militia of self-defense for *kibbutzniks* and *moshavniks*. The group took the name Bar Giora, after Shimon Bar Giora, a hero of the Jewish uprising against the Romans. Their motto was "In blood Judea fell, in blood it will rise again." Alexander Zeid was married under a wedding canopy made out of a Zionist flag. He died during one of his many shifts on watch.

With Zeid was Haim Sturman, born in a Ukrainian village, and described as "a rock" and "an old oak tree." Haim once said, "There is one thing that inspires us: defending our ability to reclaim our lost pride. The Arabs talk about us; they say that there are some Jews who cannot be driven out." And so he built the community of Tel Adashim from nothing, and when many Jews left Palestine after the beginning of English rule, Haim stayed where he was, until the very end. A legend in the labor movement, he combined labor and military self-defense. Haim's pistol was handed down to his son Moshe, who would die in the war of 1948. His grandson would die in the war of 1967, and one year later it would be the turn of another Sturman. Haim was a living wall of defense for Israel, while in Motza the Arab aggressors had slit the throats of the entire Maklef family. The only one to be saved was little Mordechai, who would become the third chief of staff of the Israel Defense Forces.

Joseph Trumpeldor is buried at Kfar Giladi. As a young man in Russia he was an ardent Zionist, influenced by Tolstoy, and imbued with socialist anarchism. He lost an arm in the Russo-Japanese war in 1904. "If Gogol and Dostoyevsky had seen the brave young Jews, they would have presented their Jewish characters in a completely different way," he told his friends. After emigrating to Palestine, Trumpeldor helped found a settlement in Galilee, and when World War I broke out, he was deported to Alexandria, where he met the revisionist leader Ze'ev Jabotinsky. He wrote letters to console the fathers who had lost sons on the battlefield. In 1920, he was sent by Hashomer to defend the Tel Chai kibbutz, near Kfar Giladi, from Arab aggression. He was mortally wounded in the effort, and before dying he reportedly said to his doctor, "It is good to die for one's country." Trumpeldor fought to bring into being an independent, free, fair, and democratic Jewish state.

These stories of Jewish pioneerism were carried in the hearts of the reservists who assembled at the Kfar Giladi kibbutz in early August 2006. In civilian life they were profes - sionals, lawyers, doctors, professors, university students; now they were paratroopers. When Israel calls, they throw some underwear into a duffel bag, grab their sleeping bags, and go—by bus, by motorcycle, hitchhiking, or in cars with the child safety seats still in them. They reassure their wives. They don't think about death.

"The siren sounded—it sounded for a minute, and they did nothing, they just stood there talking, chatting as if nothing were happening; they would live, they would all live if only . . ." recalled the head of security for the kibbutz. The reservists had gotten used to hearing sirens, and they didn't take cover. Twelve were cut down by a Katyusha rocket. One of them was Mordechai Butbul, "one of those who said that it was a just war," his wife recalled. "When we were at home, the Katyusha rockets had almost hit us; he said that when it happened, it would be fate. He told me not to stay here in the Kfar Giladi kibbutz; he was afraid for me and our son, but not for his own life. Twelve Israelis were murdered in Kfar Giladi in a single stroke. The detail of the bloodied boots shown on television wounded Israel's heart."

Shlomo Buchris had just assured his brother that he would come back safely. He bore the name of his father, who had been killed in the 1967 war. Shlomo died along with his cousin Yosef Karkash, so their relatives "didn't know which family to visit and console first." Shmuel Chalfon was forty-two years old, but he "loved the army" and insisted on taking part in the war. When the rocket hit the kibbutz, Shmuel's mother saw his shoes on television; there was no mistaking them. He left behind three children, the youngest just eleven months old. Daniel Ben-David "was always laughing" and he "loved helping others." Captain Eliyahu Elkariaf was killed that day, as was Ziv Balali, who had just completed his Middle Eastern studies. Gregory Aharonov, from Ukraine, was named after his grandfather who had been killed in war.

Yehuda Greenfeld left behind two young children. He had been active in helping the new Ethiopian immigrants who were arriving in Israel, many of whom were at the funeral to say their goodbyes. His sister Shoshi remarked that the war by Hezbollah in which Yehuda had died was one of many "pogroms against Israel." His brother Yitzhak commented, "We are at war, and this war began thousands of years ago. We have not yet had a moment of quiet. We left Egypt and arrived here in Israel, and have been fighting ever since." Yehuda's widow, Gavriella, spoke about the "messianic destiny of the kingdom of David," and ended by quoting Yehuda's exhortation, "Fight your battles with courage." The Ashkenazi chief rabbi, Yona Metzger, noted that Yehuda was "not a man of passive quiet, but rather a quiet that spoke of respect." Yehuda had studied in the best Israeli yeshivas, including Mercaz Harav, which would be hit by an attack in the spring of 2008. "Yehuda," said Rabbi Metzger, "you were never separated from the pages of the Gemara or from the Torah, for even a single day of your life."

Among the first reservists to be called into service for the war against Hezbollah in southern Lebanon was Elad Dan, who died on August 9, 2006. Members of his kibbutz said, "He was one of us. We raised him, and he paid us back through his giving and his endless good heart. If there was ever a boy you could call a 'diamond,' it was Elad." Before going into active duty in Lebanon, Yonatan Einhorn had asked his parents to be strong. "It's a battle of life or death," he told them. One of his uncles said, "He was the salt of the earth. He had dedicated his entire life to the army, to the paratroopers." His father, David, was also on active duty, another proud reservist; he was told about his son's death while he was still deployed to the front. His mother, Revital, said of him, "I know how much you loved life. You fought for your country, you loved your country, and you died for your country." Omri Elmakaias had been a reservist first in Gaza and then in Lebanon. One of his friends said that Omri "gave everything he had. He was fun, he loved to joke around." He even worked for the army on weekends, organizing social events. He was unmistakable in his Golani Brigade T-shirt.

Although Major Ron Maschiach had been eagerly awaiting the birth of a child, his brother recalls, "The last time we talked to him, he said he was happy to be going on a mission." He was another casualty of the Hezbollah war. Yehoshua Kochva came from a moshav. At his funeral, his commanding officer said, "I knew you since you were eighteen years old; you were an excellent warrior, a superb reservist." A friend of the family called him "a pilot whose love for this land was inscribed in his heart." Yehoshua had named his architecture office Sabra, honoring the hundreds of thousands of Jews born free in Israel.

A few years earlier, thirteen reservists were killed in an ambush while they patrolled the Jenin refugee camp on April 9, 2002. Oded Golomb was a farmer on a kibbutz. When asked why he took the risks he did, he would reply, "I can't send soldiers into battle without me." Menashe Hava, called back into service after the massacre at the Park Hotel in Netanya, said, "I am doing the right thing, and if I die, it will not be in vain. It will be for the State of Israel and its people." With him in Jenin was Yoram Levy had been called up on Shabbat and asked to be allowed to wait for sunset before joining his platoon. His wife, Rachel, was pregnant and didn't want him to go. He said, "If I don't go, and everyone else refuses to go, who will protect us?"

David Damelin had a degree in philosophy and taught at the military prep school in his kibbutz, the pacifist Metzer kibbutz in the Golan Heights. "How can I be a teacher in the State of Israel if I don't fulfill my duty as a reservist?" he asked. He was killed by a Palestinian sniper on March 3, 2002. David was a true Zionist who "embodied the greatest human ideals" and who "lived without cynicism," said one of the many friends who came to bid him a final farewell. "You used to say that we were fighting for the only democracy in the Middle East."

A beautiful young woman named Kochava Polanski was among those killed when a terrorist plowed a bus into a waiting crowd in February 2001. She had five months of military service left, and her father decided to complete what she could not. At the age of fifty, Eli Polanski stepped forward as a volunteer. "It was so important to her, but she didn't have the possibility of finishing it," he said. "That's why I'm doing it, for her. There are those who immortalize the memory of their children by building monuments, by giving money; I am perpetuating it by serving as a reservist. This is what she would have wanted me to do. People think that I am the one who is giving something to the army, but it is exactly the opposite: it is the army that has given something to me. Serving as a reservist has saved me. It was there that I was able to begin rehabilitation, where I started to live again, to laugh again; it was there that I was reborn. I see the soldiers, and I imagine that Kochava is among them. After the catastrophe, I didn't leave the house for more than a year. Now, thanks to my service in the reserve, I can breathe again."

After entering the reserve, Eli went to his daughter's grave in the cemetery of Ashkelon. "Yes, I was in uniform. In the first row, there were the graves of five soldiers, all of them killed on the same day, in the same attack. I went to her grave and gave the military salute. I said to her, 'Sergeant Kochava, your father.' I think she would be very proud of me." Eli Polanski was born in Chişinău, which is now the capital of Moldova. In 1978, he emigrated to Israel with his wife and child. Kochava was born in Israel. "In the Soviet Union," he explains, "they had told my wife that she would not be able to have any more children. When we came here, she underwent testing and treatment, and we had a little girl. We decided to call her Kochava, 'divine star.'"

Israel is a country built by the sweat of immigrants and living on the heroism of the "return" to Jerusalem. Jewish immigration to the land of Israel is the closest twentieth-century equivalent to the classical epics. During the 1950s, Israel absorbed a number of Jews equal to 50 percent of its population. From 1882 to 1903, more than 35,000 Jews chose Israel; from 1904 to 1914, another 40,000 arrived, mostly from tsarist Russia; between 1919 and 1923, they came from Eastern Europe, under pressure by the Christian pogroms. Another 82,000 came between 1924 and 1929, from Poland and Hungary; 250,000 arrived between 1929 and 1933, driven by the sulfurous breath of Nazism. From 1933 to 1948, up to 110,000 came; 500,000 from 1948 to 1950 with the complete emptying of Jews from Arab countries; in 1949 the Jews of Yemen, more than 49,000 persons, were transported to Israel; 113,000 fled from Iraq in 1951; 30,000 Iranian Jews fled Khomeini's totalitarian rule. Then there are the many from the former Soviet Union. Finally, there are the Jewish immigrants from a France that is once again plagued with anti-Semitism. Today, one of six citizens in Israel is an immigrant.

In 1948, at least 3,500 Jews came to Israel from all over the world as military volunteers. They were known as the Mahal, an acronym for Mitnadvei Hutz LaAretz, many of them veterans of the wars against fascism, whose grandchildren today are serving in the Israeli army. The *mahalniks* arrived on clandestine ships with the most beautiful names, like *Haganah, Hatikvah, Exodus 1947, Geula,* and *The Jewish State.* Many of them had left the United States and South Africa, England and Latin America, after the revelations about the Holocaust. They wanted to contribute to the survival of Israel. Foreign volunteers would form the beating heart of Israeli aviation and of the emergency medical services; they would be the best doctors, the first radar technicians, the first naval commanders. The first head of the Israeli naval fleet was an American, Paul Shulman, who had guided the twelve American ships that transported hundreds of Holocaust survivors to Israel. Two-thirds of the pilots killed in 1948 were non-Israelis. One of the volunteer heroes, the South African pilot Harold Simon, said, "We were the most privileged ones; we were present at the birth of our nation and at the redemption of the Jewish people after the Holocaust." Yet the *mahalniks* are virtually absent from the Israeli public memory.

David Ben-Gurion had encouraged their arrival, and he recognized them as having made an exceptional contribution to that special sense of "physical solidarity" between the Jews of the diaspora and those of Israel. The War of Independence for Israel was fought not only by Israelis, but also by Jews who had escaped the Holocaust, Jews who had fled in time from the Nazi inferno, and whom the Haganah had picked up and transported illegally to Palestine. They are, according to Ariel Sharon, the "true heroes" of Israel. "They came from the death camps, on seaborne junkers. From the internment camps, they were sent directly to the front line. They had no homes; they came from another planet. They were young like us, and yet thousands of years old."

At the military cemetery on Mount Herzl, there is a mass grave with fifty-two nameless victims. "I remember that some of them were under my command," Sharon said. "Michael Klein, a survivor in Hungary, fell in the battle of Nebi Samuel. Many years later, his sister came looking for him, but who knew him? And Joshua Mendelmacher, from Łód in Poland—no one has visited his grave since 1948. I remember a true hero, Mordechai Doziminer, who was killed after volunteering on a mission from which it was not possible to come back alive. They came without names, they fought without names, they died without names, and many of them still do not have one. In my mind, they are the true heroes." The names of 119 *mahalniks* who fell in battle are recorded on the Mahal Memorial near Sha'ar Hagai. The words of Yitzhak Rabin are engraved there: "They came to us when we needed them most, during those hard and uncertain days of our War of Independence."

Ya'akov Handeli was a Jewish volunteer from Greece. He made it through the selections in the Birkenau concentration camp, where he saw his sisters and parents for the last time before they went up through the chimney of the crematory. His brother died of starvation in the camps, but Ya'akov made it to the end, reaching Bergen-Belsen on foot in the fateful death marches. Then he came to Israel, the only survivor of his enormous family, and distinguished himself in battle.

There were also many non-Jews among the *mahalniks,* driven above all by the sufferings of the Jews in Europe. They wanted to follow the example of Orde Wingate, the greatest non-Jew in terms of Israel's history. Wingate was born in 1903 at the foot of the Himalayas, where his father was a colonel in the Indian army; his family belonged to a Christian sect that had Jewish influences and did not recognize ecclesiastical authority. It was Wingate who convinced Chaim Weizmann of the need for a Jewish force of self-defense. Wingate was also the mentor of Moshe Dayan. He spurred on his men with the story of Gideon and denounced the "swordless democracy" that had repudiated itself in Munich. In 1942, the English sent him to Burma to fight the Japanese. Winston Churchill called him "a genius," this non-Jew in love with Israel. In 1944, Wingate was in Normandy, and when he died in a plane crash, the entire Jewish community in Palestine went into mourning. In his last letter he had written, "If I forget you, Jerusalem, let my right hand wither."

For Jewish Americans, the model is Mickey Marcus, whose parents had fled to New York from Romania because of rampant anti-Semitism. Mickey graduated from the United States Military Academy at West Point in 1924 and fulfilled his active duty requirements, subsequently remaining in the reserve corps. With the outbreak of the war, he went back into uniform. He was sent to England right before D-Day and voluntarily parachuted into Normandy, helping to coordinate the landing. As part of the occupation government in Berlin, he was involved in clearing out the death camps. His first visit to Dachau convinced him that the only solution to the problem of genocidal anti-Semitism was a Jewish state. Marcus flew to Israel in 1948 and started organizing the nascent Jewish army. In a highly unorthodox move, David Ben-Gurion named him commander of the Jerusalem front; so 2,100 years after Judas Maccabeus, the Jews had a new commander to lead them in liberating their capital. One evening at headquarters, a young guard didn't recognize him. Marcus didn't understand his command in Hebrew, and the guard, not understanding Mickey's reply in English, shot him in the head. Mickey's body was taken to New York, escorted by Moshe Dayan. Ben-Gurion said, "Marcus was the best man we had." His tombstone calls him "A soldier for all humanity."

Each year, close to 120 Jews from abroad join the Mahal; the total number of volunteers over the years is around 5,000. Tziki Aud, who acts as an adoptive father for many "solitary soldiers" and is also head of the information center for new immigrants at the Jewish Agency for Israel, explains that "these are people that only ideology and Zionism are able to create. They have no financial interests, and they could have made much more money if they had stayed in America. Their friends have gone to college, but they instead decided to make the aliyah. Sometimes the soldiers come without any support from their families. Their parents are in the United States, and once they have arrived here their friends become their family." In some cases the parents have found out about their military service only with the news of their death.

Alexei Kutman came from the Urals. The Jewish Agency had helped his family settle in a kibbutz, and Alexei had found work as a truck driver so he could support his family. His wife was widowed while she was expecting their second child. German Rozhkov, who immigrated from Ukraine, was deputy platoon commander of the Nahal Brigade. His story represents the paradox of many half-Jewish Russian immigrants: his father, who still lives in Kiev, is Jewish, but his mother is not. German always felt a sense of belonging to Israel, and when he moved there he decided to enlist right away. He loved military life and was making it his career. His mother followed her only child to Israel, but since she was not Jewish, she had no right to citizenship and obtained only a residency visa. German was deeply distressed about it, so he wrote a personal letter to the prime minister, Ariel Sharon, saying, "What sense does it make that an officer who serves his country with fidelity should not find his mother waiting for him when he returns home? Must I perhaps fall in battle so that my mother's right to citizenship may be recognized?" A few days later, German was killed; and the following day, an official from the Ministry of the Interior came to see is mother.

Gregory Aharonov, also Ukrainian by birth, was killed by the Hezbollah rocket that hit Kfar Giladi. He was named after his grandfather who died in the Second World War. Gregory "had an open soul and would help everyone who asked," said his brother-in-law. "He would always do his reserve duty, and he went this time despite his fears." Igor Kublik's friends called him "a man of gold." He was an Orthodox Jew who had arrived in Israel at the beginning of the 1990s, when the collapse of the Soviet Union released thousands of "prisoners of Zion." Igor's mother was proud that he had become free and fought for his country. Ya'akov Marviza was born to a Serbian Jewish father and a Croatian Christian mother. Ten years earlier he had left his mother and sister to become an Israeli citizen, living in a kibbutz made up mainly of soldiers without parents in Israel. Asked why he decided to emigrate to Israel, Ya'akov said the country was fighting for its life and he needed to make a contribution. "He felt he was giving a hand to the nation," said Nizzim Uzan, the coordinator of his kibbutz.

Michael Levin came from the United States and died at the age of twenty-two, but today his name has an almost mythical greatness. One of his friends recalled, "We met in our Hebrew class, and it was very important to him to join the army, even though this was not obligatory. He was part of a group of lone soldiers from the United States. He had a heart of gold and gave everything to the army." His mother said that Israel meant everything to Michael.

On a visit to Mount Herzl in 2001, while he was studying in Israel, Michael was deeply moved by the grave of Yoni Netanyahu, the soldier killed in the raid on Entebbe that saved many Jewish lives. Michael was inspired to make the aliyah and enlist, so he returned to Israel the next year at age eighteen, telling his father, "Even if you cut off my legs, I will go to Israel." He was on leave in the United States when Hezbollah attacked in 2006, and he rushed back to join his unit again. Before leaving his beautiful home in Newtown, Pennsylvania, Michael said things like "if I come back," or "if I get out alive." When his parents said goodbye to him at the airport in New York, he said, "If God brings me back home, fine. Otherwise, bury me on Mount Herzl."

Michael was killed in action in Lebanon on August 1, 2006, and buried on Mount Herzl, the last home for the solitary soldiers who emigrate to Israel to fight. His uncle, Rabbi Allen Silverstein, noted that Michael was named after a relative who was decorated for his service in the Second World War. He also had a grandfather who survived the Holocaust. "We will miss you, Michael," the rabbi said, "but we will continue to take our inspiration from your love for Israel." His sister said, "Michael had a dream, and he made it come true." His story was turned into a documentary, *A Hero in Heaven*. After it was broadcast in

Israel, the TV channel was bombarded with telephone calls of condolence and affection for the Levin family.

Matanya Robinson was killed in Jenin in 2002 and buried in the Tirat Zvi kibbutz. He was the first member of the community to be killed in battle since 1973. A friend from the kibbutz recalled that they had talked about Zionism and how they were in a "second war of independence" just a few days before Matanya died. His commanding officer said he had "fought with courage and honor against a despicable enemy," and that Israel needed heroes like Matanya. His parents, Mark and Rina, had come from the United States in 1979, before he was born. "They are very much a Zionist family," recalled a friend from the kibbutz. "Mark leads seminars on the Holocaust, and Rina was a teacher in the kibbutz for years." Mark also took students to visit the concentration camps in Poland. Matanya "had the spirit of someone who was fighting for his country, like most of the children of the kibbutz," said a friend. "He was killed for the good of the country, so that the citizens could sleep in peace."

Ari Yehoshua Weiss was killed in 2002 while fighting in Nablus as part of the Nahal Brigade. He had made the aliyah from Dallas with his family ten years earlier. His father, Rabbi Stewart Weiss, was born in Chicago, and Stewart's father was a decorated member of the United States Air Force in the Second World War. Rabbi Weiss is the director of the Jewish Outreach Center in Ra'anana. His wife, Susie, is the daughter of Holocaust survivors. "They were with us when Ari was killed, visiting from America," he says. "And for them, having survived the Holocaust, it was a heavy blow."

As Rabbi Weiss sees it, "Every time a soldier dies, a little piece of us disappears along with him." He explains that "in Israel, a special honor is reserved for our soldiers, our best young people. We honor them on Yom Hazikaron, and the whole country pauses in silence while the sirens are sounded in their memory. The nation of Israel understands that we continue to exist as a country thanks to all those who pay the ultimate price for our security. The army is the great equalizer of society." He remembers those young Americans who came to Israel in 1948 to fight for independence: "Israel is a country of immigrants, although we lived in this land for thousands of years. After the dispersion of the Jewish people, when the Temple was destroyed two thousand years ago, we dreamed and worked to return to our ancient land. We never gave up the hope of returning. And when we began to do so at the end of the nineteenth century, we knew it wouldn't be easy. Every Jew has the right to citizenship in Israel because every Jew, from birth, is part of Israel. Over the past fifty years, the population of Israel has grown by 1,100 percent."

We ask him what religious significance he sees in Ari's death, and he replies, "Historically, the Jewish people have always fought against those who were seeking to destroy the Jews—from the time of the Bible, when Esau fought against Jacob, to ancient Greece, to the Spanish Inquisition and the Holocaust. The same thing is happening with Islamic hatred for Jews and Judaism. There is no rational explanation. Hitler did himself harm by persecuting the Jews and banning books written by Jews, including Einstein. Ari was called to fight against Israel's enemies in this chapter of the Jewish struggle for freedom and independence. And he fell to the terrorists of Hamas and Islamic Jihad. On a spiritual level, I believe that Ari's death is part of Israel's martyrdom and God's plan. I can't tell you why, I only know that Ari was chosen to give his life, and that he served a divine mission that has been an inspiration for thousands of people, demonstrating heroism, courage, and devotion to a higher cause. The spirit of sacrifice is itself one of the characteristics of Judaism and guarantees our eternal survival."

Weiss believes that "the just man, because of the life that he has lived and the example he is for others, lives on after his death. His name is alive. His spirit is alive. He continues to influence others even when he has left this world. In Ari's case, there are seven children who bear his name; a public park and a center will soon be dedicated to him. So he is still alive in our eyes. Physical life is brief, but heroes are immortal and never die. They live in our minds, in our hearts, in our souls."

Asked what the sanctity of life means in Judaism, and above all in a land that has known only fear, blood, and violence, Rabbi Weiss tells us, "We believe in the sanctity of life. Judaism teaches that life is the highest ideal, that if someone saves a life it is as if he had saved the whole world. Each person is a world. We are not afraid of dying; we know that sometimes, on the path of freedom and justice, people must die in order to make the world safer. Our God is the God of life. That is how we honor Ari's life, spent to help others, to bring joy to others, spreading life, happiness, and hope. Because, in the end, life and hope will triumph over death and despair."

Yehonatan Wolsiuk had come to Israel from Ukraine on his own and had been adopted by a kibbutz. The principal of his high school, Ido Argman, said that Jehonatan represented modern Zionism: "He was a fifteen-year-old boy who had emigrated to Israel without his parents, and without knowing Israeli society and culture. Thanks to his will power and his charming personality, he was able to achieve success at all levels." Yehonatan's family flew in from Ukraine when they were informed that he was missing in battle in 2002, at age twenty-one. Yulia wanted her son to be buried in Kibbutz Lahav. "He was an Israeli citizen who died doing his duty, so he will be buried here. He loved this country so much," she said. "He was a responsible young man who loved life. He wanted us to emigrate to Israel after the end of his military service. He simply loved the army, and loved Israel. He would have been discharged the following November. He had said that he might have gone to Lebanon, and the idea didn't scare him. This whole situation infuriated him. The terrorists infuriated him. He felt that he had to do something."

Noam Meierson was "a God-fearing man," his mother said. "He loved the history of the Jewish nation, the nation that had returned here from exile; he had great faith and inner strength." Noam had a habit of telling the whole story from the very beginning: the promise that God made to Abraham, Jacob leading his family into Egypt, Joseph buying up tract after tract of land, the pharaoh ordering that all the sons of the Hebrews be killed, Moses appearing on the banks of the Nile, the crossing of the Red Sea, the succession of Joshua, the Twelve Tribes, and then Judah, the monarchy, the first warrior king named Saul, David taking Jerusalem from the Jebusites, Solomon constructing the Temple, the Babylonian exile, the liberation by Cyrus of Persia, the sacking of Jerusalem, the beginning of two thousand years of exile. And finally, the return to the coastal plain once inhabited by the Philistines, to the mountains of Carmel, where the prophet Elijah built his altar, and then those of Judah, where Samson fought and David challenged Goliath, traveling over the paths walked by Hosea and Jeremiah, and the valley in Ezekiel's vision. Noam Meierson lost his life fighting Hezbollah in southern Lebanon in 2006.

Kiril Golenshin was in one of the units most at risk because of the many raids into the Palestinian Territories that it had to carry out in order to chase terrorists. Kiril was killed in the Gaza Strip in November 2006. His commanding officer noted that as an only son, Kiril could have asked for exemption from the combat units. His father mourned him as a true patriot: "I never told you, but I am proud of having raised you. When I asked you if you would stop it with all of these dangerous operations, you answered me, 'Dad, I'm with my friends, I can't hold back.'"

Alexei Naikov came from Ukraine to Israel in 1996, when he was seventeen years old. He was planning only to study in

Israel, but he fell in love with the country and joined a combat unit. He also convinced his parents, Klara and Semyon, to follow him to Israel. "He wrote home to tell us how difficult it was," says Klara, "and then he called us saying, 'Don't pay any attention to what I wrote; things have changed and I don't intend to leave Israel.' That is why we also decided to make the aliyah." Alexei rented an apartment in Haifa for his parents and helped them begin to meet the challenges of assimilation.

In October 1998, Alexei was in a jeep escorting a bus that was transporting children from Kfar Darom to the school at Neveh Dekalim in Gush Katif, a world that would not survive for a single day if not for the army protecting it. When a car loaded with explosives approached the bus, the jeep blocked it and absorbed the blast, saving the children's lives. Alexei was killed instantly and the two soldiers with him were wounded.

His father asked that Alexei be buried in Israel. "This country accepted him, and he accepted this country and wanted to defend it. He told me that he was serving in a combat unit, but I didn't know he was in Gaza. From his voice, I had guessed that he was in a dangerous place, and that he didn't want to get into the details. I don't resent Israel. I am proud that my boy did his duty. But the pain is unbearable. Just one month after I came to visit him, I returned to bury him." Alexei's mother, Klara, says, "It has been terribly painful. His death has wiped out half of our life. During the period of strict mourning, we realized that there are many families in Israel like our own. We very rapidly became part of the great Israeli family. Maybe we have even become Israeli." She adds, "We have had problems, but we feel that we are not alone."

Semyon Naikov notes a difference between Israel and his native country: "Here, respect is given to the soldiers who have given their lives for the State of Israel, and their parents are remembered. In the Soviet Union, neither the army nor the state remembers the fallen, not even for a month. Although our son went to meet his destiny, he will continue to live in the hearts of the children of Kfar Darom. Now our job is to tell people about Alexei and continue on the path that he began." Klara remarks, "A person lives on as long as people continue to talk about him." In fact, people still talk about Alexei Naikov, and a special bond has grown between his parents and the children of Kfar Darom. They visit Klara and Semyon two or three times a year, and have prepared a special commemorative album for them. Klara says, "We are proud of our son because he saved children. We can see him and feel him in each of these children." Semyon points to a tree standing at the entrance to their house. "In our village, a cherry tree was planted every time someone was born."

Their Best Dresses
and Shoes

On March 27, 2002, *Sivan Vider* was at the Park Hotel in Netanya for a Passover Seder. She was twenty years old, and a picture of her shows a young woman with her sight set on her goal. In one month she would finish her military service and then go on a long trip, as many young Israelis do after their discharge. Sivan taught the recruits how to handle weapons. She refused to be fearful. "Everything is written, if it must happen ..." she used to repeat like a mantra. Her grandmother had said, "Come to Netanya, it's less dangerous here than where you live." Sivan's fiancé was not with her at the Seder because he had to be with his family; the two had been madly in love for five years. At Sivan's grave, he said, "You were so beautiful, so funny, so intelligent. I'm still ready now, Sivan, let me come with you." Her father, Ze'ev, also died; one of his kidneys was transplanted into the body of an Arab woman in Jerusalem. "Dad wanted to save a life, and a life has no nationality," said his son Nimrod, who was out of the country on the night of the Seder. He promised his father that he would take care of his mother and his sister Gili, who was in the hospital and had lost her fiancé.

The Palestinian terrorist, carrying a suitcase, was able to sneak past the private guards at the entrance to the Park Hotel. He walked through the lobby into the dining room, where

dozens of people—whole families, many children—were listening to a reading from the Haggadah, the biblical account of the
ten plagues that struck Egypt to convince the pharaoh to
release the Hebrews from their enslavement. One of the passages says, "Tonight everyone should think of himself as someone who has left Egypt personally." What this asks for is an
effort of identification in order to celebrate that ancient liberation with greater awareness. During the Seder, symbolic actions
are performed to emphasize the central points of the event.
One of these is the eating of bitter herbs, in memory of slavery,
dipped into a sweet mixture called *charoset,* to represent how
hope for the sweetness of freedom never disappeared even
amid the bitterness of bondage. The *charoset* is a mixture of
raisins, dates, apples, prunes, and cinnamon, symbolizing the
mortar that the Israelite slaves were forced to make for their
bricks.

One text for the Passover Haggadah of 1949 says, "How is
this night different from all other nights? On the other nights,
before we came to this country, we were under the rule of hostile and foreign laws ... and now we are in our country, whose
land we cultivate and whose deserts we make bloom." A version
of that account had been written many centuries before. After
the Romans demolished the Temple of Jerusalem, a group of
scholars of the Law survived in the village of Yavneh. They met
to pray and study in an attic. The modern version of the Haggadah was born then, when the fate of Judaism depended on
the courage and perseverance of just a few people. Hope for
Israel's survival was rekindled in that school. Its students
included Rabbi Akiva, who died under torture while reciting
the Shema. Just like the Orthodox Jews in Nazi Europe, and
the Israelis gathered at the Park Hotel that night. Many Jews
repeated Rabbi Akiva's words before being swallowed up by the
gas chambers. The same ones who, in Auschwitz, were able to
set aside their piece of bread until sundown, in observance of

fasting. As Ehud Barak—the most decorated soldier in Israel's history, who lost his family at Treblinka—said, "in our blood run the genes of the Maccabees and of the zealots who died in Masada. But we also bear the legacy of Yochanan ben Zakkai, who fled from Jerusalem when it was under siege in order to preserve in Yavneh a tiny, fragile testimony of the heritage of the Torah and the Talmud."

A ritual Passover supper, like the one in Netanya, follows a complex ritual. "When the attack happened, my family and I were just sitting down around the festively set table," recalled Naomi Ragen, a writer who was at the hotel that evening. "The Seder means, literally, 'order.' You read the story of the Exodus from Egypt, the escape from slavery into freedom, and at certain points you stop and point to ritual objects: a bowl of salt water for tears; a cup of wine representing the drops of blood spilled from Jewish babies thrown in the Nile, and the revenge of G-d during the Ten Plagues; the flat breads, called the 'bread of affliction' because the Jews were chased out of Eygpt after the last plague, and the bread couldn't rise." All the plagues must be remembered with a sense of relief as well as compassion for the Egyptians, up to the last one: the terrible death of the firstborn.

When the Palestinian "martyr" entered the hotel's dining hall, the guests were listening to Exodus 12:13–14, "But the blood will mark the houses where you are. Seeing the blood, I will pass over you; thus, when I strike the land of Egypt, no destructive blow will come upon you. This day shall be a memorial feast for you, which all your generations shall celebrate with pilgrimage to the Lord, as a perpetual institution." The suicide bomber waited a moment and then set off the detonator. The hall was devastated, windows and glass panels shattered, light fixtures ripped out, the ceiling halfway collapsed. The ball bearings and nails packed into the bomb hit the people farther away. There was an enormous pool of blood—the blood of innocent Jews who had wanted to celebrate Passover together that night. A copy of the Haggadah and a piece of unleavened matzo bread were immersed in the blood, as if to illustrate one of the worst claims of anti-Semitic propaganda: that the Jews make the bread with the blood of Arab children.

Emergency workers found dozens of victims dead on the floor, their cell phones ringing wildly. "It was like ten attacks at the same time, all the plagues of Egypt," said Isaac Atsis. Thirty died in an instant. It was the largest single massacre of Jews since the Second World War. The hotel owner, Claude Cohen, remarked, "Under the laws of Vichy, I was excluded from the French schools because I was Jewish. The world wants Israel to fight like a boxer with his hands tied behind his back."

Naomi Ragen recalled, "We were waiting for my husband's parents to come up. They were downstairs using the washroom. And suddenly we heard a roll of thunder, and the floor shook. The room we were in was sort of an enclosed balcony with many windows. Suddenly all the glass shattered, and the shards flew in towards us in slow motion, like something in a cartoon. 'Get down!' my husband commanded. I began to scream the way I had in childbirth. But then I saw how that was frightening my two grown sons and my daughter-in-law, so I stopped. My daughter-in-law, still a young bride, was weeping and shaking uncontrollably. We waited, not knowing what would happen next. We wondered if there was another bomber who was on his way upstairs. My son said he heard shooting. My husband said he was going down to look for his parents and we should wait. But while he was gone, two young waitresses came up the steps. They were covered in blood. This frightened me so much that I asked my family to take a vote if we should wait or flee. We all wanted to leave.

"We made our way down the back steps with the help of the hotel manager's children (whose father had been killed in the blast, we found out later). There were electric wires hanging down, and water covering the floor. I was afraid we'd get electrocuted. Downstairs, our exit was blocked; it was the pool area. My son, an army reservist, found a way through the basement to the lobby. The floor was covered with red, and as much as I wanted to leave, I couldn't bring myself to step in it. We didn't look around, terrified of what we would see. We made our way to the street.

"The ambulances were already arriving. My in-laws were standing there, waiting for us. My father-in-law had two children gassed in Auschwitz. Now he had invited his only son and grandchildren to share the holiday with him. 'If anything had happened to you, I would never forgive myself,' he murmured. We hugged each other and made our way down the street to another hotel where people were in the middle of their Seder. They didn't seem to know what had happened. I asked them to find a room for my in-laws, and I told them to set another table so we could read the words of the Seder, and thank G-d for His deliverance."

In Israel, it is rare to go to a gathering, a party, without running across survivors of the concentration camps. Netanya is a place favored by devout elderly Jewish immigrants, and the Park Hotel was known to be where Holocaust survivors went with their families for the Seder. It was also easy prey for suicide bombers, being just a few miles from Qalqilyah. Amiram Hamami, the hotel manager and security coordinator, had been interviewed by a local television station a few days earlier and had emphasized the dangers in Netanya. "Our proximity to Tulkarem makes it easy for us to be hit by terrorists at any point in the city in a matter of seven or eight minutes. The city's security systems need to be reinforced." Amiram, called Ami, had noticed a man wearing a black overcoat, a long wig, and sunglasses even though it was nighttime, and had followed him. It seems that Ami had drawn his pistol just before the explosion. He died two days after the attack. Ami was a handsome man with gold-rimmed glasses and a kippah on his head. The guests of the hotel say that he made everyone feel at home. He left behind a wife and six children, and many friends.

Avraham Beckerman, twenty-five years old, was supposed to meet the parents of his girlfriend, Gili Vider, that night. The invitation made him a member of the family. They had been living together for a year and a half, in an apartment on an agricultural moshav, "a couple united by heaven." Avi loved scuba diving, and he loved his work in the aviation industry even more. He was a mechanic who specialized in helicopters. That had been his dream ever since high school, his brother recalled. Avi's coworkers said that helping others was a source of joy for him.

Perla Hermele, seventy-nine, had come from Stockholm, where her father had brought the whole family from Poland to escape from the Nazis. She wanted to spend Passover in Israel, as she had done for the previous twenty-five years. Since she was widowed six years earlier, she traveled with two of her friends. "I know very well that it's dangerous, but it's precisely on days like these that I need to be in Israel," Perla told one of her two children during a telephone call to wish each other a happy Passover, shortly before the attack. Always full of energy and enthusiasm, Perla worked tirelessly as a volunteer. Her son Bernt filmed a splendid documentary about her life for Swedish television, *My Mother Was Murdered by a Suicide Bomber.* "My mother knew what she was doing, and I was nervous about her decision to go to Israel on those days," Bernt said. "But her faith was very strong, and she felt that Israel was the right place to be during that time."

Shimon Ben-Aroya, age forty-two, worked for the city of Netanya in the sanitation department. His family was at the center of the explosion, and fourteen of them were injured, including two children ages nine and thirteen. "We were relaxed when we sat down, trusting in the presence of the guard at the entrance to the hotel," said his wife. "All of a sudden it went dark. I felt an electric shock through my entire body, but I don't remember hearing an explosion. I started yelling. I didn't know what had happened to my husband." His boss at work said, "Whenever I gave him a job, I knew that I could depend on him. He was an outstanding worker, industrious, intelligent," someone who "barely missed a day of work."

Irit Rashel, forty-five, loved to sing and was a member of the choir of Hadera. She went to rehearsals after finishing her job as a secretary for a psychological counseling center. That night she was at the Seder with a friend. Her husband had come from the Soviet Union during the years of the "silent Jews," and was a Zionist at a time when it meant grave danger in the USSR, as Natan Sharansky had shown. He was a representative of the Jewish Agency, working in Odessa, where he was organizing a Seder on the day of the attack. Their two daughters, ages eighteen and twenty, had just left for Budapest on a trip that Irit had planned to go on, but she backed out at the last minute, giving her ticket to her older daughter instead.

Yehudit Korman, seventy, was born and raised in Ramat Hasharon, near the beautiful upscale city of Herzliya. Her husband, Eliezer, was a builder and real estate entrepreneur who still worked on construction sites at age seventy-four. He was born in Poland, and when World War II broke out, he fled with his parents to Siberia. After the war, he searched for his brothers and sisters in Germany, Austria, and Italy, but couldn't find a trace of them. Eliezer fought in the Battle of Latrun in the 1948 war. The Kormans had celebrated Passover many times in Netanya. That year, because of their children's worries, they had decided not to go, but the hotel manager changed their minds by offering them a discount. "We have to keep living, without fear," Yehudit said. Speaking with her son on the phone a few minutes before the attack, she said, "I'm enjoying every minute. Don't forget to take the gefilte fish from the refrigerator."

Idit and Andre Fried were a beautiful and happy couple; in their pictures they are always together, smiling. They had come from Hungary in the late 1970s, to establish themselves in Netanya. Andre was a successful dentist and Idit was a nurse at the Laniado Hospital, where her coworkers wept as they tended to those injured in the attack. "Idit liked making people laugh. Both of them enjoyed life; they loved traveling abroad and helping new immigrants find their way in Israel," said friends visiting their two children in mourning at their huge home with its ocean view. Tom and Shirli, ages sixteen and twenty-one, were saved by a slight delay: they arrived at the Park Hotel a few minutes after the attack. They also lost their grandmother Anna, who was Andre's mother.

Anna had been married for twenty years to George Yakobovitch; both were Holocaust survivors, and it was the second marriage for both. That evening, they were sitting at the same table with Anna's son and daughter-in-law. Anna was able to say a few words to her grandson before losing consciousness in the hospital, where she died two weeks after the attack. George Yakobovitch was a lawyer, and was well liked among his neighbors and the Hungarian Jewish community. He was a calm, refined man of habit who inspired trust in those who met him. "We would always see him get on the bus to go to his office at the same time, and return at the same time each evening," a neighbor said. "He seemed like he was destined to be there forever."

Eva and Ernest Weiss "were like two lovebirds," said a relative who was called to identify the mutilated bodies of the elderly couple. "In the tragedy of their death, there is at least the consolation that they died together. Neither of them could have survived without the other." Born in Romania, Eva and Ernest had both experienced the Nazi concentration camps. They got married in Transylvania immediately after the war. In 1967, they moved to Israel, settling in Petah Tikva. Ernest worked as a diamond polisher, while Eva took care of the house; they had no children. After Eva's mother died, the couple had started celebrating Passover at the Park Hotel. This time, their neighbors say, "Ernest was very worried. The day before they left, he told us that he couldn't wait to return home."

Sarah Levy-Hoffman, eighty-nine years old, was a survivor of Auschwitz, where she lost her husband and a four-year-old daughter who was torn from her arms when she arrived at the camp. In Israel, she made her living with a little grocery store. She had a son who was with her on the evening of the tragedy and was injured, while her three grandchildren and daughter-in-law were saved because they were in another room at the moment of the explosion. Sarah died after eleven days in the hospital. "She was a strong woman," her family said. "She survived Auschwitz but not terrorism."

Dvora and Michael Karim had come from Iran. They were famous in the Persian community, and for years they welcomed Iranian Jews who were fleeing from the Islamic regime. They lived in Netanya, where Michael managed one of the offices of the Jewish National Fund, which has been working to make this arid land green since before the foundation of the state. Dvora was a kindergarten teacher. Michael had recently met with President Moshe Katsav to inaugurate a project to preserve Jewish-Persian culture and create a retirement home for the elderly of the community. He had donated a Sefer Torah, a scroll of the Pentateuch, to his synagogue, and a big celebration was organized in his honor. "Maybe he felt that the end was coming and he wanted to perpetuate his name," his prayer companions say. Dvora and Michael left behind two daughters, grandchildren, and a great-grandson.

Chanah Rogan, ninety years old, had come from the United States in the 1970s with her husband, Pinhas. The Laniado Hospital in Netanya remembers Chanah for her generous acts of charity, including the donation of an intensive care unit and an operating room. She used to celebrate the Seder in a nearby kibbutz, but that year she decided to stay in Netanya, together with her childhood friend Yulia Talmi, who was also killed in the explosion. Yulia was a white-haired lady who always wore pearl earrings. She lived in the most elegant building in Tel Aviv, the huge Kikar Hamedinah. She had come from Russia in the 1930s, and up until the death of her husband she loved to host the entire family for the Seder supper in their beautiful apartment. "Yulia was the anchor of our whole family, a source of support and affection for all of us," said her brother, whose wife had been killed in 1990 by a terrorist attack on a bus of Israeli tourists in Egypt.

Alter and Frieda Britvich, both in their eighties, had lived in Netanya for years, and the Park Hotel was just a few minutes on foot from their apartment. Frieda was born on the border between Romania and Czechoslovakia. She survived Auschwitz and married Alter after a courtship by letter. They loved going on walks and traveling. "They weren't apart even for a moment," said one of their granddaughters. Both were seriously injured and taken to different hospitals, where they died a few hours apart from one another.

Marianne Lehmann Zaoui, seventy-six, was born in Germany and escaped extermination by fleeing to France, where she and her sister hid in a Catholic village. After the war, she taught English in a high school in France and had three children. In 1992 she moved to Israel, joining Lucien, her second husband. Marianne's relatives are convinced that, with her death, she saved the life of her husband, who was slightly injured, and of her nine-year-old grandson, who was unharmed, because her body absorbed the impact of the explosion. Her daughter had left the dining room a moment earlier to take her own daughter to the restroom.

"There is no fruit or flower that you won't find in his garden," say the neighbors of Eliahu Nakash, age eighty-five. He had come from Syria in 1948 and had started a brisk business growing fruit and vegetables. After his first wife died, he decided that "life is too short not to enjoy it," so he married Geula. They grew flowers, went on walks, socialized with friends. A very religious man, Eliahu went regularly to the neighborhood synagogue. His neighbors say that recently he had donated a scroll of the Pentateuch. "He had no children, and that scroll was worth at least a hundred thousand dollars," they murmur with admiration. Geula was seriously injured in the attack.

Shula Abramovitch, sixty-three, had come from Poland when she was fourteen, and her family had escaped the Holocaust by taking refuge in Siberia. Two years after arriving in Israel, she met "the right man," with whom she had two daughters. Shula lived outside Tel Aviv and worked in a factory. Her family had been part of a great dynasty of wise men and rabbis, and in recent years she had "returned to the answer," as it is called when Jews return to Orthodox practice. That was why she and her husband had celebrated the Seder at the Park Hotel.

Lola Levkovitch had a contagious smile, a beautiful and full face. At age seventy, she lived alone in a beautiful residential neighborhood in Jerusalem, and her neighbors say that she was always full of affection for everyone. Her daughter, four grandchildren, and two great-grandchildren live in Paris. As soon as her daughter found out about the attack, she tried to track down Lola. Unable to find her, she got on the first flight to Tel Aviv. "I tried to embrace her and warm her up a little," she said. Miriam Gutenzgan, eighty-two, had been a nurse, and she volunteered for social work after her retirement. On the day she died, she was wearing a T-shirt with a photo of her son, a pilot who had been killed in the war of Yom Kippur.

David Anichovitch, seventy, had the face of a World War II veteran. He had suggested attending the Seder at the hotel that evening because "it's more comfortable and easier," as he told his wife, Frieda. His only son, who lived in America, rushed to the airport as soon as he heard the news. He found his mother in the hospital, asking for her husband over and over, and he had to break the news of his death.

Clara Rosenberger was the thirtieth victim at the Park Hotel. She had a number tattooed onto her arm fifty years earlier when she was deported to Auschwitz with her family, who were all gassed and incinerated. A strong young woman, she had been given the job of collecting the belongings of those who were sent to the gas chambers. After the war, she boarded a ship belonging to Bricha, the movement for clandestine immigration into Israel. Her only possession was a new pair of shoes, which she was wearing when she first set foot in Israel. After the war, Ephraim Oshry, the rabbi of Kovno, was asked if the survivors could have the numbers tattooed on their arms removed. Oshry said that would have been a victory for Hitler. Clara wore her number with pride. "I have never hurt anyone," she said from her hospital bed, adding that she didn't hate her attackers. Clara, with her number and with her story of redemption and pain, was and is the image of Israel.

Arkady Vieselman, who had immigrated from Odessa, by chance escaped the attack at the Park Hotel, where he worked as a chef. Two months later, a bomb at a market in Netanya killed him.

After this immense tragedy that, on one Passover evening, devastated dozens of families and killed many elderly people who had survived Auschwitz, the Palestinian Authority organized a school soccer tournament in Tulkarem in honor of the best suicide bombers. Isam, the brother of the Netanya bomber, was there to hand out the trophies.

Commenting on the attack, Naomi Ragen wrote, "It seemed to me to epitomize the savagery and barbarity of our enemies, who love death. They say so openly. I am not a vengeful person. But I never want to hear the word 'peace' again as long as I live. It has become a code word for leaving yourself vulnerable to the attacks of your enemies, who can only be defeated by war. People forget that Israel is home to the highest number of Holocaust survivors in the world, and when terrorists target Israelis, they are targeting survivors, and that this is a particular obscenity. Europeans build memorials to the dead victims of the Nazis, but they seem perfectly O.K. with the idea that the living victims and their children are being targeted and slaughtered by terrorist savages. In our 'Haggadah,' the book we read on Seder night, there is a line: 'Not only in one generation have they tried to annihilate us, but in every generation our enemies seek to annihilate us; but G-d who is blessed, saves us from their hands.' When I said those words on Seder night in 2002, I felt deeply the truth of that statement. It only strengthens my commitment to building a Jewish state and a Jewish army which will be strong enough to protect us from such atrocities. I don't believe there is any other way."

The massacre at the Park Hotel was behind Solly Busidan's decision to join the Israeli army. Born and raised in Brazil, Solly had never met Amit Busidan, an Israeli second cousin of his who was urgently called up to take part in Operation Defensive Shield after the attack in Netanya. Amit fell in the course of a bloody battle in Jenin. Solly's supervisor at work, an Israeli, abruptly asked him at the office, "Solly, tell me, do you still have relatives in Israel?" When he answered yes, his supervisor continued, "Do they have the same last name?" When Solly said yes again, he said, "I think it's best that you call home. A soldier with your last name has been killed in Jenin." Solly called his grandmother, who was weeping and told him, "It's my brother's grandson." Solly says, "It was hard, as if I were the one who had been hit. That's your own blood." The Jewish community of São Paulo held a demonstration in support of Israel and the Israeli army, in the face of Palestinian propaganda about Operation Defensive Shield. "During the demonstration, many people were marching and waving pictures of the thirteen soldiers killed in Jenin," Solly recounts. "Suddenly I saw an enormous photo of Amit. It was like a sign for me, it gave me the definitive push. I got the feeling that I had to come to Israel and enlist."

A few days after the bombing at the Park Hotel was Holocaust Remembrance Day. It had a particularly terrible resonance that year. "I have a feeling that I have gone through a new Holocaust," said Deborah Stein, whose mother, Marianne Lehmann Zaoui, died in the Passover attack. As a girl, Marianne had fled Germany just ahead of the Nazis and found shelter in France, pretending to be a Christian. "The fate that Hitler had prepared for them was realized by a Palestinian suicide bomber," said Menachem Rosensaft, founder of the International Network of Children of Jewish Holocaust Survivors. "Once again, Jews were killed because they were Jews." That night at the Park Hotel was like a new Shoah. Elderly survivors of the gas chambers, wearing their best dresses and shirts, hats and polished shoes, were gathered for the ritual meal ushering in one of Judaism's holiest nights. Families whose apartments were too small to accommodate large gatherings sat alongside the tourists who had dared to venture into Israel at this dangerous time. All of them died while praising God.

The images of the massacre at the Park Hotel called to mind a special Passover Seder held after the liberation from Nazism, when two hundred Jews sat down in the German State Theater on April 15, 1946, with a book that mirrored the account of the Exodus from Egypt. The Haggadah text was written by Yosef Dov Sheinson, a Hebrew teacher who survived a Lithuanian ghetto, forced labor, and the Dachau concentration camp. The Haggadah charts a journey that leads from the death camps and gas chambers directly to the Promised Land, with sweet images of fruit and trees: "We must make aliyah, build the chosen land, and make a home for ourselves and our children for eternity."

Repairing the World

Terrorism *has struck many Jewish places* of worship. In October 2001, during Sukkoth, Jewish women had gathered for prayer in Hebron when the assassins opened fire. On February 14, 2002, a terrorist killed seven people at a bar mitzvah celebration in Hadera. One month later was the carnage in the ultra-Orthodox neighborhood of Beit Yisrael, again during a bar mitzvah. Eleven were killed, a family decimated. The Mahane Yehuda market in Jerusalem, where the city goes to shop in preparation for Shabbat, has been hit repeatedly by suicide attackers and car bombs.

Talmudic students at a school in Atzmona were also killed during the same period. Atzmona no longer exists on the map today; it was one of the settlements evacuated by Ariel Sharon. Until the peace agreement with Egypt, it was a settlement in northern Sinai; when Menachem Begin gave the peninsula back to Egypt, the inhabitants moved a few miles north, to the Gaza Strip. It is the only settlement that was dismantled for a second time during the withdrawal in August 2005. Most of the demonstrators against the evacuation in Atzmona were young men dressed in orange T-shirts, the color of protest, that said: *Yehudi lo megaresh yehudi,* "A Jew does not expel a Jew." There were fathers with big backpacks on their shoulders and the Israeli flag in their hands. They reflected the resourcefulness of the Gaza greenhouses with their magically flourishing plants, their vegetables exported all over the world; they represented the superb and tragic idea of raising children in a hostile environment, the stubborn attachment to a land that they knew, deep inside, they would have to leave someday. Among those who stood defiant was Osnat Levran, a beautiful woman in her thirties living with her husband and children in Shirat Hayam, "Song of the Sea," a settlement of just sixteen families. Osnat is one of those mothers with long colorful skirts and fringed headscarves covering their hair. In their trailer there was a piano, which was played by Oz, her farmer husband who always had his pistol at his side.

On the evening of March 7, 2002, the young men were getting ready for bed at the school in Atzmona that prepares them for rabbinical studies and for the army. It was almost midnight when shots were heard in the yard. A terrorist had succeeded in penetrating the settlement, and was throwing hand grenades and shouting *"Allahu Akbar,"* seeking martyrdom. The yeshiva's rifles were under lock and key in the rabbi's cabinet. Five Jewish students were killed. Rafi Peretz, the director of the school, said that the young men "were turned into combatants without uniforms, not because they had chosen to fight, but because Providence has chosen to turn every member of this country into a warrior."

Eighteen-year-old Arik Krogliak volunteered for Magen David Adom, caring for those in need, in the little free time he had away from his studies. He had recently undergone heart surgery, which lowered his military profile, preventing him from joining active units. Instead, he had applied for the secret service, where he would be able to serve Israel without needing to be in perfect physical condition. It is said that he never lost his composure. At his funeral, his father said, "I could stay here singing Arik's praises until tomorrow, but instead I prefer to pray: God, take my son and his companions, saints like him, as the latest victims of this massacre. Enough, we are tired, we want only to live in peace."

Asher Markus wanted to study in order to become "a better Jew," to help people in danger and organize fundraising for the poor, according to his mother, Rivka, who is an archivist at the Knesset. She had tried to convince him to postpone his return to school for at least a few days because his brother, a soldier, had been wounded. Asher waited one more day, but then explained to his mother that he belonged with his classmates. "My son was killed in a pogrom," said Yitzhak Markus, his father. "Both my parents and Rivka's survived the Holocaust, but they didn't lose their faith. And we follow in their footsteps. Asher identified with the Holocaust and read the poems written by his grandmother in Auschwitz." Yitzhak added, "My boy wanted to travel blessed roads, to sanctify the name of the Holy One, blessed may he be. And us? We remain here for the time being." "For the time being" is what many of the survivors of massacres in Jewish settlements have said.

Tal Kurtzweil was an intellectual; he devoured books one after another, and he lived for the Torah. His grandfather had been one of the founders of the famous Bezalel Academy of Arts and Design in Jerusalem. Tal was tiny, with a great, sly smile. After passing the rigorous air force exam, he was supposed to begin training soon. Israel has always insisted on *Hatovim la Tayis*, "The Best for the Air Force." Tal was proud of being part of an air force that has always needed to be capable of defeating enemy forces in a few hours. In the war of 1967, Israeli pilots hit the enemy planes with such precision that no one understood how it was possible.

Ariel Zana's family had come from France, where Ariel's father directed the Jewish Agency's French office. Before arriving at the school in Atzmona, Ariel had been a leader in a branch of Bnei Akiva, a religious scouting group. He is remembered as someone who could control and teach dozens of teenagers not much younger than himself, always with a smile on his face. Ariel Zana and Eran Picard had lived in the same Jerusalem neighborhood, and they were inseparable. "When we found out that Eran was among the victims," his family said, "we were certain right away that we would find Ariel close to him."

Eran Picard's family had arrived twenty years earlier from France. Eran's mother, Rachel, is a gynecologist at Hadassah Hospital, and his father, Eli, is a physician at Shaare Zedek Medical Center in Jerusalem. One week before the attack in Atzmona, Eli had been attending to the wounded from the attack in Beit Yisrael. "We tried to flee from an anti-Semitic country," he said. "And now where do they want us to go?" At Eran's funeral, Rachel noted that her son died while studying the Torah, "a privilege granted only to the just. God called for five volunteers to redeem the sufferings of the people of Israel, and you, as always, stepped forward immediately."

This is how Dr. Picard remembers that day: "You arrive home one ordinary Thursday evening following a long day of treating sick patients. As usual, your wife shares with you the events of her day, the children present their latest requests, and mail waits to be opened. Suddenly your world collapses. A terrorist attack occurred at the college where your son is studying. You are filled with fear. Are there victims? Is your son among them? Where is he? His mobile phone doesn't answer. The tension is agonizing. News and bits of information fly all around you, some reassuring, some alarming. Every minute now feels like forever. You search in the hospitals, and unfortunately you find that your worst nightmare is reality. Your son, this smart, cheerful and optimistic adolescent has been taken from this world. The funeral and the next seven days of mourning, during which time you are surrounded by consoling friends, is all surreal and you do not internalize your tragedy. But afterwards, slowly, slowly ... the emptiness, the loneliness."

There is a flood of thoughts and problems and many endless questions, most of them without answers. "You feel a wish to find the person responsible, and at some level, even an uncomfortable desire for vengeance. Your life is forever changed, and somehow you must learn to face this sad and painful situation. You are observed by people who watch you but don't know how to look at you or how to approach you. And for yourself, how should you behave? Should you play the stoic and appear indifferent or even optimistic? Would you then be betraying your son's memory? Should you rather be candid and display your sadness, depression, and anger? Then you risk eliciting pity that you do not want. Besides, society doesn't take well to those who lament. Especially at such a difficult time you can't afford the risk of rejection." The family is confused. "Despite the heavy pain you carry, you must maintain enough strength to help your family deal with this disaster. In your professional life, you are offered no discounts. Your personal tragedy must not interfere with your productivity. Though sympathetic, your colleagues expect the same level of performance as before. How will you cope with this complex trial involving so many social, familial, professional, political, and metaphysical implications? It is a challenge you wish you were not presented."

Eran was very close to his parents and wanted to become a doctor also. "My son was a teenager like all the others; he wanted to live his life," says Dr. Picard. "Eran had just finished high school, and had decided to enroll in the school in Atzmona before starting military service. The young Israelis at the school spend a number of months deepening their knowledge of Jewish history, religion, and philosophy. Eran was brilliant and had a great future ahead of him. He loved helping others, and had a fantastic sense of humor."

The history of the Picard family began in France. "I made the aliyah from France halfway through my studies, motivated by the desire to be part of Jewish history, which lives above all here in Israel. My family's origins are in Alsace in the eighteenth century, and I can visit the graves of my ancestors in the cemetery of Wintzenheim, near Colmar. During the Second World War, the Vichy government prohibited my father from practicing his profession. He was sought by the Gestapo and was forced to hide on a farm with my mother's whole family for more than a year. His sister was killed in Auschwitz, and his sister-in-law survived the hell of the extermination camp. My father fled to Lyons, was arrested by the Gestapo twice, and was fortunately able to escape. Then he embraced the resistance. Many of his friends, including Rabbi Brunsweig and Rabbi Sammy Klein, were killed by the Germans. You never forget them."

Eli Picard explains that "in the Jewish tradition, life has supreme value, above everything else and in every circumstance, while death is considered the ultimate tragedy. That said, the fact that Eran was killed while studying the Bible in a holy place gives me and my family a minimum of consolation. At first, returning to life after what happened to me was impossible, but slowly you find the strength to go on, especially for the good of the other children who want to live a normal life. In the end, you live like a handicapped person who has to learn from the beginning every day." Eli notes that Atzmona is no longer on the map and the school has been moved. "It is hard for me not to be able to visit the place where my son's blood was shed. Before the Israeli evacuation from Atzmona, I asked some of Eran's friends to bring me some sand from the place where he was killed. And I put that sand in my garden in Jerusalem."

Asked what Israel represents for him, Eli Picard replies, "It is the land that all my grandparents dreamed about. It is the shield of the Jewish people when, even during our own time, the synagogues are being desecrated in Western countries. We have already experienced genocide, and there will not be a second one. It is time for the nations of the world to accept Israel, and the Jewish message of peace based on the most ancient and universal book in the world, the Bible. It would be good for the whole world."

The massacre of Atzmona was not the last one against the *talmidim,* the religious students with their enigmatic beauty, intensified by a vague disregard for their own safety. On March 6, 2008, a lone Palestinian gunman killed eight students at the Mercaz Harav yeshiva in Jerusalem. It was "an attack on the heart of Zionism," as the *Jerusalem Post* put it. Richard Landes, a historian at Boston University, wrote that "the deliberate attack on this venerable institution of Jewish learning, a sacred seminary, cannot be interpreted as anything but an overt act of premeditated, genocidal anti-Semitism not dissimilar from the acts of pogroms in Eastern Europe and Nazi SS raids on Jewish communities in Western Europe."

When Rabbi Avraham Yitzhak Kook founded the yeshiva in 1924, his intention was that it become "a center for the Torah and Zionism." Many leaders of Zionist revisionism have come from Mercaz Harav, starting with the commanding officer of Irgun, David Raziel (whose name is now attached to a moshav in Judea). The school is a combination of pride and piety, scripture and courage, purity and ardor. Its best students go on to study at Machon Meir, a religious studies institute in Jerusalem where a plaque is dedicated to "the souls of the martyrs who gave their lives in the sanctification of the name of God in the wars of Israel and in the settlement of the Land." The students at Mercaz Harav thought of themselves as the heirs of Rabbi Akiva, the young shepherd who became the greatest rabbi of his time. He supported the Bar Kokhba rebellion against

Rome, and later was arrested and imprisoned for breaking laws against Judaism. While Roman soldiers tore his flesh off with iron hooks, he continued to pray and recite the Shema.

The hall where the terrorist snuffed out those young lives was always full, night and day. The young students knew they were a target. Some of them had already escaped other terrorist attacks. The Israeli government instructed the media office to spread the shocking photos of the attack all over the world, including the photos with the sacred texts from the school library pierced by the projectiles.

The streets of Gaza were filled with thousands of joyful Palestinians celebrating the attack on the school. In the mosques of the Gaza Strip, many of the faithful gathered for prayers of thanksgiving. Armed men went through the streets firing into the air in rejoicing, while sweets were handed out to the passersby. Hamas released a statement in which it "blessed" the group responsible for the attack, adding that "it will not be the last."

The students killed that night were "the best of the best, pure gold," said the head of the yeshiva, Rabbi Ya'akov Shapira, at their funeral. Rabbi Yerahmiel Weiss knew all of the victims. "My heart died that horrible night. How can we eulogize not one, not two or three, but eight students? O God, you have taken eight saints." Rabbi Weiss mourned them one by one. "You have taken Yehonadav, whose kindness, innocent perfection, talent, mental power, simplicity, and inner beauty made him holy to you. You have taken Yochai, a diligent student. You took Segev, who excelled in Torah. You have taken Yonatan, a young man who loved to sit in the library. You have taken Avraham, a kind soul who delighted in chanting from the Torah. And you have taken Neria, the youngest, who came from a great family and whose light we already miss." The Mishnah clearly states that "a student of the Torah takes precedence over a king of Israel." These eight murdered young men were living branches of the oldest exegetical tradition in the world.

The Sephardic chief rabbi, Shlomo Amar, also spoke, saying that the families' pain "is shared by the whole House of Israel." Ehud Barak, the defense minister, came to express his condolences. "The terrorists did not choose this place at random, it is a place of tremendous Jewish and Zionist power."

Yehonadav Haim Hirschfeld, nineteen, came from one of the oldest families of Kochav Hashachar, a community of about three hundred families in the Binyamin region of Samaria. Kochav Hashachar means "morning star." When Yehonadav's family heard about the massacre, they looked for him the entire day. In the evening, a rabbi brought them the terrible news. Five years earlier, Yehonadav had been deeply moved by the death of a fellow settler, a mother of seven children who was shot to death in her car.

Eighteen-year-old Yochai Lifschitz, from Jerusalem, "excelled above all in his innocence," they said at his funeral. "He always wanted to search for the truth on his own, at the synagogue or at prayer in the morning, or during military service." His cousin noted that "even at his death, he was studying the Torah." Yochai was always at school before classes began. When the summer break arrived, he complained that the seminary would be closed for two months. "We could take a break for two weeks and then return to class," he said to his parents. Yochai wrote to the Ministry of Education proposing a change, and two weeks later he got a reply thanking him for the suggestion.

Segev Peniel Avichail was only fifteen years old. His father, Elyashiv, is the rabbi of Telem and Adora, and his grandfathers are both great rabbis. One is Yehoshua Zuckerman, the founder of the El Ami movement. The other is Eliyahu Avichail, the preeminent scholar of the Lost Tribes of Israel. For fifty years he has dedicated himself to finding the descendants of the tribes that made up the ancient states of Israel and Judah—the ten tribes who had lived in the northern kingdom of Israel and were exiled by a punitive Assyrian expedition in 722 BCE, dispersed as slaves on the outer edges of the Assyrian Empire, and those exiled to Babylonia after the destruction of the Temple of Jerusalem in 586 BCE. Rabbi Avichail traveled widely to identify them among the Pathans of Afghanistan and Pakistan, and of Indian Kashmir; in the Karen people of northeast Burma; among the Shinlung of northeast India, who call themselves Bnei Menashe (Children of Manasseh); in the Chiang-Min tribes of China; in Japan, in the Caucasus, and in Kurdistan. Segev's mother is a convert to Judaism.

"Segev was a pure heart, exceptionally diligent in his studies," said his uncle Yair. "He was always looking for ways to make things better. When he was told that he had been admitted to the yeshiva, he was the happiest person in the world." Segev wrote poetry. On the night of the massacre, his father found one of the poems on his table; it said that "there is justice and there is a judge." Rabbi Elyashiv Avichail recalls, "My son loved helping out in the family. He smiled at others, he took care of them and offered to help them. Since he was a child, he had a coin purse for the needy, and he collected money every month. He was like light, he saw the best in everything. He had learned to write the Torah like an adult, and his knowledge of the Talmud was enormous. He was honest, and he didn't forget easily. There was an Ethiopian worker at the school; Segev saw him working hard and wanted to thank him. After the attack, that man said that Segev had been the only one who paid attention to him."

Elyashiv's family had been marked by the Holocaust, like those of many other victims. His maternal grandmother came from a Belgian family that was exterminated in Auschwitz. His paternal grandmother had hidden in countryside villages during the roundups in France. Elyashiv lived for five years in the old section of Jerusalem, after which he started serving as a rabbi in a settlement near Hebron.

"The terrorist drove the bus for the Jewish schools, and his father was a contractor for Jewish homes," Rabbi Avichail comments. "The terrorist was not raised that way; he simply decided to kill Jews. He hated Jews and wanted to kill them. Why Mercaz Harav? Because it is a place of great faith—faith in the Jewish people, in the land of Israel and in the Torah. They hate us because we live here, in the land of Abraham, Isaac, and Jacob. Segev was the exact opposite, full of love. Three years ago we were near Adora when the terrorists fired on us. Segev was wounded; he prayed to God to save him, but he never said a word of hatred about the terrorists."

Even through his pain, Elyashiv has never lost his faith. "Everything in life strengthens the strong and weakens the weak. Nothing changes this fact. Faith in the Jewish people, in the land of Israel, and in the State of Israel weakens the projectiles. They want to break us, but the opposite is happening—we are stronger than before, even more devoted to the land and to the state. We are like the petals of a flower: alone we are weak, together we form a very strong bunch. Every war of terror is a battle between the darkness and the light. The Jews want goodness to win. The evening of the attack was supposed to be a celebration for the new month of Adar. Segev told his friends that he was going to study for 'five more minutes.' And it was in those minutes that the attacker arrived. Those who want to destroy us remember our strength. From ancient times until today. From Abraham to us. They will never get rid of us. But it's up to us to have faith."

Neria Cohen was also fifteen years old, "the light of God, a perfect soul, a son of the Torah." He had been raised in the Muslim quarter of Jerusalem. Neria spent much of his time helping the poor. His name means "candle"—the candle of Shabbat.

Yonatan Yitzhak Eldar came from Shiloh and was sixteen years old. He was buried with his inseparable copy of the

Babylonian Talmud, still covered in blood. "We decided to bury our son with it for two reasons," said his father, Dror Eldar. "The first is found in the Halakhah, the Jewish law, which requires that every drop of blood be committed to the earth. And that book was soaked in blood. And then because it had a special meaning for my son." At the funeral, Rabbi Bin-Nun of Shiloh said that Yonatan was "a young man full of joie de vivre," and that his family's tears were "tears of heroism, tears of supreme faith."

Dror Eldar, who arrived in Shiloh in 1987 when it was only a dot on the map, remarks that "Mercaz Harav was the treasure of Rav Kook, and the terrorists wanted to strike one of our most important places, a symbol of Israel. The attack strengthened instead of weakening my faith, which is fundamental in my life. My mother survived the Holocaust; our families came from Romania, from Hungary, and from Czechoslovakia, and they were decimated. When the Germans arrived in my mother's village in Transylvania, they deported all the Jews to Auschwitz. I lost my aunt in the gas chambers, all my grandparents, an uncle, and dozens of cousins. For us, therefore, such hatred and pain is nothing new: we know that there is someone who wants to destroy us."

"He felt close to God," said the friends of Roi Roth, who was eighteen. "Everyone in the *bet midrash* could hear his 'Amen.'" Roi often wept during prayers, they said, and he was always the last one to leave the classroom. The first responders found him lying on the floor, his body riddled with shrapnel, his kippah in his hand; he hadn't had time to put it back on. His mother, Orly, says the family came to live in Elkana sixteen years ago. "We had four children, we were a happy family, and we lived in a little trailer. Everything seemed perfect, with a big dog named Oz. We had visited the village a few months before. We were excited by Shabbat and by the demeanor of the residents. Everyone wished you a good Shabbat and wanted to invite you. There was a beautiful view of Samaria. It was an ideal place for us and the children. This place comes before all the rabbinical literature."

Orly talks about her son: "He smiled, he didn't talk much, he played sports. When he received a medal, he wasn't proud, he received it in silence. Roi was like that, strong and humble." Speaking of the Mercaz Harav yeshiva, she says "it is holy, it speaks of prayer, of the sanctity of Jerusalem, of closeness to God. That sanctity surrounded Roi. Our comfort is that he was taken in the holy city, in the holy yeshiva, and with the holy Talmud. Roi was the heart of our home. After he was taken away from us, there was no difference between night and day. A terrorist had invaded the very heart of the Jewish nation. This will never be forgotten."

One of the Mercaz Harav victims, Doron Meherete from Ashdod, was twenty-six and soon to become a rabbi. He had arrived in Israel along with thousands of other Ethiopian Jews who were brought into the country with Operation Solomon in 1991. His father doesn't speak Hebrew, only Aramaic. Doron wanted to get married and live in a small community. When he had a little free time, he volunteered at the Mevasseret Zion Absorption Center for immigrants, helping young Ethiopian Jews discover the biblical Israel and the Torah. Thousands of young people wrote to his family. "Doron, I love you," one little girl said. "You taught me about the Torah and Israel. I will pray to Hashem that you come back to life."

Doron represents the miracle of Israel; he had arrived on angel's wings. The passion with which Israel brought in the Jewish children of Solomon and the Queen of Sheba—about thirty thousand altogether—is an emblematic story of solidarity and fidelity. The Bricha, the rescue, is the true face of Zionism. With Operation Magic Carpet in 1949, Israel had brought to safety the Yemeni Jewish community trapped in Aden. With Operation Ali Baba beginning in 1950, Israel saved 113,000

Iraqi Jews from a promised extermination. From Europe, 100,000 Holocaust survivors arrived clandestinely in Israel. Many Israelis have died in the course of helping newcomers. One was Karine Malka, who worked with new arrivals from Ethiopia. "She was the kind of young woman who was always laughing; she always had a smile on her face," said one of her friends. "She gave everything for the children. She stayed late to help." Karine was killed by a bus bombing in 2004.

The last victim of the Mercaz Harav attack, sixteen-year-old Avraham David Moses from Efrat, is described as "pious" by his parents, who had immigrated from New Hampshire. Avraham was said to be "like an angel, of surprising integrity." His mother, Rivka, laments, "I will not be able to dance at his wedding, and I will never see his children. But I am so grateful for the fact that I was his mother for sixteen years. Avraham is a martyr. There are traditions saying that paradise is a Talmud and a candle. That was Avraham's paradise. I like gold, a glass of wine, and a novel, but for him that was paradise." His father, Naftali, recalls that Avraham David was a great scholar of the sacred books, who didn't watch television or even go to the beach. When he had to cut vegetables, he always did it with the Torah open in front of him.

One of Avraham David's teachers said that "he would have become a giant of the Torah." One student said to his parents, "You had the privilege of raising him, a holy and mature young man, a *hasid*, a *parush*, a *tzadik*, a *lamdan*. We are so far from his purity, from his Torah, from his acts of goodness." Another teacher, Avidan Weitzman, explained that "he and the others are on the wings of the *shekhinah*, together with Rabbi Akiva and the other holy martyrs." The *shekhinah* is the physical presence of God in the world, a term used for the Temple of Jerusalem and the Tabernacle. "For Avraham David, the Torah was worth more than all riches," said a friend of the yeshiva. "He died while learning the Torah, in an act of self-sacrifice."

His father recalls, "During the last months of his life, Avraham David put into practice the idea of not looking his parents and teachers in the eye. He decided to follow a precept of the medieval ethical treatise *Igeret HaRamban,* that of lowering the eyes as a sign of respect. Lowering the gaze is a Hasidic custom. This bothered me—I wanted to see his face. When anyone at the table slandered someone else, he got up and left. This is a precept written in the Torah, Leviticus 19:16. Like the *gedolim* and the *tzadikim,* the wise and the just, Avraham wanted to be completely in tune with the Torah. He slept little and ate even less—an experience reserved only for the prophets. He wanted to see the face of God, but he knew that God said 'No one can see My presence.' My son was a student devoted to the Torah; he memorized entire passages of ancient texts and tried to apply what he had learned to real life. Avraham David lived according to the Book."

Naftali tells his own story: "My family's origins are German. My father's family lived for centuries in the same village, and fled to America after the Night of Broken Glass. They were fortunate to have a brother who was working in Chicago. I grew up in New York, and I came to Israel twenty-five years ago. It wasn't an ideological decision for me to live in Judea; I was drawn by the quality of life. I believe in God and in his people, not in political entities. I chose to live in Israel because I wanted to live a fully Jewish life, surrounded by other Jews. Maybe I will die doing the same thing."

We ask Naftali what it means to live in a community like Efrat, which has been wounded by terrorism repeatedly and has lost many residents who came from France, Tunisia, and the United States. "It's an important question. I will answer by describing the commemoration of this year, which took place ten weeks after my son was killed. Every family that has lost someone because of terrorism or in the army had been invited to come to a little hall an hour before the main ceremony began. When it was my turn, I met the rabbi. Every year, a family enters this 'club.' This was our year. My wife and I sat down in a circle with ten other families, transcribing the oral history of every member of the family killed; they had interviewed us a few weeks before. But I wasn't listening, I was looking around, seeking out the familiar faces of my neighbors, knowing that we all share the same terrible secret—the secret of loss and pain."

Rabbi Yerahmiel Weiss taught seven of the seminarians who were murdered at Mercaz Harav. "The attack was a painful chapter in the history of Jewish martyrdom," he tells us. "The death of these young people was a great *Kiddush Hashem*, because they were studying the Torah, because they were immersed in the faith, in 'the sea of the Torah.' The idealistic and devout world of the young men of the yeshiva leapt to the attention of many Israelis who knew nothing about this way of life, about the holiness and purity of the students of the Torah. Unlike the terrorists, these young people didn't choose to die, but they were ready to sacrifice their own lives." Weiss has no doubt about why the yeshiva was targeted: "Because of its ideals, and because of the fact that these students are taught to combine Jewish nationalism with the Jewish faith, the heart of which is revealing to the world the *Mamlechet Kohanim VeGoy Kadosh,* the Holy Nation, elevating the world to the divine goodness."

Noting that some victims came from families marked by the Holocaust, the rabbi says, "It is human dignity to think that a family that has suffered so much, that has lost so many of its members in the Holocaust and has risen from the ashes, should not have to suffer anymore. The survivors of such horrible experiences have paid the price of a *tikkun* [repairing of the world] where evil had reigned. It is human to wonder why they should have to suffer again. But there is another aspect. Those who have survived the Holocaust and have come back to life with the strength to start again have found inner strength where they didn't even think it existed. We were able to prevail with the help of God. We know that asking questions is natural and human, but we also know that, being human, we don't know the answers. We have discovered that it is possible to rebuild in spite of everything. Looking at these ravaged families, we have learned that it is possible to grow through suffering. Maybe it is making us better people. The attack has made our religious faith stronger. There is a desire for meaning today. So the disaster has driven these people to study even more and delve into the depths of Jewish philosophy."

There were few calls for revenge—because, as Rabbi Weiss observed, "Satan has not yet created the revenge for the blood of a child." As the Talmud says, to mourn the names of its eight sons, Israel "lit candles instead of cursing the darkness." Terrorism extinguished another eight young Jewish lights, but not the spirit that lives in Mercaz Harav. "This evening, the terrorists interrupted our joy," one student said. "But they won't succeed in destroying what we believe in."

We Won't Stop Dancing

You have changed my mourning into dancing.

PSALM 30:11

The film **Sobibor, October 14, 1943, 4 P.M.,** by the French director Claude Lanzmann, was presented at the New York Film Festival on October 11, 2001, exactly one month after the triumph of death at the World Trade Center. It's the story of Yehuda Lerner, the hero of the revolt in the Sobibor concentration camp, and it shows the absolute sanctity of life amid a reign of death. In an act of fundamental liberty, motivated by superhuman courage, Lerner and his companions turned to violence in order to put an end to the massacre of innocents. Lanzmann remarked, "The lesson that I took from the revolt in Sobibor is the need for the Jews to reclaim the use of force. Yehuda Lerner, a nonviolent man, discovered that he was violent. The Holocaust was not only a massacre of innocent human beings, but of defenseless human beings. That a person like Lerner, who had never thought about taking up arms before then, should have done so has a lot to do with the roots of today's Jewish state."

New Yorkers understood that the film was unintentionally addressed to them. The morning of September 11, 2001, the only good news came from United Airlines flight 93. Todd

Beamer, a software salesman for Oracle, had left his house in New Jersey at five o'clock in the morning, moving quietly to avoid waking his children and his wife, Lisa, who was pregnant with their third child. After taking off from the airport in Newark, Todd came to understand that the day would not have a happy ending. He asked the cell phone operator to recite Psalm 23 with him: "Even though I walk through the valley of the shadow of death . . ." Then, leaving his phone open, he said, "Are you guys ready? Let's roll!" And together with some other passengers, he stopped the terrorists from plowing into another building. In their sacrifice, Todd and his fellow passengers sent America a message of hope.

This same hope nourishes Israel's vocation of freedom. On American Airlines flight 11, the first to crash into the World Trade Center, was Daniel Lewin, a former officer of the elite Israeli army unit Sayeret Matkal, which is entrusted with the most secret and dangerous missions such as the raid in Entebbe. Telephone calls revealed that Lewin tried to stop the terrorists who were breaking into the cabin. Apparently, the first victim of the attacks on September 11 was an Israeli.

The actions of Todd Beamer and Daniel Lewin would be echoed by Professor Liviu Librescu, a Holocaust survivor who had suffered under the Communist regime in Romania before emigrating to Israel, after decades of failed attempts, thanks to Prime Minister Begin's intercession with President Ceausescu. Later he went to the United States to teach aeronautical engineering at Virginia Tech. In the spring of 2007, Professor Librescu tried in vain to prevent a crazed killer from entering Norris Hall, where he was teaching a class, before being struck down by bullets fired through the door. He died, along with thirty-two students, on the same day that Israel commemorates the Holocaust. But thanks to his actions, many of his students are alive today.

Liviu Librescu was buried in the Israeli town of Ra'anana. "He saved them, he saved them," his wife, Marilena, said over and over when his body arrived in Israel. "He wanted to save everyone." Liviu's name was also celebrated by President George W. Bush at the United States Holocaust Memorial Museum in Washington. "That day we saw horror, but we also saw quiet acts of courage. We saw this courage in a teacher named Liviu Librescu," said President Bush. "On the Day of Remembrance, this Holocaust survivor gave his own life so that others may live." One of the professor's children, Arie, said, "Father, I think that at this moment you are looking down and saying, 'What is this crowd in mourning? I only did what I had to do.'" The Lubavitcher community announced that their new student center at Virginia Tech would be named after Professor Librescu. They also organized a lighting of candles all over the world for Shabbat, as Marilena had requested. It was Librescu's favorite mitzvah, or good deed. He was not religious, but he lit candles every Shabbat—as the Soviet Jews had done in the Communist prisons.

Professor Librescu was not only an accomplished researcher, but also "the most humble person I ever met," said Arie. "If my dad believed in doing something, he went ahead and did it, and he didn't care what other people might say about it. What should be done had to be done, he felt. In that sense, he looked at life in black-and-white terms." Marilena— who like her husband spent some of the war years in the Ploesti ghetto in Romania—spoke about how Liviu, at the age of twelve, supported his mother by tutoring other children in math. "He was a man who liked to help everybody," she said. "I've had letters from his former students all over the world, and so many wrote: 'I've lost my second father.'" Librescu was a quiet man who acted heroically as a matter of course. Two words jump out from his name: "Libre," which means "free" in Spanish and French, and "Rescu," short for "rescue."

The story of Liviu Librescu, and that of Israel, is summed up in the Jewish saying, *Lo amut ki echyah,* "I will not die; I will live." An intense love of life is manifested in the emphasis placed on the mitzvah of *pidyon shvuyim,* the rescue of prisoners by whatever means possible. Witness Israel's daring raid on Entebbe; the ongoing search for the Holocaust hero Raoul Wallenberg; the myriad efforts to identify the whereabouts of missing Jewish soldiers and secure their freedom. The Jewish love of life explains the *shomrin,* Israel's human shields, so different from the ones that Hamas used to the detriment of the Palestinian population in 2009 during the war in Gaza. At the doors of supermarkets and department stores, theaters and cinemas, schools and synagogues, an Israeli guard looks through the bags of any suspect person who wants to enter. The guards in Israel have risked their lives, and often lost them, to stop suicide bombers. Ital Aviksous, a bus guard who came from Argentina, admits, "Of course I'm afraid, but if I die in a confrontation with a suicide bomber I will save many human lives."

The *shomrin,* the guards, are the incarnation of a saying from the Talmud Berakhot: "There are wicked men who, although alive, are like the dead. There are just men who, once dead, are always alive." According to a prominent strain of Jewish thought, it is better to be sacrificed than to sacrifice. Traces of this radical code of ethics can also be found in the Israeli army, which does everything it can to prevent harm to civilians, avoids striking a terrorist if he has women and children around him, and has always professed inviolable respect for human life, including the enemy's life. This principle is called *tohar haneshek,* meaning "purity of arms."

Hundreds of bodyguards and security agents in Israel have been killed or wounded while trying to protect other human beings. There are many police officers, security guards, waiters, doctors, and students who have literally pulled explosive packs off the backs of terrorists. They are the heroes of an Israel that has fought against death in the restaurants and cafes, in the schools, in the clinics, in the synagogues. And in the end, they have won.

On December 5, 2005, a pregnant woman named Shoshi Attiya, a major in the police force, noticed a youth who was attempting to set off a bomb at the Hasharon Mall in Netanya. She ran after him yelling, "Terrorist! Terrorist!" The crowd moved aside while Shoshi kept running toward the terrorist. She almost succeeded in removing his hand from the pocket where he was about to activate the device. Meanwhile he also tried to latch onto Haim Amram, a working student who was guarding the entrance to the mall. Haim died in the attempt to block the terrorist with his body, while Shoshi fortunately was virtually unharmed. Even if they weren't able to stop the terrorist, their heroism saved many lives. "He wanted to save them all," Haim's family kept saying. He had survived another suicide attack a few months earlier, and he planned to get married the following summer.

Jerusalem was bustling with preparations for Shabbat on March 29, 2002. Avigail Levy was overtaken by an unusual mood, nervous and agitated. That morning she had decided to relax with her seventeen-year-old daughter, Rachel; in the afternoon she asked Rachel to go buy some things at the supermarket. The girl waiting at the entrance to the store in Kiryat Yovel was the same age, with the same straight black hair—but she was loaded with TNT, having resolved to blow herself up, killing as many Jews as possible, "to defend the al-Aqsa Mosque." Rachel was studying art in high school and had just finished preparing an exhibition of her photographs. She loved music and books, and enjoyed telling bedtime stories to her younger brother. She died holding the shopping list her mother had made.

The two hundred people in the Kiryat Yovel supermarket that day owe their lives to Haim Smadar, one of the two guards at the entrance. A few minutes before the attack, a police-woman who was going in to shop had complimented him, saying, "You're right to be on your guard with the women; the latest warnings say that suicide girls are coming." This was one reason why the young terrorist, Ayat al-Akhras, did not evade the security measures, even with an angelic face. "You're not going in—you and I are going to die right here," Haim said, stopping the girl, who decided to blow herself up at the door. Recently he had told his wife, Shoshana, "If a suicide attacker wanted to enter my school, I would stop him with my body." Shoshana remarked, "His name was Haim, and that's exactly what he gave so many people: life." She added, "It's true, a lot of people are alive thanks to him, but my children don't have their daddy anymore, and I don't have my husband."

Haim Smadar was a Tunisian Jew whose family had come to Israel when he was two years old. At age fifty-five, he had a kindly face and a big salt-and-pepper mustache. He was adored by the parents of the autistic children at the school where he had been a guard for years and had also become the general handy-man. One child remembered him like this: "Whenever I was late for school, he would say, *'Jalla jalla.* Run to class or you won't get recess.'" He was good with children, and had five of his own at home, two of them hearing-impaired. It wasn't always easy to make ends meet, so he took side jobs to supplement his income, like the one at the supermarket. Haim was a humble and quiet man. "He never told me about the medal he had received from the mayor for his work at the school," his brother Moshe said. "He was always optimistic, open, and smiling. Life didn't smile on him; it was hard to raise a deaf son and a daughter with hearing problems. But he was happy." The pupils of the school dedicated a garden to him, putting in a plaque that reads: "With his courage he saved lives. Haim Smadar, 1947–2002."

Oded Sharon also defended what he believed in with his life. "Many people owe their lives to him," said Avi Dichter, the head of Shin Bet, the domestic secret service. His friend Oded, the director of security for the Jewish settlements in Gush Katif, was killed by a suicide bomber at a checkpoint. Speaking at the funeral, Avi said, "Security ran in your blood even before you worked for us. You stopped the terrorist with your body."

Mamoya Tahio, a Jew of Ethiopian origin, was working as a policeman in Jerusalem when he was killed trying to disrupt a suicide attack. "Like all of us, he dreamed of living on holy ground," said Adisu Messele, head of the association for Ethiopian immigrants. "He prevented a disaster with his body. He is like a symbol of the assimilation of our community into Israeli society." One of the members of his unit said that Mamoya wore the uniform with great pride. Another said that "at the front he was a hero, and he saved the lives of many men, women, and children."

Valery Ahmir was an excellent doctor from Russia, but he couldn't get a job in medicine, so he worked as a guard to support his family. Although he suffered from diabetes, he was always at his post. He was killed by terrorists' gunfire as he drove home from work one night. Yair Mordechai prevented a massacre in the Sheluhot kibbutz by giving his own life. "Thank you, Yair, you saved the kibbutz," wrote the members of the community.

Among those murdered in suicide bombings are many workers from Bulgaria, Romania, Ghana, Argentina, China, and the former Soviet Union. Some were citizens, some not, and some were not even legally in Israel. These foreign workers do not come to Israel out of Zionist fervor, but they are pioneers in a special way, enduring hardship and often separation from the family they came to provide for. Many of them have been killed while performing security services. Julio Pedro Magram had recently immigrated from Argentina when he was killed by a suicide bomber while working as a security guard at a shopping mall in Kfar Saba.

Alexander Kostyuk came from Ukraine to serve in the Israeli army. He was killed at the Kfar Saba train station while preventing a massacre with his own body. His parents wanted to bury him in Odessa, his hometown, but his mother changed her mind: "My son died defending Israel, and I want him to rest here," she said. Alexander's father is Jewish but his mother is not, so he was buried in the non-Jewish Yarkon Cemetery near Tel Aviv. "When I heard that someone had stopped a terrorist with his own body, I knew it was Alexander," said a member of his unit.

When the Maxim restaurant in Haifa was blown up in October 2003, one of the victims was an Arab Christian security guard, Mutanus Karkabi. "He paid with his life in order to protect others, whether they were Arabs or Jews," said his brother. Ahmed Mazarib, an Arab Israeli policeman, was killed in 2002 by a suicide terrorist who blew himself up after being stopped for questioning on the road to Jerusalem. Israel's police commissioner, Shlomo Aharonishky, praised Mazarib's courage, adding, "If Ahmed had not blocked the terrorist's way, we would be attending more funerals today." Ahmed Mazarib was buried near one of his cousins, a soldier who had recently been killed in a terrorist attack near Kerem Shalom in Gaza.

The hero of the Caffit coffeehouse, in the German Colony neighborhood of Jerusalem, is a waiter named Shlomi Harel. Along with a security guard, he pulled a large backpack off a suicide bomber after pushing him outside the cafe, and then yanked the wire out from the detonator. Shlomi commented, "I've been told that if someone has to die, better one than many." Mikhail Sarkisov is an immigrant from Turkmenistan, toughened by poverty, like so many of those who fled from the former Soviet Union. He lives in a trailer with no bathroom or refrigerator. Working as a guard on Tel Aviv's beachfront Cafe Tayelet, armed with a fake pistol, he threw himself bodily on a suicide bomber before he could detonate the primer, saving dozens of lives.

Aharon Gozlan, a policeman, flung himself against a suicide attacker at the French Hill bus stop. It was too late to prevent the explosion, which killed seven people. Aharon's legs were mutilated and became gangrenous, so they had to be amputated. Today, Aharon walks on prostheses. Michal Franklin, the granddaughter of Holocaust survivors, was one of seven people killed in that explosion. It had been her last day of college, and she was on her way to celebrate.

A bus door closed in the face of someone attempting to board through the exit, knocking him onto the pavement. When the driver, Baruch Neuman, went out with two passengers to help the man, they discovered an explosive device strapped to his body. They held onto his hands and started yelling at the other passengers to run, before fleeing to safety themselves. The Egged bus company, which sends more than five thousand buses around Israel every day, has never received transfer requests from drivers on dangerous routes. Wearing bright blue shirts with dark blue jackets and pants, these drivers show up for their risky jobs every day.

Hadar Gitlin was twenty-one years old and had been working for a couple of weeks as a guard at the Hamakim shopping center in Afula, making about six or seven dollars an hour. She was seriously injured when she stopped a female suicide bomber loaded with ten pounds of explosives. Eight years earlier, her older sister Mor, a nurse in the paratrooper corps, had survived a twofold terrorist attack at an intersection near Netanya.

In addition to "the Wall," the one that has been turned into a symbol of Israeli abuse of power, there's the human wall of Israelis who have stopped terror from taking control of everything and everyone, body and soul. Most of them are poor people who needed a second job to make ends meet. Together with the *miluim*—the reservists who leave their businesses and families to serve in the army—the *shomrin* are the living image of

Israel. There should be a monument to these silent, humble heroes. Instead, they don't even make it to the pages of our newspapers. These "angels of Israel" are like points of life on a map of pain.

The history of the Israeli army is also full of such angels. One of them stands out above all: Major Roi Klein, who jumped onto a grenade, shouting the Shema, to save the lives of his companions during the war against Hezbollah in the summer of 2006. Roi used to say that his priorities were the Torah and the unity of the Jewish people. He was one of those 40 percent of Israeli combatants who describe themselves as "very religious." A large proportion of the special forces live in the settlements in Judea and Samaria.

The story of Roi Klein recalls the names of earlier heroes of Israel, such as Natan Elbaz, the cobbler and devoted student of Judaism who told his mother on the day he left Morocco, "I'm going to Israel to build a better future for you." In the army, Natan found what the secularized world of the kibbutz couldn't give him. Every time his unit received requests for difficult missions, Natan volunteered. He died in 1954 while saving his companions from a grenade that was about to explode. Chaim Zarfati was sent to Marseilles by the Mossad to organize the aliyah for Holocaust survivors. He died on the open sea during one of his many clandestine voyages. His remains were finally brought back to Israel in 1992. Arieh Atzmoni, who fought the Nazis in Europe and then fought in the War of Independence, represents the continuity between Israel and the Jewish partisans of the ghettos. Eliezer Feig, from Transylvania, spent his short life in many concentration camps, from Auschwitz to Mauthausen, but met his death on the coast of Israel. He worked at the Weizmann Institute, but also went on missions for the army, and fell on "Heroes' Hill." Emil Brig, a Polish Holocaust survivor, won the Medal of Valor in the 1948 war by blowing up a bridge to halt the advancing enemy.

Major Klein also received the Medal of Valor, which had not been awarded since 1973. It's not easy to stop thinking about those last seconds of his life, when he decided to jump onto the grenade. His two children will know about him through the stories they hear and the pictures that are shown to them. Roi was serving in Lebanon to guarantee a peaceful existence for his people in their own land, to safeguard the innocent lives of his children, to ensure that people could live in their own homes in tranquility and continue with their ordinary lives—shopping at the mall or eating a pizza without being blown to bits; praying at the synagogue without having to run for shelter; putting their children on a school bus without thinking about the shrapnel that will pierce them.

Americans have a Roi Klein of their own. Michael A. Monsoor was a half-Arab teenager living in the paradise that is Garden Grove in Orange County, California. At the age of twenty, he enlisted in the United States Navy, and two years later, on his second attempt, he was admitted to the elite Navy Seals. He had a tattoo of Saint Michael fighting the dragon on his shoulder, and the prayer of Saint Michael on his side. He ended up in Ramadi, Iraq, "the graveyard of the Americans" according to graffiti in the city. One day Michael went up onto a roof with three of his fellow Seals. He positioned himself close to the exit, to keep watch for surprises. Someone threw a grenade, which bounced off his chest. It had a time fuse, allowing a couple of seconds of horror. He could get away and save himself. Michael threw himself onto the grenade, absorbing almost all of the explosive shock and saving his companions, who got away with minor injuries.

This is the great difference between the martyrdom of a suicide terrorist and the martyrdom of Jewish culture—between the suicide bomber and the *shomrin,* between the *shahid* and the *Kiddush Hashem.* Roi Klein's enemy was willing to die in order to bring death and pain to as many people as possible; Roi was willing to die so as to guarantee life and liberty for others, to preserve a world in which Jews can pray in their synagogues, to fulfill the divine commandments and make the world better.

Little more than half a century had passed since the echo of the Shema resounded in the Nazi gas chambers where the Jews were gassed and then burned in the crematories, simply because they were born Jewish. Roi Klein knew the ways of these martyrs, and he died with the Shema on his lips. His relatives on his father's side had arrived in Israel after fleeing from Dusseldorf, in Germany, and then from Lille, in northern France, when it was invaded by the Germans. Two cousins on his mother's side fought with the partisans in the forests of Eastern Europe, while the rest of the family were killed in the ghettos of Lithuania.

"On the one hand, Roi was very practical; he had finished his schoolwork with excellent results," says Shlomo Mirvis, who worked at the Bnei David yeshiva in Eli, which Klein had attended. "On the other, Roi was a spiritual person who got up at five o'clock in the morning to study the Torah and pray." Klein always said that "the Torah is the order inside of reality," and that one must be humble like Isaac, who renounced everything in the presence of the divine will, and never arrogant, because "it removes us from devotion to God." He loved the natural surroundings of Samaria. He said that "abundance has a divine quality in Israel; this abundance is not material, but spiritual."

"Roi Klein was my classmate, a serene and stable man, with a profound desire for the spiritual," says Rabbi Eliezer Kashtiel. "He studied whenever he had a spare moment. He was honest and simple, a family man, not a great conversationalist, but a person who loved to help, who respected the truth." His ultimate martyrdom contains a metaphysical truth. "Life has been given to us by the Creator in order to fulfill a moral purpose. The individual's most profound imperative is to express an ideal in life; it is the aspiration to sanctity. At the same time, for the sake of realizing the ideal, we are called to sacrifice our lives, because life was given to us for that purpose. And when a person sacrifices himself for a sacred cause, it is clear that his whole life was not random, without meaning, but lived for a higher purpose."

It is not heresy to state that the actions of the guard Haim Smadar, of the guard Alexander Kostyuk, of the soldier Roi Klein, to name only a few, were the extension of the things that so many Jewish mothers did to protect their children during the Holocaust. There are stories of mothers who took actions as heroic as they were instinctual to save their children, often shielding them with their own bodies. No one will ever know the names of those women. There are also stories of ten-year-old girls comforting their mothers at the entrance to the gas chambers. No one will ever know the names of those girls. During his last days in Treblinka, a sergeant of the SS rose from the table and said to the two Jewish women who had just cooked for him, "Okay, girls, now it's your turn." One of them, Tchechia, spit back at him, "Kill us, come on, just do me one favor: don't ask us to undress." As the other woman fell to her knees, sobbing, Tchechia said to her, "Get up, don't give him this satisfaction, remember that you are a Jew."

Gigantic incinerators crackled, dozens of yards deep, and the soil of Treblinka took in the remains of 700,000 Jews. They could burn four thousand human beings a night. That place of the pine trees and old stumps is a moving landscape, alive with the shirts of the slain, their shoes, penknives, candlesticks, gold teeth, baby shoes, linens for special occasions, saucepans, children's letters, handwritten poems. As the great Communist writer Vasily Grossman wrote after the Red Army liberated many of the Nazi death camps, "From the depths of the earth come the funeral peals of countless tiny bells. And it seems that at any moment the heart might stop, overcome by a sadness, by a pain, by an anguish so great that a human being cannot bear it."

Out from a Europe turned into the mass grave of Judaism came the pioneers of the new Jewish state. One of the first manifestations of the resurgence of Jewish freedom in Treblinka was suicide. A person would ask a friend to remove the box that he was standing on and to recite the Kaddish, the prayer for the dead proclaiming the holiness of the Name. The right to die by suicide led to the right to die while fighting. It was no longer necessary to die in order to glorify the Holy Name; it was possible instead to claim the first gift that he gave to his people, life. The Jews rebelled as best they could—some with a grenade kept hidden until arrival and then detonated in the presence of the SS, some with a straight razor, some with a pole pulled from the fence, some with a knife for the ritual slaughter.

One day Edi Weinstein, who participated in the armed revolt against the Germans and was the last living survivor of Treblinka, had seen dozens of children on the edge of a pit in which hundreds of charred bodies were crackling. "All my memories of that factory of death are filled with the wonderful faces of those children." He has always been proud of the fact that he took part in the resistance: "I am proud that after five years of brutal persecution and blood, I was still able to participate in the defeat of Germany." The last words of Yakoov, one of the heroes who took up arms in Treblinka, were: "We have prepared to work and to fight in Israel. It is by building Israel that we will save our people."

The idea of Israel sustained a thousand courageous Jews who rebelled against the executioners. Of the six hundred Jews who lived through the revolt, all but forty were massacred by Ukrainian fascists or by Polish farmers. Each of those forty survivors had at least one child, and almost all of them live in Israel now. This is one of the greatest victories of the Jewish state. The meaning of Israel is found not in a tormented Star of David, but in the star resurgent as a symbol of resurrection. It is no accident that Yom Hazikaron, the Memorial Day for those who have fallen in battle, is followed immediately by the day when the founding of the state is celebrated. The abrupt transition from the somber silence of commemoration to the unbridled joy of freedom creates a psychological tension that has not yet been thoroughly examined. There is unconscious joy over the miraculous escape from danger.

The highest virtues of Judaism and Zionism were on display also after Haiti's massive earthquake. Amid the rubble-strewn streets of Port-au-Prince, three Israeli rescue teams searched through the ruins for Haitian survivors—even as Israel's enemies continued to assert that Zionism is racism. "Everywhere, the acrid smell of bodies hangs in the air," said Mati Goldstein, the head of the Zaka International Rescue Unit. The Jewish delegation took time out to recite the Shabbat prayers. Many locals sat quietly in the rubble, staring at the men as they prayed facing Jerusalem and then kissed the prayer shawls. The words of the prayer took on a deeper significance: "O King who causes death and restores life." Amid the tragedy and devastation that pervaded Port-au-Prince, a happy event took place inside the Israeli field hospital: Dr. Shir Dar, who works at Hadassah Ein Kerem, delivered the first healthy baby in the facility. The mother named her son "Israel."

In the spring of 2002, while death was knocking at the door for so many Jews in Israel, while pain was intruding into their happy homes, their festive restaurants, the buses full of students and children, there was joyful news from the United States: Adam Pearl was born, the son of the *Wall Street Journal* correspondent Daniel Pearl and his widow, Mariane. Once again life had won, forcing death to retreat. So it did also in October 2007, when children of terror victims, fifty-five boys and forty-five girls, met in Jerusalem to celebrate their bat and bar mitzvahs, their entry into the age of responsibility and freedom. The ceremony was led by the chief rabbi, Yisrael Meir Lau, who had visited their homes after each attack. Menashe Pur David, a member of the commission for the victims of terrorism, invoked a minute of silence for those who had not been saved. "The fact that you are here demonstrates that those who have tried to destroy us cannot break our spirit. You are proof that the people of Israel lives."

That day, the children of the victims of terrorism were celebrating life—as were the passengers on the ships *Crescent* and *York* when they raised anchor on December 26, 1947, and all the Jews went above deck to sing the *Hatikvah*. Never before had so many Jews gathered to sing together, as if all the generations were united in a single song. The young Russian Jews who congregated at the Dolphinarium on that evening in June 2001 were singing, laughing, wearing their finest and looking their best. They were the flowers of Israel, toasting to life. A memorial that commemorates the victims of the massacre on the beach of Tel Aviv says: *Lachaim—lo nafsik lirkode,* "Choose life—we will not stop dancing." Those young men and women have never stopped dancing. They are alive in the memory of their people.

Behind the Jewish love for life we find a society of departed spirits: the twenty teenagers who were blown up by a suicide bomber outside a disco in Tel Aviv, the soldiers who made a wrong turn and were lynched in Ramallah, the brave rabbi who died trying to save the Torah scrolls at Joseph's Tomb, the security personnel who were ambushed while trying to protect those walking home from Shabbat prayers at the Tomb of the Patriarchs in Hebron, the kindergarten teacher killed when a minibus was attacked by Palestinian gunmen. Terrorism is the loss of human face, the destruction of the moral person, the will to annihilate humanity. The dreadful "V" of terrorism's victory is impressed in the folds of the soul. If you search for something left of your son and find it under the head of the suicide bomber, what type of reaction will occur in a brittle human heart? We can touch Israel's martyrdom in the homes of survivors. An invincible people confesses its bewilderment, while the world isolates them and deepens their wounds. How long can Israel sustain a war with no fronts, a war with no end?

There was another miraculous event in 2002: the birth of a son to Meir Schijveschuurder, a survivor of the large Dutch family that was decimated by a Palestinian suicide bomber at the Sbarro pizzeria. Two of his young sisters were hospitalized with extensive injuries. Another sister, fourteen-year-old Ra'aya, died after she arrived at the hospital. Meir was unable to find his father, mother, four-year-old brother Avraham Yitzhak, or two-year-old sister Hemda. All hope gone, he went to the morgue, and that's where he found them. They were a beautiful family. Meir had just finished three years of military service in Lebanon when he suddenly had to learn how to be a father to his little sisters.

"My parents were the children of Holocaust survivors, and the stories about my many relatives who died in the gas chambers were part of our lives," says Meir. "It is precisely because all the others died that my parents wanted a big family with eight children, and in Israel. They gave us the names of those who had been killed, to keep their memory alive." And just as he had inherited the name of a relative who was murdered in

Poland, Meir named his own son Mordechai in honor of his grandfather (Meir's father), who was killed by terrorism. For the ritual of the "redemption of the firstborn," he symbolically placed a piece of jewelry that had belonged to his mother, Tzira, on his child's body. "A family has been reborn from the ashes," it was said in Israel. This new family represents the continuity of the Jewish people in the land of Israel. They embody the incredible courage and strength that are necessary to survive the horrors of life after terror. They are Israel's pillars of strength.

At first glance, Moshe Holtzberg looked like any other happy Israeli boy on the brink of his third birthday when he received his first haircut. Among the Chabad-Lubavitchers, Hasidim, and some other Orthodox groups, a boy is not given a haircut until the age of three. Moshe stood quietly, accepting chocolate bars from the bearded rabbis as they snipped his locks. But Moshe is far from normal; he is a living miracle. In December 2008, a group of Islamic terrorists stormed into his home in Mumbai, India, killing his parents and four others at the Jewish center. Moshe's nanny, Sandra Samuel, an Indian Catholic, found him sitting on the floor beside his parents' bloodied bodies. Sandra saved Moshe and was named "Righteous among the Nations," the highest Israeli award that may be presented to a non-Jew.

The terrorists in Mumbai did not inquire whether their victims were Haredi, Orthodox, traditional, or secular. All that mattered was that they represented Jewish civilization. Each of them died sanctifying God's name. "Where is the outcry in this world?" asked Rabbi Avraham Berkowitz, director of the Chabad Mumbai Relief Fund, which is helping rebuild what was once an oasis for Jewish locals and travelers. "This is a religious site. Religious leaders were murdered in cold blood here."

Two years after the devastation in Mumbai, Moshe Holtzberg's life continues, much like the life of any other boy in

Israel. "My home is in Mumbai," he likes to repeat to his grand-parents. "My father and mother are there." A photograph shows Moshe on his father's shoulders at a Mumbai beach, with a smile that will forever be part of Israel.

Israel has lost 22,570 soldiers in war, and 1,557 citizens in terrorist attacks since the Olso Accords, but the population has not abandoned the stone houses, the alleyways or restaurants of Jerusalem and Haifa, nor the beaches and bars of Tel Aviv; no one has stopped attending schools or universities; Israeli medicine, physics, and agriculture continue to produce Nobel Prizes. It is estimated that in 2080, about 81 percent of Jewish children under the age of fourteen will be living in Israel—in spite of Ma'alot, Netanya, Emmanuel, the Dolphinarium, the Sbarro, and the dozens of other massacres that have stained Israeli history in blood. This statistic is the answer to the hundreds of innocent deaths in these years of terrorism.

During the feast of Hanukkah in the fall of 2007, President George W. Bush welcomed the parents of Daniel Pearl to the White House. "During Hanukkah, we remember an ancient struggle for freedom. More than two thousand years ago, a cruel tyrant ruled Judea—and forbade the Israelites from practicing their religion. A band of brothers came together to fight this oppression. And against incredible odds, they liberated the capital city of Jerusalem. As they set about rededicating the holy temple, they witnessed a great miracle: The purified oil that was supposed to last for one day burned for eight." Every Jew commemorates that miracle by lighting the Hanukkah candles. And the Talmud says that the candelabra should be fully visible, so that all may admire its light. "The flames remind us that light triumphs over darkness, faith conquers despair, and the desire for freedom burns inside every man, woman and child."

President Bush was surrounded by many Jews who had fled from persecution in Iran, Syria, and the former Soviet Union.

"The forces of intolerance can suppress the menorah—but they can never extinguish its light." The menorah that was lit that day had belonged to Daniel Pearl's great-grandparents, Chaim and Rosa Pearl, who had brought it from Poland to Israel in 1924 when they helped establish the Orthodox community of Bnei Brak; and finally it came to the United States. "In his final moments, Daniel told his captors about a street in Israel named for his great-grandfather. He looked into their camera and he said, 'My father is Jewish, my mother is Jewish, and I am Jewish.' These words have become a source of inspiration for Americans of all faiths. They show the courage of a man who refused to bow before terror—and the strength of a spirit that could not be broken." *Ani' yehudi,* "I am Jewish," Daniel Pearl affirmed before dying. One day his son, Adam, like Moshe Holtzberg and Mordechai Schijveschuurder, will also be able to say with pride, *Ani' yehudi.*

The proud Zionist Yona Malina frequently told his parents that he didn't regret settling in Israel, even though he was paralyzed from the neck down in 1995 by a suicide bombing attack in Jerusalem. When he was in a coma, his parents—believing that he wanted to die—petitioned a district court for permission to have his respirator disconnected. But when Yona suddenly regained consciousness a few weeks later, he told his parents that he didn't want his life to be ended. He lived until 2005.

Yona was born in Bratislava, where his parents had fled on the eve of the Holocaust to escape Nazi persecution. His original name was Peter. Because his family had hidden their Jewish roots for so long, first from the Nazis and later from the Communists, he didn't know of his Jewish origins until his grandmother urged him to visit Israel in the late 1980s. Yona fell in love with the country, doing volunteer work on a kibbutz and studying Hebrew. After a long search in the municipal archive of Bratislava, he found the birth certificates of his mother, Eva, and her parents; and he decided to stop calling himself Peter, adopting the name Yona instead. He is a shining symbol of Israeli victory over terrorism. Yona was not merely part of the history and suffering of the Jewish people; he helped redeem it by his audacity and strength.

The thousands of terror victims and their families are like the Israeli flower known as "the ultimate survivor," because it can live in conditions that would kill many other plants. In the Persian buttercup, the storage roots have a unique structure for resisting drought. The cell walls offer protection from a sudden surge of water in the first winter rains, and at the same time protect the cells from dehydration. Examined under a microscope, the cells look like Stars of David.

The prophet Isaiah (41:18–19) says, "I will open up rivers on the bare heights, and fountains in the broad valleys; I will turn the desert into a marshland, and the dry ground into springs of water. I will plant in the desert the cedar, acacia, myrtle, and olive; I will set in the wasteland the cypress, together with the plane tree and the pine." David Ben-Gurion once said that "the origin of the word 'Paradise' is the Hebrew word *pardes*: an irrigated orchard. And our pioneers will succeed in making a paradise of this desert."

When one reads the passages in the Torah about Abraham's journey through the desert toward the Promised Land, what emerges is a nomadic way of life in harmony with the harsh environment. This harmony was lost for many centuries. Intensive grazing and poor management turned the once productive northern Negev region into a desert. At the time Israel won its independence, the Negev desert went all the way to Gedara, a southern suburb of Tel Aviv. After twenty centuries of exile— when the land ended up in the hands of the Romans, Byzantines, Arabs, Crusaders, Egyptians, and Turks—the Jews went back to inhabit an arid and scrubby desert, and they turned it into an Eden. More than two hundred million trees have been planted in the Jewish state during the last century. The biblical symbol of eternal life has reappeared on the hills of Judea and Galilee.

The Persian buttercup that grows in Israel is also known as the "resurrection plant," because it can live without water and then "rise again" when water becomes available. Israel is like this flower: a country that has risen again five times, and five times has emerged victorious from wars intended to wipe it from the face of the earth.

When the Nazis in Vilna ordered the Jews to assemble in order to leave the ghetto, setting out for the death camps, the great philologist Zelig Kalmanovich reassured those around him: "I am not afraid, I am not afraid." The others, astonished, asked him, "Why aren't you afraid?" And as if it were the most natural thing in the world, Kalmanovich replied, "I have a son in Israel."

Unlike Kalmanovich, Chaim Shapiro would live through the inferno. Originally from Krakow, he survived four concentration camps. Before the war, Chaim had eight children and a beautiful wife. Afterward, only one of his children remained. He was liberated from Buchenwald by the Americans, and his son Baruch joined him in Israel in 1948. Baruch volunteered under the command of Yitzhak Rabin, and died in battle. Chaim had only one request of the army: that his son be buried with honors on Mount Herzl in Jerusalem. He was the last of the Shapiros, the end of a dynasty. At the funeral, Chaim started singing the *Am Yisrael Hai,* "Israel Must Live." Addressing those present, he said, "I lost seventy relatives in one year, including seven children, my wife, and my parents. There is no grave where I can go and mourn for them; they are ashes in the skies of Europe. And I don't know why they died. But this son, I know why he died: so that we might have a home for the Jewish people in the land of Israel, and a grave. This is not a reason to weep, but to sing." Then Chaim started dancing.

When Israel was born, it was thought that the yellow star, a sign of extermination and symbol of the gas chambers, should be replaced with something that would evoke life. But the opposite view prevailed. The sign that in our days has been sanctified by suffering and terror would illuminate life and reconstruction in Israel. Before it ascended, the Star of David had to journey through the abyss, where it underwent the ultimate humiliation. But there it also won its eternal greatness. The victims of terrorism are one of the reasons why Israel exists.

A poem by the Jewish partisan Abba Kovner talks about "the day after," when the few survivors of the Holocaust returned to walk among the living, on the surface. They came out two from a city, one from a village. A woman and her son emerged from a bunker under the rubble. The partisans walked out of the forests. The survivors were released from Auschwitz. They found each other again amid heaps of ashes. In Europe, the sun began shining again after so many years.

Those who are no longer here remain alive in our hearts. The stars do not vanish when we die.

Acknowledgments

Where do I begin to express gratitude, when so many people have lent so many hands to advance the cause of this years-long project? I cannot name all who should be named. In many cases, I do not even know their names. Many helped me behind the scenes. They live in my heart.

I think mostly of Avner Weiss: I always knew that the voice of his father, the heroic Lipa, was crucial to the construction of this book. I could not have kept going without the encouragement expressed to me by people like Dr. Eli Picard. "Stay a friend of Israel," he said. "It is so rare and so unpopular that I appreciate your courage." I thank the One Family Fund, Alex Katsman, Adriana Katz, Yossi Zur, Yoav Alon, Rachel Ohana, Yaakov Cohney, Stewart Weiss, Anya Antopolosky, Susi Cohen, Laura Ben-David, Lori Mosher Vera, Jean Dayan, Audrey Gerber, Shlomo Mirvis, Kaeren Fish, and Bernice Wolf. To any other people who helped me in various small ways, thank you. I have made every effort in the text to respect the hundreds of testimonies I received. If I have erred, it is out of ignorance and not malice.

Christopher Caldwell helped me find the right way forward. I am indebted to Roger Kimball because he always believed in the importance of this book. No author could have asked for a better publishing team.

A special word must be written for my family, robbed of my presence for four years while I was holed up amid stacks of nightmares and frights. Their indulgence was indispensable. I couldn't have written this book without the love of my wife, and I will never be able to thank her enough.

To the parents of the terror victims: may their memory be a blessing for all of us. I want to dedicate to them an immortal verse by Vladimir Jankelevitch: "He who has been, from then on cannot not have been: henceforth this mysterious and profoundly obscure fact of having been is his viaticum for all eternity."

Index